REGRESSION OF *Y* ON *X* (Section 13.2)

$$b_{YX} = \frac{N\Sigma XY - \Sigma X \Sigma Y}{N\Sigma X^2 - (\Sigma X)^2}$$

$$c_{YX} = \frac{\Sigma Y - b_{YX}\Sigma X}{N}$$

STANDARD DEVIATION OF A SAMPLE (Section 3.10)

$$s = \sqrt{\frac{\Sigma X^2 - (\Sigma X)^2/n}{n-1}}$$

t–TEST FOR MEANS:

Independent groups design (Section 8.7)

$$t = \frac{\overline{X}_1 - \overline{X}_2}{\sqrt{s^2/n_1 + s^2/n_2}}$$

$$s^2 = \frac{\Sigma X_1^2 - (\Sigma X_1)^2/n_1 + \Sigma X_2^2 - (\Sigma X_2)^2/n_2}{n_1 + n_2 - 2}$$

Repeated measures/correlated samples design (Section 8.9)

$$t = \frac{\Sigma D}{\sqrt{\dfrac{N\Sigma D^2 - (\Sigma D)^2}{N-1}}}$$

VARIANCE OF A SAMPLE (Section 3.10)

$$s^2 = \frac{\Sigma X^2 - (\Sigma X)^2/n}{n-1}$$

Z – SCORES (Section 4.3)

$$z = \frac{X - \mu}{\sigma}$$

Basic
Statistics for
Behavioral
Sciences

Basic Statistics for Behavioral Sciences

Theadore Horvath

University of Windsor

 Little, Brown and Company

Boston   Toronto

Library of Congress Cataloging in Publication Data

Horvath, Theadore.
    Basic statistics for behavioral sciences.

    Includes index.
    1. Psychometrics. I. Title.
BF39.H685 1985   150′.1′5195   84–19987
ISBN 0–316–37382–6

Copyright © 1985 by Theadore Horvath

Library of Congress Catalog Card No. 84–19987

ISBN 0-316-37382-6

9   8   7   6   5   4   3   2   1

MV

Published simultaneously in Canada by Little, Brown & Company (Canada) Limited
Printed in the United States of America

Acknowledgments

Page 8: From Brian W. Aldiss, *The Eighty Minute Hour.* Copyright © 1974 by Brian W. Aldiss. Reprinted by permission of the author.

Page 192: The general procedure for ANOVA computations throughout this book is modeled after that presented by Winer (1962). Adapted by permission from B. J. Winer, *Statistical Principles in Experimental Design* (New York: McGraw-Hill, 1962).

Preface

Introductory statistics texts are not among the things that this world lacks; why then another? In my years of teaching introductory statistics, I have been unable to discover a text that my students found readable and comprehensible or that suited my preferences of organization and presentation. It may be that statistics cannot be rendered into plain English. It may be that I am malcontent. Conversations with other statistics instructors lead me to believe otherwise. In writing *Basic Statistics for Behavioral Sciences* I hoped to achieve clarity and readability without sacrificing depth of coverage or oversimplifying subtle concepts. Students' initial apprehensions about taking a course in statistics are often heightened by an intimidating and unintelligible text. I have tried to present statistics in a direct and plain language style, using understandable words and images. Introductory statistics texts are plentiful, but those that communicate effectively are rare.

Basic Statistics for Behavioral Sciences is intended for introductory courses that emphasize inferential reasoning. It is perhaps most appropriate for students majoring in psychology, but should be useful as well for students in education and other behavioral science disciplines. The text contains a good deal more than can be reasonably covered in a one-semester course; thus, instructors can select from the content those topics most relevant to their particular disciplines.

Basic Statistics for Behavioral Sciences is organized to promote students' learning and to provide instructors with maximum flexibility. I believe that students learn statistics primarily by doing problem exercises, and that such practice should occur as soon as possible after exposure to the conceptual material. Thus I have interspersed problem exercises within the chapters to promote the integration of theoretical and practical content. This organization can benefit the instructor as well in that the exercise sections are convenient points at which to conclude a particular topic. Instructors may thus pursue a topic to whatever depth they desire and they can end the discussion without creating confusion.

The first seven chapters are intended to provide the framework and conceptual basis for inferential decision making. Chapter 1 (Introduction) is conversational in tone and is intended to introduce statistics and allay some common apprehensions and misconceptions about the nature of this subject.

Chapter 2 (Data) defines terms and concepts essential to later discussions of empirical data and features a discussion of objectivity, subjectivity, and operational definitions. Chapter 3 (Some Descriptive Statistics) includes discussions of frequency distributions and graphs, averages, variance and standard deviation, and a relatively elaborate presentation of the summation operator. Chapter 4 (The Normal Distribution) discusses the normal distribution as an entree to subsequent discussion of sampling distributions and features step-by-step diagram-illustrated sample problems. Chapter 5 (Probability) begins with a discussion of the special case addition and multiplication rules; following sections knit the concept of probability to the previously discussed normal distribution and to frequency distributions in general. The treatment of probability in Chapter 5 is appropriate to serve as a conceptual basis for inferential decision making; however, instructors wishing to pursue probability in greater depth will find a discussion of the general case rules, along with problem exercises, in Appendix V. Chapter 6 (Sampling and Sampling Distributions) and Chapter 7 (Hypothesis Testing) form the conceptual core of the text in that they describe the conceptual basis upon which inferential decisions are made in empirical science. This discussion proceeds from random sampling to the concept of sampling distributions in Chapter 6 and carries on to hypothesis testing, confidence, Type I and II error, and power in Chapter 7.

Beyond Chapter 7 the sequence of topics reflects a personal preference. I find it easier to deal with correlation when students have become thoroughly familiar with inferential decision making and thus place this subject relatively late in the topic sequence. I also prefer to deal with regression after I have discussed correlation since a significant correlation is the logical basis for deriving a regression function. However, Chapter 13 (Linear Regression) contains a section describing the F-test for the regression and this section, not usually found in introductory texts, makes a precorrelation discussion of regression logically reasonable since it obviates the need for prior establishment of a significant correlation. The discussions of product-moment correlation and linear regression use a common hypothetical example so that the student can see concepts demonstrated numerically as, for example, in the section that confirms the variance interpretation of correlation.

The presentation of the t distributions and t-tests for means is approached directly and not, as in some texts, through discussion of z-tests or non-parametric techniques. I recommend this approach as both expeditious and less confusing. It seems to me that authors too often slight or ignore repeated measures designs and thus the repeated measures/correlated samples t-test procedure is given separate and equal treatment relative to the independent groups design. This approach is also used in the discussion of the independent groups and repeated measures ANOVAs. Post F-test comparisons seem to me an essential follow-up to ANOVA. Tukey's HSD and Scheffé's tests are presented in Chapter 10 to provide students with the means to deal with equal and unequal group size situations.

The discussion of two factor ANOVA is primarily conceptual and is limited to the independent groups design. In this context, however, a hypothetical example is explored thoroughly so that the concept of interaction can be properly illustrated. It is my presumption that most instructors will not ordinarily deal with two factor ANOVA in detail and thus Chapter 11 may be read for a conceptual understanding without going into the computations.

Nonparametric statistics are grouped into Chapters 14 and 15 according to the type of data used, that is, nominal or ordinal. However, special care is taken in the introduction to Chapter 14 to point out that parametric and nonparametric statistics are not defined by the type of data that they use even though the correspondence largely holds up.

Chapter 16 attempts to summarize the content of the book by means of a chart that can be used to determine the correct analysis for a given set of circumstances and objectives. A diagrammatic version of this chart appears on the inside back cover. I have found that such a decision chart can be a useful guide to students and a convenient focal point for reviewing the subject matter at the end of the course.

We all know that the microcomputer will become ubiquitous at all levels of education, but how soon and in what form is still uncertain. In my own classes I find students who have never touched a microcomputer and students with considerable skill and experience. I acknowledge the microcomputer and its potential role in data analysis by means of Appendix IV, which contains programs in BASIC for computing most of the analyses covered in the text. Each instructor is likely to be faced with a unique mix of students' access to and facility with microcomputers. I leave it to individual instructors and students to integrate these programs as they see fit into the course and into their understanding of statistics.

Many persons helped to bring this book into being. I should like to acknowledge my indebtedness to them and absolve them of any responsibility for faults or errors that may remain. I thank Michael Murton for the initial impetus, and George Bergquist for his expression of confidence at a crucial stage. I am profoundly grateful to the following people for their insightful comments, encouragement, and the care and concern with which they reviewed parts or all of the manuscript: Edward Arees (Northeastern University), Norman Berkowitz (Boston College), Jerry Cohen (University of Rhode Island), Jerome Frieman (Kansas State University), William Klipec (Drake University), Carol Lowery (University of Kentucky), Thomas E. Nygren (Ohio State University), Michael Raulin (SUNY-Buffalo), Joseph Lee Rodgers (Oklahoma University), and Anthony Walsh (Salve Regina College). I also thank my colleagues Meyer Starr, Art Smith, Martin Morf, Ged

Namikas, Ted Hirota, and Ann McCabe for our discussions on technical matters that helped clarify my thinking and prose. I thank Henry Minton, then serving as Head of the Psychology Department, for his support of this undertaking, and Dave Reynolds, current Head, for continued encouragement. Special thanks and undying gratitude go to Veronica Edwards, Lucy Brown, Cheryl Evon, Carmela Papp, and Lyn LaPorte, University of Windsor Word Processing Centre, for their skillful, professional, and always cheerful assistance with the manuscript.

I am grateful to many people at Little, Brown and Company for their competent treatment of the manuscript and its author. I wish to thank Molly Faulkner, sponsoring editor, for her professionalism and good humor. Special thanks to Virginia Shine, book editor, for her patience with me and for the competence and professionalism with which she shepherded the manuscript through production. Thanks to Denise Lee and Judy Maas, editorial assistants, for their capable and cheerful help. I thank Kathy Smith for an excellent job of copyediting, and Victor Curran for beautiful design work.

I am grateful to the Literary Executor of the late Sir Ronald A. Fisher, F.R.S., to Dr. Frank Yates, F.R.S., and to Longman Group Ltd., London, for permission to reprint Tables II, III, IV, and VII from *Statistical Tables for Biological, Agricultural and Medical Research* (6th edition, 1974).

Finally, I thank my wife, Barbara, and children, August and Brenda, for their encouragement and forbearance and for providing a secure and stable context in which I could pursue this demanding task.

T. H.

Contents

Part II   61

Concepts and Procedure in Statistical Decision Making

4 The Normal Distribution

5 Probability

6 Sampling and Sampling Distributions

Part III 145

Decisions About Differences

Part IV   249

Decisions About Relationships

12 Product-Moment Correlation

Basic
Statistics for
Behavioral
Sciences

Part I

Terminology and Description

1 Introduction

Chapter Preview

1.1 Why Learn Statistics?

Provides a rationale for making statistics a part of the education of scientists and citizens in general

1.2 What is Statistics?

Describes the ways in which statistics serves the scientist and defines statistics as a subject area

Key Terms   descriptive statistics
inferential statistics
statistics (definition)

1.3 How to Learn Statistics

Advice to the student on how to most successfully learn this subject matter

1.4 The Calculator

Advice on purchasing a hand-held calculator

1.5 The Computer

Some thoughts on computers

1.1 Why Learn Statistics?

Why are you enrolled in a statistics course? Is it because the subject has a reputation for being interesting and stimulating, or is it perhaps because you have heard that it is easy and a good way to add an A+ to your transcript? Most of the students that I meet do not have either of these expectations. Usually they are taking statistics because it is a required course in their degree program. This reason is eminently sufficient, but it is not very satisfying. If you are being required to take statistics and are wondering why, it is because you are majoring in a science.

What does science consist of, or, what is the fundamental operation that is performed by scientists in all disciplines? My answer is observation: all science boils down, in one way or another, to the process of observation. In turn, what does observation consist of, or, what is the essential event in any observation? In my view the answer is measurement. Any observation is improved by the act of measurement and the more accurately scientists can measure, the happier they are. Finally, what is the result of measurement? The answer is numerical data: most often the observations and measurements we make are expressed in numerical form.

As scientists, we observe in order to understand the relations between events and thus to discover the laws that govern natural phenomena such as human behavior. Having obtained these observations, we must make judgments and decisions as to what they mean and how broadly they apply. Thus, making decisions and judgments about numbers is part of the scientific procedure. Statistics is a methodology for extracting information and meaning from numbers, and for making decisions about them. Statistics is the intermediary between what is observed and what can be concluded about how natural events operate and thus it is a vital tool for all scientists. Stated simply, there is no way that you can claim to have a comprehension of the material of any scientific discipline without having some understanding of the rules and procedures for evaluating scientific evidence. That is why you must learn statistics.

Science, which is a systematic inquiry into the unknown, is as fascinating and diverse as the universe we live in, the creatures that share this world with us, and our own behavior. Statistics finds application wherever we investigate the unknown, and when an exciting finding is reported, it is an excitement that rests on statistical reasoning. Observations are not interesting by themselves; it is the meaning we can attach to them that is interesting. So, whether we want to predict peoples' voting behavior or whales' reproduction rates, evaluate the effectiveness of a disease vaccine or of antiaircraft artillery, determine the relationship between speed limits and traffic accidents, or between government spending and inflation (see Tanur et al., 1972), statistics plays a central role. If you adopt a positive attitude toward statistics as being potentially useful and interesting, then learning statistics can become an enjoyable and productive experience.

There is a good reason for being exposed to statistics quite apart from appreciating it as a tool of scientific research. A great deal of the information that is communicated in our culture is expressed in statistical terms; furthermore, there are many groups and individuals, from politicians to advertisers, who seek to influence your behavior with statistical arguments. You can be easily led astray if you cannot see through flawed uses of statistics or do not know how to ask intelligent questions. I think it is impossible to be a responsible citizen in our culture without having a sufficient grasp of statistics to enable you to defend yourself against specious propaganda.

We have all heard the claim that, "My group had 30 percent fewer cavities with BILBO toothpaste." Thirty percent fewer than what, than people who did not use BILBO, or people who did not use toothpaste at all? Another question to be considered is, did "my group" have 30 percent fewer teeth? As soon as such questions are asked, it is obvious that the initial claim cannot be taken at face value.

Here is another typical advertising statement, "The majority of women who had a preference chose Brand A." What if 100 were tested, only 3 had any preference, and 2 of those preferred Brand A? The original statement would still be true but the superiority of Brand A is less impressive.

An aside on "statistics" in advertising

1.2 What is Statistics?

We use statistical methods for two broad purposes: description and inference. *Descriptive statistics* consists of the techniques for organizing, summarizing, and extracting information from numerical data. Suppose we were interested in learning something about the language capabilities of children in grade four, and that we had devised a convenient way to measure the size of such a child's vocabulary. If we obtained this measure, the number of words a child comprehends, for 500 grade four children, we would end up with 500 numbers typed on a page. Not many people could look at this collection of numbers and perceive such things as the average vocabulary size, whether all the children had similar vocabulary sizes or whether there was wide variation, and what vocabulary sizes identified the upper and lower quarters of the group. This information and more could be learned by calculating appropriate terms and depicting the numbers in graphical form. Nothing would have been done to the observations except to distill some purely descriptive information. Although descriptive procedures do not occupy a large portion of this text, they are quite basic to understanding data and constitute the first stage of analysis.

descriptive statistics

inferential statistics

Inferential statistics involves generalizing the findings beyond the immediate observations. A scientist who is studying human behavior or any other natural event cannot usually observe every individual, but rather is limited to a relatively small number of cases; nonetheless, the objective is to make general statements about people or the event. Although we may directly observe only a few grade four children, we are actually seeking to know about all such persons. *Inferential statistics* is the body of rules and procedures by which general statements are made about people or events based on the observation of a relative few. Inferential statistics is thus at the heart of the scientific enterprise. If we could make statements only about those individuals or events that have been directly observed, science would be quite impractical. The acid test for how well we understand something is our ability to predict when and under what conditions it will happen in the future. Statistics provides us with procedures for making predictions based on observed data and for interpreting the outcome of experiments designed to test predictions.

statistics

Taken altogether, *statistics* may be defined as the body of rules and procedures for evaluating and making decisions about the outcome of scientific observation. Inasmuch as such observation results in numerical data, what we are really doing is evaluating and making decisions about numbers. To this end, the scientist, and the student of statistics, indulges in some complicated number manipulations. Remember though, that these numerical gymnastics are secondary to the real purpose, which is decision making.

1.3 How to Learn Statistics

To say that statistics involves the manipulation of numbers raises an issue that is central to many students' reluctance to take a course in this subject. Many anxiety-ridden students have approached me after the first class saying, in tremulous voices, "I can't do math." I tell them not to worry because I can't either and, fortunately, neither of us will have to. The point of statistics is to make decisions and not to manipulate numbers as an end in itself. In fact, the four basic arithmetic operations of adding, subtracting, multiplying, and dividing, and occasionally determining a square root represent the highest mathematics required in statistics. To be sure, these operations will be performed in some lengthy and complicated sequences, but fears of incomprehensible mathematics are unwarranted. For students who are still apprehensive, Appendix II provides a review of some basic arithmetic and algebraic operations.

Am I suggesting that your statistics course will be easy? Not for a moment! You will be required to think a bit and spend many hours working out problem exercises. I believe that one learns statistics by doing statistics, not so much by reading a text, or even by listening to your professor's lectures. I believe also that learning is promoted and interest can be maintained by applying concepts and skills as soon as possible after they are introduced. To those ends, I have provided many review exercises for you to work out, and have integrated them into the text chapters. Your professor will clarify those things that I have not communicated well, and provide you with additional examples and illustrations, but above all he or she will assign problems for homework. The secret to success is simple, do your homework regularly and keep up with the class. This is one subject you cannot cram the night before the examination. You can expect statistics to be time-consuming, but if you keep up with the homework, it should not be unusually difficult.

1.4 The Calculator

The hand-held calculator has become so inexpensive and is such a labor saving device that you really cannot justify being without one. I now expect everyone in my classes to obtain and use a calculator. Buy only what you need, however, and do not waste money on expensive features that have no immediate application to statistics. In addition to the four arithmetic functions, your calculator must have a memory capacity and a square root function. These are all the capabilities required for any statistics covered in this book and indeed for any computations short of those that would be referred to a computer. A ten-digit display capacity is preferable to an eight-digit display since we will occasionally deal with quite large numbers. The calculator that I take to class is powered by a photoelectric cell, so that it operates from ambient light and does not need batteries. This seems to me a convenient and practical feature and has the potential to be anxiety-reducing as well, since it regularly happens that someone has battery failure midway through the final exam. Most students entering college will be quite familiar with the hand-held calculator, but if you are obtaining one for the first time, read its operating manual and learn how to use its features. You will soon come to regard the calculator as a valuable and useful tool.

1.5 The Computer

Although computers have existed for decades, they have remained a mystery to the vast majority of people who do not have direct contact with them. In general, we have become accustomed to thinking of computers as large devices that require special skills for operation and are suitable for large masses of data. Such main-frame computers, as they are called, are usually found in universities. You may have access to one and might even use it to compute your homework problems for this course. More likely though, if you use any computer, it will be one of the recently emerged group known as personal computers, or microcomputers. These small, and in some cases quite inexpensive, computers use BASIC computer language. They are easy to learn to use, have impressive capacity, and will surely revolutionize life for broad masses of people in the areas of data management and education. I think that learning to construct and use BASIC computer programs to perform statistical calculations could be a useful auxiliary to the growing conceptual understanding that you will acquire as you work your way through your statistics course. With this in mind, programs in BASIC computer language for most of the computations covered in this book have been included in Appendix IV. These programs are written in Microsoft BASIC and can be adapted, where necessary, to any microcomputer. If you have a microcomputer I encourage you to explore the programs in Appendix IV. Don't just copy and use them in a dependent way, but try to improve them in terms of efficiency or by adding features; this can be a very rewarding way to learn about statistics as well as about computers.

An aside: it computes but I comprehend

Computers are so impressive in their speed and precision that there is a temptation to credit them with conceptual powers and to shift the burden of comprehension from human to machine. It is perfectly all right to let machines do the tedious work, but it is quite unacceptable to hand over the responsibility for making decisions and understanding what is going on. The more the computer does for you the greater is your need to have a clear understanding of the rationale of the computations. Remember that the responsibility to understand the meaning of the computations belongs to you and not to the computer. The computer is your servant; don't let it become your master. A lovely bit of poetry by Brian Aldiss (1975) conveys, I think, an uplifting thought in this context.

> "The biochemic interweaving force
> That we call Nature, aeons back devised,
> From cell and jell, computers light enough
> To work effectively and fast, be tough,
> And utilize a power-source micro-sized—
>   Computers called the human brain, of course."

---

2 Data

2.1 What Are We Talking About?

Unambiguous communication requires that the terminology used be clearly defined and understood. Scientists in general, and statisticians in particular, use precisely defined terms and symbols both as a convenient shorthand and as a means of accurate communication. The beginning student of statistics thus acquires a new vocabulary. In this section we will define some basic terminology. Since long-winded attempts to explain or justify the importance of each bit of terminology may not be effective at this point, we will proceed through the definitions in an orderly and quick-paced fashion. The repeated use of these terms in subsequent discussions will provide ample demonstration of the importance of the underlying concepts.

population

A *population* consists of all of the organisms, objects, or events of a specified type. Population membership must be clearly defined so it can be known with certainty whether or not any given individual or event belongs to that population. For example, we might define our population of interest as all children enrolled in grade four in the public school system of your city, or all female freshmen at your university this semester. Both of these definitions are unambiguous; any individual may be determined to be either included in, or excluded from, the population in question.

sample

A *sample* is any subgroup or subset of a population. Many populations are so large that it is impractical to observe all of the members, and scientists therefore resort to observing a relatively small number, termed a sample, which serves to represent that population. The characteristics of many populations can never be known in the sense of having been directly observed, but rather they are inferred from measures taken on samples. In order for such inferences to be accurate, the samples must accurately represent their populations. In Chapter 6 we will examine the method by which samples are drawn from populations to achieve representativeness.

An aside on sample and population

Here is another perspective on the matter of sample and population. Consider the measurement of a characteristic that is not directly observable, such as intelligence, creativity, anxiety, or honesty. We can never see a person's intelligence; we can only infer its existence through his or her behavior, which we might categorize as intelligent or nonintelligent. Stated in the simplest possible terms, an intelligence test is basically a series of items to which a person can respond intelligently or nonintelligently; if we count up the number or proportion of intelligent responses, then we have a measure of intelligence. The purpose behind this oversimplified characterization of intelligence tests is to point out that the individual's behavior during the test is regarded as a sample of the total repertoire (population) of behavior of which he or she is capable. The general conclusion regarding a person's amount or degree of intelligence is an inference because a sample of behavior is used to estimate characteristics of that person's behavior in general. The validity of this kind of inference rests on the same need for sample representativeness required for inferences from samples of subjects to their populations.

While it is sometimes convenient to think of populations as very large groups of organisms or events and samples as relatively small groups, this misses the point. Any group of organisms or events is a population if our interest is limited to those individuals. On the other hand, if our intent is to use the measures taken on some individuals as a basis for estimating the characteristics of those not directly observed, then the ones who were actually measured constitute a sample. The number of individuals is irrelevant; it is our purpose that defines whether they are a population or a sample.

A *parameter* is a numerical term that summarizes or describes a population. If, for example, the population of interest was all current members of the International Brotherhood of Teamsters, and we had measured the height of every member and calculated the average value, then that average value would be a parameter of that population.

parameter

A *statistic* is a numerical term that summarizes or describes a sample. If we had selected a sample of 100 individuals from the total membership of the International Brotherhood of Teamsters and had determined the average height of these persons, then that average value would be a statistic. Statistics are obtained from samples and are used to estimate population parameters. A parameter is a purely descriptive term, but a statistic is both a descriptive term (because it describes a sample characteristic), and an estimate of the corresponding population characteristic.

statistic

In science, observation is tantamount to measurement, and measures are usually expressed as numerical values that are termed *data*. We may define *data* as any recorded observations, although for our purposes these will invariably take numerical form. The word *data* is plural and refers to a group of observations; any particular observation such as an individual teamster's height, is a *datum*. When observations are recorded and gathered together they are termed the *raw data*. These are the observations/measures just as they were obtained and have not had anything done to them. Our various statistical procedures are performed on the raw data.

data

datum
raw data

When one uses the phrase raw data, it naturally implies its opposite, namely, cooked data. Contrary to what you might expect, cooked data does not refer to data that have been statistically analyzed. In fact, cooked data are data that

**An aside on
raw and cooked**

an unscrupulous experimenter has made up or otherwise tampered with; it refers to the deliberate falsification of observations. This is the most serious crime that one can commit in science and, when an individual is unmasked and found guilty of this behavior, the repercussions are severe.

---

variable

A *variable* is any observable/measurable property of organisms, objects, or events, such that individuals may differ in the amount, or kind, of this property. Height, reaction time, color preference, and tolerance of pain are some examples of human variables. Psychologists study behavioral variables, physiologists study body system variables, and so on. We refer to the behavior or property under investigation as the variable of interest.

quantitative variable

A *quantitative variable* is one in which the number derived from the measurement reflects the amount of the property in question. Length is a quantitative variable. Length is expressed as the number of measurement units such as centimeters or inches, and this numerical score corresponds to the actual physical size of the object. Quantitative measurement is the assignment of numerical quantity to the variable and is what we ordinarily understand the act of measurement to mean.

qualitative variable

A *qualitative variable* is a distinction of kind, and not amount. Qualitative measurement consists of classification into categories such as when people are classified as being male or female. The designations of male and female do not imply different amounts of the variable of gender but rather indicate different kinds or qualities of this variable. A qualitative measurement on the variable of hair color is the classification of people as being blonde, red-haired, brunette, and so forth. Qualitative measurement differentiates individuals in terms of their possession of specified qualities; such distinctions are frequently of great interest in behavioral science.

continuous variable

A *continuous variable* is one that may assume any value between maximum and minimum limits. Height is an example of a continuous variable since, within limits, any value is possible; if height was measured with sufficient precision, then no two people would have exactly the same height. Theoretically, a distinguishing feature of continuous variables is that they do not produce tied scores, that is, multiple occurrences of the same value, but this is only true when measurement reaches an infinite degree of precision. Since we cannot achieve infinite precision, all real-life measurement is expressed in discrete units, so that while some variables may be continuous, all actual data are discrete. Therefore, on any variable, if enough measures are taken, then tied scores will occur. If height was measured as finely as to the nearest millimeter, it would still be possible, if enough people were measured, to find two or more persons with the same height.

discrete variable

A *discrete variable* is one that can only assume certain numerical values, such as being restricted to whole numbers. Examples of discrete variables are number of children per family, score on a multiple choice test, and finish position in a race. If measures were taken of several such events, tied scores would be expected. The fact that some quantitative variables are discrete while others are continuous and that all continuous variables are expressed in discrete units does not usually pose a problem. In general, quantitative data, whether the variable is theoretically continuous or discrete, are analyzed by procedures known collectively as parametric statistics (if there are many tied scores, analysis by a nonparametric technique may be preferable). Qualitative data are analyzed by nonparametric techniques; these matters are discussed further at appropriate points in this book.

2.2 Review Exercises

1. Define or describe the following terms.

   (a) population
   (b) sample
   (c) parameter
   (d) statistic
   (e) datum
   (f) raw data

   (g) variable
   (h) quantitative variable
   (i) qualitative variable
   (j) continuous variable
   (k) discrete variable

2. Identify the following variables or measures as being either quantitative or qualitative.

   (a) color of Barbara's eyes
   (b) heart rate
   (c) Catholic
   (d) reaction time

   (e) pupil dilation
   (f) Hungarian
   (g) crop yield
   (h) paranoid schizophrenic

3. Identify the following variables or measures as being either continuous or discrete.

   (a) body temperature
   (b) atmospheric pressure
   (c) income tax bracket
   (d) sales resistance

   (e) number of books in the library
   (f) amount of money in your pocket
   (g) lung capacity
   (h) size of your cat's litter

2.3 The Essence of Science

All science may be observation but all observations are not scientific. Objectivity is the special quality of scientific observation. An *objective observation* is one that is not in any way affected by the opinions, values, or biases of the observer. This evening when you go home, someone may ask you to describe your statistics professor and you might respond (a) "He has a moustache," or (b) "He is gorgeous." Both of these statements are observations but only (a) is scientific because only it is objective. The acid test for objectivity is whether

objective

any other person viewing the same events would report the same things. This would be the case for presence of a moustache but a statement about beauty is an opinion that might not be shared by another observer.

subjective

A *subjective observation* is one that reflects the observer's personal point of view; clearly, there can be no science if the raw data are a matter of opinion. Experimenters may deal with subjective variables, such as the subjects' opinions of the performance of a political figure. Although these data represent the subjective opinions of the subjects, the crucial point is that the experimenter must maintain an objective relationship to the data and not influence the subjects' responses in any way. The essence of science is that the observer is objectively detached from the observations.

empirical

An *empirical event* is one which may be perceived by our senses (including any extension of them in the form of detection and/or recording apparatus). Science is an empirical enterprise because it deals with observable events and because its findings are based on objective observation rather than subjective impression. Behavioral scientists study not only overt responses but also internal events and processes such as emotions, motivations, and talents. Such internal events and abilities are interesting both in their own right and because they are presumed to influence overt behavior. But how can we have an objective and empirical science when we are dealing with events that are not directly observable and are completely subjective to the person experiencing them? For example, under certain conditions I experience an internal sensation that I call hunger. As a scientist, how could you study the influence of hunger on my behavior since my hunger is an event that you can never observe directly? The answer lies in an *operational definition*.

operational definition

An *operational definition* of a variable specifies the manner of measurement of the variable. Operational definitions are essential in science because they are a means by which we can achieve precision in our communication and objectivity in our data. The variable *speed* can be defined operationally as the number of kilometers or miles per hour. If someone reported that an object went by quickly or slowly we could not interpret this statement because it is subjective, but if he or she stated that the object went by at 20 km/hr or m/hr, there would be no misunderstanding about how speed was measured or how fast the object was going. Furthermore, any other person equipped with appropriate measuring apparatus would report the same speed score. Some years ago I performed an experiment that involved the measurement of fear in laboratory rats (Horvath et al., 1971). Now who can say whether rats experience a psychological state equivalent or analogous to what we humans call fear? Certainly not I. Rats ordinarily show a heart rate slowdown when exposed to a stimulus that is presumed to be fear-inducing. In this experiment the rats' heart rates were continuously monitored and fear was defined operationally as the amount of heart rate decrement in the presence of a fear-inducing stimulus relative to heart rate in a similar environment without the fear-inducing stimulation.

Operational definitions are the key to transforming subjective phenomena into observable/measurable variables. A subjective experience such as hunger cannot be observed directly; we can study hunger scientifically only if we define it operationally as a measurable event. Hunger could be defined operationally as the number of hours since having last eaten, or the amount of money one was willing to pay for a sandwich. An operational definition of success might be annual income in number of dollars and an operational definition of love for another person might be the number of kisses given per day.

It is important to appreciate the liabilities as well as the advantages of operational definitions. We have already said that operational definitions are essential because they enable unambiguous communication of exactly what was observed, assist in making observations objective by specifying overt means of measurement, and allow us to study, albeit indirectly, many purely subjective phenomena. But it is important to note that operational definitions are arbitrary ways to convert variables into objective numerical data. The need to measure may result in the reduction of subtle and complex variables into questionable oversimplifications. Ask yourself whether annual income is a valid or accurate reflection of success, or if the number of kisses per day adequately represents one person's love for another. When you read a research report, always pay close attention to how the variables were defined operationally; the writer may be talking about success but only measuring annual income.

People sometimes speak of "hard" science and "soft" science, though it is unclear whether they refer to qualities of the phenomena under study, the techniques used in experimentation, or states of mind of the investigators. This uncertainty notwithstanding, Physics would probably be termed a hard science, perhaps Psychology a soft science, and possibly Biology a lumpy science. If this characterization means anything at all, I think it refers to the relative predictability and controllability of the event under observation. Some natural events, such as chemical reactions, are less variable and consequently more repeatable than others such as behavior. Further, it is considerably more difficult to specify clear and indisputably valid operational definitions of behavioral events or internal psychological states. Thus behavioral data are in a sense less tangible than the data of some physical sciences. If hard and soft refer only to the "tangibility," as it were, of the phenomena being studied then I don't object. But some people confuse the predictability of the event being observed with the experimenter's regard for accurate measurement, and jump to the conclusion that some sciences are more rigorous than others: this is nonsense. Calling a field of inquiry a science means that its data are collected with controlled and objective procedures

An aside on the texture of science

and that these data are evaluated according to the established rules of empirical science. Science is defined by method, not by subject matter, and there are no texture gradations of correct methodology.

2.4 Review Exercises

1. Define or describe the following terms.
   - (a) objective
   - (b) subjective
   - (c) empirical event
   - (d) operational definition

2. Which of the following are operational definitions?
   - (a) popularity
   - (b) number of times Brenda is asked to dance
   - (c) anxiety
   - (d) height
   - (e) score on an I.Q. test
   - (f) degree of addiction to caffeine
   - (g) mark on an exam
   - (h) intelligence
   - (i) number of cups of coffee consumed per day
   - (j) number of seconds devoted to an item on the evening news
   - (k) amount of money earned by a racehorse during a season
   - (l) an alcohol content in the blood of 0.08 percent or greater

2.5 Types of Measurement

Behavioral science encompasses a broad spectrum of phenomena, and behavior scientists are thus interested in a diverse range of variables that cannot be represented quantitatively with equal precision. Thus, there are different types of measurement that have different properties, provide different information, and are analyzed by different methods. It is common to differentiate four types of measurement: ratio, interval, ordinal, and nominal.

ratio measurement

    Ratio measurement is quantitative; this means the numerical values are assigned in such a way that the size of the number reflects the amount of the variable being measured. Length expressed as number of measurement units such as centimeters or inches is a ratio measure, and when a thing is determined to be 15 units long or 18 units long, the numbers 15 and 18 reflect amounts of length. A ratio measure has a true zero point, which means that the number 0 reflects an absence of the variable in question, so that a thing that is 0 cm long or 0 in. long does not exist. In ratio measures, the numbers bear both a consistent interval relationship and ratio relationship to each other. By consistent interval relationship, we mean that the unit, or interval, of measurement refers to a constant amount of the variable throughout the measurement range. For example, 1 centimeter is the same amount of length regardless of whether it is the 1st, 24th, or 98th centimeter measured. Thus, 20 centimeters is as much longer than 15 centimeters as 80 centimeters is longer than 75 centimeters. By ratio relationship, we mean that the proportions of the magnitudes of the variable are accurately reflected by the proportions of the numerical scores. As an example, 30 in. is twice as long as 15 in., and 20 in. is one third as long as 60 in. A true zero point is the essential feature of ratio measurement and is the basis for the property that different numerical values represent proportionally different variable magnitudes. Other examples of ratio measures are time measured in seconds, weight measured in pounds, the number of correctly answered items on a test, and the frequency of being asked to dance. If the duration of an event is measured to the nearest second, then duration has been operationally defined as number of seconds; frequency of being asked to dance might serve as an operational definition of popularity.

Interval measurement is quantitative, meaning that it yields numbers that reflect the amount of the variable. Unlike ratio measurement, an interval measure does not have a true zero point; this means that in an interval measure the zero value is defined arbitrarily and does not reflect an absence of the variable. An example of interval measurement is temperature expressed in degrees Celsius (also in degrees Fahrenheit). Zero degrees Celsius is defined as the temperature at which water freezes; this arbitrary definition of 0°C has the effect that numerical values in the Celsius scale do not bear a ratio relationship to each other. As a result, 20°C is not half as hot as 40°C; in the Fahrenheit scale, 30°F is not three times as hot as 10°F. In interval measurement, however, the numerical values do bear a consistent interval relationship to each other. The units of measurement reflect a constant amount of the variable throughout the measurement range; thus, it is true that 20°C is as much hotter than 10°C as 40°C is hotter than 30°C, and the difference in heat between 40°F and 35°F is the same as that between 85°F and 90°F. Interval measurement can yield negative scores such as a temperature reading of minus ten degrees Celsius (−10°C), whereas in ratio measurement, negative scores are impossible. (Negative scores do not ordinarily pose any problem for statistical analysis.)

interval measurement

Here is a situation that occurs regularly in behavioral science. Suppose that subjects are asked to rate on a numerical scale, say a 10 point scale, some attribute, say attractiveness, of several stimuli. The subjects would be given verbal definitions of at least the extreme numerical values, such as 10 = extremely attractive and 0 = extremely unattractive, and would then proceed to evaluate each stimulus by assigning a number within these limits. Can such scores be regarded as interval data? Conclusively establishing that such data have interval properties would be difficult, and yet it seems likely that this is the case. Our psychological experience with numbers is based on ratio conceptions of counting and physical measures; thus, it seems reasonable that, given a definition of the extreme values, people would tend to subdivide the intervening space into approximately equal units. The technique of assigning numerical quantity to psychological attributes is known as magnitude estimation and has long been used in the areas of perception and psychophysics. Indeed, subjects may be instructed to assign numerical values that are proportional to the perceived attribute, in which case the data are treated as a ratio measure. There is some evidence (D'Amato, 1970) that this is valid.

An aside on intelligence

Intelligence is often defined operationally as the score obtained on a standard intelligence test, and such scores are usually treated as interval data. (Intelligence test scores can only be regarded as ratio data if it is assumed that a score of zero reflects a complete absence of intelligence.) Treating intelligence test scores as interval data assumes that the unit of measurement (one test score point) reflects a constant amount of intelligence throughout the range. In other words, the difference in intelligence reflected by the scores 105 and 95 is assumed to be the same as the difference in intelligence reflected by the scores 75 and 65. This is an assumption that may be subject to question.

---

ordinal measurement

Ordinal measurement consists of rank ordering. For example, an ordinal measurement of some number of individuals on the variable of beauty consists of identifying them as the first most beautiful, the second most beautiful, the third most beautiful, and so on. Ordinal measurement is not quantitative; the numbers assigned reflect ordinal position (rank) only and in no way measure or reflect the amount or magnitude of the variable. In a beauty contest, individuals may be ranked 1st, 2nd, 3rd, etc.: these numbers are not measures of beauty, although it can be said that the individual at any rank is more beautiful than lower ranking persons and less beautiful than higher ranking persons. Suppose a person ranked the desirability of five food items in the following order: lobster, steak, chicken, hamburger, and sardines. Could it be said that the person preferred lobster over steak by the same amount as he or she preferred steak over chicken, or hamburger over sardines? The answer is no. There can be no presumption of equal variable differences between pairs of adjacent ranks. We may be unwilling to regard I.Q. test scores as being a ratio or interval representation of the variable of intelligence; such scores might be used with greater, although not complete, confidence to rank individuals. Such ranks would carry no implications concerning the absolute amount of intelligence or the amount by which one individual differed from another.

Nominal measurement is classification. In nominal measurement the individuals or objects are classified as belonging to one or another of a set of categories. For example, the nominal measurement of people on the variable of gender consists of classifying each as being male or female. A nominal measurement on the variable of hair color is the classification of individuals as blonde, brown-haired, black-haired, red-haired, etc. Nominal measurement requires a set of categories, which is exhaustive, meaning that the range of categories is sufficient to encompass all individuals, and in which the categories are mutually exclusive, meaning that any individual can belong to only one category. (See *An Aside: "Friends, Romans, countrymen. ..."*) The numbers obtained from nominal measurement are the frequencies of occurrence of the nominal classes, or types. Nominal measurement is not quantitative; if one determines that a room contains 25 males and 32 females, these numbers are frequencies of occurrence and are not measures of amount or degree of masculinity or femininity. Nominal measurement is most often classification by qualitative distinctions such as gender, nationality, and political affiliation. Continuous variables are sometimes reduced to nominal distinctions when we lack confidence that we can reliably measure them in quantitative terms. For example, experimenters sometimes wish to determine whether "high anxious" and "low anxious" persons differ in their response to some situation. A typical procedure for selecting the subject groups is to administer some measure of anxiety to a large number of people and operationally define "high anxious" as those who score in the top 25 percent, and "low anxious" as those who score in the bottom 25 percent.

nominal measurement

Shakespeare's Mark Antony, in the tragedy *Julius Caesar*, began his eulogy of Caesar with the words, "Friends, Romans, countrymen. ..." It may seem at first that these three types of people are alternative classes in a nominal measurement, but in fact, these designations are not mutually exclusive; an individual could be a friend *and* a Roman. Actually, nominal measurement is occurring on three separate variables: friend or non-friend, Roman or non-Roman, and countryman or non-countryman. This serves to illustrate another facet of nominal measurement, which is that any individual may be simultaneously subjected to nominal classification on more than one variable dimension. We shall gain a fuller understanding of what is meant by mutually exclusive in Chapter 5, and we shall deal specifically with multidimensional nominal classification in Chapter 14.

An aside: "Friends, Romans, countrymen. ..."

The reference to intelligence test scores in *An aside on intelligence* points out that interval/ratio operational definitions may require assumptions about the variable that we are unwilling to grant. In such instances it may be more prudent to use a simpler form of measurement. Data may be readily transformed from a more complex to a less complex form, but not in the opposite direction. For example, if some number of people were measured on the variable height, these ratio scores could be ranked. This would require the adoption of a rule for assigning the ranks such as assigning first rank to the tallest individual. (Since such rules are arbitrary, one could as well have used the rule that first rank goes to the shortest individual). The height scores could be nominalized by simply identifying some as tall and others as short. This requires that a definition of what constitutes tall and short be arrived at, such as persons at or above 178 cm shall be deemed tall, and those below 178 cm shall be deemed short. The following chart serves to illustrate.

Height in cm (ratio)	Height ranks (ordinal)	Height classification (nominal)
175	3	short
183	1	tall
162	5	short
178	2	tall
157	6	short
165	4	short

It is clear that as we go from ratio to ordinal to nominal measurement, we have less and less information about the heights of these subjects, both in absolute terms and relative to each other. Since information is lost when data are transformed into simpler forms, this is usually not done unless there is some question as to the validity of the original form of measurement, as might be the case for intelligence test scores. If the original data have characteristics that violate the assumptions of a particular statistical analysis, then transformation into a simpler form and analysis by another method may be appropriate.

Data that are obtained from ratio and interval measurement are quantitative and permit the calculation of parameter values (such as an average score), and are suitable for use in many computational procedures. For purposes of statistical analysis, the distinction between interval and ratio data is unimportant and henceforth the term interval/ratio will be used. Nominal and ordinal data are not quantitative in nature and do not lend themselves as readily to the calculation of parameters or to arithmetical manipulation. This is not to say that nominal and ordinal measurement are not of use in science. There are many occasions when we are interested in determining whether different types of individuals, such as males compared to females, or 20-year-olds compared to 40-year-olds, differ on some behavioral measure, and in such cases nominal distinctions are at the heart of the research. Since nominal and ordinal data provide less information, interval/ratio measurement is preferred for the behavior or event that the experiment is designed to study.

2.6 Review Exercises

1. Define or describe the following terms.

    (a) ratio measurement
    (b) interval measurement
    (c) ordinal measurement
    (d) nominal measurement

2. What type of measurement is occurring in each case?

    (a) kilometers per hour
    (b) 5th ranked heavyweight
    (c) "LADIES and GENTLEMEN"
    (d) exam grades (A, B, C, etc.)
    (e) the outcome of a coin flip   –
    (f) amount of money in your bank account   *ratio*
    (g) day of the week   *nominal*
    (h) income tax bracket   *nominal*
    (i) degrees Kelvin   *interval*
    (j) top seed in a tennis tournament   *ordinal*
    (k) exam marks   *interval*
    (l) percentage of people absent from class today   *ratio*
    (m) qualifying position in prerace time trials   *ratio*

2.7 Concluding Remarks

Chapter 2 is concerned with establishing some conceptual and terminological groundwork as a basis upon which to proceed. If it seems that these terms and concepts do not form a unified whole or interconnected theme, this is not cause for alarm. Actually, we have a good deal more to learn that is of a fundamental nature before we can completely integrate and apply these concepts; I regard the first seven chapters of this book as comprising this fundamental material. We will turn next to numerical data, and to the very practical matter of making some sense out of what we have observed.

3 Some Descriptive Statistics

Chapter Preview

3.8 Averages

Describes three methods of calculating an average and compares their properties

Key Terms   mode   median
                    unimodal   arithmetic mean
                    bimodal   unbiased

3.9 Review Exercises

3.10 Variability

Describes what is meant by variability in numerical data and the manner by which this property is measured

Key Terms   variability   variance
                    range   standard deviation
                    Sum of Squares   bias

3.11 Review Exercises

3.12 Concluding Remarks

3.1 Introduction

Descriptive statistics refers to all the organizational procedures and summarizing terms that describe characteristics of the raw data. Description is a first priority when we have collected numerical data because we cannot appreciate the information contained in a mass of numbers until they have been organized in some meaningful way and useful summary terms, such as an average, have been calculated. Describing the data's characteristics can be an end in itself or just the first step to inferring the characteristics of a larger population. Since the focus of this book is inferential statistics, our discussion of descriptive procedures is intended primarily to acquaint the reader with terminology and to lay down conceptual foundations for later discussions of inferential procedures. This is not to imply, however, that descriptive procedures are not interesting or important in their own right.

3.2 Frequency Distributions and Graphs

Frequency Distributions

A *frequency distribution* is an arrangement that lists all possible data values or types, and shows the frequency of occurrence of each one. Frequency distributions enable the viewer to see aspects of the data that are not easily detected by merely scanning the raw scores, for example, whether the

frequency distribution

Table 3.2–1 Frequency distribution of age for subjects aged 17 to 35 years

Age to nearest year	Frequency
35	5
34	3
33	3
32	4
31	3
30	5
29	8
28	12
27	8
26	7
25	10
24	14
23	16
22	35
21	40
20	58
19	85
18	14
17	1
	331

Table 3.2–2 Frequency and cumulative frequency of ages for subjects aged 17 to 35 years

Age	Frequency	Cumulative frequency
35	5	331
34	3	326
33	3	323
32	4	320
31	3	316
30	5	313
29	8	308
28	12	300
27	8	288
26	7	280
25	10	273
24	14	263
23	16	249
22	35	233
21	40	198
20	58	158
19	85	100
18	14	15
17	1	1

data are bunched at one or several points or spread evenly throughout the measurement range. Assembling raw data into a frequency distribution is a purely descriptive operation; the scores are not altered or transformed in any way, but are merely organized.

In a study on physical attractiveness, Horvath (1979) tested students enrolled in undergraduate psychology courses. Table 3.2–1 shows the frequency distribution of age for the 331 subjects who were between 17 and 35 years old. An unorganized printout of the 331 age scores would be very difficult to interpret, but a glance at Table 3.2–1 shows that 19 was the most frequently occurring age, the age scores were bunched in the region of the late teens and early twenties, and there were four times as many persons aged 21 as there were aged 25.

cumulative frequency distribution

A *cumulative frequency distribution* is one in which the frequency of observations at each data value is added to the frequencies of preceding values; thus, the frequency values accumulate as one reads up the listing of the data values, or types. Table 3.2–2 illustrates a cumulative frequency distribution. Cumulative frequency distributions enable a quick determination of the percentage of observations above or below some value. For example, $308/331 \times 100 = 93.05$ percent of the subjects were less than 30 years old. They also provide an indication of where the bulk of the data lie. It can be seen in the chart that the cumulative total increases very rapidly at first but only slowly after age 28.

The identification of every possible data value sometimes results in a long list over which the raw scores are so spread out that the summarizing purpose of a frequency distribution is not achieved. The solution in such cases is to establish class intervals, which divide the range of measurement into a manageable number of units. A *class interval* is a specified range of observation values, and the resulting frequency distribution lists the number of observations in each class interval.

class interval

During the 1973 season, there were 144 players among the 26 National Football League teams who carried the ball 10 or more times (Neft, et al., 1974). These individuals ended the season with average yards-per-carry scores ranging from 1.1 to 6.6. Suppose we wished to construct a frequency distribution that showed the number of players who achieved various yards-per-carry performances. Between the known limits of 1.1 and 6.6, there are 55 discriminable values, i.e., 1.2, 1.3, 1.4, . . . 6.5, so that a total of 57 data value entries would be required if we wanted to list all of the possible scores. Although this would be the most accurate presentation of the data, it would be very lengthy and difficult to take in at a glance. In addition, 144 scores distributed over 57 performance level possibilities would not be likely to result in a smooth or informative distribution; it could also be argued that distinctions of one-tenth of a yard are too fine for summarizing purposes.

Table 3.2–3 Distribution of yards-per-carry averages by NFL players with 10 or more carries during the 1973 season

Average yards-per-carry	Frequency
7.0–7.4	0
6.5–6.9	2
6.0–6.4	5
5.5–5.9	7
5.0–5.4	7
4.5–4.9	20
4.0–4.4	28
3.5–3.9	33
3.0–3.4	21
2.5–2.9	12
2.0–2.4	6
1.5–1.9	2
1.0–1.4	1
0.5–0.9	0
	144

(Adapted from Neft, et al., 1974)

The solution to these difficulties lies in establishing yards-per-carry class intervals. The conventional practice is to adopt a class interval size that will divide the range of observations into about 10 to 15 intervals; in the present case, an interval size of 0.5 yards would be suitable. Table 3.2–3 on the previous page shows the frequency distribution of NFL players who achieved yards-per-carry averages in the indicated class intervals during the 1973 season.

The class interval boundaries must be specified with sufficient precision that every observation can be placed unambiguously into one interval. This ordinarily means that the class interval limits must be expressed with equal or finer measurement precision than the raw data. The class intervals shown in Table 3.2–3 will suffice only if the average yards-per-carry scores are expressed with accuracy to one decimal place. If the raw data had been expressed at two decimal places accuracy, then the class intervals would have been 0.50–0.99, 1.00–1.49, 1.50–1.99, ... 7.00–7.49.

When calculating summary statistics from frequency distribution data it is sometimes necessary to specify the exact limits of the class intervals. The *exact limits* are one-half unit to either side of the class interval values, as shown in the table.

exact limits

Class interval	Exact limits	Class interval	Exact limits
7.0–7.4	6.95–7.45	7.00–7.49	6.995–7.495
6.5–6.9	6.45–6.95	6.50–6.99	6.495–6.995
6.0–6.4	5.95–6.45	6.00–6.49	5.995–6.495
⋮	⋮	⋮	⋮
0.5–0.9	0.45–0.95	0.50–0.99	0.495–0.995

When class intervals are constructed in terms of exact limits, an arbitrary convention must be adopted to deal with the occurrence of a score equal to an exact limit value. The usual practice is to place such a score into the next higher interval; thus, the score 6.45 would be counted in the 6.45–6.95 interval. We shall encounter examples of the use of exact limits in the discussion of percentiles in Section 3.4 and the median in Section 3.8.

Graphs

graph
abscissa

ordinate

A *graph* may be thought of as a pictorial representation of a frequency distribution or data table. Graphs are drawn such that the *abscissa,* or horizontal axis, is marked in units representing the variable of interest, and the *ordinate,* or vertical axis, is marked in units indicating frequency or amount. The most pleasing visual result is obtained when the height of the ordinate is two-thirds to three-quarters of the abscissa length, although this rule is not inviolable. The commonly differentiated types of graphs are bar graphs, frequency polygons, and histograms.

In a *bar graph*, the frequency or amount of each type of observation is represented by a vertical bar, and the bars themselves are separated by some space. Bar graphs are useful to depict frequencies of nominal variables because the distinctness of the bars reinforces the distinctness of the nominal classes of observation.

bar graph

Suppose one kept track of the total yards gained in every game by each football team in a given league. At the end of the season these data could be organized into a table showing total yards offense by each team. Table 3.2–4 presents these data for the 13 American Conference teams of the National Football League during the 1973 season. (Students of the game will recall this as the season that Buffalo running back O. J. Simpson rushed for a record 2003 yards.) Table 3.2–4 constitutes a performance comparison of the 1973 AFC teams. The listing of the teams is alphabetical, but this is quite arbitrary; since team identity is a nominal variable, any order could be used. Figure 3.2–1a is a bar graph that presents the total yards offense by the AFC football teams during the 1973 season.

Table 3.2–4 Total yards offense by AFC teams in the 1973 season

Team	Total yards offense
Baltimore	3,777
Buffalo	4,324
Cincinnati	4,675
Cleveland	3,709
Denver	4,660
Houston	3,758
Kansas City	3,832
Miami	4,196
New England	4,193
New York	4,217
Oakland	5,121
Pittsburgh	4,300
San Diego	3,943
	54,705

(Adapted from Neft, et al., 1974)

Since the heights of the bars are proportional to the amounts or frequencies they represent, one can make relative comparisons conveniently and quickly. Note that Figure 3.2–1a shows only the tip of the iceberg, so to speak, in that the first 3500 yards of offense is not represented. Oakland appears to have gained several times as many yards as Cleveland; however, if the ordinate is marked from 0 to 5200 yards, as in Figure 3.2–1b (on page 29), the performances of the teams appear more similar. One should examine the

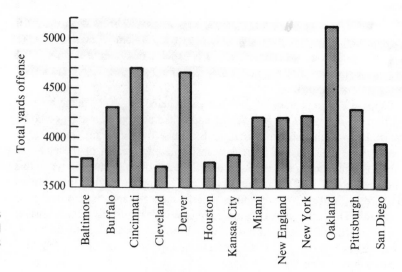

Figure 3.2–1a Total yards offense by AFC football teams during the 1973 season

values marked on the ordinate carefully in order to get a true perspective of the data being represented.

Bar graphs can be made more complex so as to present more information, as shown by Figure 3.2–2, in which total offense is divided into rushing and passing yardage by each team.

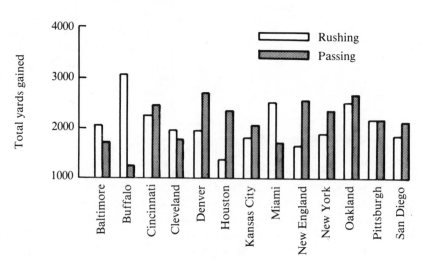

Figure 3.2–2 Total rushing and passing yardage by AFC football teams during the 1973 season

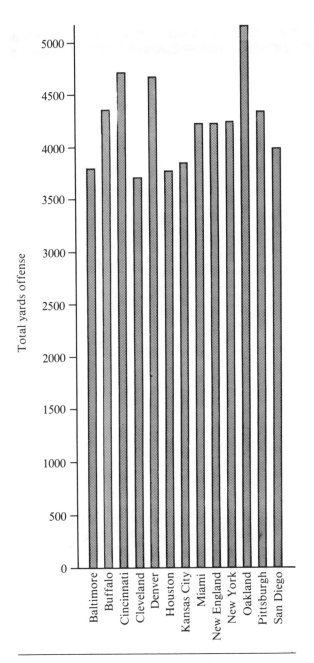

Figure 3.2–1b   Total yards offense by AFC football teams during the 1973 season

frequency polygon

A *frequency polygon* is constructed so that the frequency of each data value is plotted as a point and the points are then connected by straight lines. This creates an impression of continuity between the data points and thus frequency polygons are an appropriate way to depict interval/ratio variables. Figure 3.2–3 presents the age distribution data shown earlier in Table 3.2–1.

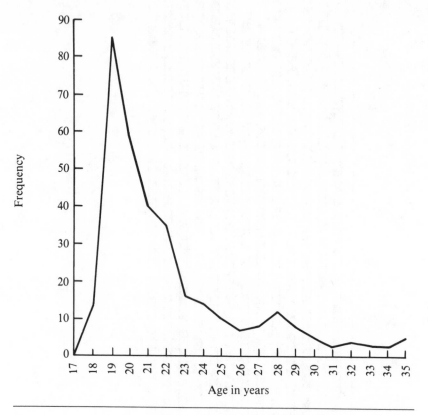

Figure 3.2–3   Frequency polygon of age distribution for subjects aged 17 to 35 years

More than one frequency polygon may be plotted on the same set of axes, thereby increasing the amount of information presented and providing a direct comparison. Figure 3.2–4 shows the age distributions of the male and female subjects separately by using different lines to represent the two groups.

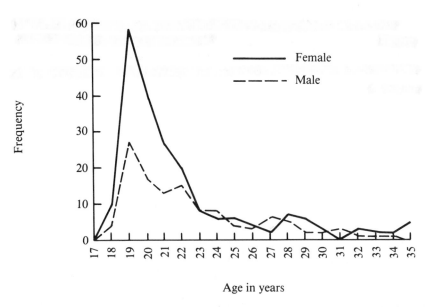

Figure 3.2–4 Age distribution of male and female subjects aged 17 to 35 years

When the frequency polygon is a representation of a frequency distribution organized by class intervals, the usual practice is to plot the frequency point over the midpoint of the class interval. This procedure is illustrated in Figure 3.2–5, which presents the average yards-per-carry data shown earlier in Table 3.2–4.

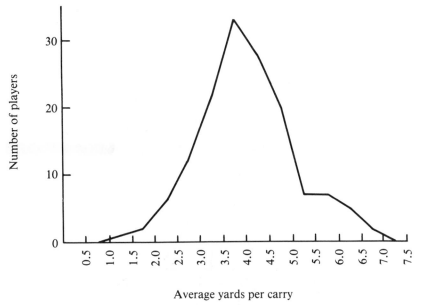

Figure 3.2–5 Distribution of yards-per-carry average by NFL players with 10 or more carries during the 1973 season

histogram

A *histogram* uses vertical bars to depict frequencies of an interval/ratio variable; it differs from a bar graph in not having spaces between the bars. When the same data are presented as a histogram and frequency polygon, the histogram will tend to emphasize the differences between the score frequencies, whereas the frequency polygon will tend to emphasize continuity between them. Figure 3.2–6 is a histogram of the age distribution data in Table 3.2–1 that was shown earlier as a frequency polygon in Figure 3.2–3.

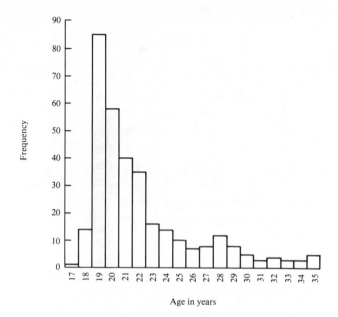

Figure 3.2–6 Histogram of age distribution for subjects aged 17 to 35 years

A distribution is termed symmetrical when the data frequencies decrease at equal rates above and below a central point. Visually this means that if the distribution is bisected, one half is the mirror image of the other, as is shown below and is fairly well the case in Figure 3.2–5. A nonsymmetrical

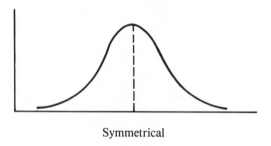

Symmetrical

distribution is termed *skewed* and appears visually as a bunching of the observations at one or the other end of the measurement range. If the observations are bunched at the lower score values, as is shown below and in Figure 3.2–3, the distribution is *positively skewed;* if the scores are bunched at the high end of the measurement range, it is termed *negatively skewed.*

skew

positive skew
negative skew

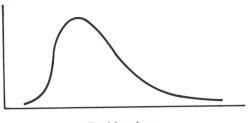

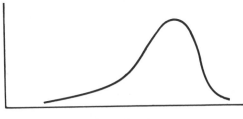

Positive skew   Negative skew

   The term *kurtosis* refers to the relative peakedness or flatness of the distribution and reflects whether the scores are more or less evenly distributed throughout the measurement range. A *leptokurtic* distribution is one in which the scores are bunched together with steeply sloping sides, and a *platykurtic* distribution is one in which the scores are more evenly spread out, as is shown below. Another way to think of it is that in a platykurtic distribution, a

kurtosis

leptokurtic
platykurtic

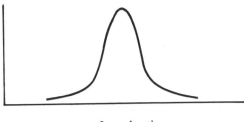

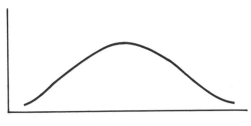

Leptokurtic   Platykurtic

relatively greater proportion of the scores fall toward the ends, or tails, of the distribution. A distribution that is neither too peaked nor too flat (but is just right) is termed mesokurtic. Kurtosis can be measured quantitatively and

Normal distribution
(mesokurtic)

mesokurtic actually refers to the kurtosis value of a theoretical frequency distribution known as the normal distribution. We shall become acquainted with the normal distribution in Chapter 4. Leptokurtic means more peaked than the normal distribution and platykurtic means more flat than the normal distribution.

In summary, frequency distributions and graphs are basic organizational devices that provide information at a glance regarding the distribution of the raw data, illustrate the point or points at which the observations are clustered, and allow comparisons between data value frequencies. The frequency distribution is most often the experimenter's first meaningful look at the raw data, and the insights thus provided may serve to direct more detailed analyses. A graph is the logical followup to the construction of a frequency distribution, both as an aid to comprehending the nature of the raw data and for communicating this information to others.

3.3 Review Exercises

1. Define or describe the following terms.

(a) frequency distribution
(b) cumulative frequency distribution
(c) class interval
(d) exact limits
(e) graph
(f) abscissa
(g) ordinate
(h) bar graph

(i) frequency polygon
(j) histogram
(k) skew
(l) positive skew
(m) negative skew
(n) kurtosis
(o) leptokurtic
(p) platykurtic

2. One hundred people who were enrolled in a physical fitness program were interviewed and measured to provide the following data: each person's weight (kg); the amount each was overweight for a person of that age and height (kg overweight); and each person's education in terms of the highest level completed. (The categories used were PS = public school, HS = high school, B = bachelor's degree, M = master's degree, and PhD = doctorate.) The raw data are shown in the chart on page 35.

(a) Construct a frequency distribution of the subjects' education data.
(b) Construct a frequency distribution of the subjects' kg overweight data.
(c) Construct a frequency distribution of the subjects' weight (kg) data.
(d) Construct a bar graph depicting the data in (a).
(e) Construct a frequency polygon depicting the data in (b).
(f) Construct a histogram depicting the data in (c).
(g) Construct a cumulative frequency distribution of the subjects' kg overweight data.

6 m

50

18 B

5 PHD   2 PS 19 HS

kg	kg overweight	Education	kg	kg overweight	Education
65	8	PS	82	13	B
75	9	HS	84	14	PhD
100	15	PS	79	10	PhD
117	18	HS	80	6	M
52	8	B	85	16	B
109	9	M	64	8	HS
93	17	PS	83	15	HS
79	11	M	87	13	HS
71	9	B	84	12	B
78	10	PS	88	15	HS
60	8	M	84	11	B
84	15	B	90	16	HS
73	11	B	95	16	HS
87	16	PS	108	18	PhD
66	13	B	95	17	B
83	14	PhD	109	20	HS
97	16	HS	72	9	M
114	16	B	89	15	M
58	7	PS	103	13	B
91	16	HS	78	11	PhD
87	14	M	74	9	B
92	14	HS	80	11	PS
93	17	HS	63	8	B
67	9	HS	86	15	B
70	9	B	81	12	HS
86	13	PS	104	15	B
91	13	HS	107	19	HS
74	10	HS	88	15	PhD
108	19	B	63	8	M
88	14	HS	110	17	B
77	8	HS	102	17	HS
83	14	B	99	16	HS
71	10	M	94	16	HS
98	18	M	80	14	B
96	17	PS	66	9	B
77	11	B	92	16	HS
106	18	HS	88	14	HS
81	12	HS	119	19	PS
76	10	HS	85	14	HS
68	9	B	89	15	B
76	12	B	82	12	B
92	14	PS	75	9	HS
86	15	PS	97	17	B
81	13	M	105	18	HS
56	7	B	79	13	M
94	17	HS	101	14	M
86	16	M	98	17	HS
73	12	HS	90	16	B
82	13	B	85	15	B
89	15	PS	76	9	HS

3.4 Percentiles, Deciles, and Quartiles

Percentiles, deciles, and quartiles can be useful ways to describe the relative position of a particular score within its distribution. They are frequently used in education to compare different individuals' performances relative to some reference group, or the same individual's performance on different tasks, again relative to some reference group or distribution.

percentile

    A *percentile* is the score value below which a specified percentage of the distribution falls. Suppose you were a member of a class of exactly 100 students; the class wrote an exam, your score was 83, and 90 other members of the class scored lower than 83. Your score of 83 would be termed the 90th percentile score because there were 90 scores (90 percent of the distribution) below 83. If a friend got a mark of 53, and 65 people scored higher than that, his mark of 53 would be termed the 34th percentile score because 34 percent of the distribution was below 53. In these examples the score 83 would be said to have a percentile rank of 90, and the score 53 a percentile rank of 34.

percentile rank

    We can raise two questions in connection with percentiles: (1) what is the *percentile rank* of any given score (that is, what percentage of scores fall below it), and (2) what score has a specified percentile rank (for example, what score has a percentile rank of 50, meaning that 50 percent of the distribution is below it). To illustrate the calculation of these values, we shall refer to the distribution of the ages of experimental subjects that is presented in Table 3.2–2. These data are shown with an additional column indicating cumulative percentage.

    The percentile rank of any given score can be read directly from the cumulative percentage column in Table 3.4–1. For example, the age score 25 has a percentile rank of 79.46, and the age score 30 has a percentile rank of 93.05.

    Let us select an arbitrary percentile rank such as the 50th percentile and determine which age score has that percentile rank. We can see from Table 3.4–1 that the age score of 21 has a percentile rank of 47.73 but there is no obvious score that has a percentile rank of 50. In order to make an exact determination of the 50th percentile score, we must digress briefly to consider an aspect of measurement.

    When a continuous variable is measured and assigned a quantity such as 10 cm, it does not mean that the thing is exactly 10 cm long, but only that it is closer to 10 cm than it is to 9 cm or 11 cm. The number 10 is merely a convenient label for the range of observations whose exact limits are 9.5 cm and 10.5 cm. Similarly, the exact limits of the range of values represented by the number 10.00 are 9.995 and 10.005. No matter how finely we measure or how precise our ruler is, every measurement value actually stands for a range of values whose exact limits are one-half unit higher and lower.

Table 3.4–1 Frequency, cumulative frequency, and cumulative percentage of subject ages

Age	Frequency	Cumulative frequency	Cumulative percentage
35	5	331	100.00
34	3	326	98.49
33	3	323	97.58
32	4	320	96.68
31	3	316	95.47
30	5	313	94.47 56
29	8	308	93.05
28	12	300	90.63
27	8	288	87.01
26	7	280	84.59
25	10 ƒ I	273	82.48
24	14	263	79.46
23	16	249	75.23
22	35	233	70.39
21	40	198	59.82
20	58	158	47.73
19	85	100	30.21
18	14	15	4.53
17	1	1	0.30

In the case of our age data, we can see from Table 3.4–1 that the age score 21 has a percentile rank of 47.73, which, since we want to identify the 50th percentile score, is too low. The age score 22 has a percentile rank of 59.82, which is clearly too high. The value we seek therefore, the unknown 50th percentile score, is somewhere in the range of values represented by the score 21, that is, somewhere between the upper and lower exact limits of 21.5 and 20.5. A convenient formula for determining the exact score value of the desired percentile score is

$$\text{Percentile score} = \text{LEL} + \left(\frac{f_{PR} - f_{LEL}}{f_{I}} \right) (S_{I})$$

where

LEL = lower exact limit of the score interval that contains the desired percentile score

f_{PR} = frequency of scores (number of raw scores) that will be below the specified percentile rank (f_{PR} = specified percentile rank times the total number of scores, divided by 100)

f_{LEL} = cumulative frequency of scores below the interval that contains the desired percentile score

f_I = frequency of scores within the interval that contains the desired percentile score

S_I = size of the interval (number of measurement units) that contains the desired percentile score

In the case of determining the 50th percentile score for the age data in Table 3.4–1, the terms can be seen to be

LEL = 20.5

$$f_{PR} = \frac{(50)(331)}{100} = 165.5$$

$f_{LEL} = 158$

$f_I = 40$

$S_I = 1$

The 50th percentile score is determined as follows.

$$\text{50th percentile score} = 20.5 + \left(\frac{165.5 - 158}{40}\right)(1.00)$$

$$= 20.5 + 0.19$$

$$= 20.69$$

Let us consider a case in which the data are grouped into a frequency distribution using class intervals. Table 3.4–2 shows the average yards-per-carry data presented earlier in Section 3.2.

Table 3.4–2　Frequency, cumulative frequency, and cumulative percentage of yards-per-carry averages by NFL players with 10 or more carries during the 1973 season

Average yards-per-carry	Frequency	Cumulative frequency	Cumulative percentage
7.0–7.4	0	144	100.00
6.5–6.9	2	144	100.00
6.0–6.4	5	142	98.61
5.5–5.9	7	137	95.14
5.0–5.4	7	130	90.28
4.5–4.9	20	123	85.42
4.0–4.4	28	103	71.53
3.5–3.9	33	75	52.08
3.0–3.4	21	42	29.17
2.5–2.9	12	21	14.58
2.0–2.4	6	9	6.25
1.5–1.9	2	3	2.08
1.0–1.4	1	1	0.69
0.5–0.9	0	0	0.00

(Adapted from Neft, et al., 1974)

The calculation of any desired percentile score follows the formula presented earlier. The 75th percentile yards-per-carry score can be calculated as follows.

$$\text{75th percentile score} = 4.45 + \left(\frac{108 - 103}{20}\right)(0.50)$$

$$\frac{75 \times 144}{100} = 108$$

$$= 4.45 + 0.13$$

$$= 4.58$$

Suppose you wished to identify the percentile rank of a given average yards-per-carry score, such as 3.3 yards-per-carry. When the data are grouped into class intervals, this cannot be done merely by reading from the cumulative percentage column. The solution may be obtained by the following formula.

$$\text{Percentile rank} = \frac{f_{\text{LEL}} + [(X - \text{LEL})/S_I][f_I]}{N} \times 100$$

where

X = the given score whose percentile rank is being determined

f_{LEL} = cumulative frequency of scores below the interval containing the given score

LEL = lower exact limit of the interval containing the given score

S_I = size of the interval (number of measurement units) containing the given score

f_I = frequency of scores within the interval containing the given score

N = total number of scores

The percentile rank of the score 3.3 yards-per-carry is

$$\text{Percentile rank} = \frac{21 + [(3.3 - 2.95)/0.50][21]}{144} \times 100$$

$$= \frac{21 + [0.70][21]}{144} \times 100$$

$$= 24.79$$

Deciles are scores that divide the distribution into tenths; the 1st decile has 10 percent of the distribution below it, the 2nd decile has 20 percent of the distribution below it, and so on. The 1st decile corresponds to the 10th percentile, the 4th decile to the 40th percentile, and so on. *Quartiles* divide the distribution into fourths: the 1st quartile has 25 percent of the distribution below it and corresponds to the 25th percentile, the 2nd quartile has 50 percent of the distribution below it and corresponds to the 50th percentile, and so on. Particular decile and quartile values may be determined using the method described earlier for percentiles; merely translate the decile/quartile value of interest into the appropriate percentile value.

decile

quartile

3.5 Review Exercises

1. Define or describe the following terms.

   (a) percentile
   (b) percentile rank
   (c) decile
   (d) quartile

2. Using the data in Table 3.4–1, determine

   (a) the percentile rank of the age scores 32, 27, and 18.
   (b) the age scores that have percentile ranks of 25, 80, and 95.

3. Using the data in Table 3.4–2, determine

   (a) the percentile rank of the yards-per-carry scores 2.1, 4.2, and 5.7.
   (b) the yards-per-carry scores that have percentile ranks of 30, 50, and 99.

3.6 Summation Notation

In this section we will take the first steps toward learning the vocabulary of symbolic notation used in statistics. The notational symbols comprise something of a second language and are used in place of words because they are convenient, precise, and allow formulas and operations to be expressed in general terms.

The upper case letter X is commonly used to represent the variable of interest, with individual scores being identified by numerical subscripts. If we measured the heights of some individuals, we could use X as the variable name for height scores, and X_1, X_2 and so on as identifiers of individual scores. If we had measured the heights of five persons, these data might be presented as follows.

Subject	X (height in cm)
1	$X_1 = 155$
2	$X_2 = 173$
3	$X_3 = 165$
4	$X_4 = 178$
5	$X_5 = 168$

In this listing, X serves as the general name for height; the height of the first subject is $X_1 = 155$ cm, the height of the second subject is $X_2 = 173$ cm, and so on.

The letter n is used to indicate the number of observations (scores) that we have gathered. In the previous example we measured the heights of five persons; therefore, $n = 5$.

A frequently used notation in statistics is the summation operator, which is symbolized by Σ (*capital Greek letter sigma*). In words, Σ means the sum of. When Σ occurs before a letter representing a variable, as in ΣX, it means the sum of all n scores of the type represented by X. In general terms we would express the meaning of ΣX as

$\Sigma (sigma)$

$$\Sigma X = X_1 + X_2 + X_3 + \cdots + X_n$$

In words, this expression states that ΣX is equal to the first X score plus the second X score plus the third X score and so on down to and including the last, or nth, X score.

In the example just given X represents the variable height and was measured on $n = 5$ persons; in this context ΣX means the sum of the five height scores. Thus

$$\Sigma X = X_1 + X_2 + X_3 + \cdots + X_n$$
$$= 155 + 173 + 165 + 178 + 168$$
$$= 839$$

The expression ΣX^2 is used often in statistics and means the sum of the squared X's, that is, the sum of the scores obtained when each X value is squared (multiplied by itself). The expression ΣX^2 reads as the sum of the squared X's because squaring has a higher priority than summing (see Appendix II). Thus

$$\Sigma X^2 = X_1^2 + X_2^2 + X_3^2 + \cdots + X_n^2$$

In terms of our data

$$\Sigma X^2 = (155)^2 + (173)^2 + (165)^2 + (178)^2 + (168)^2$$
$$= 24{,}025 + 29{,}929 + 27{,}225 + 31{,}684 + 28{,}224$$
$$= 141{,}087$$

The expression $(\Sigma X)^2$ means the square of the sum, that is, the sum of the X values squared. Thus

$$(\Sigma X)^2 = (X_1 + X_2 + X_3 + \cdots + X_n)^2$$

In terms of our data

$$(\Sigma X)^2 = (155 + 173 + 165 + 178 + 168)^2$$
$$= (839)^2$$
$$= 703{,}921$$

Note

$$\Sigma X^2 \neq (\Sigma X)^2$$

A *constant* is represented by the letter c. It is a term that can be any number, but its value remains constant (does not change) for the operation specified. The expression $\Sigma (X + c)$ means the sum of the scores obtained by adding a constant to each X value. Thus

$$\Sigma (X + c) = (X_1 + c) + (X_2 + c) + (X_3 + c) + \cdots + (X_n + c)$$

In terms of our data, if $c = 10$

$$\Sigma (X + c) = (155 + 10) + (173 + 10) + (165 + 10)$$
$$+ (178 + 10) + (168 + 10)$$
$$= 165 + 183 + 175 + 188 + 178$$
$$= 889$$

The expression ΣcX means the sum of the scores obtained by multiplying each X value by a constant. Thus

$$\Sigma cX = cX_1 + cX_2 + cX_3 + \cdots + cX_n$$

In terms of our data, if $c = 5$

$$\Sigma cX = (5)(155) + (5)(173) + (5)(165) + (5)(178) + (5)(168)$$
$$= 775 + 865 + 825 + 890 + 840$$
$$= 4195$$

If we measured the weights of our five subjects at the same time we obtained their heights, we could have represented the variable weight with the letter Y, and presented the data as follows.

Subject	X (height in cm)	Y (weight in kg)
1	155	46
2	173	68
3	165	52
4	178	81
5	168	64

The expression ΣY means the sum of all n scores of the type represented by Y. Thus

$$\Sigma Y = Y_1 + Y_2 + Y_3 + \cdots + Y_n$$

In terms of our data

$$\Sigma Y = 46 + 68 + 52 + 81 + 64$$
$$= 311$$

The expression $\Sigma(X + Y)$ means the sum of the scores obtained by adding each X value to its corresponding Y value, that is, the Y value taken from the same subject. Thus

$$\Sigma(X + Y) = (X_1 + Y_1) + (X_2 + Y_2) + (X_3 + Y_3) + \cdots$$
$$+ (X_n + Y_n)$$

In terms of our data

$$\Sigma(X + Y) = (155 + 46) + (173 + 68) + (165 + 52)$$
$$+ (178 + 81) + (168 + 64)$$
$$= 201 + 241 + 217 + 259 + 232$$
$$= 1150$$

The expression ΣXY means the sum of the scores obtained by multiplying each X value by its corresponding Y value. Thus

$$\Sigma XY = X_1Y_1 + X_2Y_2 + X_3Y_3 + \cdots + X_nY_n$$

In terms of our data

$$\Sigma XY = (155)(46) + (173)(68) + (165)(52) + (178)(81)$$
$$+ (168)(64)$$
$$= 7{,}130 + 11{,}764 + 8{,}580 + 14{,}418 + 10{,}752$$
$$= 52{,}644$$

The expression $\Sigma(X - Y)^2$ means the sum of the scores obtained by subtracting each Y value from its corresponding X value and squaring the result. Thus

$$\Sigma(X - Y)^2 = (X_1 - Y_1)^2 + (X_2 - Y_2)^2 + (X_3 - Y_3)^2 + \cdots$$
$$+ (X_n - Y_n)^2$$

In terms of our data

$$\Sigma(X - Y)^2 = (155 - 46)^2 + (173 - 68)^2 + (165 - 52)^2$$
$$+ (178 - 81)^2 + (168 - 64)^2$$
$$= (109)^2 + (105)^2 + (113)^2 + (97)^2 + (104)^2$$
$$= 11{,}881 + 11{,}025 + 12{,}769 + 9{,}409 + 10{,}816$$
$$= 55{,}900$$

The expression $\Sigma X \Sigma Y$ means the product of the sums of the X values and the Y values. Thus

$$\Sigma X \Sigma Y = (X_1 + X_2 + X_3 + \cdots + X_n)(Y_1 + Y_2 + Y_3 + \cdots + Y_n)$$

In terms of our data

$$\Sigma X \Sigma Y = (155 + 173 + 165 + 178 + 168)$$
$$\cdot (46 + 68 + 52 + 81 + 64)$$
$$= (839)(311)$$
$$= 26{,}092$$

As these examples have shown, the use of the summation operator is straightforward. Just remember to read Σ as meaning the sum of all n scores of the type in question, and be alert for the proper sequence of operations, such as squaring before summing in ΣX^2 and summing before squaring in $(\Sigma X)^2$. With a little practice the use of Σ will become second nature to you.

An aside on subscripts/ superscripts

Many authors introduce Σ with a subscript/superscript notation, that is, $\sum_{i}^{n}$. The subscript refers to the first value to be summed and the superscript identifies the last value to be summed. Thus $\sum_{1}^{n} X$ means the sum of all X scores from the first through the nth. The symbol $\sum_{4}^{15} X$ means the sum of the 4th through 15th X scores, and $\sum_{10}^{23} X$ means the sum of the 10th through 23rd X scores, and so on. The subscript/superscript notation is used to specify the addition of subgroups of the X scores. I think it is a confusing notation and that there are more convenient ways to identify subgroups of scores. For these reasons, the subscript/superscript notation is not used in this text.

3.7 Review Exercises

1. Given the data

X	Y
20	22
25	20
40	14
15	27
30	16
28	17
60	12
22	22

Calculate the value of

(a) $\sum X$

(b) $\sum Y$

(c) $\sum XY$

(d) $\sum X \sum Y$

(e) $\sum (X + Y)$

(f) $\sum (X - Y)$

(g) $\sum X^2$

(h) $\sum Y^2$

(i) $(\sum X)^2$

(j) $(\sum Y)^2$

(k) $\sum X^2 Y^2$

(l) $\sum X^2 \sum Y^2$

(m) $(\sum X)^2 (\sum Y)^2$

2. Using the raw data presented in Question 1, determine whether the following statements are true or false.

(a) $\sum X + \sum Y = \sum (X + Y)$ T

(b) $\sum X - \sum Y = \sum (X - Y)$ T

(c) $\sum X^2 + \sum Y^2 = \sum (X + Y)^2$ F

(d) $\sum (X + Y)^2 = [\sum (X + Y)]^2$ F

(e) $\sum Y^2 = (\sum Y)^2$ F

(f) $\sum (Y + c) = \sum Y + c$ (let $c = 2$)   F

(g) $\sum (Y + c) = c\sum Y$ (let $c = 2$)   F

(h) $\sum (X/c) = \sum X/c$ (let $c = 2$)   T

3. Is the following statement true or false?

$\sum c = nc$ (let $c = 5$ and $n = 8$)

$\sum x = n\bar{x}$

3.8 Averages

Averages are probably the most frequently reported descriptive statistics because curiosity about the average value is one of our first reactions to being presented with numerical data. The word average is a popular term but not a technical one. This is because there are several different statistics that may legitimately be called averages; each provides particular and different information and, depending on the characteristics of the score distribution, they can be quite different numerical values. Because it has no certain meaning, the term average is not used in statistics; its use in popular communication can be a source of misunderstanding. In this section we will discuss the mode, median, and arithmetic mean.

The Mode

The *mode* is defined as the most frequently occurring score. It is often of considerable interest to know which score occurred most frequently; however, the mode can be viewed as a typical or average score only in the sense that it occurred more often than any other. When data are presented graphically, the mode is the value of the highest bar in a histogram/bar graph or the highest

mode

point in a frequency polygon. For example, in the distribution of ages presented in Table 3.2–1, the modal age is 19 years.

To determine the mode of a set of numbers, one need only scan them to identify the score that occurred with greatest frequency. The possibility of error is greatly reduced if the scores are ordered in either ascending or descending order, and this procedure is recommended. Thus, given the numbers

$$18, 10, 8, 8, 15, 4, 4, 6, 16, 2, 9, 8, 10, 15, 12$$

arranged in ascending order,

$$2, 4, 4, 6, \underline{8, 8, 8}, 9, 10, 10, 12, 15, 15, 16, 18$$

the mode = 8

unimodal

When there is clearly one score value that occurred the most frequently, the distribution is termed *unimodal* (one mode). In a case where two adjacent values share the distinction of occurring the most frequently, the mode is the midpoint between them. Thus

$$1, 2, 4, 4, 6, \underline{8, 8, 8}, \underline{11, 11, 11}, 12, 14, 15, 20, 30$$

the mode $= \dfrac{8 + 11}{2} = 9.50$

bimodal

Although strictly speaking, one could term a distribution *bimodal* (two modes) whenever there are two most frequently occurring scores, this label is usually reserved for cases wherein the modal scores are separated by some less frequently occurring values.

To determine the mode of data that has been organized into a frequency distribution using class intervals, simply identify the class interval that contains the greatest frequency of scores. The mode of the distribution is the midpoint of that class interval. For example, in the distribution of average yards-per-carry presented in Table 3.2–4, the mode is 3.7 yards-per-carry.

The Median

median

The *median* bisects the distribution, meaning that it is the value that has half of all the scores above it and half below it. The median is the central point of the distribution in the sense of being the middle observation; there is no implication that it is the midpoint of the score range. To determine the median of a set of numbers, it is necessary to first arrange them in either ascending or descending order. If there is an odd number of scores, the middle score is the median value. Given the numbers

$$2, 4, 4, 6, 8, 8, 8, 9, 10, 10, 12, 15, 15, 16, 18$$

$n = 15$, therefore the 8th score is the median because it has 7 scores below it and 7 above.

$$2, 4, 4, 6, 8, 8, 8, |9,| 10, 10, 12, 15, 15, 16, 18$$

median = 9

If there is an even number of scores, then the median is the midpoint between the two middle scores. Thus

2, 4, 5, 8, 9, 11, 14, 15, 15, 18, 19, 20

$n = 12$, and therefore the median point is between the 6th and 7th scores

2, 4, 5, 8, 9, 11, | 14, 15, 15, 18, 19, 20

$$\text{median} = \frac{11 + 14}{2} = 12.50$$

Let us consider a case in which there are tied scores that span the median point of the distribution, as shown next.

3, 4, 7, 10, 10, | 10, 11, 12, 12, 15

The median occurs at the point indicated. In order to explain its calculation in such cases, we must reiterate some comments that were made in Section 3.4 on the nature of measurement. Any numerical score can be seen as a label that represents a range of score values with exact limits one-half unit above and below the score in question. The number 10 is merely a label for the range of observations that has exact limits of 9.5 and 10.5. Similarly, the exact limits of the range of values labeled by the number 20.00 are 19.995 and 20.005. In the previous example there are three 10s; two of the three are to be below the median point, and one is to be above. We could say that 2/3, or 0.67, of the range of values for which 10 is a label is to be below the median. The actual numerical value of the median is determined by adding this proportion to the lower exact limit. Thus

3, 4, 7, 10, 10, | 10, 11, 12, 12, 15
          0.67 | 0.33
     9.50   10.50

median = 0.67 + 9.50 = 10.17

When dealing with tied observations that span the median point, the general rule is to add the proportion of the tied scores that are to be below the median point to the lower exact limit of the tied score value.

As an additional example

5, 6, 8, 12, 12, 12, | 12, 16, 17, 20, 20, 30
        0.75 | 0.25
    11.50   12.50

median = 0.75 + 11.50 = 12.25

When determining the median of data that have been organized into a frequency distribution using class intervals, the first step is to identify the class interval that contains the median point. Then you must determine the proportion of the observations in the median class interval that is to be below the median; the numerical value of the median of the distribution is found by adding that proportion of the class interval size to the lower exact limit of the median class interval. For example, the median of the yards-per-carry distribution shown in Table 3.4–2 would be determined as follows. Since there are 144 observations, the median has 72 below it and 72 above it. If we accumulate the frequencies reading upward we find that the median will occur in the 3.5–3.9 class interval and that 30 of the 33 scores in that interval are to be below the median. The class interval has a size of 0.5 units and a lower exact limit equal to 3.45. Thus

$$\text{median} = (30/33)(.5) + 3.45$$
$$= 0.45 + 3.45$$
$$= 3.495$$

Readers who have studied Section 3.4 will appreciate that the median is the 50th percentile score; thus, the median of a frequency distribution may be determined by means of the formula on page 37.

The Arithmetic Mean

arithmetic mean

The *arithmetic mean,* referred to simply as the mean, is defined as the sum of the scores divided by the number of scores.

$$\text{Arithmetic mean} = \frac{\Sigma X}{n}$$

The mean is widely used in statistics because it is defined algebraically and can therefore be integrated into other arithmetic and algebraic operations. The mean is what people ordinarily understand by the term "average" in everyday conversation. One can think of the mean as the amount of the variable per individual measured. If some number of persons had a mean height of 168 cm, then there was, so to speak, 168 cm of height per individual observed.

A different symbol is used to represent the mean, depending on whether one is dealing with a population or a sample. Recall that a set of scores is considered a population when it consists of measures of all individuals of interest. This means that either every member of the population has been measured or the experimenter is interested only in those individuals that have been measured and does not intend to generalize the findings beyond them. A set of scores is considered a sample when the experimenter's purpose is to generalize the findings to a larger and not directly observed group, that is, when the findings are intended to be used to estimate parameter values.

The mean of a population is symbolized by μ, Greek letter *mu*.

$$\text{Mean of a population:} \quad \mu = \frac{\Sigma X}{n}$$

The mean of a sample is symbolized by the letter representing the variable with a bar on top, so that the mean of a sample of X scores is symbolized as $\overline{X}$ (X-bar) and the mean of a sample of Y scores is $\overline{Y}$ (Y-bar).

Mean of a sample: $\overline{X} = \dfrac{\Sigma X}{n}$

Since we usually deal with samples in the social sciences, sample notation ($\overline{X}$) is used in this section and generally throughout this book. The statistic $\overline{X}$ is our best estimate of μ when this parameter cannot be obtained directly. In the language of statistics $\overline{X}$ is termed an *unbiased* estimate of μ because it estimates μ without any systematic tendency to be larger or smaller than μ. If many samples were drawn from a population, their means would form a symmetrical frequency distribution about the true population mean. If every different sample that can possibly be drawn from a population was obtained and the means calculated, the mean of these sample means would equal μ. We therefore say that the expected value of $\overline{X}$ is μ (the mean of all possible $\overline{X}$s is μ) and refer to $\overline{X}$ as an unbiased estimate of μ. The calculation of the mean is illustrated next. Given the numbers

unbiased

3, 5, 9, 2, 8, 6

$\Sigma X = 33;$ $n = 6;$

$\overline{X} = \dfrac{\Sigma X}{n} = \dfrac{33}{6} = 5.50$

Note

since $\overline{X} = \Sigma X/n$, therefore $n\overline{X} = \Sigma X$

Adding or subtracting a constant to a set of numbers results in the adding or subtracting of the same constant to the mean; multiplying or dividing by a constant results in multiplying or dividing the mean by the same constant. Another interesting property of the mean is that the sum of deviations from it is always equal to zero; that is, $\Sigma(X - \overline{X}) = 0$. In fact, the arithmetic mean may be defined as that value about which the sum of deviations equals zero. Thus

X	$X - \overline{X}$
3	$3 - 5.50 = -2.50$
5	$5 - 5.50 = -0.50$
9	$9 - 5.50 = +3.50$
2	$2 - 5.50 = -3.50$
8	$8 - 5.50 = +2.50$
6	$6 - 5.50 = +0.50$

$\Sigma X = 33$ $\Sigma(X - \overline{X}) = 0.00$

$n = 6$

$\overline{X} = 5.50$

Suppose three groups, labeled A, B, and C, were all measured on variable X. We could represent the groups' means as $\overline{X}_A$, $\overline{X}_B$, and $\overline{X}_C$ respectively, and the number of subjects in the groups as n_A, n_B, and n_C respectively. If two or more groups of scores have the same number of observations in each, or equal n's, then the overall mean is equal to the mean of the group means. Thus, when $n_A = n_B = n_C$

$$\overline{X} = \frac{\overline{X}_A + \overline{X}_B + \overline{X}_C}{3}$$

When the number of observations in the different groups is not the same (unequal n's), the overall mean may be found by totaling the sums and dividing by the sum of the n's.

When $n_A \neq n_B$

$$\overline{X} = \frac{\Sigma X_A + \Sigma X_B}{n_A + n_B}$$

Although the mean is the most generally useful of the averages, it can sometimes be misleading, especially when the score distribution is markedly skewed or contains a few extreme scores. Consider the numbers

$$3, 5, 8, 8, 4, 7, 84$$
$$\text{mode} = 8; \quad \text{median} = 7; \quad \overline{X} = 17$$

In this case the mean is larger, and in fact more than twice as large, than six of the seven numbers in the distribution. If the average is being used to indicate a middle value, then the median or mode are more appropriate descriptions in this instance. The choice of which measure to use is determined by the specific information that one wishes to communicate and, to some extent, by peculiarities of the data. The mean is affected by deviant scores because it is based upon all the observations; the median is determined by one or two observations and is much less affected by an extreme score; and the mode is not affected at all.

When the distribution is unimodal and symmetrical, the mean, median, and mode are the same numerical value, as is shown in Figure 3.8–1a. As the distribution becomes more skewed the mean, median, and mode become different values, as is shown in Figure 3.8–1b. In a skewed distribution, quite different impressions could be created by citing these different statistics, all of which may go under the name average. As an example, consider the case of annual salary for all employees of a given corporation; such distributions are most often positively skewed because fewer people earn the higher salaries. The average income represented by the mode could be quite different from that represented by the mean. In order to avoid being misled one must insist on knowing which statistic is actually being reported. Knowing all

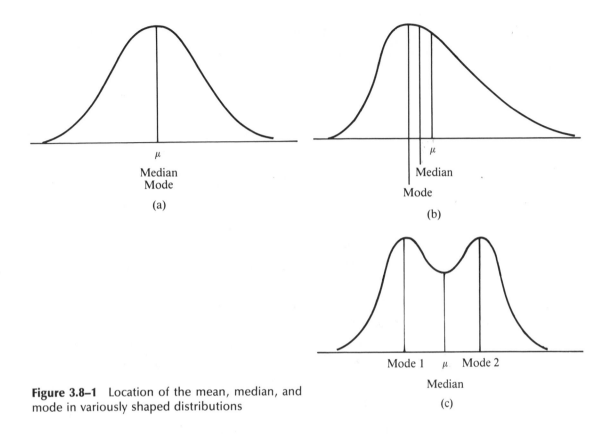

Figure 3.8–1   Location of the mean, median, and
mode in variously shaped distributions

three statistics is best, as this would indicate whether or not the the distribution
is symmetrical.

We tend to view an average as a central point about which the raw scores are
clustered, and the mean, median, and mode are often termed measures of
"central tendency." However, one should realize that there is nothing about
any average or its calculation that implies the existence of a cluster of scores,
and there is no implication that the raw scores have any tendency to assume,
or move toward, the average value. The values in any distribution are what
they are; they have no tendency to be anything else. Referring to averages
as measures of central tendency may foster the preconception that the
distribution is unimodal and symmetrical; such preconceptions can be quite
erroneous. The mode, median, and mean represent certain information but
imply nothing about the shape of the distribution.

**An aside on
"central tendency"**

3.9 Review Exercises

1. Define or describe the following terms.

   (a) mode   (d) median
   (b) unimodal   (e) arithmetic mean
   (c) bimodal   (f) unbiased

2. Given the raw data

   8, 12, 10, 32, 19, 27, 4, 16, 18, 10, 16, 20, 12, 11, 14, 10

   determine the

   (a) mode   (b) median   (c) mean

3. Given the raw data

   22, 19, 9, 14, 15, 19, 31, 29, 22, 19, 14, 10, 22, 6

   determine the

   (a) mode   (b) median   (c) mean

4. Given the raw data

   6, 7, 6, 8, 5, 6, 7, 7, 5, 6, 8, 4, 6, 8

   determine the

   (a) mode   (b) median   (c) mean

5. Four groups of 12 persons each were tested in a reaction time experiment. The mean scores of the four groups were

   Group no. 1: $\overline{X}_1 = 3.20$ seconds
   Group no. 2: $\overline{X}_2 = 1.75$ seconds
   Group no. 3: $\overline{X}_3 = 2.10$ seconds
   Group no. 4: $\overline{X}_4 = 2.20$ seconds

   What was the overall mean reaction time?

6. Using the data presented in exercise 3.9–4, determine the mean when

   (a) $c = 5$ has been added to each score
   (b) $c = 3$ has been subtracted from each score
   (c) each score has been multiplied by $c = 4$
   (d) each score has been divided by $c = 2$

7. Three classes wrote an examination with the following results.

   Class A: $n_A = 40$, $\overline{X}_A = 59.40$
   Class B: $n_B = 34$, $\overline{X}_B = 63.72$
   Class C: $n_C = 21$, $\overline{X}_C = 70.08$

   What was the overall mean mark?

8. In a group of 100 people there were 40 men and they had a mean height of 171 cm; the 60 women had a mean height of 167 cm. What was the mean height of the 100 persons?

9. For purposes of determining passenger weights on aircraft, a man is presumed to weigh 188 lb, a woman 141 lb, a child (person aged 3 to 11 years) 75 lb, and an infant (person aged less than 3 years) 30 lb. Assume that an aircraft was boarded by 30 people, consisting of 8 men, 14 women, 3 children, and 5 infants.

   (a) What was the mean weight of the passengers?
   (b) What was the median weight of the passengers?

10. Determine the mean age of the experimental subjects from the data presented in Table 3.2–1.

11. Determine the mean average yards-per-carry score from the data presented in Table 3.2–3.

3.10 Variability

People may say, "If you've seen one you've seen 'em all," but the truth is that no two things in the natural world are identical if you look closely enough. Thus it is virtually inevitable that if we take some measure on different individuals, the result will be different numerical scores. *Variability* refers to dissimilarity among the raw scores; low variability means that the scores tend to be similar to each other in magnitude, and high variability means that the differences between the scores tend to be greater. The amount of variability in the data is of immediate interest as a descriptive property of the score distribution. If the numbers have low variability, the frequency distribution will be bunched with steeply sloping sides. If variability is high, it means that the scores are more spread out over the measurement range and the distribution will appear flatter.

variability

   Apart from being a descriptive feature of the raw data, variability in the occurrence of natural events is the lifeblood of science and the reason for its existence; the causes of variability are what science seeks to understand. If human beings were identical in every respect, and thus showed no variability, then we could select anyone at random and all observations/measurements of that person would be true for the entire population. Life would be simpler, although perhaps insufferably boring, and there would be no need for inferential science. Understanding human behavior boils down to understanding the causes of different responses, or variability, between individuals, and the causes of different responses by the same individual on different occasions. Scientists in other disciplines face a similar task. Since statistics is the body of procedures for analyzing data, the occurrence of variability as a property of numerical data is perhaps the most fundamental concept in statistics.

   The *range* of a set of data is defined as the difference between the maximum and minimum scores. The range is easy to determine, and provides some useful information by identifying the size of the measurement range in

range

which the scores are dispersed. However, the range is not a generally useful statistic because it does not measure variability per se; it tells us nothing about how tightly packed or how spread out the observations are between their score limits.

Numbers that have low variability are similar in magnitude, and if we chose pairs of numbers from such a group, the differences between the numbers in each pair would tend to be small. Conversely, in a group of numbers with high variability, the differences between the members of randomly chosen pairs would tend to be larger. A measure of variability should reflect the fact that when variability is low, the numbers differ from each other by small amounts, and when variability is high, they differ from each other by larger amounts. We could imagine a measure of variability that consisted of selecting all possible pairs of scores and determining the mean difference between pairs. While this approach seems logical it would become overwhelmingly cumbersome as the number of observations increased. We can simplify the situation by transforming the differences between the numbers into differences from a fixed point.

If you take a set of scores and subtract each one from an arbitrary constant, then it will be the case that if the numbers have low variability they will all differ from the constant by similar amounts. On the other hand, if the numbers have high variability, they will deviate from the constant by highly varying amounts. The variability within a set of numbers will be reflected in the variability of their deviations from some fixed point.

Suppose we have a set of scores and calculate the mean (μ). If we then obtain the deviation of each raw score from the mean ($X - \mu$), we would find that in a set with low variability these deviations would tend to be small and of similar size because the numbers are all similar to each other and thus similar to their mean. If the scores have high variability, the deviations about the mean will tend to be large and variable because the numbers are dissimilar to each other and thus to their mean. The variability within a set of scores can be conceptualized as the average (mean) deviation of the raw scores from their mean. In principle this seems to be a good way to measure variability, but it will not work because the sum of deviations about the mean always equals zero [$\sum (X - \mu) = 0$], and thus the mean of these deviations will always equal zero as well, regardless of the amount of variability contained in the data.

This obstacle can be overcome by finding a legitimate way of circumventing the occurrence of negative signs when obtaining the deviations of the raw scores from their mean. A convenient solution is to obtain the deviations and then square them, thereby eliminating the negative signs. The sum of the squared deviations from the mean, $\sum (X - \mu)^2$, is known as the *Sum of Squares* and is always a positive value. If we divide the Sum of Squares by *n*, we have derived a statistic known as the *variance*. The *variance* is the mean

Sum of Squares

variance

of squared deviations of the raw scores from their mean, and is symbolized by σ^2, Greek letter sigma squared. Thus

$$\sigma^2 = \frac{\Sigma(X - \mu)^2}{n}$$

The following numerical example illustrates the calculation of the variance. Suppose these data represent age to the nearest year of eight persons.

X	$X - \mu$	$(X - \mu)^2$
20	−4.50	20.25
23	−1.50	2.25
18	−6.50	42.25
31	+6.50	42.25
27	+2.50	6.25
26	+1.50	2.25
21	−3.50	12.25
30	+5.50	30.25

$\Sigma X = 196$ $\Sigma(X - \mu) = 0.00$ $\Sigma(X - \mu)^2 = 158.00$

$n = 8$

$\mu = 24.50$

$$\sigma^2 = \frac{\Sigma(X - \mu)^2}{n} = \frac{158}{8} = 19.75$$

The variance is a measure of the variability within a set of scores. When calculated on different sets of data, the variance allows us to make direct comparisons concerning the relative amounts of variability. Since the variance is obtained by squaring deviations from the mean, it is a term that does not reflect the original units of measurement. If we wish to express the degree of variability in the same measurement units as the raw scores (in the previous case age to the nearest year), we simply obtain the square root of the variance; the resulting term is known as the standard deviation. The *standard deviation* is symbolized by σ, Greek letter *sigma,* and is a measure of variability expressed in the same measurement units as the raw data. Thus

standard deviation

$$\sigma = \sqrt{\frac{\Sigma(X - \mu)^2}{n}} \doteq \sqrt{19.75} = 4.44$$

We would say that the eight people had a mean age of 24.50 years, and a standard deviation of 4.44 years. The standard deviation is somewhat more useful than the variance as a descriptive term, but note that these two statistics are not different concepts; one is simply the square root of the other.

bias

The formulas for determining variance and standard deviation derived thus far are appropriate for populations; however, when dealing with samples for the purpose of estimating population variability, a slight modification is required. Variance, as defined before, has a systematic tendency to underestimate the population variance; thus it is said to be a *biased* estimate. *Bias* refers to any systematic tendency for a statistic to err as an estimate of the corresponding parameter. In the case of the variance, the bias is corrected by changing the denominator to $n - 1$ instead of n. (Note: The denominator term for sample variance $(n - 1)$ is properly called a degrees of freedom term. Clarification of the meaning of degrees of freedom is not essential at this point; however, if curious, you may refer to section 6.3.) The variance of a sample is defined as the Sum of Squares divided by $n - 1$ and is symbolized by s^2. The standard deviation of a sample is symbolized by s. This modification results in s^2 as an unbiased estimate of σ^2 but does not make s a completely unbiased estimate of σ; thus, statistical procedures involving the estimation of population variability ordinarily use the sample variance.

The variance of a population is the sum of squared deviations from the mean (Sum of Squares) divided by n.

$$\sigma^2 = \frac{\Sigma (X - \mu)^2}{n}$$

The variance of a sample is the sum of squared deviations from the mean (Sum of Squares) divided by the degrees of freedom.

$$s^2 = \frac{\Sigma (X - \overline{X})^2}{n - 1}$$

The formula for the standard deviation of a population

$$\sigma = \sqrt{\frac{\Sigma (X - \mu)^2}{n}}$$

The formula for the standard deviation of a sample is

$$s = \sqrt{\frac{\Sigma (X - \overline{X})^2}{n - 1}}$$

In general, sample notation and formulas are used throughout this book in keeping with the reality that, in the behavioral sciences, we are usually interested in generalizing our findings beyond the immediate observations and thus use statistics mainly as an inferential tool.

An aside: definition by purpose   I have tried to render the matter of whether a set of scores is a population or a sample into simple terms; however, the world is not a simple place and we must occasionally deal with situations that seem to defy simple classification. For example, statistics obtained from a group of individuals may be used to estimate population parameters, which means that we are treating the group as a sample. But we might wish to perform some subsidiary analyses to confirm a theoretical assumption in which only the properties of the data at hand are of interest, which means that the group is now being regarded as a population. The same set of scores can be a sample one minute and a population the next, depending on our purpose. Some statisticians advocate a triple notation in which σ^2 is the variance of a population, s^2 is the variance of a sample, and $S^2 = (X - \overline{X})^2/n$ is the variance of a sample when the variance is used descriptively but not inferentially. While I sympathize with the rationale behind this system, I believe that it has more potential for confusion than clarity and therefore have not incorporated it into this book. Let us reiterate that "sample" and "population" are labels that we apply to data as a function of our purpose; if our purpose changes, then so can the label.

The calculation of the Sum of Squares by obtaining all the deviations from the mean, squaring each one, and then summing them is a cumbersome procedure. The following formula is algebraically equivalent and more efficient to use.

$$\text{Sum of Squares} = \Sigma X^2 - \frac{(\Sigma X)^2}{n}$$

The algebraic equivalence of these formulas may be demonstrated as follows

$$\Sigma(X - \overline{X})^2 = \Sigma(X^2 - 2X\overline{X} + \overline{X}^2)$$
$$= \Sigma X^2 - \Sigma 2X\overline{X} + \Sigma \overline{X}^2$$
$$= \Sigma X^2 - 2\Sigma X\overline{X} + n\overline{X}^2$$
$$= \Sigma X^2 - 2\Sigma X\left(\frac{\Sigma X}{n}\right) + n\left(\frac{\Sigma X}{n}\right)^2$$
$$= \Sigma X^2 - 2\left[\frac{(\Sigma X)^2}{n}\right] + n\left[\frac{(\Sigma X)^2}{n^2}\right]$$
$$= \Sigma X^2 - 2\left[\frac{(\Sigma X)^2}{n}\right] + \frac{(\Sigma X)^2}{n}$$
$$= \Sigma X^2 - \frac{(\Sigma X)^2}{n}$$

The formulas for determining variance and standard deviation may be written as

Sample variance:
$$s^2 = \frac{\Sigma X^2 - \dfrac{(\Sigma X)^2}{n}}{n - 1}$$

Sample standard deviation: $s = \sqrt{\dfrac{\sum X^2 - \dfrac{(\sum X)^2}{n}}{n - 1}}$

Population variance: $\sigma^2 = \dfrac{\sum X^2 - \dfrac{(\sum X)^2}{n}}{n}$

Population standard deviation: $\sigma = \sqrt{\dfrac{\sum X^2 - \dfrac{(\sum X)^2}{n}}{n}}$

The following numerical example illustrates the calculation of sample variance and standard deviation using both formulas for determining the Sum of Squares. The raw data are the same as in the previous illustration for calculation of σ^2 and σ; note that s^2 and s are larger values as a consequence of dividing the Sum of Squares by $n - 1$.

X	$X - \bar{X}$	$(X - \bar{X})^2$	X^2
20	−4.50	20.25	400
23	−1.50	2.25	529
18	−6.50	42.25	324
31	+6.50	42.25	961
27	+2.50	6.25	729
26	+1.50	2.25	676
21	−3.50	12.25	441
30	+5.50	30.25	900
196	0.00	158.00	4960

$$n = 8$$
$$\sum X = 196$$
$$\bar{X} = 24.50$$
$$\sum (X - \bar{X})^2 = 158.00$$
$$\sum X^2 = 4960$$

$$s^2 = \frac{\sum (X - \bar{X})^2}{n - 1} = \frac{158.00}{8 - 1} = \frac{158.00}{7} = 22.57$$

$$s^2 = \frac{\sum X^2 - \dfrac{(\sum X)^2}{n}}{n - 1} = \frac{4960 - \dfrac{(196)^2}{8}}{8 - 1} = \frac{4960 - 4802}{7}$$

$$= \frac{158}{7} = 22.57$$

In both cases

$$s = \sqrt{22.57} = 4.75$$

The variance, and standard deviation, are direct measures of variability, which means that their numerical values increase as variability increases. The lower limit for variability is no variability at all, that is, when the data are all some constant value. In that case, every score will be equal to the mean and the Sum of Squares will equal zero, thus s^2 and s will also be equal to zero. But as variability increases, so does the numerical value of s^2 and s.

Given any set of scores, what would be the effect on s^2 and s of adding or subtracting a constant to each raw score? Earlier we said that variability was the tendency of numbers to be dissimilar. Adding or subtracting a constant changes the absolute size of numbers but does not affect the amount by which any two differ. This should not affect a good measure of variability and this is the case for s^2 and s; adding or subtracting a constant does not change the value of the variance or the standard deviation. On the other hand, if a set of numbers is multiplied or divided by a constant, then the size of the differences between numbers is affected, as well as their absolute size. We should expect s^2 and s to be affected by these operations, and this is indeed the case. Multiplication by a constant results in multiplication of s by the same constant and in multiplication of s^2 by the square of the constant. Division by a constant results in the division of s by the constant, and division of s^2 by the square of the constant.

3.11 Review Exercises

1. Define or describe the following terms.
   - (a) variability
   - (b) range
   - (c) Sum of Squares
   - (d) variance
   - (e) standard deviation
   - (f) bias

2. Determine s^2 and s for each of the following sets of scores.
   - (a) 7, 5, 9, 10, 7, 9
   - (b) 4, 9, 11, 8, 7, 5
   - (c) 6, 2, 9, 8, 1, 12
   - (d) 6, 10, 10, 14, 4, 12, 10, 6, 8, 12, 18

3. Determine s^2 and s for each of the following sets of scores.
   - (a) 7, 2, 4, 6, 9, 0, 1, 5, 8, 3
   - (b) 5, 9, 9, 10, 11, 12, 14, 15, 17, 21
   - (c) 56, 59, 61, 65, 58, 57, 62, 59, 60, 55
   - (d) 4, 8, 7, 12, 9, 7, 10, 6, 7, 5, 9

4. Using the numbers in 2(d)
   - (a) add $c = 2$ to each score and determine s^2 and s.

   (b) multiply each score by $c = 5$ and determine s^2 and s.

5. Using the numbers in 2(d)

   (a) subtract $c = 3$ from each score and determine s^2 and s.
   (b) divide each score by $c = 4$ and determine s^2 and s.

6. Take all the numbers in 2(a), (b), and (c) as one group of scores and determine s^2 and s.

7. Take all the numbers in 3(a), (b), and (c) as one group of scores and determine s^2 and s.

8. The following are low temperatures recorded in degrees Celsius during a week in January. Determine $\overline{X}$ and s.

     5, 8, 4, −2, −6, −5, 2

Convert these scores into temperatures in degrees Fahrenheit using the formula $°F = (9/5)\,(°C) + 32$ and determine $\overline{X}$ and s in °F.

9. The following are high temperatures recorded in degrees Fahrenheit during a week in July. Determine $\overline{X}$ and s.

     75, 81, 80, 85, 87, 82, 80

Convert these scores into temperatures in degrees Celsius using the formula $°C = (5/9)\,(°F − 32)$ and determine $\overline{X}$ and s in °C.

3.12 Concluding Remarks

Chapter 3 contains a seemingly diverse collection of terms, symbols, and concepts. Of course, the procedures and statistics discussed have a common theme in that they are all aimed at describing one or another property of numerical data. The reader will by now have noticed that in statistics the concepts and terminology build upon one another very quickly. Many of the terms first defined in Chapter 2 are now comfortably familiar to you; indeed, in this chapter the summation operator (Σ), which was first introduced in Section 3.3, is by this time second nature. This characteristic, wherein each concept quickly becomes the basis upon which additional new concepts are developed, is a main reason why, as a student, you must work at statistics consistently and not in isolated spurts.

    In the next chapter we will encounter a theoretical distribution known as the normal distribution. We will apply some of the terms, formulas, and concepts learned thus far to make descriptive statements about normal distributions, and will acquire important notions about theoretical distributions in general, which we will use later to develop the rationale of inference in statistics.

Part II

Concepts and Procedure in Statistical Decision Making

4 The Normal Distribution

Chapter Preview

4.1 Normal Distributions in Nature

The normal distribution is a theoretical frequency distribution defined by a mathematical equation.* The normal distribution seems to have penetrated the public mind more than most mathematical concepts, as people will occasionally be heard making reference to "the bell curve." It has nothing to do with bells per se, but, being a symmetrical distribution, when it is depicted graphically it seems to raise that image in peoples' minds. Its importance for us as scientists lies in the fact that many natural events yield frequency distributions that closely approximate the normal distribution. For this reason the normal distribution is an important theoretical reference; knowing its general properties enables us to make specific statements about normally distributed variables on which we have gathered data. In a broader sense, the normal distribution is only one of several theoretical distributions that are useful in statistics. Getting to know the normal distribution will serve as an introduction to theoretical distributions in general. The student should become acquainted with the normal distribution so that reference to it in later work will, if you will pardon the pun, ring a bell of familiarity.

Did you know that just over 68 percent of North American men are between 168.5 and 181.5 cm tall (about 66.5 to 71.5 in.), or that 4.8 percent of women are shorter than 152 cm (5 ft)? Men's and women's heights are normally distributed. If a variable is normally distributed we need only determine the mean and standard deviation to enable specific statements to be made about the proportions of the observations that lie above, below, or between given score values. We will see how this is done in a later section, but for now, let us consider why measures of naturally occurring events tend to yield normal distributions.

An aside on "normality"   In the context of the normal distribution, the term "normal" does not mean typical, usual, or conventional; it is not the opposite of abnormal. Normal is simply a technical name or label that is given to this particular mathematical function. The normal distribution is a theoretical function and probably no natural event will produce a frequency distribution that is *exactly* normal; however, many natural events approximate the normal distribution closely enough that, for all practical purposes, they can be termed normally distributed. It is with this understanding that the phrase "normally distributed" is used with reference to natural events.

---

*$Y = (1/\sigma\sqrt{2\pi})e^{-(X-\mu)^2/2\sigma^2}$ where Y = height of curve for particular values of X, $\pi = 3.1416$, and $e = 2.7183$ (base of natural logarithms).

The key to the following discussion is the *Central Limit Theorem,* which may be stated as: *the distribution of sums or means of a multitude of sufficiently large and equal sized random samples will be normal, irrespective of the shape of the population distribution.** No attempt will be made to prove the Central Limit Theorem; however, an example using an ordinary deck of playing cards may help to illustrate why natural events tend to be normally distributed.

If we assign the numerical values 11, 12, and 13 to the jacks, queens, and kings, respectively, a deck of cards becomes a population of 52 numerical values consisting of four sets of the numbers from 1 to 13. The frequency distribution of this population would be termed rectangular because all numerical values occur with equal frequency. Suppose we shuffled this deck and dealt four cards, which we may term a sample, and noted the sum of the numerical values of these four cards. The minimum possible sum would be 4, when we happened to deal the four aces, and the maximum possible sum would be 52, when we happened to deal the four kings. If we dealt a large number of such four-card samples (dealing each from a full deck) and recorded the sum of each, we would expect the mean of the sample sums to be 28. This follows from the fact that the mean numerical value of the deck is 7; since we are dealing four cards, we expect the mean of four-card sums to be $4 \times 7 = 28$. Now would a sample sum equal to 4, or one equal to 52, occur as often as a sum equal to 28? Certainly not! There are 270,725 different samples of four cards that can be drawn from a deck of 52 (see Section 5.8). Only one of these samples yields a sum of 4, and only one yields a sum of 52, but there are 14,361 four-card combinations (samples) with a sum of 28. Sample sums close to the expected mean of 28 will occur more often than sums farther from the mean simply because there are more four-card combinations that can produce them. If we drew a large number of four-card samples and entered their sums into a frequency distribution, this distribution would be symmetrical and have mean equal to 28 (this distribution would not be normal because of the small sample size).

The point of this example is to show that, when a datum is based on a combination of contributing factors, scores close to the mean are more likely to occur than those that are extreme departures from the mean. In the playing cards example, each sample sum was a term that summarized the values of four independently varying factors (cards). As the number of contributing

---

*Strictly speaking, the Central Limit Theorem applies to the distribution of all possible sample means or sums, but for our present purposes the notion of a large multitude will suffice. The Central Limit Theorem is referred to again in Chapter 6 in the context of sampling distributions.

factors, or sample size, increases, the distribution of sums or means derived from the samples will more and more approximate the normal distribution.

An aside on "sufficiently large"

The Central Limit Theorem, as defined in the text, requires that the samples from which the sums/means are derived be "sufficiently large" in order for the distribution of the sums/means to be normal. What constitutes sufficiently large is not clear-cut. If the population is normal, then even quite small samples can produce normal distributions, whereas if the population is markedly non-normal, as in a deck of cards, then larger samples are required. Sample sizes greater than 10 are generally presumed to yield approximately normal distributions of sums/means, but arbitrary dividing lines should not obscure the fact that the shape of the distribution of the sample sums/means is jointly determined by the population distribution as well as the sample size.

An analogous situation holds when we take measurements in the natural world. At first the variable height may seem to be a unitary measure, but in fact it is a score based on a host of contributing factors. These factors include hereditary inputs from each parent (consisting of an unknown number of genetic factors); nutritional history (the extent to which an unknown number of specific nutritional requirements have been fulfilled); disease history (the influence of an unknown number of disease possibilities), and so on. There are clearly dozens, if not hundreds of specific factors that contribute to the determination of the height of any person. A specific height score merely summarizes the particular combination of contributing factors that occurred in that person at the time of measurement.

Just as there are more four-card combinations that yield a sum of 28 than there are four-card combinations that yield a sum of 50, there are more combinations of height-determining factors that yield a person of average height than would produce, say, a Wilt Chamberlain. In the case of height, the number of contributing factors, which is analogous to sample size, is sufficiently large that the distribution of height scores approximates the normal curve.* Consider the multitude of contributing factors that might influence the cubic volumes of human brains, the number of needles on pine trees, the amount that people err when estimating the passage of time, or a person's score on an intelligence test. In these cases, and for most measures of natural events, *the score obtained represents the sum of the set of determining factors*

---

*This would hold for the distribution of heights of men or women; however, since women tend to be shorter than men, if both genders are included, the distribution of height scores will ordinarily be more platykurtic than the normal distribution, and possibly bimodal.

Height as a Normally Distributed Variable

Listed are the heights to the nearest inch as reported by fifty female students in my undergraduate classes.

63	67	64	65	63
64	65	70	69	66
67	64	65	64	66
65	68	67	67	64
68	65	63	62	68
66	66	65	67	66
61	62	64	69	62
65	65	66	65	65
63	64	62	65	67
65	63	66	68	64

$$\mu = 65.20 \qquad \sigma = 2.01$$

Frequency distribution

Height	Frequency
71	0
70	1
69	2
68	4
67	6
66	7
65	12
64	8
63	5
62	4
61	1
60	0

Frequency polygon

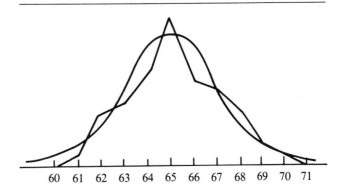

You can see that this distribution is not perfectly symmetrical and appears somewhat more leptokurtic than the normal distribution; nonetheless, the approximation is fairly good. With a larger number of subjects, the approximation to the normal distribution would be greater.

as manifested by a particular individual at a particular time. In a sense then, such a measure is like a sample sum. If departures from the mean are equally likely in either direction, and the contributing factors have approximately equal weight, the Central Limit Theorem implies that any empirical datum that is multideterminate will tend to approximate the normal distribution.

4.2 Properties of the Normal Distribution

Since the normal distribution is defined by a specific equation, all sets of normally distributed observations have certain characteristics. A typical normal distribution is shown in Figure 4.2–1. It can be seen that the normal distribution is symmetrical. The mean, median, and mode are the same numerical value and bisect the distribution, dividing it into equal parts. Half of the observations are above and half are below the mean value, as is shown in Figure 4.2–2.

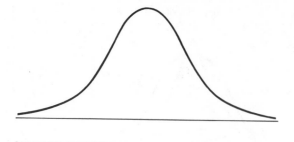

Figure 4.2–1 The normal distribution

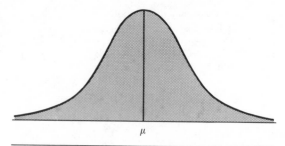

Figure 4.2–2 In a normal distribution the mean, median, and mode are the same numerical value and bisect the distribution

The two extremes or tails of the normal distribution, which is also referred to as the normal curve, do not actually touch the abscissa. The tails of the normal curve meet the abscissa at infinity, which implies that in order for a distribution to be normal, both infinitely large and infinitely small values must theoretically be possible. The fact that this may never be true in real life does not diminish the utility of the normal curve as a reference distribution for natural events. However, since the tails of the normal distribution are open-ended, we use the central point, or mean, as the reference from which to make statements about scores in a normal distribution.

It is useful to think of normal distributions in terms of proportions of the area under the curve. In Figure 4.2–2, the shaded region represents the total area under the curve; this area is equivalent to the total number of observations in the distribution. Thinking in terms of the area under the curve becomes convenient if one views the total area as being equal to one. We can then say that 0.50 of the area under the normal curve is above the mean, and 0.50 of the area is below the mean. This is equivalent to saying that 0.50 of the scores in a normal distribution are above the mean, and 0.50 of the scores are below the mean. The normal distribution is defined in such a way that the height of the curve above any point on the abscissa is a function of the distance of that point from the mean. The effect is to establish specific proportions of area under the curve between the mean and abscissa values. For example, it is the case that 0.3413 of the area under the normal curve lies between the mean and a point one standard deviation above the mean, and that 0.4772 of the area under the normal curve lies between the mean and a point two standard deviations above the mean.

In a truly monumental report, Clauser et al. (1972) described 125 anthropometric measures taken on over 1900 U.S. Air Force women. As a concrete example with which to illustrate the general properties of the normal curve, let us consider the data from one of these measures, namely, foot length. These data formed a normal distribution with mean equal to 241 mm and standard deviation equal to 11 mm.* Since we know that 0.3413 of the area under the normal curve is between the mean and one standard deviation above the mean, we can say that 0.3413 or 34.13 percent of women have feet between 241 mm and 252 mm (241 + 11). Because normal distributions are symmetrical, it is also true that 0.3413 of women have feet between 241 mm and 230 mm (241 − 11). (Note: In this text, to avoid tedious qualification, I use the Clauser et al. data as though it represents women in general when in fact it was derived from U.S. Air Force personnel. The Air Force women might well be an accurate representation of North American women, but this is not known for certain.) Figure 4.2–3 shows the distribution of foot length (incidentally, each subject's right foot was measured) and indicates the proportions of scores, which are equivalent to proportions of areas under the curve, between points one standard deviation apart.

As can be seen from Figure 4.2–3, 0.1359 of women have feet between 252 mm and 263 mm long, 0.0215 of women have feet between 208 mm and 219 mm long, and 0.0013 of women have feet larger than 274 mm.

The obvious question is, where did this information concerning area proportions come from? The proportions of the normal distribution between the mean and abscissa values can be worked out and entered into a table. One need only consult such a table to obtain the information of interest; we will proceed to this operation in the next section. The point being made here is that the normal distribution has certain fixed properties in terms of its proportions between abscissa values, and these general properties may be applied to any specific case of normally distributed scores to obtain information of interest.

---

*As is inevitable with real-life data, these scores were not *perfectly* normally distributed; the actual statistics reported were $\mu = 240.7$ mm and $\sigma = 11.3$ mm (Clauser et al., 1972). I have used approximations in the interest of convenience.

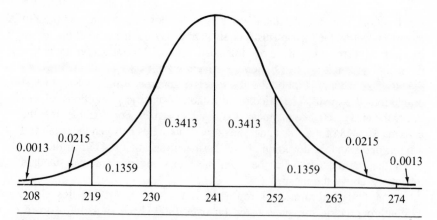

Figure 4.2–3 The distribution of women's foot length scores and proportions of scores between values one standard deviation apart (adapted from Clauser et al., 1972)

4.3 z-scores

Although many natural events generate approximately normal distributions, different measures are not expressed in the same or comparable units. How can one compare a weight score of 82 kg (181 lb) with a height score of 170 cm (67 in.), or with an exam mark of 60 percent? Obviously, such scores have no direct comparability because the measurement units are totally different, and also because the amount of variability in the different raw data distributions is likely to be dissimilar.

Suppose, for example, that Gus wrote exams in statistics and Greek. He got a mark of 60 in statistics and a mark of 70 in Greek. The distribution of statistics marks had a mean of 50 and a standard deviation of 5 and the distribution of Greek marks had a mean of 55 and a standard deviation of 10, as shown below.

Statistics marks	Greek marks
$\mu = 50$	$\mu = 55$
$\sigma = 5$	$\sigma = 10$
$X = 60$ (Gus's mark)	$X = 70$ (Gus's mark)

In which exam did he do better? At first it may appear that the Greek performance was better since the mark of 70 is higher than the mark of 60 obtained in statistics. Also, the Greek mark is 15 points above the mean Greek score while the statistics mark is only 10 points above the class mean. Both of these impressions are misleading because, relatively speaking, the statistics mark is considerably better than the Greek mark. To understand this we must view the raw score (Gus's mark) in terms of the number of standard deviation units by which it differs from its mean.

Recall that the standard deviation is a measure of variability in the raw data; any two groups of scores are likely to differ in this respect. If we regard the standard deviation as a unit, whatever its numerical size, then we can say that a given score is so many standard deviation units above or below the mean. This enables us to compare the positions of scores in different distributions that have different means and variabilities by simply comparing their distances from their respective means in number of standard deviation units. If we return to the case of Gus, we can see that the Greek mark was 15 points above the mean in a distribution in which the standard deviation was 10; therefore, that mark was $15/10 = 1.50$ standard deviation units above its mean. The statistics mark was 10 points above the mean in a distribution in which the standard deviation was 5; therefore, that mark was $10/5 = 2.00$ standard deviation units above its mean. When the different amounts of variability are taken into account, the statistics mark is farther above the mean performance in its group than the Greek mark is above the mean of its group, and thus we can say that Gus did better in statistics. (Note: In order to be completely appropriate, this kind of comparison assumes that the two reference groups, which in this case are the Greek and statistics classes, are composed of similar or comparable individuals. It is also assumed that the distributions of the two sets of scores are similar so that, for example, a score one standard deviation above the mean has the same percentile rank in both distributions.)

When we expressed the raw scores as number of standard deviations from the mean, we created what are known as z-scores, or standard scores. A *z-score* is a transformation of a raw score such that the difference between the raw score and the mean is divided by the standard deviation. Thus

z-score

$$z = \frac{X - \mu}{\sigma}$$

In this transformation, the standard deviation, whatever its numerical value, is treated as a unit and the raw score is expressed as the number of these units by which it differs from the mean. Raw scores that are higher than the mean have positive z-score values; scores that are below the mean have negative z-score values. The numerical example on page 72 illustrates the transformation of a set of raw data into z-scores.

When a set of data has been transformed into z-scores, the z-scores can be treated like any other group of numbers. You will find that the z-scores for any set of data always have mean equal to zero ($\mu_z = 0$) and standard deviation equal to one ($\sigma_z = 1.00$). You should not take my word for this. Make up an arbitrary set of numbers, calculate μ and σ, convert the raw scores into z-scores, and then calculate the mean and standard deviation of the z-scores.

X	$X - \mu$	$z = (X - \mu)/\sigma$
40	+5	+2.28
35	0	0.00
37	+2	+0.91
33	−2	−0.91
35	0	0.00
35	0	0.00
36	+1	+0.46
33	−2	−0.91
32	−3	−1.37
34	−1	−0.46

$$\Sigma X = 350 \qquad\qquad\qquad\qquad\qquad \Sigma z = 0.00$$
$$n = 10 \qquad\qquad\qquad\qquad\qquad\qquad n = 10$$
$$\mu = 35 \qquad\qquad\qquad\qquad\qquad\quad \mu_z = 0.00$$
$$\sigma = 2.19 \qquad\qquad\qquad\qquad\qquad \sigma_z = 1.00$$

Such an exercise will give you practice in deriving z-scores and also confirm that they always have a mean of zero and a standard deviation of one.

If you think back to the discussion of the standard deviation in Section 3.8, you will recall that $\Sigma(X - \mu) = 0$. Since $\Sigma z = \Sigma[(X - \mu/\sigma] = \Sigma(X - \mu)/\Sigma\sigma$, it is clear that the numerator term will always be equal to zero; thus, it will be the case that $\Sigma z = 0$ and consequently that $\mu_z = 0$. Recall also that dividing raw scores by a constant has the effect of dividing the standard deviation by the same constant. In the previous example the raw scores had $\sigma = 2.19$, and in the derivation of the z-scores, the deviations from the mean, the $X - \mu$ terms, were each divided by that value, 2.19. The result is necessarily that the standard deviation of the z-scores is equal to one.

Z-scores provide a common basis with which to compare raw scores taken from different distributions when the distributions in question have similar shapes. Assuming this to be the case, we transformed raw scores into z-scores, and this enabled us to evaluate whether Gus performed relatively better or poorer in statistics than in Greek. We could use z-scores to determine whether a person's weight has a position in the distribution of weight scores similar to the position his or her height has in the distribution of height scores, or make whatever other comparisons might be of interest.

If we can assume that the variable in question is normally distributed, then z-scores are the key to determining the frequency with which any given raw score occurs. Any normally distributed set of data can be represented with the values on the abscissa expressed as z-scores. Consider the distribution of women's foot length scores shown in Figure 4.3–1.

It is characteristic of the normal distribution that 0.3413 of the area under the curve, which is equivalent to 0.3413 of the scores in the distribution, lies between the mean and one standard deviation in either direction. It fol-

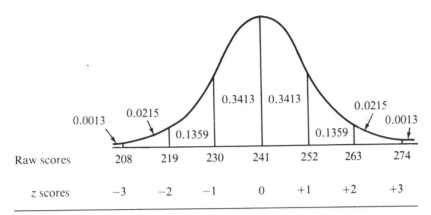

Figure 4.3–1   The distribution of women's foot length scores (adapted from Clauser et al., 1972)

lows that 0.6826 (0.3413 + 0.3413) of the area lies between $z = +1.00$ and $z = -1.00$. Since 0.1359 of the area lies between $z = -1.00$ and $z = -2.00$, then a total of 0.4772 (0.3413 + 0.1359) of the area lies between the mean and $z = -2.00$. You can see that a host of such statements could be made just from the information shown in Figure 4.3–1.

An aside: positive and negative skew

In Section 3.2 it was stated that nonsymmetrical distributions in which the data are bunched at the lower end of the measurement range are termed positively skewed, and those in which the data are bunched at the higher end of the measurement range are termed negatively skewed. Reference to Figure 4.3–1, in which the abscissa is also labeled in z-scores, will provide a way to remember the use of the adjectives "positive" and "negative." In a distribution having a positive skew, the data are bunched away from the positive z-scores, and in a distribution having a negative skew, the data are bunched away from the negative z-scores. If this strikes you as a backwards rationale, you are right. Actually, the index commonly used to measure skewness is such that when the data are bunched at the lower end it is a positive value, and when the data are bunched at the higher end it is a negative value. This is the real basis for characterizing skewness as "positive" and "negative" (see Ferguson, 1981).

Earlier it was said that the area proportions under the normal curve between the mean and points on the abscissa have been calculated and entered into a table; it is now time for you to learn to use the information contained

P. 351

in such a table. Please turn to Table A and refer to it as you read this paragraph. Table A contains numbers in three columns such that the left column is z-scores, the middle column is the proportion of the area under the normal curve between the mean and the given z-score, and the right column is the proportion of the area under the normal curve that lies beyond (toward the tail from) the given z-score. For example, at $z = 1.00$, the area between μ and z is 0.3413, and the area beyond z is 0.1587; this is how we can say that 0.3413 of the observations in any normal distribution lie between the mean and one standard deviation above the mean, and that 0.1587 of the observations are greater than one standard deviation above the mean. Referring to Figure 4.3–1, we can say that 0.3413 of women have feet between 241 mm and 252 mm, and 0.1587 of women have feet longer than 252 mm.

Check Table A for $z = -2.00$. You will not find negative z-scores in Table A but this poses no problem because the normal curve is symmetrical, and anything true of the positive side is also true of the negative side; therefore, simply use the information associated with $z = +2.00$. The area between μ and z is 0.4772, which means, in the case of women's foot length scores, that 0.4772 of women have feet between 241 mm and 219 mm long; also, the area beyond z is 0.0228, which means that 0.0228 of women have feet smaller than 219 mm. Note that this same entry in Table A also tells us that 0.4772 of women have feet between 241 mm and 263 mm long, and that 0.0228 of women have feet larger than 263 mm.

We will now proceed through a set of example questions that will serve as models for using the information contained in Table A. You should adopt the habit of illustrating each problem with a small diagram as this makes the situation much clearer and easier to understand. You will also have noticed that population notation is used for the mean (μ) and standard deviation (σ) throughout this chapter. This is because our work with normal distributions at present is purely descriptive; we are describing the characteristics of hypothetical normal distributions of data but are not seeking to generalize these findings to unobserved populations.

Question 1: *What proportion of the area under the normal curve lies between the mean and z = +1.73?*

Solution: Read Table A for $z = 1.73$ and find that the area between μ and z is 0.4582; therefore, 0.4582 of the area under the normal curve lies between the mean and $z = +1.73$.

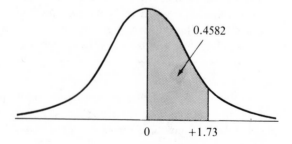

0.4582

0   +1.73

Question 2: *What proportion of the area under the normal curve is to the left of* z $= -0.88?$

Solution: Read Table A for $z = 0.88$ and find that the area beyond z is 0.1894; therefore, 0.1894 of the area under the normal curve is to the left of $z = -0.88$.

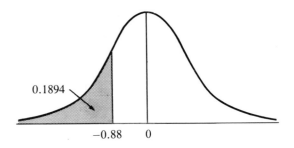

Question 3: *What proportion of the area under the normal curve lies between* z $= \pm1.96?$

Solution: Read Table A for $z = 1.96$ and find that the area between μ and z is 0.4750. Since 0.4750 of the area lies between μ and $z = +1.96$ and 0.4750 of the area lies between μ and $z = -1.96$, then the total proportion of the area under the normal curve that lies between $z = \pm1.96$ is $0.4750 + 0.4750 = 0.9500$.

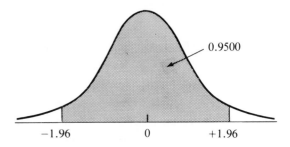

Question 4: *What proportion of the area under the normal curve lies between* z $= +0.25$ *and* z $= -2.11?$

Solution: Read Table A for $z = 0.25$ and find that the area between μ and z is 0.0987. Read Table A for $z = 2.11$ and find that the area between μ and z is 0.4826. Therefore the total area between $z = +0.25$ and $z = -2.11$ is $0.0987 + 0.4826 = 0.5813$.

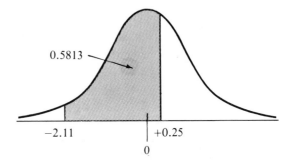

Question 5: *What proportion of the area under the normal curve lies between* z $= +0.66$ *and* z $= +1.34?$

Solution: Read Table A for $z = 1.34$ and find that the area between μ and z is 0.4099. Read Table A for $z = 0.66$ and find that the area between μ and z is 0.2454. Therefore the area between $z = +1.34$ and $z = +0.66$ is $0.4099 - 0.2454 = 0.1645$.

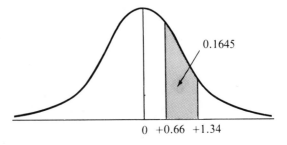

Question 6: *What z-score contains 0.2500 of the area under the normal curve between the mean and itself?*

Solution: In Table A, scan the column of area proportion between μ and z until you find the entry closest to 0.2500; the z-score associated with that entry is the best answer. In this case the closest area entry is 0.2486 and is associated with $z = 0.67$. Therefore $z = +0.67$ (or $z = -0.67$) contains 0.2500 of the area under the normal curve between the mean and itself.

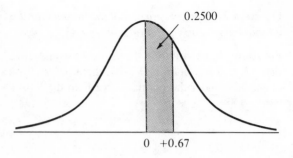

Question 7: *What z-score cuts off the bottom 0.1500 of the area under the normal curve?*

Solution: In Table A, scan the column of area proportion beyond z until you find the entry closest to 0.1500; the z-score associated with that entry is the best answer. In this case, the closest entry is 0.1492 and is associated with $z = 1.04$. Therefore the z-score that cuts off the bottom 0.1500 of the area under the normal curve is $z = -1.04$.

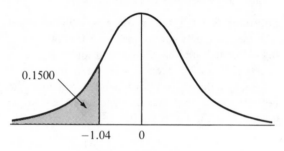

Question 8: *What z-scores contain the middle 0.8000 of the area under the normal curve?*

Solution: Since we seek the middle 0.8000 of the distribution, there must be 0.4000 of the area to each side of μ. Read Table A and search the column of area proportion between μ and z until you find the entry closest to 0.4000; the z-score associated with that entry is the best answer. In this case, the closest entry is 0.3997 and is associated with $z = 1.28$. Therefore, the z-scores that contain the middle 0.8000 of the area under the normal curve are $z = \pm1.28$.

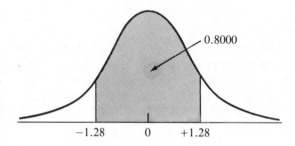

4.4 Review Exercises

1. Define or describe the following terms.
   (a) Central Limit Theorem
   (b) area under the normal curve
   (c) z-score (standard score)

2. What proportion of the area under the normal curve lies between μ and
   $z =$

   (a) $+0.90$ (c) $+3.00$ (e) -0.05
   (b) -2.58 (d) -1.11 (f) $+1.96$

3. What proportion of the area under the normal curve lies to the

   (a) right of $z = +1.80$ (e) right of $z = -1.96$
   (b) right of $z = +2.24$ (f) right of $z = -2.73$
   (c) left of $z = -1.41$ (g) left of $z = +1.68$
   (d) left of $z = -0.99$ (h) left of $z = +0.77$

4. What proportion of the area under the normal curve lies between $z =$

   (a) ±0.50 (c) ±2.58 (e) ±2.00
   (b) ±1.96 (d) ±1.30 (f) ±0.95

5. What proportion of the area under the normal curve lies between $z =$

   (a) $+2.00$ and -1.00 (e) $+1.77$ and $+2.77$
   (b) -1.94 and $+0.94$ (f) -0.50 and -2.00
   (c) -2.35 and $+0.47$ (g) -1.09 and -1.99
   (d) $+1.43$ and -1.76 (h) $+1.61$ and $+1.69$

6. What z-score contains _____ of the area under the normal curve
   between μ and itself?

   (a) 0.2000 (c) 0.4500 (e) 0.4750
   (b) 0.3000 (d) 0.0900 (f) 0.4950

7. What z-score cuts off the _____ of the area under the normal curve?

   (a) upper 0.2500   (e) upper 0.7500
   (b) lower 0.3800   (f) lower 0.6200
   (c) upper 0.5000   (g) lower 0.9000
   (d) lower 0.0500   (h) upper 0.9900

8. What z-scores enclose (contain) the middle _____ of the area under
   the normal curve?

   (a) 0.5000 (c) 0.8400 (e) 0.9500
   (b) 0.9000 (d) 0.3700 (f) 0.9900

4.5 Application

If you have completed the exercises in Section 4.4, you should be quite
skilled in reading and extracting information from Table A. Putting this capa-
bility to use in real-life situations requires only the additional step of transforming raw scores into z-scores, and vice versa. In this section we will see
how this is done by considering three typical problems.

Let us assume that North American women have a mean height of 162 cm
(64 in.) with a standard deviation of 6 cm (2.4 in.), and that North American

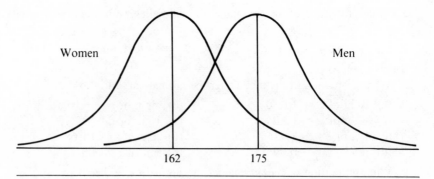

Figure 4.5–1   Height distributions of North American women and men

men have a mean height of 175 cm (69 in.), with a standard deviation of 6.5 cm (2.6 in.).* These distributions are normal and are depicted in Figure 4.5–1. Let us assume that the curves in Figure 4.5–1 represent 2000 female height scores and 1000 male height scores. Thus

Women's heights	Men's heights
$\mu = 162$	$\mu = 175$
$\sigma = 6.00$	$\sigma = 6.50$
$n = 2000$	$n = 1000$

Question 1: *How many women are shorter than 152 cm?*

Solution: We seek to determine how many women are to the left of (shorter than) 152 cm, as represented by the shaded area in the diagram. We cannot work directly with the number 152 because it has no meaning outside of its specific distribution. We must transform the raw score of 152 cm into a form that is usable to extract information from Table A. Our procedure is to convert 152 into a *z*-score and then read Table A to find the proportion of the area under the normal curve that is to the left of that point. Since proportion of area under the normal curve is equivalent to proportion of observations in a normal distribution, we need only convert the proportion that is to the left of 152 into a number to know exactly how many women it represents; this is done

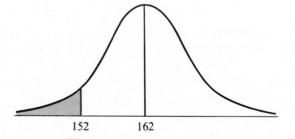

*Various anthropometric sources suggest that these values closely approximate the population parameters.

by multiplying the proportion by the number of scores in the distribution.

$$z = \frac{X - \mu}{\sigma} = \frac{152 - 162}{6} = -1.67$$

Now read Table A for $z = 1.67$ and find that the area beyond z is 0.0475. Thus, 0.0475 of women are shorter than (to the left of) 152 cm. The exact number of these women is found by multiplying the proportion by n; thus $0.0475 \times 2000 = 95$. Therefore we can say that 95 women are shorter than 152 cm.

It might occur to you to ask about the woman who is exactly 152 cm tall. Is she part of the shaded area to the left of 152 cm or is she part of the distribution to the right of 152 cm? In other words, is this woman included among the 95 or not? The answer is that the cutting score, or dividing line score, is always part of the area toward the mean of the distribution. In order to be in the shaded area (bottom (0.0475) one must be less than 152 cm; thus, a woman who is exactly 152 cm is not included in the 95.

Question 2: *How many men are as tall as or taller than the average woman?*

Solution: Since the average woman is 162 cm, the question becomes how many men equal or exceed that height, as represented by the shaded area in the diagram. Again, we must work through the medium of z-scores.

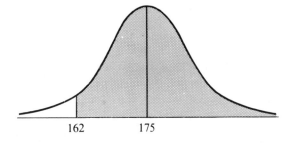

$$z = \frac{X - \mu}{\sigma} = \frac{162 - 175}{6.50} = -2.00$$

Read Table A for $z = 2.00$ and find the area between μ and z to be 0.4772. Thus, 0.4772 of the men are between 162 cm and 175 cm in height. We add 0.4772 to the entire right half (0.5000) of the distribution to find the total proportion represented by the shaded area, which is the total proportion of men whose height is 162 cm or taller. Thus, $0.4772 + 0.5000 = 0.9772$, and we can therefore say that 0.9772 of the men are as tall as or taller than the average woman. The exact number of these men is: $0.9772 \times 1000 = 977.2$ The answer is that 977.2 men are as tall as or taller than the average woman (162 cm).

Question 3: *How tall must a woman be in order to be among the tallest 10 percent of women?*

Solution: The question is what height cuts off the upper 0.1000 of the women's height distribution, as represented by the shaded area in the diagram. Our procedure is to find the z-score that cuts off the upper 0.1000 of the area under the normal curve and then convert it into a height score in the women's distribution. Read Table A and find the entry closest to 0.1000 in the area beyond the z column; the closest entry is 0.1003 and is associated with $z = 1.28$. Since we are dealing with a proportion to the right of the mean we must use this z-score as a positive value. The next step is to convert $z = +1.28$ into a height score in the women's distribution.

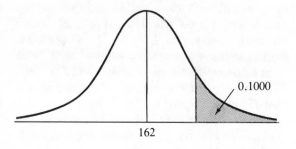

Since $z = \dfrac{X - \mu}{\sigma}$ then $X = z\sigma + \mu$

$X = (+1.28)(6.00) + 162$

$\quad = 169.68$

We have found that the height score 169.68 cm cuts off the upper 0.1000 of the women's distribution; therefore, in order for a woman to be among the tallest 10 percent of women, she must be taller than 169.68 cm.

You will encounter references to the normal distribution many times throughout the rest of this book because many statistical procedures are based upon the assumption that the raw data being analyzed are normally distributed. For the moment, the important thing is that you should acquire an understanding of the basic properties of the normal distribution and a competence in applying these properties to real-life situations. The exercises in Section 4.6 will serve this purpose.

4.6 Review Exercises

1. Marks on an examination were normally distributed with a mean of 60 and a standard deviation of 5. There were 40 students in the class, a passing

$z = \frac{x - \mu}{\sigma}$

mark was 50, and Dave got 56. How many students got a lower mark but still passed?

2. Two hundred people ran in a race. Their finishing times were normally distributed with a mean of 15 minutes 30 seconds, and a standard deviation of 4 minutes 10 seconds. The slowest 25 percent were declared physically unfit. What was the slowest finishing time that was judged physically fit?
   score

3. An experimenter obtained writing speed measures on 300 right-handed persons and 100 left-handed persons. The right-handed group had $\mu = 100$ and $\sigma = 8$, and the left-handed group had $\mu = 84$ and $\sigma = 10$. Assuming normality of the distributions, how many left-handed persons wrote faster than the average right-handed person?

4. A thing's value may be defined as the amount that someone is willing to pay for it. One thousand people were asked to name the maximum price they would pay for a particular painting. These data were normally distributed with $\mu = \$225.00$ and $\sigma = \$45.00$.

   (a) How many people were willing to pay more than $300.00?
   (b) What was the maximum price that a person in the bottom 10 percent of the group was willing to pay?

5. A measure of anxiety was taken on 1000 men and 1000 women. The data were found to be normally distributed with the men having $\mu = 80$ and $\sigma = 10$, and the women having $\mu = 95$ and $\sigma = 15$.

   (a) How many people altogether got a score greater than 100?
   (b) What score would a woman have to get in order to be in the least anxious 15 percent?
   (c) What score would a man have to get in order to be more anxious than three-quarters of the women?

6. Scores on a particular test were normally distributed with $\mu = 69$ and $\sigma = 11$. A letter grade system of F (fail), P (pass), or P+ (excellent), was used with the proportions 0.20, 0.50, and 0.30 of the class getting the three grades respectively. What were the mark intervals for the three letter grades?

7. Suppose "average" is defined operationally as the middle 4 percent of the distribution. Women's heights are normally distributed with $\mu = 162$ cm and $\sigma = 6$ cm. What range of heights defines the average woman?

8. Assume that intelligence test scores are normally distributed with $\mu = 100$ and $\sigma = 15$.

   (a) In order to become a member of Mensa (a club for high I.Q. types) one must score in the top 2 percent of the distribution. What is the minimum acceptable score?

(b) There is an even more exclusive high I.Q. club called Sigma-Four. The name means that an intelligence test score equal to or higher than four standard deviations above the mean is required for admission. Assuming that the population of North America is 300 million, how many people qualify for Mensa but are too stupid for Sigma-Four?

9. The mean life of stockings issued by the army is 40 days with a standard deviation of 8 days and follows a normal distribution. If 1000 pair are issued

   (a) How many will need replacement before 35 days?
   (b) How many will last longer than 46 days?

10. Let us assume that male and female marathon runners differ in endurance, or how far they go before quitting. For men, assume that the mean is 18 miles with a standard deviation of 2.5 miles, and for women assume that the mean is 15 miles with a standard deviation of 4 miles. Both distributions are normal. A marathon was attempted by 100 men and 100 women.

    (a) After 20 miles, how many people are still running?
    (b) How far would a man have to go to outdistance 99 percent of the women?
    (c) After 75 men have dropped out, how many women are still running?

11. A factory that produced meter sticks made a batch of 500. The actual lengths of these sticks varied and formed a normal distribution with $\mu = 1000$ mm and $\sigma = 4$ mm.

    (a) If we accept sticks that differ from a true length of one meter by no more than plus or minus 1 mm as being accurate, how many in this batch were inaccurate?
    (b) How many sticks in this batch mismeasure a meter by 3 or more millimeters?

12. The number of mushroom fragments was counted on 2000 large-size and 1500 small-size pizzas. These data yielded normal distributions with $\mu = 290$ and $\sigma = 38$ for the large-size pizzas and $\mu = 220$ and $\sigma = 24$ for the small-size pizzas.

    (a) How many small pizzas had more mushroom fragments than the average large pizza?
    (b) How many pizzas had 200 or fewer mushroom fragments?
    (c) How many mushroom fragments did small pizzas in the top 1 percent contain?

13. A production batch of 800 automobiles was subjected to a two-year followup study to determine repair frequency. The data were normally distributed with $\mu = 19$ and $\sigma = 6$.

    (a) If a "lemon" is defined as a car that needed more repairs than 1.30 standard deviations above the mean, what repair frequency defines a lemon?

    (b) If a "lemon" is defined as a car that needed 24 or more repairs in two years, how many were lemons?

    (c) The terms "lemon," "poor," "acceptable," and "good," are applied to cars with repair frequencies in the top 15 percent, next 20 percent, next 40 percent, and bottom 25 percent of repair frequency. What repair frequencies identify these classes?

4.7 Normalizing Distributions: *T*-Scores

The proportions of the score distributions lying between the mean and a given raw score, and beyond the raw score toward the tail of the distribution, which we have been using in this chapter are only correct for normal distributions. In a distribution that is skewed, the proportion of scores between μ and $z = +1.00$ will not be 0.3413, and the other normal curve values will not hold. Many statistical procedures assume that the raw data are normally distributed and if this is found not to be the case, then it may be desirable to normalize the scores before proceeding with analysis.

    In general, when we are concerned with individuals' positions in the distributions, making relative comparisons of raw scores in different distributions by transforming them into z-scores assumes that the distributions have similar shapes. Any shape is fine as long as both distributions are approximately the same, because this will result in the z-scores having comparable proportions of scores lying above and below them. If two distributions have different shapes, then it may be appropriate to normalize them in order to achieve a basis for raw score comparisons.

    In this section, we shall consider a means to normalize a set of non-normal scores and transform them into *T*-scores, which are used quite often in education to compare individuals' performances relative to different reference groups. It would be well at this time to sound a precautionary note. Transforming scores to normalize or otherwise alter data may be an acceptable procedure, but we should be mindful that any alteration of the basic characteristics of the raw data must be in some sense a misrepresentation. Normalizing two distributions to achieve comparability of scores does not make them equivalent in any larger sense. For example, if a group of Greek exam marks and statistics exam marks were normalized to allow comparison of an individual's performance in the two exams, it would not be the case that equivalent scores represent equivalent knowledge of the two subjects. Prior to normalizing data for statistical analysis, we should ask ourselves whether there is a suitable nonparametric analysis which, because normality of the data is not assumed, would not require any score transformation.

We shall illustrate the normalization of a set of skewed data by recalling once again the distribution of experimental subject ages presented in Sections 3.2 and 3.4. Table 4.7–1 shows the frequency distribution and cumulative frequencies of the subject ages, along with several new data columns, which are explained below.

Table 4.7–1 Frequency, cumulative frequency, midpoint cumulative frequency, midpoint cumulative proportion, and normalized z-scores of subject ages

Age	Frequency	Cumulative frequency	Midpoint cumulative frequency	Midpoint cumulative proportion	Normalized z-score
35	5	331	328.5	0.9924	2.43
34	3	326	324.5	0.9804	2.06
33	3	323	321.5	0.9713	1.90
32	4	320	318	0.9607	1.76
31	3	316	314.5	0.9502	1.65
30	5	313	310.5	0.9381	1.54
29	8	308	304	0.9184	1.39
28	12	300	294	0.8882	1.22
27	8	288	284	0.8580	1.07
26	7	280	276.5	0.8353	0.98
25	10	273	268	0.8097	0.88
24	14	263	256	0.7734	0.75
23	16	249	241	0.7281	0.61
22	35	233	215.5	0.6512	0.39
21	40	198	178	0.5378	0.09
20	58	158	129	0.3897	−0.28
19	85	100	57.5	0.1737	−0.94
18	14	15	8	0.0242	−1.97
17	1	1	0.5	0.0015	−2.96

In order to normalize a set of scores, we must determine the midpoint cumulative frequencies, which are shown in column 4 of Table 4.7–1, and are derived as follows. Let us consider the persons aged 21 years old. They are assumed, as are all age groups, to be evenly distributed between upper and lower exact limits, in this case between 20.5 and 21.5 years. The midpoint of this range is 21.0 and to determine the cumulative frequency of scores below this midpoint, we add half the frequency of scores at 21 years ($40/2 = 20$) to the cumulative frequency of all scores below 21 years (158) and arrive at a midpoint cumulative frequency of 178. Similarly, there were 263 people below 25 years, and 10 people at 25 years, and thus the midpoint cumulative frequency for 25 years is $263 + 10/2 = 268$. Column 5 in Table 4.7–1 represents the midpoint cumulative proportions and these are obtained by dividing each midpoint cumulative frequency by N ($N = 331$ in this case).

The normalized *z*-scores are obtained from Table A in Appendix I. For example, the midpoint cumulative proportion for the age score 17 years is 0.0015; looking at Table A we can see that the nearest *z*-score that cuts off the bottom 0.0015 of any normal distribution is $z = -2.96$. Similarly, the midpoint cumulative proportion of the age score 24 years is 0.7734 and thus we seek the *z*-score that cuts off the bottom 0.7734 of the normal distribution. This *z*-score will have 0.2734 of the area between the mean and itself; therefore, the appropriate *z*-score is $z = +0.75$. Please note that the normalized *z*-scores are not derived from the raw data; they are obtained from Table A based strictly on the midpoint cumulative proportions.

Normalizing a set of data results in a reshaping of the original distribution into a normal distribution shape. The proportions of the original distribution associated with given score values are identified as equivalent proportions of the normal distribution; the normalized *z*-scores are simply the *z*-score values that identify these proportions. Figure 4.7–1 shows this process using the distribution of subject ages in Table 4.7–1.

T-scores are a transformation of the normalized *z*-scores according to the following formula.*

$$T\text{-score} = 10z_n + 50$$

where z_n = normalized *z*-score

Normalized *z*-scores, like all *z*-scores, have mean = 0 and standard deviation = 1.00; *T*-scores have mean = 50 and standard deviation = 10.00. Since one would almost never encounter a raw score less than $z = -5.00$, *T*-scores will ordinarily all be positive values, and will usually range from 25 to 75. *T*-scores are only one of the possible ways to transform normalized *z*-scores; they are described here because they are used in educational circles and the reader may encounter reference to them.

If one wished to normalize a set of scores and express the values in terms of the original measures, one would use μ and σ as obtained from the original raw data to make the transformation. Thus

$$\text{Normalized score} = \sigma z_n + \mu$$

where

  z_n = normalized *z*-score

  σ = standard deviation of the score distribution

  μ = mean of the score distribution

For the 331 subject ages, $\mu = 22.12$ and $\sigma = 3.96$; therefore, the normalized value for the age score 24 years is $(3.96)(0.75) + 22.12 = 25.09$.

---

*If the original distribution is normal, *T*-scores are a direct transformation of the *z*-scores such that *T*-score $= 10z + 50$.

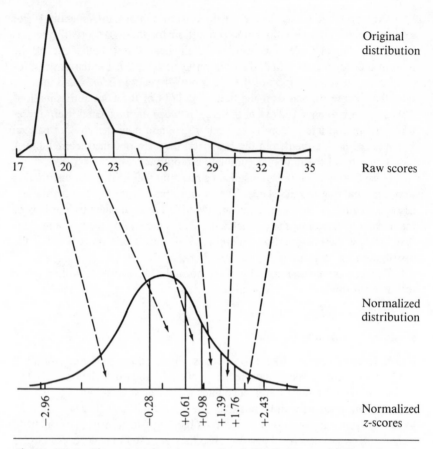

Figure 4.7–1 The original and normalized distributions of subject ages (note that not all age scores are shown)

4.8 Concluding Remarks

In Chapter 4 we applied the properties of the theoretical normal distribution to particular sets of normally distributed real-life data and learned to make various kinds of descriptive statements about such data. Although this is a useful end in itself, there is a more far-reaching purpose behind these exercises. Making decisions in science involves the testing of hypotheses; the decisions consist of retaining or rejecting the particular hypothesis under consideration, and they are made by reference to theoretical distributions. The important general concept of Chapter 4 to remember is the notion that you can view an individual score as a term in a theoretical distribution of known properties and thereby determine its relative frequency of occurrence. This in turn indicates its relative likelihood of occurrence, and is the general basis upon which we decide whether or not a given outcome is in line with the expectation of our hypothesis. We are getting ahead of ourselves here, as we still have some building blocks to put into place before we can test inferential hypotheses. It is sufficient to say for now that being comfortable with theoretical distributions is one of these fundamental building blocks; another important one is the notion of probability, to which we now turn in Chapter 5.

5 Probability

Chapter Preview

5.1 The Nature of Probability

Introduces and defines probability as the ratio of frequencies and explains how an event's probability of occurrence can be determined

Key Terms   probability
theoretical determination of probability
empirical determination of probability

5.2 This or That

Describes the addition rule for the probability of occurrence of any of several mutually exclusive events

Key Terms   addition rule
mutually exclusive

5.3 Review Exercises

5.4 This and That

Describes the multiplication rule for the probability of the joint occurrence of two or more independent events

Key Terms   multiplication rule
independent events

5.5 Review Exercises

5.6 The Normal Distribution Revisited

Recalls the normal distribution to underscore the point that proportion of area under the normal curve is equivalent to the probability of occurrence of scores in that range

5.7 Review Exercises

5.8 Permutations, Combinations, and Binomial Probability Distributions

Describes how, for events with two outcomes, the probabilities of all possible outcome combinations form a probability distribution

Key Terms permutations
combinations
binomial expansion
binomial probability distribution

5.9 Review Exercises

5.10 Concluding Remarks

5.1 The Nature of Probability

The probability of an event is the likelihood that it will happen. Everything that can possibly happen has some probability of happening; sometimes this likelihood is very high, such as the probability that the sun will rise tomorrow morning, and sometimes it is quite low, such as the probability that you will win the Irish Sweepstakes Lottery. In everyday conversation when we say that something will probably happen, such as "it will probably rain tomorrow," we usually only mean that we think it is more likely to happen than not. In science we must have more precision, so we attach numerical quantity to our use of probability; thus, *probability* may be defined as the quantitative expression of the likelihood of occurrence of an event.

probability

We have defined statistics as a body of rules and procedures for describing data and making decisions about the outcome of scientific observation. These decisions concern such things as the likelihood that a particular experimental outcome is reliable, or in other words, determining the probability that the same result would occur if the experiment were to be repeated. We use sample data to estimate population parameters but we can never be completely certain of the parameter values. Inferential science is only possible because we are able to estimate the probabilities associated with error in generalizing from samples to populations. Some familiarity with the nature of probability is necessary in order to understand the implications and limitations of decisions in science.

In addition to the role of probability in inferential science, much of our behavior is governed by probability-based decisions. You might decide to ask Chris or Pat for a date depending on which one you think is more likely to accept. Students sometimes base their choice of an optional course on an estimate of the probability of receiving a high grade. In a baseball game, in the bottom of the ninth inning with one out and a runner on first, the manager may have several strategy options; he or she chooses the one that experience has shown to have the highest probability of success. This is known as the "percentage play." People, and baseball managers, often fail to choose the wisest option available to them because of a misunderstanding of the nature of probability and how it is determined. This exposure to the basic rules of probability may improve your decision-making skills.

If the weather forecaster says that the probability of rain is 25 percent, exactly what does this mean? Will it rain on one quarter of the world but not on the other three-quarters? During the next 24 hours, will it rain for 6 hours but not for 18? Will it rain everywhere, but will only one out of every four people get wet? Actually, the statement means that if current conditions were repeated 100 times, rain would occur on 25 of those occasions at the place where the measures were taken. The probability of an event is the proportion of times it will occur when all conditions are reproduced a large number of times. Probability is a ratio in which the numerator is the frequency of occurrence of the event of interest, and the denominator is the total number of opportunities for the event to happen, or the total number of different possible outcomes. The probability of rain is 25 percent if the frequency of rain is 25 for every 100 times current conditions are repeated ($25/100 = 25$ percent).

Since probability is the ratio of frequency of the event of interest over the total number of opportunities or possibilities, the limiting numerical values are zero and one. If an event happens every time it is possible for it to happen, the numerator is the same value as the denominator. Such a ratio is equal to one, the probability of the event is 1.00, and the event may be termed a certainty. If an event never happens, regardless of how many opportunities it is given, the numerator value is zero. Such a ratio is equal to zero, the probability of the event is 0.00, and the event may be termed impossible. Based on past experience, the probability that the sun will rise tomorrow morning is 1.00; the probability that the sun will evaporate overnight is 0.00. All probabilities have numerical values between 0.00 and 1.00, reflecting the range of likelihood from impossibility to certainty.

In casual conversation probability is often expressed as a percentage, but for statistical work we express a probability value either as a decimal fraction (probability of rain is 0.25), or as a proper fraction (probability of rain is 1/4). A probability is written as a lowercase letter P with the event of interest in parentheses. For example, the probability of rain may be written as $p(Rain)$. The statement, "Probability of rain equals one in four," may be written as $p(Rain) = 1/4$, or $p(Rain) = 0.25$.

There are two ways to determine the probability of an event and we will *theoretical determination of probability* refer to these as theoretical and empirical approaches. The *theoretical determination of probability* is possible if all possible outcomes and their relative likelihood are known. Consider an ordinary coin: one side is designated "head," and the other side "tail." If the coin is tossed in the air, it must land with one or the other side facing up (landing on the edge is assumed to be impossible); thus, there are only two possible outcomes. If the coin is fair, that is, not weighted in such a way that one side is more likely to land face-up than the other, then on any toss each side is equally likely to land face-up. We could say that the probability of a head on a single toss of a fair coin is p(Head) $= 1/2 = 0.50$. The denominator in the probability ratio is 2 because there are a total of two possibilities (head and tail), and the numerator is 1 because only one of these possibilities (head) is the event of interest. We could arrive at the statement p(Head) $= 0.50$ without ever having seen a coin tossed; we could also predict that over a large number of tosses, half the outcomes would be heads.

As another example, consider a die (one member of a pair of dice). A die is a cube with each of its six sides marked with one, two, three, four, five, or six spots. If the die is fair (not weighted so that any side is more likely to land face-up than any other) one could say, without ever having seen such an object, that the probability of any particular side landing face-up is one in six, for example, $p(4) = 1/6 = 0.1667$. Such theoretical determinations of probability are based on the knowledge of the number of possible outcomes and an assumption concerning their relative likelihood; these must be verified by actual observation if there is any doubt as to their validity. It is seldom possible to specify the probabilities of natural events in this theoretical fashion because often we do not know all the possible outcomes or their relative likelihoods.

The *empirical determination of the probability* of an event may be accomplished by observing its frequency of occurrence relative to the total number of opportunities. The question might be, "What is the probability that the next person you encounter will be black-haired?" This is identical to asking what proportion of people have black hair; we need only observe some number of individuals and note how many have black hair. If we examined 85 persons and found that 13 had black hair, the proportion of black-haired types of the total is $13/85 = 0.1529$; therefore, the probability that any given person selected from that group will be black-haired is p(Black-haired) $= 13/85 = 0.1529$. This probability, or proportion, is known with certainty only for the sample of people observed. We cannot be sure that it is accurate for the population at large but it is the best estimate we have until more data are gathered. Empirically determined probabilities must be derived from representative samples that are of adequate size in order to be valid and usefully generalized beyond the events actually observed. The matter of sampling from populations is discussed in Chapter 6.

empirical determination of the probability

One final point to remember is that the probabilities of all possible outcomes sum to one. A fair coin tossed in the air has two possible outcomes; each has probability equal to $1/2$ and, taken together, add up to 1.00. A fair die has six possible outcomes, each of which has probability equal to 1/6, and altogether sum to 1.00. The reason that the probabilities of all the possibilities always add up to 1.00 is that on any trial or occasion, something must occur; since there is a certainty that something will happen, the probabilities of all the possible happenings must add up to certainty.

5.2 This or That

addition rule

mutually exclusive

A basic operation in the use of probabilities is the *addition rule,* which states that *the probability of occurrence of any of several mutually exclusive events is the sum of their separate probabilities. Mutually exclusive* events are such that only one event can happen at any given time. Stated another way, the occurrence of any one event excludes the simultaneous occurrence of any other event.* The two sides of a coin are mutually exclusive; a coin may land head-up or tail-up but both cannot occur at the same time. Similarly, the six sides of a die are mutually exclusive; any are possible but only one can be face-up on a given toss. If you draw a card from an ordinary deck of playing cards, it might be a heart but it cannot at the same time be a spade, club, or diamond; thus, the suits in a deck of playing cards are mutually exclusive. A person can be male or female but not both, blonde-haired or black-haired but not both, and so on.

The addition rule is used when we seek the probability that any of several mutually exclusive alternatives will occur. The general form of the question is: What is the probability of occurrence of this event or that event? The key word is *or,* and, when the alternative outcomes are mutually exclusive, the answer is the sum of the probabilities of the alternative events of interest.

The symbol $\cup$ is used to represent the word *or*. If we consider the mutually exclusive events A and B, then

> probability of A: $p(A)$
> probability of B: $p(B)$
> probability of A *or* B: $p(A \cup B)$

When A and B are mutually exclusive events

$$p(A \cup B) = p(A) + p(B)$$

What is the probability of obtaining a 1 *or* a 3 on a single toss of a fair die? Since the sides of a die are mutually exclusive, the answer is

$$p(1) = 1/6$$
$$p(3) = 1/6$$

---

*This discussion is limited to mutually exclusive events. For a more general treatment the reader is referred to Appendix V.

$$p(1 \cup 3) = p(1) + p(3)$$
$$= 1/6 + 1/6$$
$$= 1/3$$
$$= 0.3333$$

If a single card is drawn from a well-shuffled deck, what is the probability that it will be a spade (S), *or* club (C). Again, because card suits are mutually exclusive, we need only add the separate probabilities. Thus

$$p(S) = 13/52$$
$$p(C) = 13/52$$
$$p(S \cup C) = p(S) + p(C)$$
$$= 13/52 + 13/52$$
$$= 1/2$$
$$= 0.5000$$

The addition rule may be extended to any number of mutually exclusive events. Thus

$$p(A \cup B \cup C) = p(A) + p(B) + p(C)$$

and

$$p(A \cup B \cup C \cup D) = p(A) + p(B) + p(C) + p(D)$$

What is the probability that a single card drawn from a well-shuffled deck will be a heart (H), diamond (D), or black seven (B7)?

$$p(H) = 13/52$$
$$p(D) = 13/52$$
$$p(B7) = 2/52$$
$$p(H \cup D \cup B7) = p(H) + p(D) + p(B7)$$
$$= 13/52 + 13/52 + 2/52$$
$$= 7/13$$
$$= 0.5385$$

5.3 Review Exercises

1. Define or describe the following terms.
   (a) probability
   (b) the numerator term of a probability fraction
   (c) the denominator term of a probability fraction

    (d) the theoretical approach to determining an event's probability

    (e) the empirical approach to determining an event's probability

    (f) the meaning of the statement: "In San Francisco during February the probability of snow is 0.08."

    (g) mutually exclusive events

    (h) $p(A \cup B)$ when A and B are mutually exclusive

2. On a single toss of a fair die, what is the probability of obtaining

    (a) a 5 or 6

    (b) an even number

    (c) anything but a 2

    (d) anything but an odd number

3. If a single card is dealt from a well-shuffled deck, what is the probability that it will be

    (a) a diamond or club or heart

    (b) a king or queen

    (c) an ace or black jack

    (d) a ten, jack, queen, king, or ace

    (e) a black picture card or a red number card

4. An urn contains 8 white balls, 3 red balls, 10 green balls, 4 black balls, 18 blue balls, 6 yellow balls, 12 pink balls, and 1 purple ball. What is the probability that a single ball selected from the urn will be

    (a) pink or black

    (b) yellow, green, or purple

    (c) red, white, or blue

    (d) anything but yellow

    (e) anything but black or blue

5. Assume that in the population 20 percent of people are blonde-haired, 30 percent are brown-haired, 15 percent are red-haired, 25 percent are black-haired, and 10 percent are bald. What is the probability that the next person you will see will be

    (a) red-haired or black-haired

    (b) blonde-haired, red-haired, or bald

    (c) anything but bald

    (d) anything but red-haired or blonde-haired

    (e) anything but brown-haired or black-haired

6. You approach a vending machine that has 9 selector buttons such that 3 dispense cola, 2 ginger ale, 2 root beer, 1 orange, and 1 grape. It turns out, however, that the selector mechanism is broken and no matter which button you press, the machine is equally likely to dispense from any of the 9 slots. What is the probability that you will get

    (a) a grape or cola

    (b) an orange, grape, or root beer

(c) a ginger ale, root beer, or cola

(d) anything but a cola

(e) anything but orange, grape, or root beer   .25

7. Assume that in horse races the horse by the rail wins one time in four, the number 2 position horse wins one time in five, the number 3, 4, and .10 5 position horses win one time in ten, the number 6, 7, and 8 position horses win eight times in one hundred, and the number 9 position horse .01 wins one time in one hundred. What is the probability that the winner of a given race will be

(a) number 1, 2, or 3

(b) number 2, 4, or 6

(c) anything but number 1

(d) number 5, 4, 3, 2, or 1

(e) number 1, 2, 8, or 9

8. A peace conference is attended by 20 Americans, 16 Chinese, 7 Englishmen, 10 Italians, 22 Russians, and 1 Canadian. Just when things are going smoothly the fire alarm goes off and everyone rushes headlong for the exit mindless of anything but his or her own survival. What is the probability that the first person out the door will be

(a) the Canadian

(b) a Russian or Chinese

(c) an Englishman, Italian, or American

(d) anything but an Italian

(e) anything but a Russian, American, or Canadian

9. A Martian biologist visits Earth for the purpose of collecting a human to take home for observation. It goes to a university and snatches a student; the age distribution of students at this particular university is that presented in Table 3.2–1. What is the probability that the person captured will be

(a) 18-years-old

(b) 30 or older

(c) between 20 and 25 inclusive

(d) under 20 or over 30

(e) an odd number of years old

5.4 This and That

It is often of interest to identify the probability of a specific combination or sequence of outcomes. Such a probability may be determined by the use of the *multiplication rule,* which states that *the probability of the joint occurrence of two or more independent events is the product of their separate probabilities.*

multiplication rule

independent events

Independent events are those in which the outcomes are not connected in any way. Two events are independent if the outcome of one does not affect the outcome of the other.*

Coin tosses provide a good illustration of independent events. If a single coin is tossed in the air it may land head-up or tail-up. If tossed a second time, the coin again may land head-up or tail-up, but the outcome on the first toss in no way affects the outcome on the second toss; thus, the two tosses are independent events. The same applies if two coins are tossed in the air at the same time. How the coin on the left lands does not affect how the coin on the right lands; thus, the two tosses are independent events.

The multiplication rule is used to determine the probability of the joint, or combined, occurrence of a number of independent events. It is the probability of the combination of outcomes that is of interest, and not any individual event. If two coins are tossed in the air, one might ask: What is the probability that the left one will land head-up and the right one will land tail-up? If three coins are tossed, the question might be: What is the probability that the left one will land tail-up, the middle one head-up, and the right one tail-up? The key word in these questions is *and*. When we seek the probability of this *and* that, both outcomes must occur in order to satisfy the requirement; this is referred to as the joint occurrence of events. Sometimes the joint occurrence of interest is a specified sequence of outcomes; in such cases it is the probability of occurrence of the particular sequence that is at issue. For example, if a single coin is tossed twice we might ask: What is the probability of a head on the first toss *and* a tail on the second toss?

Whether we seek the probability of a combination of outcomes of simultaneous events or of a sequence of outcomes of an event that is repeated, if the events are independent, the answer consists of multiplying together the probabilities of all the individual outcomes. The symbol ∩ is used to represent the word *and;* thus,

probability of A: $p(A)$
probability of B: $p(B)$
probability of A *and* B: $p(A \cap B)$

When A and B are independent events

$p(A \cap B) = p(A) \times p(B)$

If a fair coin is tossed twice, what is the probability of a head on the first toss *and* a tail on the second toss?

$p(H) = 1/2$
$p(T) = 1/2$

---

*This discussion is limited to independent events. For a more general treatment, the reader is referred to Appendix V.

$$p(H \cap T) = p(H) \times p(T)$$
$$= 1/2 \times 1/2$$
$$= 1/4$$
$$= 0.2500$$

The denominator of the probability ratio is the number of outcome sequences that are possible. In the example of two coin tosses, the four sequences are H–H, H–T, T–H, and T–T.

If a card is drawn from a well-shuffled deck, then replaced and the deck reshuffled, and a second card is drawn, what is the probability that the first card will be an ace *and* the second card will be a seven? (Note: This question could just as well have been written as follows: If a single card is drawn from each of two well-shuffled decks, what is the probability that the card drawn from the left deck will be an ace *and* the card drawn from the right deck will be a seven?)

$$p(A) = 4/52$$
$$p(7) = 4/52$$
$$p(A \cap 7) = p(A) \times p(7)$$
$$= 4/52 \times 4/52$$
$$= 1/169$$
$$= 0.0059$$

The multiplication rule may be extended to any number of independent events. Thus

$$p(A \cap B \cap C) = p(A) \times p(B) \times p(C)$$
$$p(A \cap B \cap C \cap D) = p(A) \times p(B) \times p(C) \times p(D)$$

If a fair die is tossed in the air four times, what is the probability of obtaining four ones, that is, One *and* One *and* One *and* One?

$$p(1 \cap 1 \cap 1 \cap 1) = p(1) \times p(1) \times p(1) \times p(1)$$
$$= 1/6 \times 1/6 \times 1/6 \times 1/6$$
$$= 1/1296$$
$$= 0.000772$$

Imagine that you played a game in which a coin that you knew to be fair was tossed and each time it landed head you won a dollar, and each time it landed tail you lost a dollar. Suppose the coin landed tail 99 times, what is the probability of head on the 100th toss? It is the same as the probability of head on any toss, namely, one-half. People often think that an unlikely

An aside on gambler's fallacy

sequence of events ("bad luck") must be balanced by an opposite result. They raise their bet, believing that the next outcome, whether in cards, roulette, bingo, dice, or whatever is somehow more certain to be in their favor. This utter nonsense is called "gambler's fallacy." The truth is that independent events have the same probability on every trial. People often refer to the "law of averages" (have you ever seen this law written down?) and evidently understand it to mean that the game will break even in the long run, or "on average." True, a fair coin will land head 50 percent of the time in the long run, but "long run" means an infinite number of tosses! Meanwhile, when dealing with independent events, don't ever alter your betting strategy on some wishful belief that the probability of the next outcome is affected by the previous outcomes.

Sometimes we seek the probability of any of several sequences of outcomes. If a die is tossed twice, what is the probability of a 2 on the first toss *and* 4 on the second toss, *or* a 3 on the first toss *and* a 6 on the second toss? Since the outcomes of the tosses are independent and different sequences are mutually exclusive, we can combine the multiplication and addition rules. Thus

$$
\begin{aligned}
p[(2 \cap 4) \cup (3 \cap 6)] &= [p(2) \times p(4)] + [p(3) \times p(6)] \\
&= [1/6 \times 1/6] + [1/6 \times 1/6] \\
&= 1/18 \\
&= 0.0556
\end{aligned}
$$

If a die is tossed twice, what is the probability of a 1 *or* a 2 on the first toss *and* a 5 *or* a 6 on the second toss? Again, since the outcomes on any toss are mutually exclusive and the tosses are independent events, we can combine the addition and multiplication rules. Thus

$$
\begin{aligned}
p[(1 \cup 2) \cap (5 \cup 6)] &= [p(1) + p(2)] \times [p(5) + p(6)] \\
&= [1/6 + 1/6] \times [1/6 + 1/6] \\
&= 1/9 \\
&= 0.1111
\end{aligned}
$$

When all outcomes are mutually exclusive and all events are independent, the general rules may be written as

$$
p[(A \cap B) \cup (C \cap D)] = [p(A) \times p(B)] + [p(C) \times p(D)]
$$

and

$$
p[(A \cup B) \cap (C \cup D)] = [p(A) + p(B)] \times [p(C) + p(D)]
$$

Let us now consider situations in which we seek the probability of some combination of outcomes, but the sequence, or order of occurrence, is not specified. In such cases, if the combination of outcomes can happen in more than one sequence, we must include all acceptable sequences in the calculation of the overall probability. Suppose a man puts 3 quarters, 4 dimes, and 2 nickels into his pocket. The pocket has a hole in it and one coin falls out; he picks it up and returns it to the pocket and after taking a few steps, one coin again falls out. What is the probability that the 2 coins that fall out will total 15 cents? In order to lose 15 cents, the man must lose 1 dime and 1 nickel; this could happen in the order nickel-dime or dime-nickel. If we assume that all coins in the pocket at any one time were equally likely to fall out, the solution is as follows

$$p(N) = 2/9$$
$$p(D) = 4/9$$
$$p[(N \cap D) \cup (D \cap N)] = [p(N) \times p(D)] + [p(D) \times p(N)]$$
$$= [2/9 \times 4/9] + [4/9 \times 2/9]$$
$$= 16/81$$
$$= 0.1975$$

If a fair coin is tossed three times, what is the probability that the result will be one head and two tails? Again, since the order of occurrence of the outcomes is not specified, we must consider all the possible sequences, which are: H–T–T, T–H–T, and T–T–H. Any sequence is acceptable; that is, we seek the probability of occurrence of the first sequence *or* the second sequence *or* the third. Thus

$$p[(H \cap T \cap T) \cup (T \cap H \cap T) \cup (T \cap T \cap H)]$$
$$= [p(H) \times p(T) \times p(T)] + [p(T) \times p(H) \times p(T)]$$
$$+ [p(T) \times p(T) \times p(H)]$$
$$= [1/2 \times 1/2 \times 1/2] + [1/2 \times 1/2 \times 1/2]$$
$$+ [1/2 \times 1/2 \times 1/2]$$
$$= 3/8$$
$$= 0.3750$$

As you can see, it is possible to integrate questions of this *and* that with this *or* that to form larger questions. The best way to avoid confusion is to formulate a clear statement of what is required, and then substitute the probability values, additions for *ors,* and multiplications for *ands.*

5.5 Review Exercises

1. Define or describe the following terms.
    (a) independent events
    (b) joint occurrence

   (c) $p(A \cap B)$ when A and B are independent

   (d) gambler's fallacy

2. If a coin is tossed repeatedly, what is the probability of

   (a) H–H–H–H   (c) T–T–T–T–T–H

   (b) T–H–H–T   (d) T–H–T–H–T–H–T–H

3. If a die is tossed three times, what is the probability of

   (a) 1–1–1

   (b) 2–4–6

   (c) odd, even, and odd number

   (d) anything but 6 on every toss

4. Assume that 40 percent of people wear glasses, 30 percent have brown hair, 15 percent have moustaches, 50 percent are male, and 25 percent are good looking. If these variables are independent, what is the probability that the next person you see will be a

   (a) man wearing glasses

   (b) woman who does not have brown hair

   (c) good-looking woman who does not wear glasses

   (d) good-looking man with a moustache, brown hair, and glasses

5. Suppose that in the human population, the distribution of hair color is 30 percent blonde-haired, 50 percent brown-haired, and 20 percent red-haired; that 25 percent of people are smart and 75 percent are dull; and that 15 percent are skinny, 75 percent are chubby, and 10 percent are just right. If hair color, intelligence, and weight are independent, what is the probability that the next person you see will be

   (a) smart, brown-haired, and just right

   (b) red-haired, and chubby or skinny

   (c) blonde-haired or red-haired, and chubby or skinny

   (d) anything but blonde-haired, chubby, and dull

6. Assume that it rains on 2 days in 5, snows on 3 days in 10, hails on 1 day in 20, and is sunny on the remainder of days. Types of weather are mutually exclusive and the weather on any day is independent of that on any other. What is the probability that the next two days will be

   (a) hail and snow in that order

   (b) rain and sunny in any order

   (c) sunny and sunny in any order

   won't ask — (d) rain or hail, and snow or sunny in that order

   → (e) snow or rain, and snow or hail in any order

   (f) rain or snow or hail on both days

7. A card is drawn from a well-shuffled deck, then replaced and the deck is reshuffled. This procedure is repeated until four cards have been drawn.

What is the probability that the four cards will consist of

(a) four aces
(b) four picture cards
(c) heart, spade, diamond, and club in that order
(d) three hearts and a spade in that order
(e) three hearts and a spade in any order
(f) two queens and two kings in any order

8. In a consumer preference study, 15 children were asked to indicate their first choice of several soft drink flavors: 4 chose grape, 3 chose root beer, 6 chose cream soda, 1 chose cola, and 1 chose lemon. What is the probability that the next 5 children to order a drink (independently) will choose

(a) all cream soda
(b) cola, root beer, grape, cream soda, and cola in that order
(c) lemon, lemon, lemon, lemon, and cola in that order
(d) lemon, lemon, lemon, lemon, and cola in any order
(e) grape, grape, lemon, lemon, and lemon in that order
(f) grape, grape, lemon, lemon, and lemon in any order

Note: In the remaining problems pay particular attention to whether or not the sequence of occurrence of the outcomes is specified.

9. Assume that a litter of 11 rabbits consists of 5 black, 3 white, 1 grey, and 2 spotted individuals. Molly reaches into the nest and pulls one out, but it gets away and runs back inside, so she reaches in again and grabs one a second time. What is the probability that the two will be
(a) anything but spotted
(b) the first grey and the second spotted
(c) one black and the other white
(d) the first grey and the second white or black
(e) one black or grey and the other spotted or white

10. Two purses each contain 2 quarters, 5 dimes, 9 nickels, and 4 pennies. If one coin is drawn from each, what is the probability of obtaining

(a) 50 cents or 2 cents
(b) 15 cents
(c) 15 cents or 20 cents
(d) 26 cents, 30 cents, or 35 cents
(e) 11 cents, 30 cents, or 6 cents

11. In a particular lake, the probability of catching a bass is 0.05, a trout 0.01, a sunfish 0.15, and a catfish 0.21. Assume that these are the only things that can be caught and that the supply of each type is infinite.

(a) If Carmela, Cheryl, Lucy, and Veronica go fishing, what is the probability that none will catch anything?

(b) If Irene and Anne each catch 1 fish, what is the probability that they will consist of 2 catfish or 2 bass?

(c) If Nick catches 3 fish, what is the probability that they will be a catfish and 2 bass or a sunfish and 2 trout?

(d) If Barbara and Brenda each catch 2 fish, what is the probability that they will be 2 trout and 2 bass?

12. When you go to the beauty parlor the chances are 1 in 20 that you will come out beautiful, 4 in 20 that you will come out improved, 9 in 20 that you will look the same, and 6 in 20 that you will look worse. If Teresa, Mary, and Dorothy emerge from the beauty parlor, what is the probability that

(a) all will be the same or worse

(b) all will be beautiful or improved or the same

(c) one will be beautiful or improved and the other two will be the same or worse

(d) one will be beautiful or improved, one the same or worse, and one beautiful or worse

5.6 The Normal Distribution Revisited

In Chapter 4 you learned to identify what proportion of a normal distribution lies above, below, and between given score values, and what scores cut off or contain given proportions. It follows from the definition of probability cited earlier that the probability of occurrence of an event or characteristic is equal to its proportion in the population. If 0.2000 of the population weighs less than 60 kg, then the probability that any given person will weigh less than 60 kg is 0.2000. Thus the kinds of questions asked in Sections 4.4 and 4.6 could be questions about probabilities of occurrence as well as about proportions.

Assume that a large number of students write an examination that produces a normal distribution of scores with $\mu = 65$ and $\sigma = 10$. What is the probability that Michelle or any given individual will get a mark over 90? The solution consists of determining the proportion of the distribution that was greater than 90; this proportion is the probability that any given student will score greater than 90.

$$z = \frac{X - \mu}{\sigma} = \frac{90 - 65}{10} = 2.50$$

From Table A, read area beyond z for $z = 2.50$ and find 0.0064. Therefore the probability that Michelle will score over 90 is 0.0064. (See Figure 5.6–1.)

When the variable measured is normally distributed, then the z-scores form a normal population with $\mu_z = 0.00$ and $\sigma_z = 1.00$. The probability

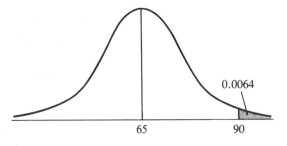

Figure 5.6–1 The probability that any given student will score over 90

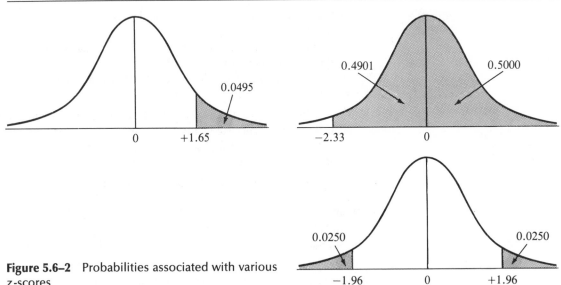

Figure 5.6–2 Probabilities associated with various z-scores

of occurrence of z-scores above and below any point can be read directly from Table A. For example, the probability that a z-score selected from a normal population will be greater than $z = +1.65$ is 0.0495, and the probability that any selected z-score will be greater than $z = -2.33$ is 0.9901 (0.4901 + 0.5000). The probability that any selected z-score will be numerically greater than $z = 1.96$ is 0.05 because 0.0250 of the normal distribution lies beyond $z = +1.96$ and 0.0250 lies beyond $z = -1.96$; thus a score greater than $+1.96$ or smaller than -1.96 has 0.0500 (0.0250 + 0.0250) probability of occurrence. (See Figure 5.6–2.)

> 1.96 eg 1.97
asking for > 1.96
at both ends of
distribution ∴
must add the
proportions

5.7 Review Exercises

1. One thousand people compete in an oyster-eating contest. Their scores (number of oysters eaten) are normally distributed with $\mu = 51$ and $\sigma = 11$.

(a) What is the probability that a given individual will eat more than 70?

(b) What is the probability that a given individual will eat between 60 and 65 inclusive (assume that oysters are eaten all-or-none)?

(c) What is the probability that a given individual will eat less than 29 or more than 72?

2. Five hundred U.S. citizens are given a list of Canadian cities and asked to pinpoint their geographical location. The measure taken is the mean number of km between the actual locations and the points selected on the map. These data are normally distributed with $\mu = 550$ and $\sigma = 225$.

(a) What is the probability that a given subject will average less than 100 km error?

(b) What is the probability that a given subject will average between 500 and 700 km error inclusive?

(c) What is the probability that a given subject will average less than 109 km or more than 991 km error?

3. A wildlife biologist traps and tags 1000 ferrets, of which 600 are female and 400 male. Each is measured for length in cm, the males having $\mu = 22$ and $\sigma = 4$, and the females having $\mu = 19$ and $\sigma = 6$. Both distributions are normal.

(a) What is the probability that a female will be longer than the average male?

(b) What is the probability that a ferret will be longer than 30 cm?

(c) What is the probability that a female will be shorter than 90 percent of the males?

4. One thousand men and 1000 women rate their own attractiveness on a 100-point scale, wherein higher numbers reflect greater attractiveness. For men $\mu = 65$ and $\sigma = 15$, and for women $\mu = 55$ and $\sigma = 10$. Both distributions are normal.

(a) What is the probability that a male will rate himself higher than the average female?

(b) What is the probability that a person will rate himself or herself over 75?

(c) What is the probability that a male will rate himself more attractive than 95 percent of women?

5. The marks of 500 students who write an exam are normally distributed with $\mu = 64$ and $\sigma = 12$.

(a) What is the probability that a given student will fail (get less than 50)?

(b) What is the probability that a given student will get an A (80 or higher)?

(c) If twin sisters Brenda and Beth write the exam, what is the probability that both will get a B (70 to 79 inclusive)?

6. On the evening news the number of seconds devoted to individual news items follows a normal distribution with $\mu = 75$ seconds and $\sigma = 15$ seconds. If two items are selected at random, what is the probability that

   (a) both will be shorter than 50 seconds
   (b) both are between 70 and 90 seconds inclusive
   (c) neither is longer than 80 seconds

5.8 Permutations, Combinations, and Binomial Probability Distributions

Permutations may be thought of as arrangements; when we speak of the number of permutations of things, we are referring to the number of ways they may be arranged, ordered, or sequenced. *The number of permutations (arrangements) of* n *objects, or events, is* n!. The notation $n!$ is read as "*n* factorial," and means the number multiplied by one less than itself, then by one less than that number, and so on, down to 1. Thus

permutations

$$n! = n \times (n - 1) \times (n - 2) \times (n - 3) \times \cdots \times 1$$

The number of permutations of five objects or events is 5!

$$5! = 5 \times 4 \times 3 \times 2 \times 1$$
$$= 120$$

If five people form a line, there are 120 different possible lines.

Suppose a table was set to receive eight people, say, Grandma, Grandpa, Mom, Dad, and four children; how many different seating arrangements are possible? Imagine that they sit down one at a time; the first person can choose from eight chairs. The second person can choose from seven chairs, but has seven choices for *each* of the eight possible chairs selected by the first. Thus, there are $8 \times 7 = 56$ possible different ways the first two can sit down. The third person has six choices for *each* of these 56 ways, and thus the first three people have $8 \times 7 \times 6 = 336$ different ways to sit down, and so on. For the total of eight people there are $8! = 8 \times 7 \times 6 \times 5 \times 4 \times 3 \times 2 \times 1 = 40,320$ different seating arrangements. Have you ever sat at a table with eleven other people, say at a Christmas dinner or maybe at the student pub? The number of different seating arrangements for twelve is $12! = 12 \times 11 \times 10 \times 9 \times 8 \times 7 \times 6 \times 5 \times 4 \times 3 \times 2 \times 1 = 479,001,600$: makes one think, doesn't it?

Combinations may be thought of as selections. Combinations are the number of different selections of r objects that can be made from a group of n objects, or the number of different subsets of size r that can be drawn from a set of size n. The notation to express the number of combinations of size r from a set of size n is $\binom{n}{r}$.

combinations

$$\binom{n}{r} = \begin{array}{l} \text{number of combinations (different samples) of size } r \\ \text{that can be obtained from a set (population) of size } n. \end{array}$$

$$\binom{n}{r} = \frac{n!}{r!(n-r)!}$$

Suppose that five children are playing ball and accidentally break a neighbor's window. They decide that two of them must go and inform the neighbor of the damage. How many different twosomes could be selected? If we identify the five children as A, B, C, D, and E, then the possible groups of two are

AB	BC	CD	DE
AC	BD	CE	
AD	BE		
AE			

Obviously, there are 10 combinations of 2 that can be selected from a group of 5. In this example the numbers are small enough that we can easily enumerate all the combinations; however, as n and r increase in size, this soon becomes impractical. The combinations expression, $\binom{n}{r}$, gives us this information directly and conveniently. Thus

$$\binom{n}{r} = \frac{n!}{r!(n-r)!}$$

$$n = 5$$

$$r = 2$$

$$\binom{5}{2} = \frac{5!}{2!(5-2)!}$$

$$= \frac{5!}{2!\,3!}$$

$$= \frac{5 \times 4 \times 3 \times 2 \times 1}{(2 \times 1)(3 \times 2 \times 1)}$$

$$= \frac{120}{(2)(6)}$$

$$= \frac{120}{12}$$

$$= 10$$

As expected, we have arrived at the same answer of 10 twosomes.

Combinations are not concerned with order, only with the number of different groups of size r that can be obtained from a group of size n. If r is the sample size and n is the population size, then the combinations expression gives us the total number of different samples of size r that can be drawn from a population of size n.

If we dealt four cards from an ordinary deck, how many different four-card samples are possible?

$$n = 52$$
$$r = 4$$
$$\binom{52}{4} = \frac{52!}{4!(52 - 4)!}$$
$$= \frac{52!}{4!\,48!}$$
$$= 270,725$$

As you can see, the number of possible samples can be surprisingly large when n and r increase in size.

An aside on human uniqueness

Humans may be predictable to the extent that they share common qualities, but they are interesting to the extent they are unique. Every person develops from a genetic blueprint estimated to consist of from 20,000 to 40,000 units of hereditary instruction or genes, each of which may occur in alternative forms. If we take the most conservative numbers, that is, 20,000 genes and 2 alternative forms of each, there are potentially $2^{20,000}$ different human genetic blueprints. This number is unimaginably large. Except for identical twins, which are genetically identical, our recognition of each individual's uniqueness is well placed. There can be no real doubt that, genetically at least, every person is different from any other living person, different from any person who ever lived in all of past human history, and different from any person who will ever live in all of future human history!

Many events, such as coin tosses, have only two possible outcomes; for others, we can categorize outcomes into the two classes of favorable and unfavorable. For example, we might classify the weather on any day as being rainy or not-rainy and thereby lump together all the alternatives to rainy as being unfavorable (not of specific interest) outcomes. Quite often we are interested in knowing the overall probability of occurrence of some number of favorable events, given some total number of opportunities or trials. Such probabilities may be determined by means of the *binomial expansion*, as is shown next.

binomial expansion

$$p(r \text{ favorable events in } n \text{ opportunities}) = \binom{n}{r}p^r q^{n-r}$$

where
  n = the number of trials or opportunities for the favorable event to occur
  r = the number of occurrences of the favorable event
  p = the probability of the favorable event
  q = the probability of all alternatives to the favorable event ($q = 1 - p$)

Suppose a coin is tossed 5 times, what is the probability of occurrence of 2 heads? The binomial expansion will be used to answer this question. The binomial expansion has three parts; the first part is the number of combinations of size r from a set of size n. In this case it would be $\binom{5}{2}$ and would give us the number of combinations of occurrence of 2 heads in 5 tosses, or, the number of different ways that one could obtain 2 heads in 5 tosses [$\binom{5}{2} = 10$; the actual sequences are H–H–T–T–T, H–T–H–T–T, H–T–T–H–T, H–T–T–T–H, T–H–H–T–T, T–H–T–H–T, T–H–T–T–H, T–T–H–H–T, T–T–H–T–H, T–T–T–H–H]. The second part is p^r, which is the probability of the favorable event raised to the power of its frequency of occurrence; in this case $p^r = (0.5)^2 = 0.25$. The third part of the binomial expansion is q^{n-r}, which is the probability of all the alternative, or unfavorable, events raised to the power of the frequency of their occurrence. In this case, $q^{n-r} = (0.5)^{5-2} = (0.5)^3 = 0.125$. The three parts are multiplied together, so that the answer to our question is

$$\binom{5}{2}(0.5)^2(0.5)^3 = (10)(0.25)(0.125)$$

$$= 0.3125$$

Clearly, the binomial expansion can be used to determine the overall probability of r favorable outcomes in n trials for any event as long as p is known.

If we solve the binomial expansion for all possible frequencies of favorable events (all possible values of r), the probabilities thus obtained form a *binomial probability distribution*.

binomial probability distribution

p(0 Heads in 5 tosses) = 0.03125
p(1 Head in 5 tosses) = 0.15625
p(2 Heads in 5 tosses) = 0.31250
p(3 Heads in 5 tosses) = 0.31250
p(4 Heads in 5 tosses) = 0.15625
p(5 Heads in 5 tosses) = <u>0.03125</u>
                          1.00000

You will notice that, as will always be the case given sufficient precision, the probabilities of all the possible outcomes sum to 1.00. A histogram of this binomial probability distribution is shown in Figure 5.8–1.

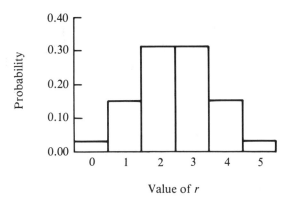

Figure 5.8–1 Histogram of binomial probability distribution when $p = 0.50$ and $n = 5$

Value of r

Let us consider another example. Suppose that on a given day, 16 babies are born at a particular hospital, and that there is a 0.5 probability of each baby being either gender. What is the probability that 11 of the 16 babies will be female?

$$\binom{16}{11}(0.5)^{11}(0.5)^5 = (4368)(0.00049)(0.03125)$$

$$= 0.06689$$

The complete binomial probability distribution for this case is listed next.

$p(0$ females in 16 births$)$ $= 0.00002$
$p(1$ female in 16 births$)$ $= 0.00025$
$p(2$ females in 16 births$)$ $= 0.00184$
$p(3$ females in 16 births$)$ $= 0.00858$
$p(4$ females in 16 births$)$ $= 0.02787$
$p(5$ females in 16 births$)$ $= 0.06689$
$p(6$ females in 16 births$)$ $= 0.12262$
$p(7$ females in 16 births$)$ $= 0.17518$
$p(8$ females in 16 births$)$ $= 0.19707$
$p(9$ females in 16 births$)$ $= 0.17518$
$p(10$ females in 16 births$)$ $= 0.12262$
$p(11$ females in 16 births$)$ $= 0.06689$
$p(12$ females in 16 births$)$ $= 0.02787$
$p(13$ females in 16 births$)$ $= 0.00858$
$p(14$ females in 16 births$)$ $= 0.00184$
$p(15$ females in 16 births$)$ $= 0.00025$
$p(16$ females in 16 births$)$ $= 0.00002$

The histogram of this probability distribution, shown in Figure 5.8–2, reveals that as n increases, the binomial probability distribution becomes smoother

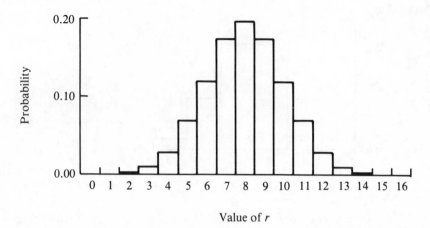

Figure 5.8–2 Histogram of binomial probability distribution when $p = 0.50$ and $n = 16$

and more continuous in appearance. If it looks familiar, that is because when $p = 0.5$, the binomial probability distribution approximates the normal distribution quite rapidly. When $p \neq 0.5$, the binomial probability distribution is skewed; theoretically, no matter what the value of p, when n becomes infinitely large, the binomial probability distribution becomes equivalent to the normal distribution. When $p = 0.5$ this approximation becomes quite good with n as low as 20 (Hays, 1973), or even 10 (Roscoe, 1975).

If we total the probabilities associated with 12, 13, 14, 15, and 16 females, we find that they sum to 0.03856. We could say that in 16 births the probability of occurrence of more than 11 females is 0.03856. Inspection of Table A shows that the nearest z-score that cuts off the upper 0.0386 of a normal distribution is $z = +1.77$; thus, the score 11 can be said to have an approximate z-score value of $+1.77$. A more precise way to determine the z-score value of any particular frequency of the favorable event is

$$z = (X_{EL} - \mu_b)/\sigma_b$$

where

μ_b = the mean of the binomial (favorable event) frequencies ($\mu_b = np$)
σ_b = the standard deviation of the binomial (favorable event) frequencies ($\sigma_b = \sqrt{npq}$)
X_{EL} = the exact limit of the frequency of the favorable event: the upper exact limit if the frequency is greater than μ_b, and the lower exact limit if the frequency is less than μ_b.

The z-score value of 11 in the example of 11 females in 16 births would thus be determined as follows

$$\mu_b = (16)(0.5) = 8$$
$$\sigma_b = \sqrt{(16)(0.5)(0.5)} = 2$$

$$X_{\text{EL}} = 11.5$$

$$z = \frac{(11.5 - 8)}{2}$$

$$= 1.75$$

Clearly, when a binomial probability distribution closely approximates the normal distribution, we can apply the properties of the normal distribution to make interpretations concerning score probabilities, just as we have become accustomed to doing in connection with score frequencies.

The point behind this exposition of the binomial expansion and the binomial probability distribution is not principally to calculate probabilities, although this is a useful procedure in some instances, but rather to show the derivation of the family of binomial distributions that constitute theoretical references for two-outcome cases in which p can be specified, and to show that distributions of the probabilities of all outcome combinations resemble ordinary frequency distributions. In fact, a frequency distribution becomes a probability distribution as soon as raw frequencies are converted to proportions of the total number of scores.

5.9 Review Exercises

1. Define or describe the following terms.
   (a) permutations
   (b) combinations
   (c) binomial expansion
   (d) binomial probability distribution

2. Derive the binomial probability distribution for the occurrence of tails in 10 tosses of a fair coin.

3. Derive the binomial probability distribution for the occurrence of ones in 10 tosses of a fair die.

4. You are standing at the main door of the university library. Assuming that male and female students are equally likely to be inside, what is the probability that of the next 20 people to emerge
   (a) more than 15 will be female
   (b) less than 6 will be male

5. If a fair coin is tossed 15 times, what is the probability that there will be
   (a) more than 13 heads
   (b) less than 5 tails

6. If a single card is dealt from each of 25 well-shuffled decks, what is the probability that there will be

    (a) more than 20 that are hearts or diamonds

    (b) less than 10 that are spades or clubs

7. If fifty babies are born on a particular day at a large city hospital, what is the probability that there will be

    (a) more than 29 females

    (b) less than 18 males

5.10 Concluding Remarks

In this chapter we have become acquainted with the two most basic rules of probability and have seen how probability serves to describe the likelihood of occurrence of particular events. It is important to have some familiarity with probability as a concept because all decisions in science are based on probabilities. We have also integrated the concepts of probability and frequency distribution by describing the occurrence of terms in normal distributions in probabilistic terms and by generating probability distributions with the binomial expansion. Decision making in science can be roughly characterized as the determination of probabilities of occurrence of obtained statistics viewed as individual terms in theoretical frequency distributions. Thus, the notion of frequency distribution assumes a conceptual generality far beyond its original presentation as a descriptive device. The next major item on our agenda concerns the matter of drawing representative samples from populations, also a probability-based process, to which we now turn in Chapter 6.

6 Sampling and Sampling Distributions

Chapter Preview

6.1 Random Sampling

A population consists of all individuals or instances of a defined type of objects, organisms, or events, and a sample is any subset of a population. Since most populations of interest, such as members of the United Auto Workers, grade one children, or monarch butterflies, are so large that studying every member is impractical, scientists resort to observing samples of individuals and inferring the characteristics of the population from sample data. The accuracy of these inferences clearly depends on the extent to which the sample of observed individuals reflects population characteristics. When a scientist sets out to collect a group of subjects to serve in an experiment, the foremost concern must be that the sample of individuals obtained is representative of the population to which the results are to be applied.

random sample

How does one select samples that are representative of their populations? The most generally useful procedure is known as *random sampling;* indeed, many statistical methods are based on the assumption that the subject groups are random samples. A sample is random when every member of the population has an equal probability of being selected, and the selection of every member of the sample is independent of the selection of any other. In everyday use the word "random" may carry an implication of haphazard, or unsystematic, but in statistics the term has a precise meaning; random sampling is in no way haphazard. On the contrary, random sampling is a systematic procedure designed to insure that all members of the population have an equal likelihood of being chosen and that the selection of any member does not affect the selection of any other. Random sampling is very useful and important in science because random procedures select individuals from the population such that, as a group, they have no systematic tendency to manifest any particular characteristic; thus, random samples have the best prospect of being representative.

Suppose the population of interest is defined as all the registered full-time first year students at a given university, and that this population consists of 1000 persons. If we wished to draw a random sample of 50 individuals from this population, it might be done in the following manner. Each of the 1000 persons' names is written on a slip of paper and put into a large container, then the container is mixed and someone reaches in blindly and pulls out one slip. The container is mixed again and the person pulls out another slip, and so on. On any draw, every slip of paper in the container could be presumed to have an equal probability of being chosen. (The slips of paper must be identical in size and texture so that none is more or less likely to be chosen than any other.) The identity of the first person selected in no way affects the identity of the second person, and so on; thus, the procedure is random. Note that in this example, as in virtually all real-life cases, sampling is being done without replacement; that is, the selected individuals are not returned to the population prior to the next draw. This does not destroy the true random nature of the selection; the critical point is that on each draw the remaining members of the population have equal probability of being chosen.

Many contests and giveaways require the entrants to send in a postcard or envelope, the winner being selected "at random" from the pile of entries. Some people seem to be luckier than others at having their entry chosen, and it is said that a few even earn their livelihood by this means! Such people are not as lucky as they might at first seem. Remember that at some point the selection is made by a person, and people are influenced by the characteristics of any stimulus. If you send in a standard size plain white envelope that is indistinguishable from a million others, your entry will have at best a chance probability of being selected. But, if your entry is vividly colored with, say, bold stripes (aimed at the selector who scans the pile visually), and is a bizarre shape such as a circle, or better a triangle, or star (aimed at the selector who uses touch), then it is far more likely to be noticed. Anything that makes your entry noticeable relative to the others changes its probability of being selected, and most likely increases it. This is how those "lucky" people do it.

An aside on the luck of the draw

The process of selecting a sample could be made more convenient by the use of a table of random digits, such as Table K. A table of random digits consists of the numbers from 0 to 9 arranged in a random order, meaning that all values have an equal probability of occupying any position. The digits in Table K may be read in groups of any size, starting at any point, and going in any direction. Using a table of random digits to select a sample involves assigning a number to each member of the population and then reading a sequence of digits in the table to identify which individuals will be chosen. If our 1000 first year students had each been assigned a number, then the digit sequence in the table of random digits would be read in groups of three, with each such group of three identifying a selected individual. Suppose we used Table K, started at the top left corner of the table, and read groups of three digits from left to right. The first person selected would be number 807, the second number 718, the third number 192, the fourth number 442, and so on, as illustrated by the excerpt from Table K shown next.

```
8 0 7 7 1 8 1 9 2 4   4 2 6 2 2 2 5 8 1 1   1 6 3 3 6 0 1 0 1 9
6 0 6 3 3 3 1 2 5 0   8 1 5 0 4 0 0 4 9 7   6 6 9 3 3 5 9 9 7 1
3 4 7 4 6 5 9 7 6 0   3 2 9 5 7 8 6 1 0 1   4 3 1 2 8 3 1 4 1 3
```

Is a random sample always and inevitably representative of its population? The answer is no. A random procedure has the highest probability of gener-

Sample Size and Representativeness

Suppose we have a population of 25 persons, of whom 15 are Democrats and 10 are Republicans, as is shown.

#1–D	#6–D	#11–D	#16–R	#21–D
#2–R	#7–R	#12–D	#17–D	#22–D
#3–D	#8–D	#13–R	#18–R	#23–D
#4–R	#9–D	#14–D	#19–R	#24–D
#5–R	#10–D	#15–R	#20–D	#25–R

Using the random digits in Table K, the following five samples of size five ($n = 5$) were drawn.

Sample no. 1:   #18–R,   #19–R   #24–D,   #22–D,   #11–D: D = 3;   R = 2
Sample no. 2:   #16–R,   #10–D,   #19–R,   #11–D,   #13–R: D = 2;   R = 3
Sample no. 3:   #12–D,   #9–D,   #21–D,   #8–D,   #17–D: D = 5;   R = 0
Sample no. 4:   #5–R,   #1–D,   #12–D,   #14–D,   #13–R: D = 3;   R = 2
Sample no. 5:   #25–R,   #12–D,   #22–D,   #6–D,   #24–D: D = 4;   R = 1

You can see that two of the five samples matched the population ratio of 3 Democrats to 2 Republicans. Over the five samples the means were $\overline{D} = 17/5 = 3.40$ and $\overline{R} = 8/5 = 1.60$.

Again using Table K, five samples of size ten ($n = 10$) were drawn.

Sample no. 1:   #6–D,   #17–D,   #7–R,   #19–R,   #20–D,
                #8–D,   #14–D,   #18–R,   #21–D,   #22–D: D = 7;   R = 3
Sample no. 2:   #13–R,   #11–D,   #24–D,   #10–D,   #2–R,
                #5–R,   #22–D,   #23–D,   #15–R,   #8–D: D = 6;   R = 4
Sample no. 3:   #8–D,   #24–D,   #22–D,   #1–D,   #12–D,
                #10–D,   #4–R,   #17–D,   #20–D,   #18–R: D = 8;   R = 2
Sample no. 4:   #23–D,   #22–D,   #7–R,   #13–R,   #8–D,
                #3–D,   #5–R,   #20–D,   #1–D,   #18–R: D = 6;   R = 4
Sample no. 5:   #11–D,   #21–D,   #13–R,   #24–D,   #18–R,
                #23–D,   #25–R,   #1–D,   #2–R,   #19–R: D = 5;   R = 5

It just happened that again two of the five samples matched the population ratio of Democrats to Republicans. Notice, however, that over these five samples, the means were $\overline{D} = 32/10 = 3.20$ and $\overline{R} = 18/10 = 1.80$. The finding that the means for Democrats and Republicans based on samples of size 10 were closer to the true population ratio values is a reflection of the fact that larger samples tend to more accurately reflect population characteristics. The other lesson that might be drawn from this simple example is that if the purposes of the experiment require that the ratio of Democrats to Republicans in the sample match that in the population, then stratified sampling would be advised.

ating a representative sample, but there is no certain guarantee that this will happen on every occasion. For example, if the 1000 first year students to which we have been referring consisted of 620 women and 380 men, could we expect a randomly chosen sample of 50 to consist of 31 women and 19 men? If the selection procedure were random, with the selections equiprobable and independent, then a ratio of 31 women to 19 men is the most probable outcome. It could easily happen that, by chance, our sample of 50 consisted of, say, 28 women and 22 men. It is important to distinguish randomness from representativeness; one refers to a selection procedure and the other to the fidelity with which a sample reflects its population.

Experimenters sometimes perform what is called stratified random sampling. If it is thought necessary to ensure that the ratio of certain types of individuals in the sample exactly match the known ratio in the population, then each sub-group (stratum) can be separately randomly sampled for the appropriate number of individuals. For example, the 620 women could be treated as population and randomly sampled for 31 individuals; similarly, 19 men could be randomly sampled from the population of 380. When these two groups are combined, the sample of 50 is a *stratified random sample*. This procedure could be used when the variable for which stratified sampling was done was crucial in the experiment, and when the proportions in the population are known. Stratified sampling insures exact representation by the sample for the stratified variable and thereby increases the accuracy with which the sample estimates population characteristics. Note that a stratified sample's match to the population is only perfect for the stratified variable; for subject characteristics that are unrelated to the stratified variable, a stratified sample is no more likely to be a perfect match than a totally random sample.

stratified random sample

Suppose the people whose names are listed in the telephone directory are taken to be a population.* If a single individual is randomly selected from this population (say by means of a table of random digits), and, using this first person as a reference, every 100th name is selected, working forward and backward along the listing, would such a sample be random? The answer is no because, while the first individual was randomly chosen, and every name in the book had an equal probability of being that first one, the remainder of the sample is dependent upon the identity of the first selection. If a truly random sample of 500 persons were to be drawn from the telephone directory, one possible sample would be the first 500 names, but the procedure described could not produce that sample. For any specified population size and sample size there is a specific number [i.e., $\binom{n}{r}$] of *different* samples that can be obtained. The number of different possible samples can be surprisingly large;

---

*For the purposes of this illustration, we would assume that no individual is listed more than once in the telephone directory. In reality this does occur when a person owns a business and is listed under the business name as well as his or her own.

for example, there are 2,598,960 different five-card samples (poker hands) that can be dealt from a deck of 52 cards (see Section 5.8). Perhaps the most elegant definition of a random sampling procedure is that it makes each of the different possible samples equally probable.

Assume that there are 3000 registered students at a given college and on a particular afternoon every one of them has an equal probability of being in the library. Furthermore, assume that each person leaves independently of all others; thus each student that leaves the library is a random selection from those inside, so any student is equally likely to be first, second, or third out the door. An experimenter stations herself outside the main exit and, beginning at some arbitrary time, takes the first person to exit and every tenth one thereafter until the desired sample size has been reached. Is this a random sample? The answer is yes because, even though the selection was every nth, or tenth in this case, person, since the people were not ordered or arranged in their departure in any systematic way, all conceivable combinations of people were equally probable. Selecting every nth individual will not produce a random sample if they are systematically arranged to begin with, such as alphabetically as in the telephone directory, but it is acceptable procedure if the order of appearance of the individuals is random to begin with. The method described in the library example would be equivalent to writing every person's name on a slip of paper, putting the papers into a container and mixing it, and then dumping them out and selecting every tenth slip. Such a procedure is random.

Suppose an experiment is performed using college students (very often the case) who were enrolled in the Introductory Psychology course (very often the case) and who volunteered to serve as subjects (also very often the case). Are college students a random sample of humanity? Are enrollees in Introductory Psychology a random sample of college students? Are volunteers a random sample of Introductory Psychology students? It is important to read the part of the research report that identifies the subjects of the experiment and the manner in which they were obtained. Research findings can only be generalized with confidence to populations from which the experimental subjects can be considered a representative sample. The tendency to extend results far beyond the range of the individuals on whom the data were gathered has been a weakness of behavioral science. Now, in fairness to experimenters, the practical limitations of time, money, and other experimenter resources often dictate that something less than pure random sampling will be used to select subjects. This does not mean that the research is useless; the key point after all is representativeness and not randomness for its own sake. It may be that volunteers from an Introductory Psychology course are eminently representative of humanity in certain respects. If, as it seems, we will have research based on non-random samples, then the interpretation of such findings must be reasonable and not overextended; furthermore, the independent confirmation of research results by other investigators is most important in behavioral science so that we can have confidence in the generality of findings.

6.2 Sampling Error and Sampling Distributions

We have said that even a randomly selected sample might not be a perfect representation of its population. We will now consider this matter further. Suppose there are 50 students in your statistics class and that we regard this group as a population. We are interested in the variable of height, and, with a population this small, it is feasible to determine parameter values. Let us say that we measured all 50 persons in the class and found the mean height to be 168 cm (66.14 in.). Now suppose we drew a random sample of 10 people from this population by selecting names from a hat, and calculated the mean height. Could we expect this sample mean to be exactly 168 cm? At first, it seems to be a reasonable expectation but, in reality, a sample mean almost always differs from its population mean by some amount. Why won't it be exactly the same? Well it could be, of course, but it is more likely to be in error by some amount, as the following discussion will try to illustrate.

There are 10,272,278,170 different samples of 10 that can be drawn from a population of 50. It is true that samples whose mean equals the population mean are more numerous than samples whose mean equals any other single value; nonetheless, samples whose mean equals the population mean are a small minority of the total possible samples. Thus the probability is greater that a sample mean will differ by some amount from the population mean than it is that the two will be equal. It is also true that large differences between the sample and population means are less probable than small differences. It could happen that, by chance, our random procedure selected the 10 tallest or 10 shortest people in the class; then the sample mean would differ considerably from the population mean. Such an outcome, although possible, is relatively unlikely, so we are left with a situation that the most probable occurrence is a sample mean that differs, but not extremely so, from the population mean.

The difference between a statistic derived from a sample and the corresponding population parameter is known as *sampling error*. Sampling error does not imply any sampling procedure fault or incorrect technique; it refers to the discrepancy between sample and population values. As we have said, even randomly chosen samples cannot be expected on every occasion to yield values that exactly match the population values. To the extent that there is a difference between sample and population values the sample may be said to be in error, and thus such differences are termed sampling error. We must expect some sampling error to occur every time we draw a sample from a

sampling error

population. The larger the size of the sample, the less sampling error there will tend to be; the limit of this tendency is reached when the sample size equals the population size, at which point there is no error.

Since we use samples to infer the characteristics of populations, it is crucial that our samples represent population characteristics faithfully. But having concluded that estimates of population parameters based even on random samples are likely to be in error by some amount, how can inferences be made with any accuracy or confidence? It begins to look as though science is impossible! Actually, we can cope with sampling error if we have a way of estimating its magnitude. If we can estimate the amount by which a given sample statistic is likely to differ from the unknown population parameter (estimate the amount of sampling error), then we can make accurate inferences concerning population parameters.

An aside: the final count is anticlimactic

On national election night the television news networks often assert the victory of one candidate over another on the basis of a few percent of the ballots counted. This must surely baffle many viewers (and, in others, arouse paranoid suspicions of manipulation by Eastern Syndicates). These predictions are made on the basis of samples. In every district, the voting result at a sample of the district's individual precincts is monitored and the pattern there observed is projected to the entire district. The accuracy of such projections clearly depends on the adequacy with which the sample of precincts represents the district, or in other words, on the amount of sampling error. Even with allowance for sampling error, such projections can be made on a surprisingly small proportion of the voting populace of the district. Other factors, such as past voting patterns and conditions affecting voter turnout, enter into these projections, but in essence this process mirrors science's inference of population characteristics from small samples.

If a sample were drawn from a population with unknown parameters, how could one estimate the amount of sampling error? A more accurate estimate of the value of the population parameter, and thus of the amount of sampling error, could be obtained by repeated sampling. Returning to our example of the population (class) of 50 students, let us assume that the parameter (mean height) is unknown. Suppose we drew a random sample of 10 students and found their mean height to be 165 cm. At that point, 165 cm is our best estimate of the unknown population mean height, but we cannot know whether it is actually that value or some other. If we drew a second sample of 10 (for these purposes we would sample with replacement, that is, the members of the first sample would be returned to the population prior to drawing the second), and found the mean height to be 170 cm, our best estimate of the population mean would now be $(165 + 170)/2 = 167.5$ cm. But there is no certainty that the parameter is that value, or even that it is between 165 cm and 170 cm. If we drew a third, fourth, and fifth sample of 10 and found the means to be 166 cm, 163 cm, and 178 cm respectively, our best estimate of the population mean would now be $(165 + 170 + 166 + 163 + 178)/5 = 168.4$ cm. Again, it must be pointed out that the true population mean is not necessarily 168.4 cm, and not necessarily between the highest and lowest sample values, but intuition suggests that our estimate of the unknown population mean will become steadily more accurate as the number of samples on which it is based increases. (A numerical illustration of this process appears later in this chapter but it will be helpful to first introduce some important concepts in connection with repeated sampling.)

Since every member of the population is equally likely to be included in a random sample, such samples have no systematic tendency to err in any direction. The sample mean is referred to as an *unbiased estimate* of its parameter because any given sample mean is as likely to be higher than as lower than the population mean; thus, a group of sample means will form a distribution that is symmetrically distributed about the population mean. As the number of samples drawn increases, the likelihood increases that the parameter (μ) value is approximated by the mean of the sample means. This is directly analogous to the statement that there is less error associated with larger samples; here we are saying that there is less error associated with larger numbers of samples.

unbiased estimate

We could repeat the process of drawing samples of size 10 from this population and calculating the mean of each sample until we had accumulated a great many numerical values, with each being the mean of a different sample. If we entered these numbers into a frequency distribution, it would be called a sampling distribution. More specifically, it would be called the sampling distribution of the mean because each term is the mean of an independent sample. The concept of a sampling distribution is fundamental and very important in statistics because virtually all statistical tests are conducted with reference to a sampling distribution.

A *sampling distribution* is the frequency distribution of the statistics derived from all possible samples of a given size.* Every term in a sampling distribution is a statistic, that is, every term is derived from an independent sample, and the sampling distribution consists of all possible values of the

sampling distribution

---

*The distribution formed by the statistics derived from all possible samples is often termed the theoretical sampling distribution. This is in contrast to an empirical sampling distribution, which is one that has actually been constructed by drawing repeated samples. Empirical sampling distributions may contain the same sample repeatedly, do not necessarily contain all the possible different samples, and may consist of any number of samples.

statistic in question. For example, there are 270,725 different samples of size 4 that can be drawn from a population of 52. If all were actually drawn, the sum calculated for each, and the sums entered into a frequency distribution, it would be the *sampling distribution of the sum*. There are 2,598,960 different samples of size 5 that can be drawn from a population of 52; if all were actually drawn, the mean calculated for each, and the means entered into a frequency distribution, it would be the *sampling distribution of the mean*.

The *expected value* of a statistic is the mean of its sampling distribution. The expected value of an unbiased statistic is equal to the parameter. Thinking back to our problem of the unknown mean height of the population of 50 students, if we drew all possible samples of size 10 and created the sampling distribution of the mean, then the mean of that sampling distribution, which we could term the mean of the means, would equal the population mean, that is, $\mu_{\bar{X}} = \mu$. Our intuitive impression that the estimate of the parameter becomes more accurate as more sample means are considered was appropriate because, when we reach the limit of this process in the sampling distribution, the mean of the means (expected value of the mean) equals the population mean.

Every statistic that can be obtained from a sample, such as the sum, mean, variance, etc., has a sampling distribution. We might say that the sampling distribution depicts the behavior of the statistic over repeated sampling. Now here is the critical part: any sample statistic we obtain can be viewed as a term in a hypothetical sampling distribution, and if we know the shape and certain parameters of that hypothetical sampling distribution, such as its expected value and variability, we can locate the position of our term in it, in other words, determine the amount of sampling error and its probability of occurrence. In essence, statistical tests are conducted by determining the probability of occurrence of an obtained statistic in its hypothetical sampling distribution.

In Chapter 4 we referred to the Central Limit Theorem as a way to understand why many natural events yield normal distributions. The Central Limit Theorem, which states that the sampling distribution of means of sufficiently large and equal-sized random samples is normal, applies directly to the present discussion. If one knows the mean and standard deviation of a normal distribution, the location and probability of occurrence of any particular score can be determined. With some qualifications concerning population shape and sample size (see *An aside on "sufficiently large"* in section 4.1), the Central Limit Theorem tells us that the sampling distribution of $\bar{X}$ is normal. We know and can readily demonstrate that the mean of the sampling distribution of $\bar{X}$ is μ. We will now consider the matter of variability.

If we calculate the standard deviation of a sampling distribution, it is called the *standard error*. A *standard error of the mean* is the standard deviation of the sampling distribution of the mean. If we think of the terms

The Expected Value of $\overline{X}$

Consider the following six numbers to be a population

2, 3, 5, 6, 8, 9

$\mu = 33/6 = 5.50$

For samples of size 2 there are $\binom{6}{2} = 15$ different samples that can be drawn from this population. The means of these 15 samples comprise the sampling distribution of the mean (when $n = 2$). These 15 samples and their means are shown next.

Sample #1: 2, 3: $\overline{X}_1 = 2.50$
Sample #2: 2, 5; $\overline{X}_2 = 3.50$
Sample #3: 2, 6; $\overline{X}_3 = 4.00$
Sample #4: 2, 8; $\overline{X}_4 = 5.00$
Sample #5: 2, 9; $\overline{X}_5 = 5.50$
Sample #6: 3, 5; $\overline{X}_6 = 4.00$
Sample #7: 3, 6; $\overline{X}_7 = 4.50$
Sample #8: 3, 8; $\overline{X}_8 = 5.50$
Sample #9: 3, 9; $\overline{X}_9 = 6.00$
Sample #10: 5, 6; $\overline{X}_{10} = 5.50$
Sample #11: 5, 8; $\overline{X}_{11} = 6.50$
Sample #12: 5, 9; $\overline{X}_{12} = 7.00$
Sample #13: 6, 8; $\overline{X}_{13} = 7.00$
Sample #14: 6, 9; $\overline{X}_{14} = 7.50$
Sample #15: 8, 9; $\overline{X}_{15} = 8.50$

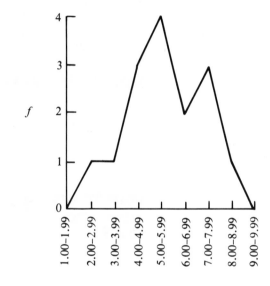

$\mu_{\overline{x}} = 82.50/15 = 5.50 = \mu$

This simple example merely serves to demonstrate that the expected value of $\overline{X}$ is μ. Note that, because the population is small and non-normal and the sample size is also very small, the sampling distribution of the mean is non-normal.

*standard error
of the mean*

comprising the sampling distribution as a population, then we would express the standard error of the mean as $\sigma_{\bar{X}}$. If a sampling distribution has a small standard error this indicates low variability; conversely, a large standard error indicates high variability. In a situation where sampling error is small (the sample values tend to differ by only small amounts from the parameter), the different samples will generate values that, taken as a group, show low variability; thus the sampling distribution will have a small standard error. When sampling error is large, the samples will produce more dissimilar values and such a sampling distribution will have a larger standard error. Thus the standard error, or variability over repeated sampling, gives us an indication of how much sampling error is associated with a given situation.

Calculating a standard error would be an impractical task if one had to actually generate the sampling distribution; fortunately, this is not necessary. When the population standard deviation is known, the standard error of the mean may be obtained by using the data obtained from a single sample.

$$\text{standard error of the mean} = \frac{\text{population standard deviation}}{\text{square root of sample size}}$$

$$\sigma_{\bar{X}} = \frac{\sigma}{\sqrt{n}}$$

If the population standard deviation is unknown, then an estimate of the standard error of the mean ($s_{\bar{X}}$) may be obtained by using the data from a single sample.

$$\text{estimated standard error of the mean} = \frac{\text{sample standard deviation}}{\text{square root of sample size}}$$

$$s_{\bar{X}} = \frac{s}{\sqrt{n}}$$

Suppose a sample of 10 students drawn from a population of 50 yielded the following height data (in cm)

$$n = 10$$
$$\bar{X} = 168$$
$$s = 7.30$$

The estimated standard error of the sampling distribution of the mean is

$$s_{\bar{X}} = \frac{7.30}{\sqrt{10}} = 2.31$$

As with any statistic, as sample size increases, the estimated standard error of the mean more and more approximates the true standard error of the mean, that is, $s_{\bar{X}}$ more and more approximates $\sigma_{\bar{X}}$.

Sample Size and Representativeness: A Further Illustration

Listed are the heights to the nearest inch as reported by 50 female students in my undergraduate classes. For our present purposes, these 50 individuals may be regarded as a population.

63	67	64	65	63
64	65	70	69	66
67	64	65	64	66
65	68	67	67	64
68	65	63	62	68
66	66	65	67	66
61	62	64	69	62
65	65	66	65	65
63	64	62	65	67
65	63	66	68	64

$\mu = 65.20$ $\sigma = 2.01$

The following five random samples of size five ($n = 5$) were drawn from this population.

#1:   69, 62, 65, 67, 63: $\overline{X} = 65.20$, $s = 2.86$, $s_{\overline{x}} = 1.22$

#2:   63, 68, 62, 64, 65: $\overline{X} = 64.40$, $s = 2.30$, $s_{\overline{x}} = 0.98$

#3:   67, 63, 64, 65, 65: $\overline{X} = 64.80$, $s = 1.48$, $s_{\overline{x}} = 0.63$

#4:   68, 68, 62, 67, 64: $\overline{X} = 65.80$, $s = 2.68$, $s_{\overline{x}} = 1.15$

#5:   65, 65, 67, 64, 64: $\overline{X} = 65.00$, $s = 1.22$, $s_{\overline{x}} = 0.52$

The following five random samples of size ten ($n = 10$) were also drawn from the population.

#6:   65, 64, 63, 69, 67, 65, 64, 67, 65, 65: $\overline{X} = 65.40$, $s = 1.78$, $s_{\overline{x}} = 0.56$

#7:   67, 65, 62, 64, 63, 65, 65, 67, 66, 69: $\overline{X} = 65.30$, $s = 2.06$, $s_{\overline{x}} = 0.65$

#8:   67, 62, 64, 62, 64, 65, 67, 64, 67, 65: $\overline{X} = 64.70$, $s = 1.89$, $s_{\overline{x}} = 0.60$

#9:   63, 65, 64, 66, 68, 66, 65, 68, 65, 62: $\overline{X} = 65.20$, $s = 1.93$, $s_{\overline{x}} = 0.61$

#10:   65, 65, 62, 70, 66, 66, 64, 64, 64, 63: $\overline{X} = 64.90$, $s = 2.18$, $s_{\overline{x}} = 0.69$

When the results from the larger samples are compared to those from the smaller samples, it is evident that larger samples produce means that are less variable, as is reflected by the smaller $s_{\overline{x}}$ terms. This indicates that there is less sampling error associated with the larger samples, which is to say that they tend to produce more accurate estimates of the parameter. This can be confirmed from the previous data by simply determining the mean of the sample means when $n = 10$ and when $n = 5$; it will be found that $\overline{X}_{\overline{x}}$ more accurately estimates μ when n is larger.

In our discussion of the normal distribution in Chapters 4 and 5 we saw that if we know the mean and standard deviation of a normally distributed population, we can locate any given term in that distribution and identify its probability of occurrence. In the case of the sample mean, we know that its sampling distribution is normal and we can estimate its standard error. The expected value of the sampling distribution of the mean is equal to the population mean, and although it is ordinarily unknown, we can make some statements about this parameter. This procedure is known as constructing confidence intervals for the population mean, and will be presented in Section 8.3.

Let us review the major points of this discussion. We began with the problem of wanting to estimate the magnitude of sampling error in order to make accurate estimates of population parameters. The amount of error associated with any statistic will be reflected in the nature of its sampling distribution, which we may say depicts the behavior of the statistic over repeated sampling. It is ordinarily impractical to actually produce the sampling distribution; fortunately, it is unnecessary to do so. If we know in advance that the sampling distribution is normal or fits any other theoretical function whose properties are familiar, and if we can from a single sample estimate the standard error of the statistic (its variability over repeated sampling), then we have the information needed to make statements concerning the population parameter.

Not all statistics have normal-shaped sampling distributions, but the concept of a sampling distribution is important because most statistical tests are performed in reference to theoretical sampling distributions such as the normal distribution, binomial distributions, and others that you will encounter as we go along. If you know the shape and certain parameters of its sampling distribution, you can determine the probability of occurrence of any statistic you have in hand. This is the basis for much statistical decision making, as you will see in later chapters. For now, remember that a sampling distribution is no great mystery but is merely the frequency distribution of statistics derived from all possible independent samples.

6.3 Degrees of Freedom

Since we have been discussing the general question of sampling and using sample data to infer population characteristics, this is an appropriate place to discuss the concept of degrees of freedom. Suppose you and a friend are watching a horse race, and your friend suggests that you each write down a prediction of the outcome, and that the person with the most accurate prediction wins a dollar from the other. Knowing that Shadowfax is favored, you write "Shadowfax wins." Your friend writes "Shadowfax wins, and, the others all finish second or worse." In fact this is exactly what happens; Shadowfax does win and the other horses all run second or worse. Your friend claims two correct predictions to your one, and gleefully departs with your dollar. Clearly, there is something amiss here! Your prediction was an independent event, but your friend's two predictions were not independent because the first one necessitated the second. Therefore these two statements are actually based on only one independently-made prediction that Shadowfax wins. Your friend's two predictions are in fact different ways of saying the same thing. This rather trivial example serves to point out that there is, or can be, a difference between the number of events and the number of independent events. We use the term *degrees of freedom* to refer to the number of independent events. We would say that both your prediction and your friend's predictions were based on one degree of freedom and, of course, the two of you demonstrated equal predictive skill because the estimate of predictive skill is based on one degree of freedom in each case.

degrees of freedom

Consider the following five numbers.

$$
\begin{array}{rl}
 & 9 \\
 & 13 \\
 & 4 \\
 & 11 \\
 & \underline{8} \\
\Sigma X = & 45 \\
n = & 5 \\
\overline{X} = & 9
\end{array}
$$

There is nothing remarkable about five numbers that have mean equal to 9; in fact, one could imagine many other combinations of five that met this requirement such as $7, 7, 20, 1, 10$, and $15, 3, 4, 31, -8$. If you should try to make up a combination of five numbers that have $\overline{X} = 9$ (or any other arbitrarily specified mean), you will find that in selecting the first four you are free to choose any value that comes to mind. Once four have been chosen, however, the fifth is determined by the overall requirement that $\overline{X} = 9$. We would say that the fifth number is not free to vary. If we specify that there are to be five numbers that must have mean equal to 9, then only four of those numbers are free to vary and we would say that there are four degrees of freedom associated with this situation. As stated earlier, degrees of freedom is simply the number of terms that are free to vary, or, the number of independent terms. The specification that $\overline{X} = 9$ costs, so to speak, one degree of freedom.

In general, n observations may be thought of as having $n - 1$ degrees of freedom. In previous discussions we have said that larger samples provide more accurate estimates of population parameters; a better way to express this is to say that there is less error associated with estimates based on larger numbers of degrees of freedom (larger numbers of independent observations).

The layman is often skeptical of scientists' readiness to make confident generalizations based on a small number of subjects. Our statistical procedures take account of number of degrees of freedom and provide us with quite reliable decisions. Even we, however, can be taken aback by experimenters who carry the inferential process to the limit, as in the case of an article entitled, "Reversal Learning by Horse and Raccoon," (Warren & Warren, 1962) in which the subjects were two horses and one raccoon!

In our discussion of variance in Section 3.10, we saw that the formulas differed for populations as compared to samples, that is, $\sigma^2 = \Sigma (X - \mu)^2/n$, and $s^2 = \Sigma (X - \overline{X})^2/n - 1$. If one has a purely descriptive purpose and is treating the data as a population, then variance is defined as the Sum of Squares (sum of squared deviations from the mean) divided by the number of observations. This is because μ is known and a population by definition consists of all the individuals of interest. However, if one regards the data in hand as a sample and uses it to estimate the population variance, then sample variance is defined as the Sum of Squares divided by the number of degrees of freedom. This is because μ is unknown and is estimated by $\overline{X}$. Estimating μ from $\overline{X}$ specifies its value for the purpose of determining the Sum of Squares; this specification (estimation) entails a cost of one degree of freedom (Howell, 1982). With n in the denominator there is a systematic tendency to underestimate the parameter; when the denominator is $n - 1$ the statistic is unbiased and has an expected value equal to the parameter, that is, the expected value of s^2 is σ^2.

6.4 Review Exercises

1. Define or describe the following terms.
    (a) random sample
    (b) stratified random sample
    (c) sampling error
    (d) unbiased estimate
    (e) sampling distribution
    (f) sampling distribution of the sum
    (g) sampling distribution of the mean
    (h) expected value
    (i) standard error
    (j) standard error of the mean
    (k) degrees of freedom

6.5 Concluding Remarks

Chapter 6 contains some of the most important conceptual material for an understanding of inferential statistical reasoning. Random sampling is fundamental to research because it provides us with an unbiased context, in the form of subject groups that are in general representative of their populations and not systematically different from each other, within which we can perform our experimental manipulations. Sampling error, which we must regard as ubiquitous, seems at first to defeat inferential science, but we saw that, if we can estimate and predict the magnitude of sampling error itself, then we are back in business. In fact we do just that by reference to hypothetical sampling distributions. Sampling distributions may be characterized as representing the behavior of the statistic over repeated sampling. I would say that the notion of sampling distributions is the single most important concept in statistics. Treating an obtained statistic as a term in a hypothetical sampling distribution enables estimation of its probability of occurrence, which is the pivot upon which scientific decisions turn. We have one major conceptual bridge to cross before we begin to actually perform inferential statistical tests; this concerns the meaning and evaluation of scientific hypotheses, to which we now turn in Chapter 7.

7 Hypothesis Testing

Chapter Preview

7.1 Some Research Terminology

Introduces the basic terminology of scientific research

Key Terms
- experiment
- independent variable
- dependent variable
- treatment type independent variable
- classification type independent variable
- experimental group
- control group
- confounding
- experimental research
- correlational research

7.2 Testing Hypotheses

Discusses and illustrates the rationale of scientific decision making

Key Terms
- hypothesis
- null hypothesis
- alternative hypothesis

7.3 Confidence, Type I and Type II Error, Power

Describes the limitations of scientific decisions and the ways they may be in error

Key Terms
- significance
- confidence level
- Type I Error
- alpha
- Type II Error
- beta
- power

7.4 Review Exercises

7.5 Concluding Remarks

7.1 Some Research Terminology

If one accepts the premise that a main function of statistics is decision making, then hypothesis testing is a central issue because statistical decisions are decisions about hypotheses. Our discussion of this subject will be easier if we can use concrete examples and, to that end, we must become acquainted with some of the basic terminology of research. The purpose of this section is to introduce that terminology.

We can define an *experiment* as any contrived circumstance in which data, or observations, are gathered. The purpose of experimentation in science is to observe events and learn something about them that was not previously known. The care and precision used to set up the conditions and record the data are vital to obtaining unambiguous results. A thorough discussion of research procedure is outside the scope of this book, but let us appreciate the fact that good research is no accident.

experiment

We have used the word variable to refer to the event of interest; we must now distinguish between independent variables and dependent variables. The *independent variable* is the thing that the experimenter manipulates. The independent variable can be the conditions or circumstances under which the data are gathered or merely the different types of individuals from which data are obtained. The *dependent variable* is the thing that the experimenter measures. The dependent variable is the behavior or event that is actually observed, measured, and recorded. In an experiment designed to test whether alcohol ingestion has any effect on motor coordination, the independent variable is the amount of alcohol ingested, and the dependent variable is some measure of motor coordination, such as the ability to stack small blocks. In an experiment designed to test whether men and women differ in pain tolerance, the independent variable is gender and the dependent variable is some measure of pain tolerance. (Note: Both independent and dependent variables require operational definitions so it is clear exactly what was manipulated and measured. For example, "amount of alcohol ingested" might be defined operationally as the consumption of 50 ml as compared to 0 ml of 100-proof grain alcohol, and "pain tolerance" might be defined operationally as the number of minutes a person can stand a specified painful stimulus, such as immersion of a hand in ice-cold water. The reader may wish to review the discussion of operational definitions in Section 2.3.)

independent variable

dependent variable

In some experiments the independent variable is a treatment type, which means that it is literally some kind of treatment or procedure that can be applied to any randomly selected subject. Amount of alcohol ingestion is an example of a *treatment type independent variable,* as are such things as methods of instruction, type of reward, and ambient noise level. In other cases, the independent variable is a classification type, which means that the different groups of subjects that serve in the experiment were selected by

treatment type independent variable

classification type
independent variable

virtue of belonging to different classes or subsets of the population. Gender is an example of a *classification type independent variable,* as is religous affiliation, nationality, and hair color. An experimenter can be said to manipulate a classification type independent variable only in the sense that he or she deliberately selects subjects of the different types for comparison.

experimental group
control group

A relatively simple experiment uses two groups of subjects. If the independent variable is a treatment type, then the two subject groups are commonly called the *experimental group* and the *control group*. The members of the experimental group are exposed to the independent variable condition and the members of the control group are not; thus, the control group represents a basis for comparison of the effect, if any, of the independent variable on the dependent variable measure. The control group and experimental group subjects must be treated identically in every respect other than exposure to the independent variable in order for the outcome of the experiment to be unambiguous. If the independent variable is a classification type, the groups are not ordinarily referred to as the control and experimental groups (they may be called Group A and Group B), but it is equally vital that they be treated identically. In essence, the independent variable is the only thing that can be allowed to vary between the two groups. If this is not accomplished and the subjects in the two groups differ in some systematic way, in addition to the independent variable difference, or if there is some systematic difference in the conditions under which the experimental and control data are gathered, the

confounding

experiment is termed confounded. *Confounding* means that some other factor in addition to the independent variable has systematically varied between the experimental and control conditions. This co-varying factor, which might be a subject, procedural, or environmental variable, is said to have confounded the independent variable. When this has happened, the experiment is uninterpretable because one cannot know whether any observed effect is attributable to the independent variable or to the confounding variable. Suppose an experiment was conducted to test the effect of alcohol ingestion on motor coordination so that members of the experimental group consumed some alcohol while control group subjects did not; suppose also that the experimental group consisted of men and the control group of women. Obviously, gender has confounded the independent variable and any results obtained cannot be attributed to alcohol ingestion because they might actually be a function of gender. This example is blatant, but confounding by procedural or environmental factors can be far more subtle. The procedures for isolating the independent variable as the only varying factor are generally grouped under the heading of experimental control procedures. A discussion of these matters is beyond the scope of this presentation and the reader is referred to a text in research design such as D'Amato (1970) and Meyers & Grossen (1978).

The distinction between treatment and classification type independent variables is important for the interpretation that can be given to the experiment's outcome. If the independent variable is a treatment type and complete control (equality) has been achieved over all extraneous variables, meaning that only the independent variable has been allowed to vary between the experimental and control groups, then the independent variable may be said to have caused the difference in the groups' dependent variable scores. For example, given the degree of control just specified, one could conclude that alcohol ingestion affected motor coordination. By using the word "affect" the researcher implies that the independent variable was a causative factor in determining the dependent variable scores but that other unknown factors may also have been operating. Research that uses treatment type independent variables is known generally as *experimental research* and is the only type of research by which science can establish a causal connection between an independent variable and a dependent variable.

experimental research

A distinguishing feature of experimental research is that when the experiment begins, the experimental group and the control group are undifferentiated in any way except that they have been given different names. In other words, the experimental and control groups may each be regarded as an independent random sample from the population. In the previous chapter we discussed random selection of samples as the basis for estimating population characteristics. If an experiment were to be conducted using an experimental group and a control group of ten individuals each, the experimenter would not actually draw two random samples of ten; rather, he or she would draw a random sample of twenty and then randomly assign individuals to the experimental and control groups. This random assignment of individuals to the various treatment conditions is functionally equivalent to having randomly sampled the groups separately and is the essential basis upon which the comparison of the effects of the different treatments rests. Random selection of subjects is crucial to inferring population characteristics from sample data: random assignment of subjects to the experiment's treatment groups is crucial to correct interpretation of independent variable effects.

If the independent variable is a classification type such as males compared to females, or smokers compared to nonsmokers, one can establish that the independent variable is related to the dependent variable, meaning that the different subject types yielded differing dependent variable scores, but it cannot be known whether this relationship is causal. For example, men might differ from women in an infinite number of ways in addition to being of different genders, and any one of these other differences could be the real causal basis for an observed difference in pain tolerance. Thus gender can be said to be related to pain tolerance (the two genders differ in pain tolerance) but the reason for the difference between the genders cannot be attributed to the gender difference itself and, in fact, remains unknown. Does cigarette smoking cause lung cancer in humans? It may, but for obvious ethical reasons this independent variable cannot be manipulated as a treatment; its causal connection to respiratory system disease cannot be established by comparing smokers with nonsmokers. (Note: This is not an endorsement of smoking. The relation between smoking and various unpleasant diseases is well established and could well be causal, it is just that relationship per se does not establish causality.) Research that uses classification type independent variables is *correlational research* known generally as *correlational research*.

In essence, experimental research is an active manipulation of some treatment followed by a measure of its effect on some dependent variable. Correlational research is fundamentally a measurement of two variables (a classification type independent variable is really a nominal measure of subject type) for the purpose of seeing whether differences in one are accompanied by differences in the other. When we have discussed hypothesis testing and move on to specific analysis procedures we shall be careful in our phrasing of hypotheses and interpretations to reflect the nature of the independent variable. There are many classification type independent variables whose relation to behavior might be of interest; furthermore, ethical considerations prohibit the performance of many treatment type independent variable experiments on human subjects. Since much of the evidence is necessarily indirect, knowledge in human behavioral science accumulates slowly; it is difficult to confirm or refute theories, and certainty of understanding of fundamental laws is rare. This is not reason for despair but rather a challenge to researchers' ingenuity in collecting and interpreting data. Advances in statistical technology over the past decades have had a powerful impact on our ability to interpret and gain information from our research efforts.

7.2 Testing Hypotheses

An hypothesis is defined as a supposition; it is a statement about an event that is unproven but assumed to be true for purposes of argument. Inferential statistical procedures are tests of hypotheses. Experimenters begin with an hypothesis and then try to construct an experiment that will provide a clear test and allow a decision to be made whether to reject or retain the hypothesis.

hypothesis
null hypothesis
alternative hypothesis

In science an *hypothesis* is a statement about one or more population parameters. We must differentiate between a *null hypothesis* and its logical opposite, which is generally termed the *alternative hypothesis*. A null hypothesis specifies the value of some population parameter(s); the alternative hypothesis states the parameter value(s) to be something other than that specified by the null hypothesis. The distinction between the null hypothesis and alternative hypothesis is not trivial. The null hypothesis specifies a parameter value and leads to a specific quantitative prediction that can be compared to the quantitative result of the experiment; thus, the null hypothesis is directly testable. In contrast, the alternative hypothesis does not generate a specific quantitative prediction and therefore cannot be evaluated relative to the quantitative outcome of the experiment; the alternative hypothesis is not directly testable. Thus, all statistical tests are tests of a null hypothesis and the decision made in every case is whether to reject or retain the null hypothesis. Let us examine this process by means of a few examples.

Suppose the population of North American men has a mean height of 175 cm and a standard deviation of 6.50 cm ($\mu = 175$ and $\sigma = 6.50$), and that a sample of 64 policemen has a mean height of 180 cm ($\overline{X} = 180$). We want to decide whether policemen differ in height from men in general, that is, from the population mean. The 64 policemen actually measured are not the issue. What we want to know is whether the population of policemen differs in height from the population of men in general, in other words, is $\mu_{policemen}$ the same as or different from $\mu_{men\ in\ general}$? The null hypothesis in this case is that $\mu_{policemen} = \mu_{men\ in\ general}$, or, that $\mu_{policemen} = 175$ cm. The alternative hypothesis is that $\mu_{policemen} \neq \mu_{men\ in\ general}$, or, $\mu_{policemen} \neq 175$ cm. You can see that the null hypothesis leads to a specific quantitative expectation, namely that policemen have a mean height of 175 cm, whereas the alternative hypothesis does not produce any specific quantitative expectation about the mean height of policemen. We have obtained a sample of policemen and found their mean height to be 180 cm. This is a value we can compare with that predicted from the null hypothesis. Based on this comparison, we can make a decision to reject or retain the null hypothesis. However, the alternative hypothesis does not lead to a specific prediction of the mean height of policemen and so we have nothing to compare to our sample mean. Thus we say that the null hypothesis is directly testable while the alternative hypothesis is not.

If the null hypothesis is true and if there is no sampling error, we would expect a random sample from the population of policemen to have a mean height of 175 cm. We cannot make a decision about the null hypothesis merely because our sample of policemen has a mean height other than 175 cm because we do not know how much sampling error is associated with this sample and consequently we do not know the value of $\mu_{policemen}$. We proceed by assuming the null hypothesis to be true and determining the probability that sampling error alone would produce a sample of 64 policemen with a mean height of 180 cm. If this probability is below some specified value, we conclude that sampling error is too unlikely to be responsible for the discrepancy between the observed mean and that predicted by the null hypothesis. Our decision is then to reject the null hypothesis and retain the alternative hypothesis. The exact procedure for this type of problem is presented in Section 8.5.

Suppose we drew two random samples from a population and set up an experiment to test whether or not amount of alcohol ingestion affects motor coordination. Assuming a suitable operational definition for both the independent variable of amount of alcohol ingestion and the dependent variable of motor coordination, we would end up with two sets of dependent variable scores, those of the experimental group (that ingested alcohol and that we can label X_E), and those of the control group (that did not ingest alcohol and that we can label X_C). In general, with a treatment type independent variable, the null hypothesis may be stated in the form that the independent variable does not affect the dependent variable. The null hypothesis in this experiment is that amount of alcohol ingestion does not affect motor coordination. Let us consider this statement more closely. The control group is presumed to be a random sample from the natural untreated population and therefore $\overline{X}_C$ is an estimate of μ_C. The experimental group is presumed to be a random sample from the hypothetical population of treated individuals. In other words, $\overline{X}_E$ is an estimate of μ_E where μ_E is the mean score obtained when every member of the population is given the alcohol ingestion treatment and measured on the motor coordination dependent variable. The null hypothesis is that $\mu_E = \mu_C$; this is equivalent to saying that the independent variable, or amount of alcohol ingestion, did not affect the dependent variable, motor coordination.

When the null hypothesis is true, and when there is no sampling error, we expect that $\overline{X}_E = \overline{X}_C$, and consequently that $\overline{X}_E - \overline{X}_C = 0$. However, in any particular case this will usually not happen because, owing to sampling error, $\overline{X}_C$ is unlikely to exactly equal μ_C; $\overline{X}_E$ is unlikely to exactly equal μ_E; and ordinarily $\overline{X}_E \neq \overline{X}_C$ and $\overline{X}_E - \overline{X}_C \neq 0$. In deciding whether or not amount of alcohol ingestion affects motor coordination we assume the null hypothesis to be true and determine the probability that the observed difference between the experimental and control groups' means ($\overline{X}_E - \overline{X}_C$) would happen as a function of sampling error. The null hypothesis views the two sets of scores as though they were independent random samples from the same population; thus, we determine the probability that two samples drawn from the same population will show a difference in means equal to our observed difference between $\overline{X}_E$ and $\overline{X}_C$. If this probability is below some criterion value, we reject the null hypothesis and retain the alternative hypothesis that the amount of alcohol ingestion does affect motor coordination. The actual statistical procedure that would be used in this case is presented in Section 8.7.

An aside: idealized research

Throughout this discussion of hypothesis testing I take the position that differences in dependent variable scores between two subject groups can only be a function of the independent variable or sampling error (the less than perfect representation of populations by samples). Of course, variation among the individual subjects is ubiquitous (Section 3.10) and produces variability in the raw data within each group. There is another class of factors, namely procedural and situational variables, which, if not adequately controlled, could confound the independent variable. This discussion assumes perfect experimental control over such extraneous situational variables.

Suppose we obtained a random sample of men and a random sample of women and tested each person for pain tolerance, thereby generating a set of scores for the men (X_m) and a set for the women (X_w). In general terms, with a classification type independent variable, the null hypothesis may be stated in the form that the independent variable is not related to the dependent variable. The null hypothesis in this case is that gender is not related to pain tolerance, meaning that men do not differ from women in pain tolerance. Once again, you must realize that the null hypothesis is that the population of men does not differ from the population of women in pain tolerance, that is, $\mu_m = \mu_w$.

When the null hypothesis is true and there is no sampling error, we expect that $\overline{X}_m = \mu_m$, $\overline{X}_w = \mu_w$, and therefore that $\overline{X}_m = \overline{X}_w$ and $\overline{X}_m - \overline{X}_w = 0$. The null hypothesis views the men and the women as independent random samples from the same population. Again, we come to a decision by assuming the null hypothesis to be true and determining the probability that the obtained difference between the mens' and womens' mean scores ($\overline{X}_m - \overline{X}_w$) would happen as a function of sampling error. If this probability is small we say that sampling error is too unlikely to be responsible, and our decision would then be to reject the null hypothesis and retain the alternative hypothesis that gender is related to pain tolerance.

Characterizing the alternative hypothesis as a statement of effect or relationship and the null hypothesis as a statement of no effect or no relationship will suit our purposes in this book. Strictly speaking however, the null hypothesis is not necessarily the absence of relationship between the independent and dependent variables, but rather the form of relationship that should be assumed to exist until empirical evidence dictates otherwise. In science this means that one assumes the simplest state of affairs until empirical evidence requires the adoption of a more complex interpretation; of course, the assumption of no relationship is the simplest position of all. But as knowledge in a given area accumulates, then basic assumptions concerning interrelationships between events may also change, and with them the specifics of a null hypothesis (Guttman, 1977).

An aside on the meaning of "null hypothesis"

Let us summarize the basic process of hypothesis testing. If proper experimental control has been exercised in the research, then the outcome can only be a function of the independent variable or sampling error; that is, the null hypothesis is either false or it is true. The null hypothesis is directly testable because when it is assumed to be true we have a specific quantitative expectation concerning the experimental results. The probability that the result is a function of sampling error represents the degree of certainty we can have that the null hypothesis is true. If the difference between the observed outcome and what was predicted by the null hypothesis is found to have a probability of occurrence as a result of sampling error that is below some criterion value, then it is concluded that sampling error was not responsible; the null hypothesis is then rejected and the alternative hypothesis is retained.

Now here is a subtle and important point. A decision to reject the null hypothesis is a decision to retain the alternative hypothesis; however, retention of the null hypothesis is not based on rejection of the alternative hypothesis. Retaining the null hypothesis is not per se evidence that the alternative hypothesis is false but rather is merely a statement that there was insufficient evidence to reject the null hypothesis. Consider the null hypothesis, "alcohol ingestion does not affect motor coordination." We might perform an experiment in which experimental group members consumed some amount of alcohol while control group members did not, and all were measured on some motor coordination dependent variable task. If the alcohol ingestion group's mean score was radically different from the control group's mean score, we would have evidence to reject the null hypothesis and retain the alternative. However, if there were no substantial difference between the two groups' mean scores, would this be evidence that the null hypothesis is true? No, it would just mean that the effect, if any, of alcohol ingestion on motor coordination was not demonstrated in this particular experiment. With a different amount of alcohol, or a different dependent variable task, the outcome may have been quite different.

7.3 Confidence, Type I and Type II Error, Power

significance

When experiments are described in the research literature or at a scientific convention, the authors often say the results were significant. As a statistical term, *significant* does not mean important, remarkable, or even noteworthy; it means reliable. A result is called significant if it has been shown that chance, in the form of sampling error, is unlikely to have produced the outcome. When a result is statistically significant it means only that it had a low probability of happening by chance. If the experiment were to be repeated, the probability is high that the same decision would be made; this is what we mean by reliability. It would be more appropriate to call such results statistically reliable rather than statistically significant, but the latter term is entrenched in scientific vocabulary, to the confusion of students and laymen.

Statistical tests are often referred to as significance tests. A significance test cannot tell us for certain whether or not sampling error produced the result in question; that is something we can never ultimately know. Such tests can only tell us the probability that sampling error was responsible. In practice, we test the null hypothesis by reference to an arbitrary probability criterion known as a *confidence level*. In behavioral science the most commonly used confidence levels are 0.05 and 0.01. When we say that a given result is significant at 0.05 confidence level, this means that we have rejected the null hypothesis because we have shown that there is a 0.05 or less probability that we would obtain this particular result purely as a function of sampling error. In other words, if the null hypothesis were true, the probability that sampling error alone would produce the observed result is 0.05 or less. All decisions in science are made in this probabilistic manner.

confidence level

The experimenter chooses the confidence level, or probability, at which he or she will reject the null hypothesis arbitrarily and in advance of collecting the data. If the experimenter chooses a confidence level of 0.20, then the null hypothesis will be rejected if the probability that sampling error alone would produce the observed outcome is as high as 0.20; if the experimenter chooses 0.001 as a confidence level, then the probability that sampling error alone would produce the observed outcome must be 0.001 or less to reject the null hypothesis. Clearly, the decision to reject the null hypothesis is one in which we have different degrees of confidence in these two cases. It is never sufficient to say that a result was significant; one must include the confidence level associated with that decision.

If one hears the claim that patients experienced "significantly" more pain relief with Brand A than Brand B, what does this mean? Two groups could be tested, one with A and the other with B, and the result could be significant at 0.50 level. This means that the probability was one-half that sampling error was responsible for the difference in pain relief! Obviously, you should never accept an assertion of "significance" without knowing the confidence level attached to that decision.

An aside on "significant"

In life there may be a few certainties such as the inevitability of death and taxes, but in science we cannot make decisions with absolute certainty. We can never completely eliminate the possibility that the null hypothesis is true; that is, we can never be completely certain that sampling error is not responsible. This means that any decision we make can be either correct or incorrect. If we reject the null hypothesis at 0.05 confidence level, we have a 0.05 probability of being in error because, by definition, there is a 0.05 probability that sampling error alone could produce such a result when the null hypothesis is true. Rejecting the null hypothesis when it is in reality true is called a *Type I Error*, and consists of concluding that the independent variable affected or was related to the dependent variable, when in reality there was no influence or

Type I Error

alpha

relationship. The probability of making a Type I Error is equal to the confidence level of the significance test and is symbolized by α, Greek letter *alpha* [p(Type I Error) $= \alpha$].

Tests of significance consist essentially of comparing an obtained value to its expected value when the null hypothesis is assumed to be true. If the difference between the obtained and expected values is small and likely to occur as a function of sampling error, then the null hypothesis is retained. But there is no way to know that the difference was not a function of the independent variable; just because it was small does not mean that sampling error was necessarily responsible. Thus, a decision to retain the null hypothesis can also be in error. Retaining the null hypothesis when it is in reality false is called

Type II Error

a *Type II Error,* and consists of concluding that the independent variable did not affect or was not related to the dependent variable, when in fact there was some influence or relationship. The probability of making a Type II Error is

beta

symbolized by β, Greek letter *beta* [p(Type II Error) $= \beta$]. The value of β is determined by α, sample size, and the true expected value of the statistic being tested.

The following chart shows the four possible decision outcomes, correct and erroneous, of any significance test.

		Experimenter's decision	
		Retain null hypothesis	Reject null hypothesis
Reality	Null hypothesis true	correct $p = 1 - \alpha$	Type I Error $p = \alpha$
	Null hypothesis false	Type II Error $p = \beta$	correct $p = 1 - \beta$

Other things being equal, as the probability of a Type I error is reduced, the probability of a Type II error is increased; thus, the selection of the confidence level for a test of significance is a compromise in trying to avoid both types of error. In general, science views a Type I error as more to be avoided than a Type II error. One rationale for this is that the publication of a false independent/dependent variable relationship may stimulate additional research that will turn out to be wasted effort. On the other hand, Bakan (1966) suggests that Type I errors are more serious for just the opposite reason, namely that a "significant" result tends to be accepted as genuine and has the effect of stopping investigation; thus Type I errors tend not to be uncovered. Failure to detect an effect that is real, a Type II error, may be considered less serious because there is sufficient redundancy in science that, if the phenomenon is genuine, some other experimenter will discover it. The choice of a confidence level for the significance test may also reflect other considerations. If one were testing a new medicine, how certain should one be of its effectiveness before recommending its use? If one were dealing with a life-threatening ailment, then it could be argued that any reasonable evidence of effectiveness must be taken seriously, so that a 0.20 confidence level might be acceptable. If one were testing this new medicine for possible harmful side effects, then one might well demand a 0.001 confidence level that no harmful side effects exist before declaring it safe for use. Suppose that one were testing a new medicine against an existing treatment. If the new medicine were judged more effective, then as a consequence, future patients could be denied the existing treatment in preference for the new medicine. One would want to be quite confident that the new medicine was indeed more effective. Obviously, a certain amount of judgment must come into play in such situations.

The *power* of a statistical test is the probability that the null hypothesis will be rejected when it is in reality false. A test's power is its ability to discriminate independent variable effects from sampling error. Power is defined as $1 - \beta$, or $1 - p(\text{Type II error})$. An exact determination of the power of a particular test depends on knowing α, sample size, and the true expected value of the statistic being tested. Sample size and α are no problem, of course, as these are set by the experimenter. The third variable is the expected mean of the statistic being tested; a clearer way to put this is that one must specify the population mean score of the dependent variable measure assuming the alternative hypothesis to be true. In other words, one must specify the magnitude of the effect the independent variable has on the dependent variable measure relative to control scores. This can be a rather difficult thing to do in advance. A technique used in this connection is to specify a range of hypothetical expected values (a range of independent variable effect magnitudes) and determine the test's power at all values in this range. Such calculations would indicate what sample size is necessary to achieve a good degree of power given a particular α, and might be used as partial basis for selecting α itself. When an experiment has been performed and the data analyzed, the power associated with the analysis may be estimated using the experimental condition mean score as an estimate of the population mean. Various ways have been suggested to then derive an index of the size of the independent variable effect that is free, or independent, of the original measurement units. Given such an index, power may be read from specially prepared tables for any specific α and sample size. Other things being equal, power increases as α increases (goes from 0.01 to 0.05), and, other things being equal, power increases as sample size increases. We have seen that power is difficult to determine in advance and so experimenters have tended to approach power through their setting of α and sample size. Since the convention concerning α has grown into regarding 0.05 as a maximum, experimenters

power

have tended to increase power by selecting the largest sample size that is practical under the circumstances. However, this is not always appropriate. The power of a test is a greater concern when the independent variable effect is small or expected to be small and consequently difficult to discriminate from sampling error. It is under such conditions that using larger samples would be most beneficial. More thorough discussions of power and its calculation in specific instances may be found in Hays (1973), Glass & Stanley (1970), and Cohen (1977).

The rejection of the null hypothesis is not an assertion that the alternative hypothesis is true; it is merely a statement that sampling error had a low probability of producing the observed result under the specific set of conditions manipulated in that experiment. This last qualification is extremely important to keep in mind. One cannot be absolutely certain of variable relationships, even in the context in which they were manipulated and measured, and correspondingly less so in other contexts. Similarly, the retention of a null hypothesis is in no way proof that the independent variable and dependent variable are unrelated; it means only that the relationship, if any, was not demonstrated under the conditions of this particular experiment. Our convictions regarding variable relationships or the lack of them are built up slowly and depend on many replications and demonstrations of consistent findings. Recognizing that there is no ultimate proof in science, we nonetheless accept certain givens as a basis for dealing with the world and for further scientific inquiry, but such "facts" represent the accumulation of many independent confirmations.

An aside: Type I Error?

Most veterans of Introductory Psychology will have heard of the planaria research performed by James V. McConnell and his colleagues (see McConnell, 1977). In one of the more celebrated experiments, planaria were conditioned in a maze task and then chopped up to be eaten by naive planaria who subsequently required fewer trials to learn the task; they appeared to have ingested some knowledge! Follow up experiments appeared to identify RNA as the knowledge-carrying substance. This research has always been somewhat controversial and I will not comment on that aspect; however, one of the more charming offshoots deserves mention. Some experimenters conditioned rats on a task and then injected RNA from their brains into naive rats who then required fewer trials to learn the task. [The staggering implications of this finding no doubt occasioned some anxiety among university professors!] Attempts to confirm this finding ended mostly in failure amid controversy over procedural matters and debates on the plausibility that injected RNA could affect the host rats' nervous systems in this fashion, whether it carried any "knowledge" or not. I have often wondered whether this controversy was started by a Type I Error.

7.4 Review Exercises

1. Define or describe the following terms.

 (a) experiment
 (b) independent variable
 (c) dependent variable
 (d) treatment type independent variable
 (e) classification type independent variable
 (f) experimental group
 (g) control group
 (h) confounding
 (i) experimental research
 (j) correlational research
 (k) hypothesis
 (l) null hypothesis
 (m) alternative hypothesis
 (n) significance
 (o) confidence level
 (p) Type I Error
 (q) alpha
 (r) Type II Error
 (s) beta
 (t) power

7.5 Concluding Remarks

These remarks will serve to conclude the introductory material in this text. Hypothesis testing was the last remaining conceptual building block and now we can proceed to the statistical tests themselves. The first seven chapters comprise the fundamental essentials for understanding virtually any descriptive or inferential statistical procedure; the remainder of this book consists of a selection of statistical procedures appropriate to an introductory course. While you will certainly encounter new terminology and concepts, the basis for your understanding of the operation of these procedures is already in place. In a sense then, this is a point of departure into what I hope will be a fascinating experience of coping with particular experimental design and interpretation situations. A word of caution: don't fall into the easy habit of computing solutions and doing homework exercises mechanically. Think about what you are doing. My best suggestion is to really imagine yourself as the experimenter, the person who has worked to collect the data and wants to know what it means. If you view the problem from the inside, so to speak, it will have more life, more satisfaction when completed, and leave you with a more lasting grasp of the processes involved. Even statistics can be fun, if you let it, and the fun is about to begin!

Part III

Decisions About Differences

8 Significance Tests Using the *t* Distributions

Chapter Preview

8.1 Introduction

Imagine that you are a nurse at a blood donors' clinic and that one day the whole University of Warsaw basketball team comes in to donate blood. As a matter of routine, you measure and record each donor's pulse (heart rate) and, when the team has gone, you look over their heart rate scores and find that the mean ($\overline{X}$) was 65 beats per minute. We have learned over the years that the mean heart rate for people in general (μ) is 72 beats per minute. The question is: Does the mean heart rate of these basketball players differ significantly from the general population mean? If this were found to be the case, and if this team could be viewed as a random sample of basketball players in general, then these data would indicate that the heart rate of basketball players differs from that of the general population.

The cranial capacity of modern humans (homo sapiens) has a mean (μ) of 1350 cubic centimeters (cm^3). An archaeologist makes a spectacular discovery of nine ancient fossil skeletons and is able to determine that their mean cranial capacity ($\overline{X}$) is 1100 cm^3. The question that immediately arises is whether the cranial capacity of these nine fossils differs significantly from that of contemporary humans because if this were true, it would suggest that they represent a different species.

Suppose someone discovered a manuscript of a play whose author is unknown but believed by some experts to be Shakespeare. One way to help settle the debate would be to make a comparison of the new manuscript with known works of Shakespeare. The new manuscript could be divided into passages (a passage could be defined as a 200-word segment), and then a random sample of passages could be drawn. Similarly, passages could be randomly sampled from known works of Shakespeare. Some dependent variable measure could then be taken on all passages; for example, the number of interrogative pronouns might be counted. If analysis showed that there was a significant difference in the occurrence of interrogative pronouns in the new manuscript as compared to known works of Shakespeare, this evidence would imply different authorship and support the view that the new manuscript was not written by Shakespeare.

On a given Wednesday a group of merchants counted the number of individuals that entered their stores. The following week, the Tuesday evening newspaper carried a full-page advertisement of sales and bargains at these stores and the next day each merchant again counted the number of persons who entered his or her store. If there were no significant difference between the number of customers after the advertisement, as compared to before the advertisement, it would indicate that this form of advertising was not effective.

The hypothetical situations just described have one thing in common: they all involve the determination of whether there is a significant difference between two groups or sets of data. In the cases of the basketball players and the fossils, we sought to know whether a sample mean differed from a known population mean. In the case of the manuscript, we wished to know whether two samples of writing differed from each other. Finally, in the case of the merchants, we sought to determine whether preadvertisement sales differed from postadvertisement sales. The techniques presented in this chapter are used to decide whether a significant difference exists between two sets of scores; this is one of the most frequently made decisions in behavioral science. We shall begin by discussing a family of theoretical sampling distributions that serve as the reference distributions for such decisions.

8.2 The *t* Statistic and *t* Distributions

The *t* statistic is derived in a manner analogous to a *z*-score. You will recall that a *z*-score is defined as $z = (X - \mu)/\sigma$ and that *z*-scores always have mean equal to zero ($\mu_z = 0.00$) and standard deviation equal to one ($\sigma_z = 1.00$). If many samples were drawn from a population and the mean ($\overline{X}$) of each calculated, the $\overline{X}$ terms could be converted into *z*-scores ($z_{\overline{X}}$) by subtracting the population mean (μ) and dividing by the standard error of the mean ($\sigma_{\overline{X}}$). Thus

$$z_{\overline{X}} = \frac{\overline{X} - \mu}{\sigma_{\overline{X}}}$$

A $z_{\overline{X}}$ score is a ratio in which the numerator is a random variable, because the size of $\overline{X}$ varies randomly from sample to sample, and the denominator is a constant. The Central Limit Theorem tells us that the sampling distribution of $\overline{X}$ is normal; thus the sampling distribution of $z_{\overline{X}}$ will also be normal and will have mean equal to zero ($\mu_{z_{\overline{X}}} = 0$) and standard deviation equal to one ($\sigma_{z_{\overline{X}}} = 1.00$).

t statistic

Suppose we drew many samples and obtained the $\overline{X}$ terms, but the population variance (σ) was unknown. We could not derive $z_{\overline{X}}$, but if we use $s_{\overline{X}}$ as an estimate of $\sigma_{\overline{X}}$, we obtain a value known as a t *statistic*. Thus

$$t = \frac{\overline{X} - \mu}{s_{\overline{X}}}$$

A *t* statistic is a ratio in which the numerator is a random variable (as in $z_{\overline{X}}$), and the denominator is also a random variable because $s_{\overline{X}}$ is derived from s ($s_{\overline{X}} = s/\sqrt{n}$), which varies randomly from sample to sample.

t distribution

The t *distributions* are a family of theoretical distributions depicting the sampling distribution of the *t* statistic. The *t* distributions are the appropriate theoretical reference when the population variance is unknown; since this is ordinarily the case, these distributions are important tools in inferential science. There is a different *t* distribution for each different number of degrees of freedom (*df*), that is, for each different sample size. All *t* distributions are symmetrical and unimodal; as *df* increases, they more and more approximate the normal curve so that the *t* distribution at $df = \infty$ is identical to the normal distribution. As *df* decreases, relatively more of the area under the curve occurs toward the tails of the distribution, as is shown in Figure 8.2–1. The *t* distributions are different for different sample sizes, and progressively depart from the normal distribution as sample size (*df*) decreases because there is progressively more error associated with $s_{\overline{X}}$ as an estimate of $\sigma_{\overline{X}}$ as *df* decreases.

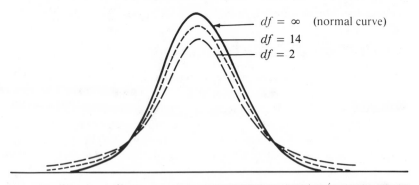

Figure 8.2–1 The *t* distributions for *df* = 2, *df* = 14, and *df* = ∞ (normal curve)

A simple demonstration of the effect of estimating as compared to knowing σ can be obtained by using an ordinary deck of playing cards with the
jacks, queens, and kings being given the numerical values of 11, 12, and 13
respectively. Suppose samples of size three ($n = 3$) were drawn from this
population. It can be readily determined that $\mu = 7$, $\sigma = 3.74$, and
$\sigma_{\bar{X}} = 3.74/\sqrt{3} = 2.16$; of course, $\bar{X}$ and $s_{\bar{X}}$ can be calculated for each sample. The following data were obtained from ten such samples.

$$\mu = 7.00; \qquad \sigma = 3.74; \qquad \sigma_{\bar{X}} = 2.16; \qquad s_{\bar{X}} = s/\sqrt{n}$$

Sample			$\bar{X}$	s	$t = (\bar{X} - \mu)/s_{\bar{X}}$	$z_{\bar{X}} = (\bar{X} - \mu)/\sigma_{\bar{X}}$
4,	9,	7	6.67	2.51	−0.23	−0.15
11,	4,	10	8.33	3.79	+0.61	+0.62
3,	13,	5	7.00	5.29	0.00	0.00
5,	12,	5	7.33	4.04	+0.14	+0.15
1,	4,	5	3.33	2.08	−3.05	−1.70
9,	4,	3	5.33	3.21	−0.90	−0.77
13,	11,	8	10.67	2.52	+2.51	+1.70
10,	5,	10	8.33	2.89	+0.80	+0.62
6,	7,	10	7.67	2.08	+0.56	+0.31
10,	4,	8	7.33	3.06	+0.19	+0.15

These data simply show that the *t*-scores $[(\bar{X} - \mu)/s_{\bar{X}}]$ are more variable
than the *z*-scores $[(\bar{X} - \mu)/\sigma_{\bar{X}}]$. If a large number of such samples were
drawn, and the distributions of t and $z_{\bar{X}}$ were plotted, these curves would show
the general form of the difference between the normal distribution and a small
sample *t* distribution, which is a greater relative proportion of the area toward
the tails in a *t* distribution. Figure 8.2–2 shows a plot of t and $z_{\bar{X}}$ terms
obtained from 100 samples of three cards drawn from a deck. Of course, the
$(\bar{X} - \mu)/\sigma_{\bar{X}}$ curve is not a normal distribution, nor is the $(\bar{X} - \mu)/s_{\bar{X}}$ curve

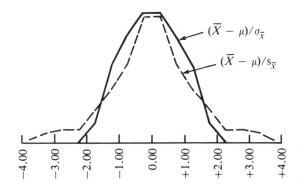

$(\bar{X} - \mu)/\sigma_{\bar{X}}$

$(\bar{X} - \mu)/s_{\bar{X}}$

−4.00 −3.00 −2.00 −1.00 0.00 +1.00 +2.00 +3.00 +4.00

Figure 8.2–2 The distribution of $t[(\bar{X} - \mu)/s_{\bar{X}}]$
and $z_{\bar{X}}[(\bar{X} - \mu)/\sigma_{\bar{X}}]$ obtained from 100 samples of
$n = 3$ drawn from a deck of cards.

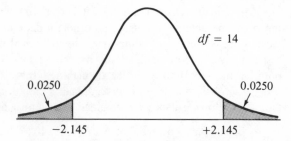

Figure 8.2–3 The probability of occurrence of a *t* value greater than +2.145 or less than −2.145 is 0.05 when *df* = 14.

a *t* distribution at *df* = 2; however, as just described, these curves do portray the general nature of the difference.

In a normal distribution, every *z*-score identifies a certain proportion of the total distribution lying above and below itself. (We can determine these proportions by reference to Table A.) The *t* distributions have mean equal to zero, and *t* values provide similar information in *t* distributions as *z*-scores do in normal distributions. For example, in the *t* distribution for *df* = 14, the values *t* = ±2.145 enclose the middle 95 percent. This means in turn that 0.05 (or 5 percent) of the observations in that distribution have *t* values either above +2.145 or below −2.145. Thus the probability is 0.05 that a score drawn at random from this distribution will have a *t* value that is numerically greater than 2.145. Figure 8.2–3 illustrates this situation.

Since there is a different *t* distribution for each different *df*, the numerical value of *t* associated with any given proportion, such as that which cuts off the extreme 5 percent and encloses the middle 95 percent, is not constant. This makes the construction of tables that show the proportions above and below different *t* values somewhat complicated. In practice, such tables are set up so that the *t* values for a few selected probability levels are presented for all the *t* distributions that are likely to be of interest. If you refer to Table B as you read the rest of this paragraph the matter will become clear. For the time being, we will be concerned only with entries under the two-tailed heading. The row headings down the left side of Table B are *df*; each row represents a different *t* distribution. The column headings are confidence levels and specify the probability of occurrence of values in each column. The values in the column headed by 0.05, for example, have a 0.05 probability of occurring by chance; for any given *df*, the probability is 0.05 or less that a *t* value randomly sampled from that distribution will be numerically equal to or larger than that in the table. You can see that when *df* = 14, the 0.05 level value is *t* = 2.145, as was shown earlier. Observe that when *df* = ∞, the 0.05 level value is *t* = 1.960, which is identical to the value of *z* that cuts off the extreme 5 percent of the normal distribution; this shows that the family of *t* distributions approximate the normal distribution as *df* increases. In fact, the normal distribution may be regarded as a special case of the *t* distributions when *df* = ∞.

An aside:
"Student's *t*"

The *t* statistic and its sampling distributions have historically been referred to as "Student's *t*" in memory of the man who derived them. W. S. Gosset (1876–1936) worked for Guinness Breweries of Ireland. One story is that he was involved in quality control and needed a way to estimate brewing batch (population) parameters from small samples; another goes that he was involved in consumer preference studies and needed to estimate consumer population taste preferences from small samples. In any event, he was faced with the problem of unknown population variance and derived the *t* distributions. The original paper was published in 1908 and because the company prohibited its employees from publishing research, he contributed his mathematical insights to the learned journals under the pen name "Student."

8.3 Confidence Intervals for the Population Mean

This section describes a procedure by which data from a single sample are used to identify a range of values known as a confidence interval, which has a specified probability of containing the unknown population mean. We are operating under conditions wherein a sample has been obtained from a population whose mean (μ) and standard deviation (σ) are unknown; nonetheless, we are able to make some statements regarding the value of the population mean, as the following discussion will show.

Suppose we went to a particular golf course and dug up 25 earthworms and found their mean length to be 14 cm, with a standard deviation of 4 cm. Thus

$$\overline{X} = 14$$
$$s = 4$$
$$n = 25$$
$$df = n - 1 = 24$$

Assuming that our 25 worms are a random sample, our best estimate of the mean length of the population of earthworms inhabiting this golf course is 14 cm, but this estimate is likely to be in error by some unknown amount. We could estimate the standard error of the sample mean as follows

$$s_{\overline{X}} = s/\sqrt{n} = 4\sqrt{25} = 0.80$$

If we know the population mean length (μ), we could convert our sample mean into a *t* value using the formula

$$t = \frac{\overline{X} - \mu}{s_{\overline{X}}}$$

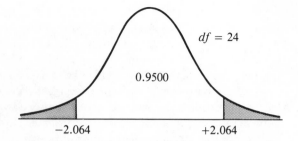

Figure 8.3–1 The t values ±2.064 enclose the middle 0.9500 when $df = 24$.

The t value thus obtained would be a single term in the t distribution at $n - 1 = 24$ degrees of freedom. If we read Table B for $df = 24$ and confidence level = 0.05, we find the entry 2.064; thus the t values ±2.064 enclose the middle 0.9500 of this distribution as shown in Figure 8.3–1. If many samples of 25 were drawn and their means converted to t values, 95 percent of them would be between $t = ±2.064$. In other words, the probability is 0.95 that

$$+2.064 \leqslant \frac{\overline{X} - \mu}{s_{\overline{X}}} \leqslant -2.064$$

or

$$p\left[+2.064 \leqslant \frac{\overline{X} - \mu}{s_{\overline{X}}} \leqslant -2.064 \right] = 0.95$$

We can rewrite this expression as

$$p[\overline{X} - (+2.064)(s_{\overline{X}}) \leqslant \mu \leqslant \overline{X} - (-2.064)(s_{\overline{X}})] = 0.95$$

If we substitute $s_{\overline{X}} = 0.80$, and $\overline{X} = 14$, then

$$p[(14 - (+2.064)(.80)) \leqslant \mu \leqslant 14 - (-2.064)(.80)] = 0.95$$
$$p[12.3488 \leqslant \mu \leqslant 15.6512] = 0.95$$

We have arrived at the statement that there is a 0.95 probability that the range of values 12.3488 to 15.6512 inclusive contains the unknown population mean. An important conceptual point here is that this statement is not a statement about the probability of μ; it is a statement about the interval. (Since the interval is a direct derivative of the sample, plus the inclusion of a t value to define the degree of confidence, this statement is literally about the probability of a sample. See Hays, 1981.) In other words, this statement means that the probability is 0.95 that the specified interval contains μ. The interval we have calculated is based on one sample; a different sample would generate a different interval. If many samples were drawn and an interval calculated from each, 95 percent of these intervals would contain the unknown population mean; it follows that any given interval has a 0.95 probability of containing the population mean. We term this the 0.95 confidence interval even though the t values are selected from Table B under the 0.05 confidence level heading. Do not be disturbed by this seemingly anomalous language; we could just as easily call it the 0.05 confidence interval and say that the probability is 0.05 that the interval 15.6512 to 12.3488 does not contain μ.

The procedure described in this section assumes the population standard deviation to be unknown. If σ is known, then $\sigma_{\bar{x}}$ may be calculated. The sampling distribution of $\bar{X}$ is normal even for small samples if the population is normal, and generally regardless of the population distribution if sample size is 20 or larger; thus, z-scores may be used in the formula in place of t values ($z = \pm 1.96$ and $z = \pm 2.58$ for the 0.95 and 0.99 confidence intervals respectively). Texts frequently introduce confidence intervals with the z-score method and then go to the t value method for dealing with cases in which σ is unknown. I have gone directly to the t value method because I believe that σ is unknown in the vast majority of real-life cases and I do not feel there is anything to be gained, in a pedagogical sense, by approaching t's through z's.

It is generally felt that when $n > 30$, then $s_{\bar{x}}$ is a sufficiently good estimator of $\sigma_{\bar{x}}$ that z-scores may be used in place of t values to determine the confidence interval. However, it seems to me that convenience is insufficient justification for imprecision, however slight, and my own view is that the t value method should always be used when σ is unknown. To this end, Table B contains critical values for t that will handle most practical needs. Those who are following along in Appendix IV will note that Program 2 uses critical values for t throughout.

An aside on
t's and z's

The procedure presented here for determining confidence intervals is not a test of significance (that is, a rejection or retention of a null hypothesis) in the usual sense, although it is conceptually equivalent. Strictly speaking, a null hypothesis states a parameter value and is formulated before data are collected and then it is either rejected or retained as a function of the disparity between the obtained results and those predicted by the null hypothesis. In the case of confidence intervals, we could say that the hypothesis that the upper and lower limits of the confidence interval, which in our case are 12.3488 to 15.6512 inclusive, contain the unknown population mean may be retained with 0.95 confidence. Obviously this hypothesis is derived from the data and is not formulated prior to its collection. (Note: The statement that $12.3488 \leq \mu \leq 15.6512$ could be used as a null hypothesis to be retained or rejected as a function of data gathered from subsequent samples.)

A more general rule for calculating the confidence interval limits for the population mean is

Confidence interval for $\mu = \overline{X} \pm (t_\alpha)(s_{\overline{X}})$

where α is the level of confidence attached to the interval and t_α is used as a positive value. The 0.99 confidence interval for the earthworm population mean length based on our sample is shown next. Again note that degrees of freedom used to select the *t* value is $n - 1 = 24$.

Upper limit of confidence interval for $\mu = 14 + (2.797)(0.80)$

$$= 16.2376$$

Lower limit of confidence interval for $\mu = 14 - (2.797)(0.80)$

$$= 11.7624$$

Thus

$$p[11.7624 \leqslant \mu \leqslant 16.2376] = 0.99$$

Note that the 0.99 confidence interval is larger than the 0.95 interval; you must specify a larger range if you wish to be more certain that it contains the population mean.

8.4 Review Exercises

1. A sample of 36 rats had a mean weight of 170 gm with a standard deviation of 13 gm.

    (a) Calculate the estimated standard error of the mean.
    (b) Determine the 0.95 confidence interval for the population mean weight.
    (c) Determine the 0.99 confidence interval for the population mean weight.

2. A random sample of 25 people was measured to determine the amount that they were overweight for their age and height. It was found that $\overline{X} = 12$ lb and $s = 2.70$ lb. Determine the 0.95 confidence interval for the mean number of pounds that members of the population are overweight.

3. Sixteen autos randomly selected from an assembly line were found to have a mean of 21 defects with a standard deviation of 5. If you buy a new car, you can thus be 95 percent sure that it will have between _____ and _____ defects.

4. If 30 randomly selected Pygmies have a mean height of 4 ft 2 in. with a standard deviation of 3 in., what range of heights has a 0.99 probability of containing the population mean?

5. Twenty leopards had a mean of 900 spots with a standard deviation of 110 spots. Suppose a "trophy" is defined as an animal with 1000 spots. Is there a 0.95 probability that the average leopard in the population is a "trophy?"

6. If 18 pygmie rattlesnakes had a mean length of 25 cm with $s = 4$ cm, could you be 99 percent sure that an individual of 27.5 cm did not represent the population mean?

7. If you were willing to accept a probability of one in twenty of being wrong, what range of values would you specify as containing the mean wingspan of monarch butterflies, given that a sample of 36 had $\overline{X} = 8$ cm and $s = 1.4$ cm?

8. If you were willing to accept a 0.05 probability of being incorrect that the mean of a sample of 46, with $s = 3$, would fall between 7.72 and 9.50, what would be the value of that sample mean?

9. A random sample of 24 had a mean measurement of 89.73 cm with standard deviation of 5.70 cm. There is less than one chance in a hundred that any individual selected at random will exceed _____ cm.

8.5 Testing the Difference Between Population and Sample Means

There are occasions when the mean value of some variable in the population is known and we wish to determine whether the mean score of a particular group differs significantly from the population mean. For example, suppose that intelligence test scores in the general population have $\mu = 100$, and that we measured the intelligence of 20 nurses and found that $\overline{X} = 103$ and $s = 12$. The question is: Do the nurses differ significantly in intelligence from the general population? In other words, should they be regarded as a sample from the general population or as a sample from the population of nurses, which differs in mean intelligence from the general population? The null hypothesis is that $\mu_{nurses} = 100$ (that is, $\mu_{nurses} = \mu_{general\ population}$). We could state the null hypothesis as "Nurses do not differ in intelligence from the general population," and test it by converting our sample mean into a t value. Thus

Null hypothesis: Nurses' mean intelligence does not differ from the general population mean ($\mu_{nurses} = \mu_{general\ population}$).

$\mu = 100$

$n = 20$

$\overline{X} = 103$

$s = 12$

$s_{\overline{X}} = 12/\sqrt{20} = 12/4.47 = 2.68$

$$t = \frac{\overline{X} - \mu}{s_{\overline{X}}}$$

$$= \frac{103 - 100}{2.68}$$

$$= 1.12$$

If the null hypothesis is true, then we expect that $\overline{X} = \mu$ and $t = 0$; however, sampling error will usually result in $\overline{X}$ being different from μ, and $t \neq 0$. We will test the null hypothesis at 0.05 confidence level by determining whether the t value obtained ($t = 1.12$) has a 0.05 or less probability of occurrence as a function of sampling error. Since our sample consisted of 20 nurses, we have $df = n - 1 = 20 - 1 = 19$ associated with this t value. If we refer to Table B, we find that the critical value for t at $df = 19$ and 0.05 confidence level is $t = 2.093$. In other words, a t value must be equal to or larger than 2.093 in order to have a 0.05 or less probability of occurrence in the t distribution at $df = 19$, as is shown in Figure 8.5–1. Since our obtained t value is less than the critical value found in Table B, it means that its probability of occurrence as a function of sampling error is greater than 0.05. This result is termed not significant and we therefore retain the null hypothesis that nurses do not differ in intelligence from the general population. Note that what has literally happened is that we have failed to reject the null hypothesis: the retention of a null hypothesis is always understood to be on this basis rather than because of any evidence for its validity. Had the calculated t value exceeded 2.093, our decision would have been to reject the null hypothesis and retain the alternative hypothesis that the nurses do differ in intelligence from the general population.

If the population standard deviation is known, then $\overline{X}$ may be converted into a z-score since $\sigma_{\overline{X}}$ may be calculated and the sampling distribution of $\overline{X}$ will be approximately normal. The null hypothesis is rejected if the z-score thus obtained exceeds the critical value for the confidence level chosen, for example, 1.96 for 0.05 confidence level and 2.58 for 0.01 confidence level.

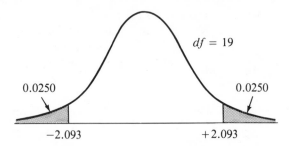

Figure 8.5–1 When $df = 19$ a t value must be numerically greater than 2.093 to have probability of occurrence = 0.05 or less.

Testing a Sample vs. Population Mean

Let us consider a situation similar to one presented earlier in this chapter concerning the heart rates of the members of the University of Warsaw basketball team. Suppose we know that the mean heart rate in the general population is 72 beats per minute, and that a random sample of 15 basketball players was found to have a mean heart rate of 65 beats per minute with a standard deviation of 6 beats per minute. The question of interest is: Does the mean heart rate of basketball players differ significantly from the general population mean?

Null hypothesis: The mean heart rate of basketball players does not differ from the population mean

$$(\mu_{\text{basketball players}} = \mu_{\text{population}})$$

$\mu = 72.00$

$\overline{X} = 65.00$

$s = 6.00$

$n = 15$

$s_{\overline{X}} = 6/\sqrt{15} = 6/3.87 = 1.55$

$$t = \frac{\overline{X} - \mu}{s_{\overline{X}}} = \frac{65 - 72}{1.55} = -4.52$$

1. $df = n - 1 = 15 - 1 = 14$

2. The critical value for t at 0.05 confidence level = 2.145

3. Therefore the result is significant.

4. Interpretation: The mean heart rate of basketball players differs from the population mean

$$(\mu_{\text{basketball players}} \neq \mu_{\text{population}}).$$

8.6 Review Exercises

In each of the following situations, identify the null hypothesis and determine whether the sample mean differs significantly from the population mean at 0.05 confidence level.

1. The overall mean annual income is 15,000 dollars; a group of 36 steel workers had a mean income of 17,000 dollars, with a standard deviation of 5000 dollars.

2. The mean Fido College Entrance Examination score is 200 for all entering freshmen in a given year, but the mean of 25 graduates of the Los Angeles high schools was 198, with a standard deviation of 20.

3. A plant produces light bulbs that have a mean life of 110 hours. A sample of 20 bulbs produced on Friday afternoons was found to have a mean life of 101 hours, with a standard deviation of 10 hours.

4. The overall mean repair frequency of North American-produced automobiles is 4.75 per 10,000 kilometers, while a sample of 46 rental company cars had a mean repair frequency of 6.29 per 10,000 km with a standard deviation of 2.71.

5. Fish taken from Lake Ontario have a mean mercury content of 0.95 parts per million, with a standard deviation of 0.18 parts per million. A sample of 30 caught in the Niagara River estuary had a mean content of 0.99 parts per million.

6. North American women have a mean weight of 127.28 pounds, with a standard deviation of 16.59 pounds. A group of 27 lady wrestlers had a mean weight of 134.68 pounds.

8.7 The *t*-Test for Means: Independent Groups

independent groups experiment

In an *independent groups experiment,* separate randomly sampled groups of individuals serve as subjects. In this section, we shall explore a procedure, called the *t*-test for means, which enables us to decide whether there is a significant difference between the mean scores of two independently randomly sampled groups. It may be that members of one group were exposed to some independent variable treatment while the second group served as a control, or it may be that the groups differed in terms of some qualitative dimension, such as one being composed of males and the other of females. In either case, we want to know whether the groups differed on the dependent variable measure.

Let us imagine a hypothetical experiment in which 10 randomly selected Girl Guides and 10 randomly selected Boy Scouts each visited 5 different houses selling boxes of cookies. The independent variable is Girl Guides as compared to Boy Scouts, and the dependent variable is number of boxes of cookies sold. This experiment tested the null hypothesis that Guides and Scouts do not differ in ability to sell cookies. Let us suppose that the 10 Girl Guides, whom we may term group #1, sold a total of 75 boxes of cookies; thus $\overline{X}_1 = 7.50$. The 10 Boy Scouts, whom we will term group #2, sold a total of 60 boxes of cookies; thus $\overline{X}_2 = 6.00$. While it is clear that the Girl Guides had a higher sales mean than the Boy Scouts, we cannot conclude from a comparison of these means that Girl Guides in general are significantly better salespersons than Boy Scouts.

If the null hypothesis is true and Guides and Scouts do not differ in cookie selling ability, the mean sales scores of the two groups should be identical. In actual practice, this will seldom happen because the null hypothesis really means that the populations of Guides and Scouts do not differ. The subject groups in our experiment were random samples from these populations and we must expect sampling error in both instances. As a result, these samples could not be expected to be precisely like their populations, or like each other. Even when the null hypothesis is true, we expect that $\overline{X}_1$ will usually differ from $\overline{X}_2$ by some amount. We must decide whether the difference between the means of the two groups is a function of sampling error or if it may be attributed to the independent variable; that is, we need to determine whether Guides and Scouts are genuinely different on this measure. There is never any way to know with certainty that the independent variable is responsible for, or related to, the difference in the dependent variable scores of the two groups. The best that we can do is to determine the probability that the result we have obtained would happen as a function of sampling error. If this probability is below some criterion level, such as 0.05 or less, then we reject the null hypothesis and retain the alternative.

If the null hypothesis is true and Girl Guides and Boy Scouts do not differ in cookie selling ability, then, in terms of that characteristic, Guides and Scouts are part of the same population. Imagine that two independent random samples are drawn from a population and arbitrarily labeled as sample #1 and sample #2, but otherwise are not treated differently in any way. If each subject were measured for some dependent variable and the two group means calculated, we could subtract one mean from the other to obtain the difference between them $(\overline{X}_1 - \overline{X}_2)$ and refer to this term as the difference between means. If we repeated this procedure a great many times and entered the $\overline{X}_1 - \overline{X}_2$ values into a frequency distribution, it would be a sampling distribution of the difference between means. Since labeling the samples on each occasion as #1 and #2 was arbitrary, positive differences between the means would occur as often as negative differences. It follows that the expected value (mean) of the sampling distribution of the difference between means (all possible $\overline{X}_1 - \overline{X}_2$ terms) is zero, that is, $\mu_{(\overline{X}_1 - \overline{X}_2)} = 0$. The standard deviation of this sampling distribution would be termed the standard error of the difference between means, and symbolized as $\sigma_{(\overline{X}_1 - \overline{X}_2)}$. The standard error of the difference between means would reflect the variability of $\overline{X}_1 - \overline{X}_2$ over repeated occurrences.

We can convert any particular $\overline{X}_1 - \overline{X}_2$ (difference between means) term into a *t* value by subtracting the mean of its sampling distribution $[\mu_{(\overline{X}_1-\overline{X}_2)} = 0]$ and dividing by the estimated standard error of the difference between means $[s_{(\overline{X}_1-\overline{X}_2)}]$. Thus

$$t = \frac{(\overline{X}_1 - \overline{X}_2) - [\mu_{(\overline{X}_1-\overline{X}_2)}]}{s_{(\overline{X}_1-\overline{X}_2)}}$$

$$= \frac{(\overline{X}_1 - \overline{X}_2) - 0}{s_{(\overline{X}_1-\overline{X}_2)}}$$

$$= \frac{\overline{X}_1 - \overline{X}_2}{s_{(\overline{X}_1-\overline{X}_2)}}$$

The estimated standard error of the difference between means is derived from a variance term based on both groups of scores.

$$s_{(\overline{X}_1-\overline{X}_2)} = \sqrt{s^2/n_1 + s^2/n_2}$$

where

$$s^2 = \frac{\sum X_1^2 - (\sum X_1)^2/n_1 + \sum X_2^2 - (\sum X_2)^2/n_2}{n_1 + n_2 - 2}$$

Notice that s^2 is a pooled variance term that reflects the variability of both the X_1 and X_2 scores. This becomes slightly more apparent if the formula is written as

$$s^2 = \frac{\sum X_1^2 - (\sum X_1)^2/n_1 + \sum X_2^2 - (\sum X_2)^2/n_2}{(n_1 - 1) + (n_2 - 1)}$$

When the two groups have equal *n*'s, then $s^2 = (s_1^2 + s_2^2)/2$. It is not necessary to have equal *n*'s, but experimenters prefer this because it reduces the risk of violating underlying assumptions. (These are discussed in Section 8.11.)

The most convenient computational formula for *t* is

$$t = \frac{\overline{X}_1 - \overline{X}_2}{\sqrt{s^2/n_1 + s^2/n_2}}$$

The *t* value thus obtained is a term in the *t* distribution at $df = n_1 + n_2 - 2$. We can refer to Table B and determine the critical value for *t* at 0.05 confidence level; the probability is 0.05 or less that a *t* value selected at random from this *t* distribution will equal or exceed the critical value. The null hypothesis predicts that $\overline{X}_1 - \overline{X}_2 = 0$, and consequently that $t = 0$. If our calculated *t* equals or exceeds the value obtained from Table B, it means that it has 0.05 or less probability of occurrence, which tells us that if the null hypothesis is true, our $\overline{X}_1 - \overline{X}_2$ term has 0.05 or less probability of occurrence as a function of sampling error. On that basis, we reject the null hypothesis and retain the alternative hypothesis.

The independent groups t-test for means analysis is illustrated in the following numerical example in which we will imagine having actually conducted the hypothetical experiment where 10 Girl Guides and 10 Boy Scouts each visited 5 different houses trying to sell as many boxes of cookies as possible. The presentation of this numerical example follows a standard format; it is highly recommended that the student follow this format as it will simplify and clarify the steps in the analysis procedure. Thus

> Independent variable: Girl Guides compared to Boy Scouts
>
> Dependent variable: cookie selling ability (defined operationally as number of boxes sold)
>
> Null hypothesis: Girl Guides and Boy Scouts do not differ in cookie selling ability ($\mu_{\text{Guides}} = \mu_{\text{Scouts}}$).

The raw data were

X_1 (Girl Guides)	X_2 (Boy Scouts)	X_1^2	X_2^2
9	6	81	36
9	7	81	49
5	5	25	25
10	8	100	64
6	5	36	25
8	6	64	36
6	7	36	49
7	5	49	25
9	4	81	16
6	7	36	49

$$\sum X_1 = 75 \qquad \sum X_2 = 60 \qquad \sum X_1^2 = 589 \qquad \sum X_2^2 = 374$$

$$n_1 = 10 \qquad n_2 = 10$$

$$\overline{X}_1 = 7.50 \qquad \overline{X}_2 = 6.00$$

$$
\begin{aligned}
s^2 &= \frac{\sum X_1^2 - (\sum X_1)^2/n_1 + \sum X_2^2 - (\sum X_2)^2/n_2}{n_1 + n_2 - 2} \\[2mm]
&= \frac{589 - (75)^2/10 + 374 - (60)^2/10}{10 + 10 - 2} \\[2mm]
&= \frac{589 - 5625/10 + 374 - 3600/10}{20 - 2} \\[2mm]
&= \frac{589 - 562.50 + 374 - 360}{18} \\[2mm]
&= 2.25
\end{aligned}
$$

$$t = \frac{\overline{X}_1 - \overline{X}_2}{\sqrt{s^2/n_1 + s^2/n_2}}$$

$$= \frac{7.50 - 6.00}{\sqrt{2.25/10 + 2.25/10}}$$

$$= \frac{1.50}{\sqrt{0.225 + 0.225}}$$

$$= \frac{1.50}{0.67}$$

$$= 2.24$$

When t has been calculated, the next step is to test it for significance by reference to Table B. The significance test consists of three steps: (1) identifying the appropriate number of degrees of freedom, (2) determining the critical value for t from Table B at whatever level of confidence we wish to conduct the significance test, and (3) stating the result. Thus

1. $df = n_1 + n_2 - 2 = 10 + 10 - 2 = 18$
2. The critical value for t at 0.05 confidence level = 2.101
3. Therefore the result is significant.

interpretation   The last step in analysis is to interpret the result. An *interpretation* is a statement that expresses the meaning of the result in terms of the independent and dependent variables. For our hypothetical experiment, the interpretation involves rejecting the null hypothesis and retaining the alternative hypothesis, and would be stated as "Girl Guides differ from Boy Scouts in ability to sell cookies." This statement is understood as $\mu_{\text{Girl Guides}} \neq \mu_{\text{Boy Scouts}}$, and does not mean that every individual Guide differs from every individual Scout.

In the formula for t, the numerator term $(\overline{X}_1 - \overline{X}_2)$ determines the sign of the t value; whether one ultimately arrives at a positive or negative t value is dependent upon which set of scores was labeled X_1 and which scores were labeled X_2. Since this labeling is purely arbitrary, the sign of the t value is of no consequence in the significance test. In order to be significant, the calculated t value must merely equal or exceed in numerical magnitude the critical value obtained from Table B.

It would seem that the control group scores should be identical, and likewise the experimental group scores, because within each group the subjects are treated identically. The scores typically vary because the subjects are different individuals and do not behave identically, and also because it is practically impossible to hold environment and measurement conditions literally constant for different subjects. The score variability within the subject groups is not a function of the independent variable or any deliberate procedure of the experimenter. This variability among the scores within the groups

Independent Groups *t*-Test

Suppose a manuscript is discovered whose author is unknown but believed by some to have been written by Shakespeare. Six passages (a passage was defined as a 200-word segment) were randomly selected from known works of Shakespeare and six passages were randomly selected from the new manuscript; in each the number of interrogative pronouns was counted. The raw data are shown next.

Independent variable: Shakespeare's passages as compared to the new manuscript's passages.

Dependent variable: Number of interrogative pronouns

Null hypothesis: Shakespeare's passages do not differ from the new manuscript's passages in number of interrogative pronouns ($\mu_{Shakespeare} = \mu_{new\ manuscript}$).

X_1 (Shakespeare)	X_2 (new)	X_1^2	X_2^2
13	7	169	49
6	9	36	81
10	5	100	25
8	7	64	49
9	5	81	25
8	6	64	36
$\sum X_1 = 54$	$\sum X_2 = 39$	$\sum X_1^2 = 514$	$\sum X_2^2 = 265$

$n_1 = 6, \quad \overline{X}_1 = 9.00: \qquad n_2 = 6, \quad \overline{X}_2 = 6.50$

$$s^2 = \frac{514 - (54)^2/6 + 265 - (39)^2/6}{6 + 6 - 2} = 3.95$$

$$t = \frac{9.00 - 6.50}{\sqrt{3.95/6 + 3.95/6}} = 2.17$$

1. $df = n_1 + n_2 - 2 = 6 + 6 - 2 = 10$
2. The critical value for t at 0.05 confidence level = 2.228
3. Therefore the result is not significant.
4. Interpretation: Shakespeare's passages do not differ from the new manuscript's passages in the number of interrogative pronouns ($\mu_{Shakespeare} = \mu_{new\ manuscript}$).

Note that the retention of the null hypothesis does not prove that $\mu_{Shakespeare} = \mu_{new\ manuscript}$; we merely continue to retain this assumption because there was insufficient evidence to reject it. In a broader sense, this result does not prove the view that Shakespeare authored the new manuscript; it merely does not contradict it.

is the basis upon which the estimated standard error of the difference between means $[(s_{(\bar{X}_1-\bar{X}_2)}]$ is calculated and represents the background noise against which the difference between the groups' means is evaluated. The magnitude of t is a function of the difference between $\bar{X}_1$ and $\bar{X}_2$ and the amount of variability occurring within the groups. Experimenters treat subjects as identically as possible to keep the "background noise" to a minimum and obtain subjects by random sampling so the noise generated by individual differences will be at the same level for the two groups.

8.8 Review Exercises

The situations and data in the following problem exercises are hypothetical. Treat them as research problems and try to determine the experimenter's objective in each case. It will help to proceed systematically; thus in each problem you should:

(a) identify the independent variable
(b) identify the dependent variable
(c) state the null hypothesis being tested
(d) complete the analysis at 0.05 confidence level using the steps shown in Section 8.7
(e) clearly interpret the result

1. Eight Siamese and eight Manx cats were tested for their ability to catch mice. Each test consisted of releasing a mouse one meter from the cat and counting the number of seconds until capture. The raw data were as follows

      Siamese cats: 4, 8, 5, 7, 6, 6, 5, 7
      Manx cats: 4, 3, 4, 5, 4, 3, 4, 5

2. A person caught 12 mosquitos, randomly divided them into two groups of 6, and put the two groups into separate but similar containers. Into one container she sprayed a half-second burst of Raid, and into the other container a half-second burst of Black Flag. The number of seconds required for each mosquito to die was as follows

      Raid: 2.5, 0.5, 1.0, 1.5, 2.0, 1.5
      Black Flag: 2.0, 1.5, 1.0, 1.0, 2.5, 4.0

3. Ten randomly selected men and 10 randomly selected women participated in an experiment in which each person was shown a photograph of a typical downtown scene for 15 seconds. Following this each subject was given a list of 50 items and was asked to indicate which items had appeared in the photo. The number of correct identifications by each subject was as follows

Women: 5, 17, 10, 12, 8, 10, 20, 15, 9, 14
Men: 28, 15, 19, 10, 10, 20, 26, 18, 9, 25

4. When the loudness of sounds increases to a certain point, the experience becomes painful. Ranking among the loudest sound sources in our culture is the rock band up close, and the popularity of such concerts implies that some masochism may be part of the experience. Measurements clearly show that the pain threshold is exceeded regularly in the front row, and thus the following experiment was performed. Twenty-four randomly selected front row patrons were given ear plugs to wear during the concert. Half of these were designed to filter out sound volumes above the pain threshold, while the other half were merely ornamental. Each of the 24 subjects was later asked to rate his or her enjoyment of the concert on a 20-point scale, on which larger numbers indicated greater enjoyment. The raw data were as follows

Ornamental plugs: 20, 20, 15, 18, 19, 14, 17, 16, 20, 16, 18, 17
Filtering plugs: 15, 14, 19, 16, 10, 18, 11, 17, 16, 16, 10, 18

5. Persons applying to graduate schools are commonly required to write the Graduate Record Examinations (GRE), which include an Advanced Test that is presumed to be a measure of one's mastery of a subject area such as psychology. In one study, a group of people who had just completed Introduction to Psychology, and a group of people who had just completed their senior year as psychology majors were given the advanced test. The scores were as follows

Completed introductory course: 550, 210, 300, 600,
426, 250, 380
Senior year complete: 700, 590, 560, 400, 642, 610, 530

6. We rely on random sampling to produce two groups of subjects who are, if not precisely equal, at least not systematically different in any respect. An advertising agency solicited two groups of 9 people each from the telephone directory to evaluate two television commercials that promote an arthritis pain relief medicine. Since people of different ages may have different degrees of concern over arthritis pain, the experimenter decided to establish whether the two groups of subjects differed in this respect. The ages of the two samples were

No. 1:   60, 52, 25, 38, 24, 35, 40, 44, 33
No. 2:   27, 36, 25, 66, 51, 41, 32, 55, 45

7. On a given Sunday the total number of yards gained by each team in the American Football Conference (AFC) and the National Football Conference (NFC) of the National Football League was recorded. The raw data were

AFC: 390, 340, 280, 410, 330, 310, 380, 300,
          240, 300, 460, 330, 260, 280
NFC: 380, 320, 300, 340, 220, 350, 400, 370,
          390, 450, 410, 500, 290, 350

8.   A person tested a bolt-action and auto-loading rifle as follows: each gun was mounted in a vise and fired at a target nine times. The accuracy (number of cm from dead center) was scored on each shot. The raw data were

Bolt-action: 2.0, 1.5, 0.0, 0.5, 3.1, 2.7, 1.4, 1.2, 1.0
Auto-loading: 1.5, 2.5, 1.7, 3.0, 2.4, 1.8, 3.2, 3.8, 2.0

8.9 The *t*-Test for Means: Repeated Measures/Correlated Samples

repeated measures experiment

A *repeated measures experiment* uses a single group of subjects upon which the dependent variable measure is obtained twice. The difference between the conditions under which the two sets of scores are gathered constitutes the independent variable. For example, we may wish to evaluate a treatment by making a before and after comparison, such as measuring peoples' weights before and after participation in a diet program to determine whether significant weight change occurred. In such a case the independent variable is the diet program, the before scores are the control data, and the after scores are the experimental data. In a learning experiment we may test the subjects' mastery of the task after 10 training trials and after 20 training trials, and compare these data to see whether performance differed. In this case, the independent variable is the number of training trials. When the independent variable is a treatment that subjects could experience in either order, that is, *A–B* or *B–A*, then care must be taken to counterbalance the order of exposure by using the reverse sequence for half the subjects. If this is not done, then order of exposure to the independent variable (*A* on the first occasion and *B* on the second occasion) and/or a practice effect on the dependent variable task will confound the independent variable and render the results uninterpretable.

correlated samples experiment

A *correlated samples experiment* is one in which the subject groups consist of different individuals, but each member of one group is paired or matched with a specific member of the other group. The correlated samples experimental design is also known as the matched groups design. For example, suppose we used pairs of identical twins as subjects and randomly assigned one twin of each pair to the control group and the other to the experimental group. The result would be that for each member of the control group there is a person in the experimental group who is matched or equated for genetic inheritance; thus, the two groups consist of matched pairs of individuals. An experimenter might select a random sample from the population, but instead of randomly dividing it into a control and an experimental group, he or she could create two groups matched on some variable such as age. The procedure would be to determine the age of every member in the original sample, select the two oldest, and randomly assign one to the experimental group and the other to the control group. Then the next two oldest are randomly assigned, with one going to each group, and so on. When completed, the experimental and control groups would be said to be matched for age. You can use this kind of control over an extraneous variable when it is known, or strongly suspected, to affect the dependent variable measure.

In an independent groups experiment, each dependent variable score can be regarded as independent of any other score in its group and in the other group. This is true because the two groups of subjects are independently randomly sampled or a single random sample is randomly divided into two groups. In a repeated measures experiment, the two scores obtained from each subject cannot be regarded as being independent of each other because the behavior of any individual under different conditions will tend to be more consistent than the behaviors of separate randomly sampled persons. The same is true for the correlated samples experiment; the scores of the paired (matched) individuals will tend to be more consistent than those of independently sampled persons. Thus, in a repeated measures/correlated samples experiment, the data may be seen to occur in pairs and the analysis focuses on the difference between the scores in each pair.

The raw data consist of pairs of scores; the null hypothesis is that the two scores in each pair have the same expected value (are drawn from the same population). When the null hypothesis is true, the two scores in each pair should be identical. If we subtract one from the other and represent the difference by the symbol D, then our expectation for any subject is that $X_1 - X_2 = D = 0$. Overall then, we expect that $\Sigma D = 0$, and that $\overline{D} = 0$. Of course, when the null hypothesis is false, there would be some systematic difference in the two scores in each pair leading to the result that $D \neq 0$ for any subject, and that $\overline{D} \neq 0$ overall. Unless the dependent variable measure is very crude, we cannot expect a given subject, or two matched subjects, to yield identical scores even when the null hypothesis is true. In a correlated samples experiment, the subjects in the two groups are different individuals and will manifest some differences no matter how well matched they are. In a repeated measures experiment the subjects, being composed of living tissue, change from moment to moment and thus are not completely identical on the two measurement occasions. Thus it is virtually inevitable that the two scores obtained from each subject, or from matched subjects, will differ to some extent. The decision we must make is whether the differences observed can be attributed to chance fluctuations of organismic or environmental variables, or to the influence of the independent variable.

For the sake of convenience, the remainder of this discussion will use a repeated measures experimental design as a vehicle for presentation; however, a similar rationale applies to the correlated samples design. Suppose that one drew a random sample from a population and simply took the same measure twice on each subject but treated the subjects identically, to the extent that this is possible, on the two measurement occasions. By subtracting the second measure from the first we could obtain a *D* score for each subject and a mean difference ($\overline{D}$) for the group. If this procedure were repeated many times and the $\overline{D}$ values so obtained were entered into a frequency distribution, it would be a sampling distribution of the mean difference. Inasmuch as the chance fluctuations that result in $D \neq 0$ for any subject are as likely to produce positive *D* values as negative ones, it follows that the $\overline{D}$ term obtained in any given case is equally likely to be positive or negative. Thus the expected mean value of the sampling distribution of $\overline{D}$ (all possible $\overline{D}$ terms) is zero, that is, $\mu_{\overline{D}} = 0$. If one calculated the standard deviation of the sampling distribution of $\overline{D}$, it would be termed the standard error of the mean difference, and symbolized as $\sigma_{\overline{D}}$.

We can convert any observed $\overline{D}$ value into a *t* by subtracting the mean of its sampling distribution ($\mu_{\overline{D}} = 0$) and dividing by the estimated standard error of the mean difference ($s_{\overline{D}}$).

$$t = \frac{\overline{D} - \mu_{\overline{D}}}{s_{\overline{D}}} = \frac{\overline{D} - 0}{s_{\overline{D}}} = \frac{\overline{D}}{s_{\overline{D}}}$$

The *t* value thus obtained is a term in the *t* distribution with $df = N - 1$ where *N* is the number of pairs of scores. The null hypothesis predicts that $\overline{D} = 0$, and consequently that $t = 0$. If we consult Table B and find that a given *t* value has 0.05 or less probability of occurring by chance, it means that if the null hypothesis is true, there is 0.05 or less probability that sampling error would produce the observed result. On this basis we reject the null hypothesis and retain the alternative. A convenient computational formula is

$$t = \frac{\sum D}{\sqrt{\dfrac{N \sum D^2 - (\sum D)^2}{N - 1}}}$$

These formulas for *t* are equivalent, as is shown next

$$t = \frac{\overline{D}}{s_{\overline{D}}} = \frac{\sum D / N}{\sqrt{\dfrac{\sum D^2 - (\sum D)^2 / N}{N - 1}} \Big/ \sqrt{N}}$$

$$= \frac{\sum D / N}{\dfrac{1}{\sqrt{N}} \times \sqrt{\dfrac{\sum D^2 - (\sum D)^2 / N}{N - 1}}}$$

$$= \frac{\Sigma D/N}{\dfrac{1}{\sqrt{N}} \times \sqrt{\dfrac{N\Sigma D^2 - (\Sigma D)^2}{N(N-1)}}} = \frac{\Sigma D/N}{\dfrac{1}{\sqrt{N}} \times \dfrac{\sqrt{N\Sigma D^2 - (\Sigma D)^2}}{\sqrt{N(N-1)}}}$$

$$= \frac{\Sigma D/N}{\dfrac{1}{\sqrt{N}} \times \dfrac{\sqrt{N\Sigma D^2 - (\Sigma D)^2}}{\sqrt{N} \times \sqrt{N-1}}} = \frac{\Sigma D/N}{\dfrac{\sqrt{N\Sigma D^2 - (\Sigma D)^2}}{N \times \sqrt{N-1}}}$$

cancel *N*'s and

$$= \frac{\Sigma D}{\dfrac{\sqrt{N\Sigma D^2 - (\Sigma D)^2}}{\sqrt{N-1}}} = \frac{\Sigma D}{\sqrt{\dfrac{N\Sigma D^2 - (\Sigma D)^2}{N-1}}}$$

The repeated measures/correlated samples *t*-test for means is illustrated by the following numerical example of a hypothetical repeated measures experiment. Suppose a random sample of nine people was drawn from a population and confronted with the task of memorizing a list of nonsense syllables. The experimenter read the list aloud, after which the subject wrote down as many as he or she could remember, and this procedure was repeated over and over. On each trial the subject was scored in terms of the number of correct syllables written down. Assume that these are the data from the fourth and sixth trials. Thus

Independent variable: Four compared to six training trials.

Dependent variable: Task performance (defined operationally as the number of correct syllables identified).

Null hypothesis: Performance after four trials does not differ from that after six trials ($\mu_{4 \text{ trials}} = \mu_{6 \text{ trials}}$).

Four trials	Six trials	D	D^2
7	9	−2	4
8	11	−3	9
10	12	−2	4
9	11	−2	4
8	9	−1	1
12	11	+1	1
8	10	−2	4
11	11	0	0
9	12	−3	9
$N = 9$		$\Sigma D = -14$	$\Sigma D^2 = 36$

Note that ΣD is obtained by adding the *D* values, with regard to sign, so that positive and negative signs must be taken into account. It must be clearly understood that the data in each row belong to a particular subject; thus, subject #1 identified 7 correct nonsense syllables after four training trials and had 9 correct after six trials, and so on. (Note: In a correlated samples experiment, the data in each row belong to a matched pair of subjects.) Thus

$$t = \frac{\sum D}{\sqrt{\dfrac{N \sum D^2 - (\sum D)^2}{N - 1}}}$$

$$= \frac{-14}{\sqrt{\dfrac{(9)(36) - (-14)^2}{9 - 1}}}$$

$$= \frac{-14}{\sqrt{\dfrac{324 - 196}{8}}}$$

$$= \frac{-14}{\sqrt{16}}$$

$$= -3.50$$

We may now test the t value for significance by referring to Table B according to the routine established in Section 8.7.

1. $df = N - 1 = 9 - 1 = 8$
2. The critical value for t at 0.05 confidence level = 2.306
3. Therefore the result is significant.
4. Interpretation: Performance after four training trials differs from performance after six training trials.*

In the repeated measures/correlated samples analysis, the sign of the t value is determined by which set of scores is subtracted. Precisely the same numerical result would occur if the four-trial scores were subtracted from the six-trial scores except that the t value would be positive. The sign of the t value is determined by an arbitrary act of labeling and is of no consequence to the significance test. To be significant, the t value must numerically equal or exceed the critical value obtained from Table B.

The repeated measures/correlated samples analysis is based on the D scores, which represent the differences in subjects' responses between the control and experimental conditions. Since only the change in responding is

---

*Again, it is understood that the literal meaning of this interpretation is that $\mu_{\text{four trials}} \neq \mu_{\text{six trials}}$ (at 0.05 confidence level); we will dispense with reiterating this throughout the remainder of this book.

Repeated Measures/Correlated Samples *t*-Test

Suppose that on a given Wednesday each of five merchants in a shopping mall counted their total number of walk-in customers. The following Tuesday they placed a joint, full-page advertisement announcing sales in their stores in the evening paper. Then on the next day, Wednesday, they again counted their total number of walk-in customers. The raw data are shown next.

Independent variable: Preadvertisement as compared to postadvertisement

Dependent variable: Number of walk-in customers

Null hypothesis: The advertisement of sales does not affect the number of walk-in customers ($\mu_{\text{preadvertisement}} = \mu_{\text{postadvertisement}}$).

X_1 (preadvertisement)	X_2 (postadvertisement)	D	D^2
30	35	−5	25
78	80	−2	4
47	54	−7	49
56	59	−3	9
61	70	−9	81
$N = 5$		$\sum D = -26$	$\sum D^2 = 168$

$$t = \frac{-26}{\sqrt{\dfrac{(5)(168) - (-26)^2}{5 - 1}}} = -4.06$$

1. $df = N - 1 = 5 - 1 = 4$
2. The critical value for t at 0.05 confidence level = 2.776
3. Therefore the result is significant.
4. Interpretation: The advertisement of sales does affect the number of walk-in customers ($\mu_{\text{preadvertisement}} \neq \mu_{\text{postadvertisement}}$).

analyzed, the absolute size of the scores is irrelevant, and in this sense it can be said that individual differences in absolute response tendency are eliminated. Thus it is said that in a repeated measures experiment, each subject acts as his or her own control. It is the variability between individuals in the amount of response change from control to experimental conditions that gives variability to the D scores and serves as the basis for calculating $s_{\overline{D}}$. The magnitude of the t value is a function of the magnitude of the mean difference and the consistency of the differences between control and experimental condition scores.

An aside: a different perspective

The repeated measures/correlated samples *t*-test evaluates the null hypothesis that $\mu_{\overline{D}} = 0$ by determining whether $\overline{D}$ differs significantly from zero. This can be done using the procedure shown in Section 8.5. Using the data from the previous illustration example, if the D scores are treated as a sample it will be found that $\overline{X} = -1.5556$, $s = 1.3333$, $n = 9$, and $s_{\overline{X}} = 0.4444$. Since $\mu_{\overline{D}}$ is assumed to be zero, then $t = (\overline{X} - \mu)/s_{\overline{X}} = (-1.5556 - 0)/0.4444 = -3.50$, and is tested at $df = n - 1 = 8$.

8.10 Review Exercises

The situations and data in the following problem exercises are hypothetical. Proceed systematically and:

(a) identify the independent variable
(b) identify the dependent variable
(c) state the null hypothesis being tested
(d) complete the analysis at 0.05 confidence level using the steps shown in Section 8.9
(e) clearly interpret the result

Note that in the presentation of the raw data, the first score in each row belongs to subject #1, the second to subject #2, and so on.

1. An experimenter tested 10 childrens' preferences for brightly colored toys as compared to toys painted medium gray. The children were released for 30 minutes into a room containing both types of toys and observers recorded the number of minutes each child played with each type. The raw data were as follows

   Colored toys: 20, 15, 16, 15, 18, 10, 20, 16, 16, 10
   Grey toys: 10, 15, 12, 10, 12, 8, 15, 10, 14, 11

2. An experimenter was interested to know whether men drive faster, as measured by the number of speeding tickets received, when they were

alone as compared to when their wives were along. He located nine men who had each received 10 or more speeding tickets during the past year and determined how many were received under each condition. The raw data were

Wife along: 6, 7, 6, 8, 9, 8, 12, 10, 7
Alone: 4, 7, 5, 3, 2, 4, 8, 6, 3

3. Six infants were fed cold formula for the first four weeks of life and warm formula for the next four weeks. Six others were fed warm formula for the first four weeks and cold formula for the second four weeks. The number of kilograms of weight gain was recorded for each child during the warm and cold formula periods. The raw data were

Cold: 1.0, 3.1, 2.5, 2.0, 2.7, 1.8, 1.5, 2.9, 1.6, 2.2, 2.0, 1.7
Warm: 1.2, 2.8, 2.4, 1.8, 3.0, 2.0, 1.9, 2.4, 1.5, 2.4, 2.6, 1.2

4. A scoutmaster taught his nine scouts to tie a particular knot. He had them practice the knot once each week for ten consecutive weeks and each time he recorded the number of seconds each scout required to complete the knot. The data from the fifth and tenth weeks were

Fifth week: 20, 10, 14, 18, 25, 17, 15, 12, 14
Tenth week: 16, 9, 15, 12, 19, 15, 13, 11, 10

5. In a study to test two new sedatives, eight insomniacs were given Drug A for five nights and eight were given Drug B for five nights. The mean number of hours of sleep was recorded for each subject for the five nights. The two groups were matched for age. The raw data were

A: 8, 10, 9, 10, 8, 6, 7, 9
B: 5, 4, 6, 6, 3, 5, 4, 8

6. Eleven nurses took a special course in how to jab people with a hypodermic needle. Injection efficiency was measured as the number of patients jabbed per minute. These data were compared to similar scores obtained from 11 nurses who had not taken this course. The two groups were matched for years of experience. The raw data were

No course: 4, 4, 4, 6, 5, 4, 3, 4, 2, 6, 5
Course: 4, 6, 5, 8, 7, 7, 6, 5, 4, 8, 6

7. Seven college girls wore "Sudden Death" perfume for one week and "Asbet" for one week. Each kept a count of the number of times she was attacked by mosquitos. The raw data were

Sudden Death: 15, 7, 20, 12, 16, 10, 16
Asbet: 18, 10, 19, 14, 20, 11, 16

8. Forty-two kindergarten children were given a reading comprehension test. The eight lowest scorers were assigned to a special remedial reading class

and retested for reading comprehension after ten weeks. The raw data were

1st test: 7, 10, 11, 8, 11, 10, 12, 9
2nd test: 9, 11, 11, 10, 12, 13, 13, 11

9. The best way to appreciate the similarities and differences between the independent groups and repeated measures/correlated samples analyses is to subject a set of data to both procedures and compare the outcomes. Suppose the following data were obtained from an experiment in which subjects were asked to thread as many needles as possible during a ten minute period after having consumed either 100 ml of colorless, odorless, and tasteless 80-proof grain alcohol (X_1 scores) or 100 ml of distilled water (X_2 scores).

X_1: 5, 6, 3, 4, 4, 4, 6, 5, 2, 5
X_2: 6, 6, 4, 6, 3, 5, 9, 6, 4, 6

(a) Analyze these data as an independent groups experiment.
(b) Analyze these data as a repeated measures/correlated samples experiment.

The following exercises may be the most valuable in this chapter. Each one presents a hypothetical experiment and provides summary terms from the raw data that enable you to perform either an independent groups or a repeated measures/correlated samples analysis. It is essential that you understand the nature of the experiment so as to be able to decide which analysis is appropriate. Proceed systematically and:

(a) identify the independent variable
(b) identify the dependent variable
(c) state the null hypothesis being tested
(d) complete the analysis at 0.05 confidence level
(e) clearly interpret the result

10. An instructor taught a day and evening section of the same course. Both classes had 31 students. At the end of the semester, each student indicated his or her evaluation of the text on a 100-point scale, wherein higher values constituted a more favorable opinion. Summary terms from the raw data were

$$\overline{X}_{day} = 68, \qquad \overline{X}_{evening} = 60, \qquad s^2 = 248,$$
$$\Sigma D = 250, \qquad \Sigma D^2 = 3000$$

11. An experiment was set up to determine whether electroshock or chemotherapy is more effective in alleviating psychotic symptoms. Ten psychotics served as subjects; each was observed for two weeks while receiving

one form of treatment and was then switched to the other form of treatment and observed for another two weeks. The order of treatment exposure was counterbalanced with half of the group receiving a reversed sequence. Five of the subjects were male and five were female. Observers counted each subject's number of symptom manifestations during each therapy period. Summary terms from the raw data were

$$\overline{X}_{chemo} = 6, \quad \overline{X}_{electro} = 7.1, \quad s^2 = 2, \quad n = 10$$
$$\Sigma D = 11, \quad \Sigma D^2 = 22$$

12. A comparative psychologist collected 15 bullfrogs and tested them for their response to mealworms as food objects. The measure taken was the number of seconds between presentation and striking at the mealworm (variable X_1). After the test, the frogs were tagged with numbered tags and released. A week later, a second group of 15 bullfrogs was collected and given the same test with potato grubs as the food object (variable X_2). However, it turned out that 12 of the 15 frogs in the second group had tags from the first test. The data from 3 frogs were discarded from each set of scores and the summary terms from the raw data were

$$\overline{X}_1 = 1.67, \quad \overline{X}_2 = 1.0, \quad s^2 = 0.24,$$
$$\Sigma D = 8, \quad \Sigma D^2 = 9$$

13. A kindergarten teacher had a morning class and an afternoon class, each with 21 students, and wished to develop interest in art. Some research had shown that the amount of time spent in drawing was an influential variable, so the teacher's task became one of getting the children to spend more time drawing. During the morning period, she decided to use intrinsic motivation; she convinced the children that drawing is fun. During the afternoon period, she used an extrinsic reinforcer; she gave a candy for each 15 minutes spent drawing. Subsequently a measure was obtained from each child on how interesting drawing is; in this measure larger numerical scores reflect greater interest. Summary terms from the raw data were

$$\overline{X}_{morning} = 20, \quad \overline{X}_{afternoon} = 17, \quad s^2 = 10.5,$$
$$\Sigma D = 63, \quad \Sigma D^2 = 300$$

14. Margaret went shopping with a list of 16 items. She went to Sam's department store and determined the prices, and then went to Fred's department store and determined the prices of the very same items. Summary terms from the raw data were

$$\overline{X}_{Sam} = 11.11, \quad \overline{X}_{Fred} = 7.98, \quad s^2 = 8,$$
$$\Sigma D = 50, \quad \Sigma D^2 = 340$$

15. An experimenter drew two samples of 10 individuals from a population. In his intended experiment, the dependent variable was a jumping measure and he therefore wanted the two groups to have similar average heights so that this factor would not confound the independent variable. He relied on random sampling to accomplish this in his two groups, but when he examined their height scores before beginning his experiment, he saw that group #1 had a mean of 168 cm and group #2 had a mean of 175 cm. He thus had to determine whether or not he could safely proceed. Other summary terms from the raw data were

$$s^2 = 45, \qquad \Sigma D = 70, \qquad \Sigma D^2 = 600$$

16. Thirteen men and 13 women tested a weight reducing plan. Each person was weighed (variable X_1) and then put on a special diet and exercise routine for three weeks, following which they were reweighed (variable X_2). Summary terms from the raw data were

$$\overline{X}_1 = 182, \qquad \overline{X}_2 = 179, \qquad s^2 = 104,$$
$$\Sigma D = 80, \qquad \Sigma D^2 = 400$$

17. Fifteen people entered a contest for "most beautiful moustache." Each moustache was appraised and given a score by a female judge and then independently by a male judge, thus yielding two sets of scores. Summary terms from the raw data were

$$\overline{X}_{female} = 8.7, \qquad \overline{X}_{male} = 7.4, \qquad s^2 = 3,$$
$$\Sigma D = 20, \qquad \Sigma D^2 = 120$$

18. A newspaper reporter went to a local pub on the evening before the government announced the new budget and asked 10 people to rate the government's performance to date. The evening after the budget was announced she returned to the same pub and again asked 10 people to rate the government's performance. When she got back to her office, however, she found that six of the persons interviewed on the second night were ones that had been interviewed on the first night. She discarded the data from four subjects from each night's collection and proceeded with the analysis. Summary terms from the raw data were

$$\overline{X}_1 = 7, \qquad \overline{X}_2 = 3, \qquad s^2 = 3,$$
$$\Sigma D = 24, \qquad \Sigma D^2 = 126$$

8.11 Assumptions Underlying the *t*-Test

The *t*-test is based on certain assumptions concerning the raw data. When one refers to assumptions underlying a statistical test, it is meant that the accuracy of the decision reached depends upon certain conditions being fulfilled.

Decision-making accuracy refers to having a true probability associated with the decision that is equal to the confidence level used in the significance test. For example, when we reject a null hypothesis at 0.05 level of confidence, it means that there is a 0.05 or less probability that the observed outcome would happen as a function of sampling error. But if the assumptions upon which our procedure is based have been grossly violated, the probability of a Type I error may be higher than the confidence level used. Thus departures from the required underlying conditions can cause erroneous decisions to be made. Given that the raw data represent interval/ratio measurement, the underlying assumptions of the *t*-test are: (1) that the subjects were obtained by random sampling, (2) that the groups of scores are random samples from normally distributed populations, and (3) that the groups of scores are samples from populations that have equal variances.

The random selection of subjects, and their random assignment to treatment groups in the case of independent groups experiments, insures that the scores obtained are independent of each other. The null hypothesis is tested with reference to sampling error probabilities based on random sampling, and if the data are not obtained from randomly selected and randomly assigned individuals, the validity of the test may suffer. The second assumption is that both sets of scores are random samples from normally distributed populations. The control scores are assumed to be a random sample of the scores that would be obtained if all members of the population were measured for the dependent variable. It is assumed that the distribution so obtained would be normal, meaning that the dependent variable measure is assumed to be normally distributed in the population. The experimental scores are assumed to be a random sample from the distribution of scores that would be obtained if every member of the population were exposed to the independent variable and then measured for the dependent variable. This distribution is also assumed to be normal, which means that the independent variable is presumed not to alter the shape of the distribution of scores produced under its influence relative to untreated subjects' scores. The third assumption is that the two groups of scores represent populations with equal (not significantly different) variances. This assumption may be tested by determining whether the two sample variances are significantly different. Such procedures are known as tests for homogeneity of variance and should be applied whenever there is concern that the variances may be grossly dissimilar (see Section 9.3).

It is probable that one or more of the underlying assumptions is violated to some extent in every real-life case. The *t*-test is termed a *robust* statistical procedure, which means that moderate violations of some of the underlying assumptions do not affect the accuracy of decisions reached. Glass and Stanley (1970) state that violation of the assumption of normality in the *t*-test has "only trivial effects" and is "no cause for concern." Violation of the assumption of equal variance is also not considered serious if n_1 and n_2 are equal; this

robust

is the principal reason that experimenters prefer equal *n*'s in independent groups experiments. Thus, the *t*-test can be used with fair confidence in a wide range of circumstances. Please note however, that violation of underlying assumptions can be moderate or gross, and no analysis, regardless of how robust, should be used without regard for its fundamental underlying requirements. The assumption that the raw scores are independent, which is the direct consequence of random selection and random assignment of subjects, is crucial, however, and may not be violated with impunity.

An aside: be alert to underlying assumptions

A colleague of mine performed an experiment in which the subjects were two groups of laboratory rats, the independent variable was amount of reward, and the dependent variable was running speed down a straight runway. The data were analyzed by an independent groups *t*-test and a report was submitted for publication. The editor suggested that while there is no lower limit to rats' running speed, there is an upper limit when they are going as fast as they can, and this speed is about the same for all rats. Thus, the population distribution is skewed and the raw scores cannot be regarded as samples from normal populations; consequently, analysis by *t*-test was inappropriate. The editor's view prevailed and the data were reanalyzed.

The lessons for us all are that the responsibility for valid decisions rests with the experimenter, not with the statistical analysis, and that we should pause and consider the kind and nature of the data we collect rather than automatically assume that the assumptions required for analysis have been met. I sometimes get the impression that many students do not question whether their data meets underlying assumptions out of fear that the answer could be no, and then all would be lost. This is not a realistic fear; there are ways to normalize distributions and homogenize variances, and one always has recourse to nonparametric analyses such as are presented in Chapters 14 and 15. Be alert to situations wherein the population distributions might be nonsymmetrical and/or non-normal, and at least inspect the raw data visually to see whether it seems that variances are grossly different.

8.12 One-Tailed and Two-Tailed Tests

We have so far chosen critical values for significance from the columns in Table B that are labeled two-tailed tests. We judged a *t* to be significant if it equaled the tabled value or exceeded it in either a positive or negative direction, or in other words was beyond the cutoff point at either the positive or *two-tailed test* negative tail of the reference distribution. In the *two-tailed test,* the direction of the effect is of no concern; the null hypothesis predicts that *t* = 0, and we reject the null hypothesis if our calculated *t* is sufficiently different from 0 in

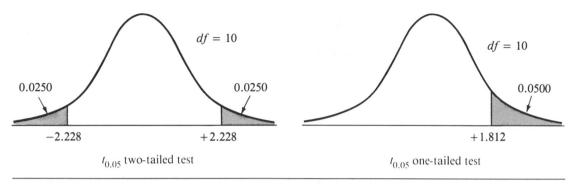

Figure 8.12–1   Two-tailed and one-tailed critical values for *t* when *df* = 10.

either a positive or negative direction. Thus we worded null hypotheses in terms such as, "alcohol ingestion does not affect motor co-ordination," and were not concerned with whether alcohol ingestion improved or worsened motor co-ordination.

In a *one-tailed test,* the direction of the effect is of concern. Whereas the 0.05 level two-tailed test critical value for *t* cuts off 2.5 percent of the reference distribution at each tail, in the case of the one-tailed test, the 0.05 level critical value cuts off 5 percent of the reference distribution at one tail only, as is shown in Figure 8.12–1. Inspection of Table B will confirm this since, for any *df*, the one-tailed test critical value at alpha level of confidence equals the two-tailed test critical value at twice alpha level of confidence.

one-tailed test

One-tailed hypotheses not only state whether the two sets of scores will differ but specify in addition the direction of that difference. For example, a one-tailed alternative hypothesis might be, "alcohol ingestion will worsen motor coordination," and a one-tailed null hypothesis might be, "alcohol ingestion will not worsen motor coordination." Keep in mind that the interpretation is always a rejection or retention of the null hypothesis being tested so that the interpretation of a one-tailed test also has this directional quality. Furthermore, the null hypothesis is formulated before data are collected. Experimenters must therefore reject or retain the null hypothesis they started with and not fabricate an appropriate one after the analysis has been completed.

Since the direction of an effect would seem always to be a matter of concern, and since the one-tailed critical value is smaller and it is therefore easier to obtain a significant result, one might think that one-tailed tests would be preferred. This is not necessarily the case, however, because it has been suggested that the one-tailed test is less robust with respect to violation of the assumption of normality than the two-tailed test (Ferguson, 1981). Thus some consider it better scientific practice to use the two-tailed test. Of course the direction of any observed effect remains an important matter, but, having established a significant difference using the two-tailed test, there is nothing to prevent an experimenter from stating the direction of the difference by reference to the raw data. One might say, "alcohol ingestion affects motor coordination, and inspection of the raw data indicated that motor coordination was poorer under the alcohol ingestion condition," or, "Girl Guides differ from Boy Scouts in cookie selling ability and inspection of the raw data indicated that Girl Guides sold more cookies." In this way one can communicate a complete picture of what happened.

8.13 Review Exercise

1. Define or describe the following terms.
    (a) *t* distribution
    (b) independent groups experiment
    (c) interpretation
    (d) repeated measures experiment
    (e) correlated samples experiment
    (f) robust
    (g) two-tailed test
    (h) one-tailed test

9 Single Factor Analysis of Variance

Chapter Preview

9.1 Introduction

Many research problems are not necessarily confined to the comparison of two groups or sets of scores. For example, if you were curious about whether different breeds of cats differed in mouse-catching ability, as in Exercise 8.8–1, you could test Persian, Burmese, and Korat cats in addition to Siamese and Manx. The experiment would then involve five subject groups and would provide much more information about the relationship, if any, between breed and mouse-catching ability than an experiment limited to two groups. In an experiment designed to explore the relationship between training and task performance, as in the illustration example used in Section 8.9, the measure of task performance could be taken after two, four, six, and eight training trials instead of just after four and six trials. Again, such an experiment would yield much more information than could be learned from a comparison of any two training levels. Experiments involving three or more groups or sets of scores are frequently evaluated using statistical procedures known as analysis of variance. We shall examine these procedures in Sections 9.4 and 9.6, but first it is necessary to become acquainted with the conceptual foundation for this form of analysis and Sections 9.2 and 9.3 provide this introduction.

9.2 The *F*-Ratio and *F* Distributions

Imagine that two independent random samples are drawn from a population, arbitrarily labeled Sample 1 and Sample 2, but are not treated differently in any way. A measure is obtained on every subject and the variances of the two samples are calculated (s_1^2 and s_2^2 for Sample 1 and Sample 2 respectively). Since each variance term is based on an independent random sample, each is an estimate of the population variance (σ^2), and, if no sampling error was associated with either sample, we would expect that $s_1^2 = \sigma^2$, $s_2^2 = \sigma^2$, and $s_1^2 = s_2^2$. We could form a ratio of the two sample variances by arbitrarily placing s_1^2 in the numerator and s_2^2 in the denominator; the ratio of two variances is known as an F-*ratio,* or simply as *F*. Thus

F-*ratio*

$$F = \frac{s_1^2}{s_2^2}$$

If there were no sampling error, we would expect that $F = 1.00$; however, both samples are likely to contain sampling error and s_1^2 is unlikely to be exactly equal to s_2^2. Thus, the *F*-ratio will sometimes be larger than 1.00 and sometimes smaller. Suppose the process in which two independent random samples are drawn and their variances calculated and expressed as an *F*-ratio is continued until all possible combinations of pairs of samples have occurred. The frequency distribution of *F*-ratios thus obtained would be termed the sampling distribution of *F* (the sampling distribution of s_1^2/s_2^2), or F *distribution,* and might have the appearance of the curve shown in Figure 9.2–1.

F *distribution*

Notice that the sampling distribution of *F* is positively skewed with a mode between 0.00 and 1.00. The nonsymmetrical shape results from the fact that a variance has no upper limit but does have a lower limit equal to zero when the scores are a set of constants. Thus for any denominator variance (s_2^2), the numerator variance (s_1^2) may range upward as far as infinity but downward only as far as zero; consequently, the *F*-ratio may range upward from 1.00 to infinity but downward only from 1.00 to 0.00. Since we are dealing with independent random samples and identifying them as Sample 1 and Sample 2 arbitrarily, s_1^2 has an equal probability of being larger or smaller than s_2^2. If *F* has an equal probability of being larger or smaller than 1.00, the median of an *F* distribution should be 1.00, with half of the distribution lying above, and half below, this value. Such a distribution will be positively skewed.

This conceptual picture of the sampling distribution of *F* is oversimplified; unfortunately, the real world is more complicated. Remember that *F* is the ratio of two variances, s_1^2 and s_2^2, which are calculated from samples

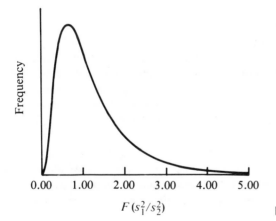

$F(s_1^2/s_2^2)$

Figure 9.2–1   A typical *F* distribution

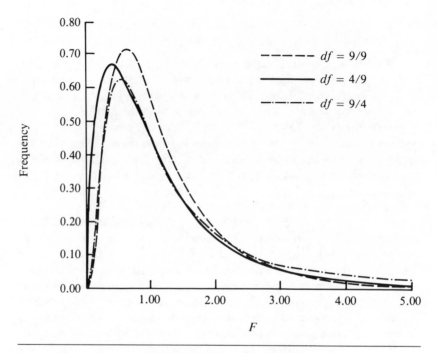

Figure 9.2–2   Distribution of F at $df = 9/9$, $4/9$, and $9/4$

of sizes n_1 and n_2, and thus have degrees of freedom equal to $n_1 - 1$ and $n_2 - 1$ respectively. This means that every F-ratio is associated with two degrees of freedom terms. For example, if $n_1 = 10$ and $n_2 = 10$, the F-ratio has a numerator variance based on 9 degrees of freedom ($df_1 = 10 - 1 = 9$), and a denominator variance based on 9 degrees of freedom ($df_2 = 10 - 1 = 9$); such an F-ratio is a single term in the sampling distribution of F at $9/9$ degrees of freedom. Similarly, if $n_1 = 5$ and $n_2 = 10$, then F, as the ratio of s_1^2/s_2^2, is a term in the sampling distribution of F at $4/9$ degrees of freedom. The F distribution at $df = 4/9$ is different from the one at $df = 9/9$. There is a different sampling distribution of F for each combination of numerator and denominator degrees of freedom. The family of F distributions is a large one and the curves that comprise it vary in their degree of skewness. Figure 9.2–2 presents several F distributions and indicates something of this range of shapes.

The F distributions occur in a range of shapes because the accuracy of s^2 as an estimate of σ^2 is a function of its degrees of freedom. With smaller degrees of freedom the variability of s^2 increases and its sampling distribution becomes more positively skewed. The expected value (mean) of F is determined by the degrees of freedom of s_2^2 [expected $F = df_2/(df_2 - 2)$ where

$df_2 > 2$]; the shape of the sampling distribution of F is determined jointly by the shapes of the sampling distributions of s_1^2 and s_2^2, and is different for each combination of df_1 and df_2.

A simple approximation to a sampling distribution of F can be generated using an ordinary deck of playing cards with the jacks, queens, and kings being given the numerical values of 11, 12, and 13 respectively. Suppose a sample of size three is drawn from the deck, the cards replaced and shuffled, and then a second sample of three is drawn. The first sample can be labeled #1 and the second #2, and an F-ratio determined. The following data were obtained from 10 such pairs of samples.

Sample #1/Sample #2	$s_1^2/s_2^2 = F$
6, 5, 8/3, 5, 7	2.33/4.00 = 0.58
12, 8, 2/11, 4, 10	25.33/14.33 = 1.77
8, 3, 2/4, 6, 7	10.33/2.33 = 4.43
6, 6, 9/12, 11, 4	3.00/19.00 = 0.16
11, 1, 6/7, 1, 5	25.00/9.33 = 2.68
4, 10, 6/9, 12, 8	9.33/4.33 = 2.15
13, 8, 12/12, 12, 5	7.00/16.33 = 0.43
7, 11, 11/4, 10, 2	5.33/17.33 = 0.31
6, 8, 11/7, 3, 6	6.33/4.33 = 1.46
5, 12, 5/11, 4, 10	16.33/14.33 = 1.14

You can see that, although the s^2 terms are quite variable, the F-ratios tend to be small and skewed toward the lower end of their range. Figure 9.2–3 shows a plot of F-ratios obtained from 50 pairs of samples of three cards drawn from a deck as described earlier. It is evident that this distribution resembles the typical shape of F distributions; if the process were continued, the curve would smooth out and eventually approximate the sampling distribution of F at $df = 2/2$.

Table D contains critical values for F at 0.05 and 0.01 confidence levels in F distributions identified by reading columns and rows for numerator variance and denominator variance degrees of freedom respectively. The entries in Table D cut off the confidence level proportion of the sampling distribution at the upper, or right-hand, tail. For example, in the F distribution at $df = 9/9$ $[(n_1 - 1)/(n_2 - 1) = 9/9]$, the 0.05 confidence level critical value for F is 3.18. In other words, the probability is 0.05 or less that an F-ratio drawn at random from this distribution will equal or exceed 3.18. When $df = 4/24$, the critical value for F at 0.05 confidence level is 2.78, as shown in Figure 9.2–4.

The entries in Table D are one-tailed critical values. We will use the F distributions to test hypotheses in connection with analysis of variance procedures, and for this purpose one-tailed critical values are appropriate. (The

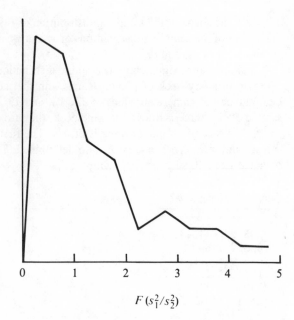

Figure 9.2–3 The distribution of *F*-ratios obtained from 50 pairs of samples ($n_1 = n_2 = 3$) drawn from a deck of cards

$$F(s_1^2/s_2^2)$$

rationale for this is explained in Section 9.4). As a point of information, however, the critical value for *F* that cuts off the confidence level proportion of the left tail of the distribution is the reciprocal of the entry in Table D. Thus, when $df = 9/9$, the value of *F* that cuts off the bottom 0.0500 of the distribu-

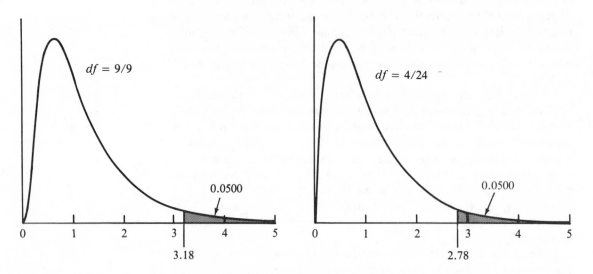

Figure 9.2–4 The 0.05 confidence level critical values for *F* when $df = 9/9$ and 4/24

tion is $1/3.18 = 0.3145$. Similarly, when $df = 4/24$, the value $1/2.78 = 0.3597$ cuts off the bottom 0.0500 of the distribution.

9.3 Homogeneity of Variance

Procedures for determining whether two or more variances differ significantly are known generally as tests of homogeneity of variance. The sampling distribution of F may be used to test whether two variances are significantly different; this may be termed a simple F-*test*. The deviation of any F from its expected value is a function of the difference in magnitude between s_1^2 and s_2^2; for example, in order that $F = 2.00$, s_1^2 must be twice as large as s_2^2. Since the sampling distributions of F for different df_1/df_2 combinations are known, one can determine the probability of occurrence of any given F-ratio. An F-ratio with a low probability of occurrence indicates that the difference between s_1^2 and s_2^2 has a low probability of occurrence. Determining whether F is significant is a test of the null hypothesis that $\sigma_1^2 = \sigma_2^2 = \sigma^2$. A significant F-ratio means that s_1^2 and s_2^2 are estimates of different population variances ($\sigma_1^2 \neq \sigma_2^2$), which in turn means that s_1^2 differs significantly from s_2^2. The essential logic of the F-test is that any two independently obtained variances may be expressed as an F-ratio and tested for significance.

For example, suppose that two samples, each having $n = 5$, were found to have variances of $s_1^2 = 19.50$ and $s_2^2 = 3.00$. The resulting F-ratio is $19.50/3.00 = 6.50$ and may be tested for significance by reference to Table D at $df = 4/4$. The 0.05 confidence level critical value for F is 6.39 and therefore this result is significant. Remember that the entries in Table D are one-tailed. The null hypothesis being tested, therefore, is also one-tailed and is that s_1^2 is not larger than s_2^2; that is, σ_1^2 is not larger than σ_2^2. A significant F-ratio, as obtained in this example, means that s_1^2 is significantly larger than s_2^2. If we had placed s_2^2 in the numerator, then the critical value for F would have been $1/6.39 = 0.16$, and our F-ratio would have been $3.00/19.50 = 0.15$. The result is again significant* and we can reject the null hypothesis that s_2^2 is not smaller than s_1^2. The two-tailed null hypothesis that σ_1^2 does not differ from σ_2^2 may be tested at 0.05 level of confidence by placing the larger variance in the numerator and selecting the 0.025 confidence level critical value for F. This procedure constitutes a two-tailed test because the identification of the numerator variance is random, since either of the two could be the larger, and the 0.025 confidence level critical value cuts off 0.0250 of the F distribution at the right tail, the direction of increasing F-ratio magnitude. In any

F-test

---

*It may seem anomalous that in this case a result is significant when it is smaller than the critical value. Remember that the F distributions have a lower limit of zero as compared to $-\infty$ for the normal and t distributions; thus, given a lower tail critical value, a significant term would be one that is closer to zero, or smaller.

two-tailed test, the critical value cuts off one-half alpha proportion of the distribution at each tail.

Numerous methods exist for testing homogeneity of variance among three or more variances. They are not delineated in this text because they are generally not very sensitive and are not robust with respect to departures from normality, and are therefore of limited utility (see Winer, 1971; Glass & Stanley, 1970). This matter will be raised again in Section 9.9.

9.4 Single Factor Analysis of Variance: Independent Groups

Analysis of variance may be used to determine whether significant differences exist among the means of three or more groups of scores. In behavioral science, many independent variables of interest can occur at more than two levels; examples of this are methods of training, type of reinforcement, income tax bracket, and religious affiliation. Identifying all possible significant differences among several groups of scores by means of t-tests would not only be cumbersome but also would increase the overall probability of a Type I error because conducting several tests provides more opportunities for a Type I error to occur. For example, if five breeds of cat were tested for mouse-catching ability, $\binom{5}{2} = 10$ different t-tests would be required to examine all possible pairs of breeds for possible significant differences. The overall probability of occurrence of one Type I error could thus be as high as $\binom{10}{1}(0.05)^1(0.95)^9 = 0.315$. The analysis of variance (ANOVA), which is a single significance test, overcomes this problem.

single factor

Single factor analysis of variance refers to designs using one independent variable that is presented at several levels or strengths. An experiment might have a control group and three experimental groups each receiving a different dosage concentration of a drug; in this case, the independent variable would be the amount of the drug administered. The phrase "independent groups" indicates that a separate randomly sampled group of subjects is tested under each independent variable level or condition. If an experiment involves k groups of subjects, the ANOVA tests the null hypothesis that $\mu_1 = \mu_2 = \cdots = \mu_k$; that is, that the k groups of scores are all random samples from the same population and the k means are all estimates of the same population mean. In terms of the independent and dependent variables, the null hypothesis is that the independent variable does not affect, or is not related to, the dependent variable. The logic of this process will be presented briefly and then examined in more detail with the aid of a numerical example.

An aside on terminology

The discussion of analysis of variance will be more comprehensible if you keep in mind the meaning of variability and variance. The term variability is used to refer to the conceptual notion of differences among raw data scores.

The term variance encompasses both the notion of variability and refers to a specific measure of it. Its use is therefore somewhat more restricted, for example, an *F* term is a ratio of variances, not a ratio of variabilities.

The analysis of variance takes the total variability in the complete set of dependent variable scores and divides that total variability into components that can be attributed to different sources. The variances (amounts of variability) attributed to these different sources are then used to form *F*-ratios, which can be tested for significance. ANOVA is often referred to as the *F*-test. Since the numerator and denominator variances represent different sources of variability, the *F* term reflects the relative amounts of variability that can be attributed to these sources. A significant *F* term is taken to mean that the different sources contribute significantly different amounts to the total variance. In this way, one can make decisions regarding the relative influences of the sources of variability.

A typical case might involve three groups of subjects, such as a control group and two levels of some independent variable. The ANOVA divides the total variance into within groups and between groups components. *Within groups variance* refers to the amount of variability among the scores within each group; this can only be a function of sampling error, that is, chance differences between subjects. *Between groups variance* refers to the amount of variability occurring between the groups, that is, the scores in one group compared to those in another. Between groups variability could be a function of sampling error or the effect of the independent variable. If the independent variable is having any effect on the dependent variable scores, it will appear as differences between the groups of scores. When the null hypothesis is true, that is, when the independent variable does not affect the dependent variable, the within groups variance and the between groups variance are both the result of sampling error. This means that they are merely different ways of estimating the population variance and therefore should be approximately equal. If the null hypothesis is false, the effect of the independent variable will be to increase the between groups variance. Thus an *F*-ratio that has between groups variance in the numerator and within groups variance in the denominator will increase in magnitude as the effect of the independent variable becomes more pronounced. A significant *F*-ratio means that between groups variance is significantly larger than within groups variance and is the basis for rejection of the null hypothesis.

As you read through the computational procedure, keep in mind the definition of variance: variance is the Sum of Squares (the sum of squared deviations from the mean) divided by the degrees of freedom. The general computational model for the single factor independent groups design proceeds as follows.

within groups variance

between groups variance

Group #1	Group #2	Group #3	
$X_{1,1}$	$X_{2,1}$	$X_{3,1}$	
$X_{1,2}$	$X_{2,2}$	$X_{3,2}$	
$X_{1,3}$	$X_{2,3}$	$X_{3,3}$	
$X_{1,4}$	$X_{2,4}$	$X_{3,4}$	
$X_{1,5}$	$X_{2,5}$	$X_{3,5}$	
T_1	T_2	T_3	$\sum X$

k = number of treatments (number of groups of scores)

n = number of scores in each group

N = total number of scores

The subscripts associated with the X's identify group membership and the individual subject's raw scores. For example, $X_{1,1}$ is the first subject's score in Group #1 and $X_{2,3}$ is the third subject's score in Group #2.* The symbol T represents group sum; T_1 is the sum of all Group #1 scores, T_2 is the sum of all Group #2 scores, and so on. The term $\sum X$ means the sum of all N scores (Note: $\sum X = \sum T$). The symbol k is used to identify the number of groups, or the total number of experimental treatments, including any control condition; in this case, $k = 3$. The symbols n and N are used to refer to the number of scores in each group and the total number of scores respectively; in this case, $n_1 = n_2 = n_3 = 5$, and $N = 15$. It is not necessary that the k groups have equal n's, but experimenters prefer this because ANOVA is more robust under this condition and also it makes certain followup analyses more convenient. (These will be discussed in Chapter 10).

The ANOVA computational procedure begins with the calculation of three terms.

(1) $\sum X^2 = X_{1,1}^2 + X_{1,2}^2 + X_{1,3}^2 + \cdots + X_{3,5}^2$

(2) $(\sum X)^2/N = (X_{1,1} + X_{1,2} + \cdots + X_{3,5})^2/N$

(3) $\sum (T^2/n) = T_1^2/n_1 + T_2^2/n_2 + T_3^2/n_3$

These terms are then combined to form the Sums of Squares of the between groups and the within groups variances.

$$SS_{\text{between groups}} = \sum (T^2/n) - (\sum X)^2/N$$

$$SS_{\text{within groups}} = \sum X^2 - \sum (T^2/n)$$

*Subscript notation systems are not consistent from one text to another and sometimes not even within a given text. The rule of thumb adopted here is that the last number identifies the subject and previous numbers identify group membership or independent variable level.

The variance attributable to differences between the groups of scores is termed the between groups Mean Square ($MS_{\text{between groups}}$) and is obtained by dividing the between groups Sum of Squares ($SS_{\text{between groups}}$) by the between groups degrees of freedom, which is one less than the number of groups ($k - 1$). The variance attributable to differences within the groups of scores is termed the within groups Mean Square ($MS_{\text{within groups}}$) and is obtained by dividing the within groups Sum of Squares ($SS_{\text{within groups}}$) by the within groups degrees of freedom, which is equal to $N - k$. When the k groups have equal n's, the within groups degrees of freedom may be understood as $k(n - 1)$. The F-ratio in this analysis is defined as $MS_{\text{between groups}}$ divided by $MS_{\text{within groups}}$.

$$MS_{\text{between groups}} = SS_{\text{between groups}}/k - 1$$

$$MS_{\text{within groups}} = SS_{\text{within groups}}/N - k$$

$$F = \frac{MS_{\text{between groups}}}{MS_{\text{within groups}}}$$

The analysis of variance is presented in a standard tabular format.

Source of Variation	Sum of Squares	df	Mean Square	F
Between groups	$\sum (T^2/n) - (\sum X)^2/N$	$k - 1$	$\dfrac{SS_{\text{between gps}}}{k - 1}$	$\dfrac{MS_{\text{between gps}}}{MS_{\text{within gps}}}$
Within groups	$\sum X^2 - \sum (T^2/n)$	$N - k$	$\dfrac{SS_{\text{within gps}}}{N - k}$	

Suppose that 40 randomly selected people were randomly divided into 4 groups of 10. Each person was set to work on a set of arithmetic and verbal reasoning problems and testing took place in a pressure chamber, which could be adjusted to simulate atmospheric pressure at various altitudes. The control group worked at sea level pressure, while members of the experimental groups worked at simulated altitudes of 1000, 2000, and 3000 meters respectively. The measure taken was the total number of problems correctly solved in a 45-minute period. The null hypothesis being tested was that atmospheric pressure does not affect problem-solving efficiency, that is, $\mu_{\text{sea level}} = \mu_{1000 \text{ m}} = \mu_{2000 \text{ m}} = \mu_{3000 \text{ m}}$. [Note: The presentation of this numerical example follows a standard format. It is highly recommended that the student follow this step-by-step format when working out practice exercises, as it will simplify and clarify the analysis procedure.] Thus

Independent variable: Atmospheric pressure (simulated)

Dependent variable: Problem-solving efficiency (defined operationally as the number of problems correctly solved in 45 minutes)

Null hypothesis: Atmospheric pressure does not affect problem-solving efficiency ($\mu_{\text{sea level}} = \mu_{1000 \text{ m}} = \mu_{2000 \text{ m}} = \mu_{3000 \text{ m}}$).

#1 (sea level)	#2 (1000 m)	#3 (2000 m)	#4 (3000 m)
12 *144*	16	16	8
15 *225*	14	11	7
14 *196*	16	17	13
14 *196*	17	13	12
16	14	13	11
19	18	15	15
15	12	11	11
17	17	10	12
15	10	16	13
15	12	11	9

$T_1 = 152$ $T_2 = 146$ $T_3 = 133$ $T_4 = 111$ $\Sigma X = 542$

$$k = 4, \quad n = 10, \quad N = 40$$

(1) $\quad \Sigma X^2 = 7650.00$

(2) $\quad (\Sigma X)^2/N = (542)^2/40$

$$= 7344.10$$

(3) $\quad \Sigma (T^2/n) = (152)^2/10 + (146)^2/10 + (133)^2/10 + (111)^2/10$

$$= 7443.00$$

$$SS_{\text{between groups}} = \Sigma (T^2/n) - (\Sigma X)^2/N$$
$$= 7443.00 - 7344.10$$
$$= 98.90$$

$$SS_{\text{within groups}} = \Sigma X^2 - \Sigma (T^2/n)$$
$$= 7650.00 - 7443.00$$
$$= 207.00$$

Source of Variation	Sum of Squares	df	Mean Square	F
Between groups	98.90	3	32.97	5.73
Within groups	207.00	36	5.75	

1. $df = (k - 1)/(N - k) = (4 - 1)/(40 - 4) = 3/36$
2. The critical value for F at 0.05 confidence level $= 2.86$
3. Therefore the result is significant.
4. Interpretation: Atmospheric pressure affects problem-solving efficiency.

Since the calculated F term ($F = 5.73$) is significant, that is, equal to or larger than the critical value for F at 3/36 degrees of freedom, the null hypothesis may be rejected and the result interpreted to mean that atmospheric pressure does affect problem-solving efficiency. This outcome only enables us to retain the general alternative hypothesis that atmospheric pressure affects problem-solving efficiency. We have no information about any particular comparison, for example, whether the sea level scores differ from the 1000 meter scores. All that we know is that among the k treatment groups, at least one pair are significantly different at 0.05 confidence level. The identification of precisely which groups differ from which others requires an additional procedure that we shall encounter in Chapter 10.

It may happen on occasion that Table D does not contain entries for the particular degrees of freedom that you seek. In this situation you may either consult a more complete set of statistical tables in the library or use the critical value at the next smaller degrees of freedom. The reason for using the next smaller df, rather than simply the nearest, is that critical values for significance increase as df decreases; choosing the next smaller value will not increase the risk of a Type I error. For example, suppose that you seek the critical value for F at $df = 2/87$, and that your calculated F term is 3.10. If you use the critical value at $df = 2/100$, the result will be judged significant, but if you use the critical value at $df = 2/60$, it would be judged non-significant. The point is that you cannot know for certain whether $F = 3.10$ is significant at $df = 2/87$. You should choose the more conservative option, that is, use the critical value at the smaller degrees of freedom because this action will reduce rather than increase the probability of a Type I error. This rule of thumb applies as well when you are seeking critical values for other statistics.

An aside: a time to be conservative

The remainder of this section explains the rationale behind the subdivision of the total variance into between groups and within groups components. By referring to the numerical example, we will show the derivation of $SS_{\text{between groups}}$ and $SS_{\text{within groups}}$ from the raw data. Earlier it was stated that all ANOVA procedures divide the total variance in the data into components attributable to different sources. Remember that the numerator term of any variance is a Sum of Squares, which is literally the sum of squared deviations about the mean. When we have a set of observations subdivided into groups, the deviation of any individual score from the overall mean may be subdivided into two parts: the deviation of the observation from the mean of its group, and the deviation of that group mean from the overall mean. Thus

$$X - \overline{X}_{overall} = (X - \overline{X}_{group}) + (\overline{X}_{group} - \overline{X}_{overall})$$

In terms of the symbols we have been using, this expression may be written as

$$X - \overline{X} = [X - (T/n)] + [(T/n) - \overline{X}]$$

If we select any observation, such as $X_{2,1}$, it can be shown that this is true. Note:

$$\overline{X} = 542/40 = 13.55$$

and

$$T_2/n = 146/10 = 14.60$$

Thus

$$(16 - 13.55) = (16 - 14.60) + (14.60 - 13.55)$$
$$2.45 = 1.40 + 1.05$$

This relationship for individual scores can be generalized to Sums of Squares. Thus

$$\Sigma (X - \overline{X})^2 = \Sigma (X - T/n)^2 + \Sigma (T/n - \overline{X})^2$$

This is the symbolic way of saying that the total Sum of Squares can be divided into a Sum of Squares reflecting variability within the groups, $\Sigma (X - T/n)^2$, and a Sum of Squares reflecting variability between the groups, $\Sigma (T/n - \overline{X})^2$.

If we wanted to calculate the total Sum of Squares for our numerical example it would be

$$SS_{total} = \Sigma X^2 - (\Sigma X)^2/N = 7650 - (542)^2/40 = 305.90$$

If we examine the results of the ANOVA, we find that

$$SS_{total} = SS_{between\ groups} + SS_{within\ groups}$$
$$305.90 = 98.90 + 207.00$$

Let us consider the within groups variance. Examination of the raw data indicates that variability exists within each of the treatment groups. Yet there is no reason for this variability to exist since the members of each treatment group receive identical experimental procedures. The scores differ because people differ, and the within group variability is simply the result of chance differences among randomly selected people. If one were to calculate the variances of the groups of scores separately, the following results would be obtained.

(1)   (sea level): $s_1^2 = \dfrac{2342 - (152)^2/10}{10 - 1} = 31.60/9 = 3.51$

(2)   (1000 m): $s_2^2 = \dfrac{2194 - (146)^2/10}{10 - 1} = 62.40/9 = 6.93$

(3)   (2000 m): $s_3^2 = \dfrac{1827 - (133)^2/10}{10 - 1} = 58.10/9 = 6.46$

(4)   (3000 m): $s_4^2 = \dfrac{1287 - (111)^2/10}{10 - 1} = 54.90/9 = 6.10$

Observe that

$$SS_{\text{within groups}} = SS_1 + SS_2 + SS_3 + SS_4$$
$$207.00 = 31.60 + 62.40 + 58.10 + 54.90$$

and that

$$MS_{\text{within groups}} = (s_1^2 + s_2^2 + s_3^2 + s_4^2)/k$$
$$5.75 = (3.51 + 6.93 + 6.46 + 6.10)/4$$

The $SS_{\text{within groups}}$ is simply the sum of the Sums of Squares of the k groups of scores, and the $MS_{\text{within groups}}$ is equal to the mean of the variances of the k groups of scores. Since each s^2 is an estimate of σ^2, the expected value of $MS_{\text{within groups}}$ is σ^2.

Let us now consider the between groups term in the ANOVA. Variability between the groups of scores is manifested by variability among the treatment mean ($\overline{T}$) values. We must ask ourselves why these means differ. One possible reason is the effect of the independent variable, which, if it is influencing subjects' behavior, will result in scores that differ from those in the control condition. This would appear as greater variability among the treatment means. But even if the null hypothesis were true, we could not expect the treatment means to be identical because the four groups represent independent random samples from the population and, as some sampling error is inevitable, the treatment means would show some differences as a function of chance. If we were to calculate the variance of the four treatment means we would obtain

$$\overline{T}_1 = 15.20 \qquad \overline{T}_2 = 14.60 \qquad \overline{T}_3 = 13.30 \qquad \overline{T}_4 = 11.10$$
$$\overline{T} = 13.55$$

$$s_{\bar{T}}^2 = \frac{\sum \bar{T}^2 - (\sum \bar{T})^2/k}{k - 1}$$

$$= \frac{744.30 - (54.20)^2/4}{4 - 1}$$

$$= 9.89/3$$

$$= 3.297$$

If we multiply this result by n, we obtain $3.297 \times 10 = 32.97$, which is the $MS_{\text{between groups}}$ in the ANOVA. Thus, the $MS_{\text{between groups}}$ is the variance of the treatment means multiplied by the number of observations making up each mean.

$$MS_{\text{between groups}} = ns_{\bar{T}}^2$$

There is an obvious logic to this since each treatment mean is derived from n scores. Since $s_{\bar{T}}^2$ is an estimate of $\sigma_{\bar{X}}^2$, which in turn is equal to σ^2/n, it can be seen that the expected value of $ns_{\bar{T}}^2$ is σ^2, $(n\sigma_{\bar{X}}^2 = \sigma^2)$.

The point behind this exposition is to demonstrate that $MS_{\text{between groups}}$ is a variance term that reflects the variability of the treatment means taking into account that each is based on a number of observations. When the null hypothesis is true, this term, like the $MS_{\text{within groups}}$, is an estimate of population variance and, roughly speaking, the $MS_{\text{between groups}}$ and $MS_{\text{within groups}}$ should be approximately equal. Thus when the null hypothesis is true, the F-ratio should approximate unity, with allowances for the factors that determine the expected value of F as outlined in Section 9.2. When the null hypothesis is false, $MS_{\text{between groups}}$ will increase relative to $MS_{\text{within groups}}$, and the F-ratio will become larger. The null hypothesis may be rejected if it is found that the obtained F-ratio had 0.05 (or whatever confidence level is chosen) or less probability of occurring as a function of sampling error.

You will remember from Section 9.2 that the sampling distributions of F are skewed. The significance test for F is conducted only on the right-hand tail, and the critical values for F obtained from Table D are cutoff points for the confidence proportion of the distribution at the upper end. The ANOVA is often referred to as a one-tailed test with the power of a two-tailed test; this apparent bit of double-talk may be understood as follows. If the independent variable affects the dependent variable, the consequence for the data can only be to increase between group variability; no other outcome is possible! Therefore, the null hypothesis can be rejected only on the right side of the distribution. This is because the right side of the F distributions contain the increasing F values, and the F-ratio in ANOVA is so constructed that the F term increases as the null hypothesis becomes less probable. What is happening is that the effect, if any, of the independent variable is being tested in the only direction that it can take.

Single Factor Independent Groups ANOVA

A computer manufacturer, who wanted to test the ease of use of three different keyboard layouts, produced five of each type. Fifteen randomly selected persons with no previous keyboard experience were each given one computer to use for one week; at the end of this period all computers were returned. Internal clocks and counters recorded the total time the computer was switched on and the total number of keystrokes during the one-week trial period. Previous data gathered by the manufacturer had shown that keyboards that are relatively easier to use result in a greater number of keystrokes per minute of use; thus, the measure taken was the mean number of keystrokes per minute over the trial period. The raw data are shown next.

Independent variable: Keyboard layout

Dependent variable: Ease of use (defined operationally as the mean number of keystrokes per minute)

Null hypothesis: Keyboard layout does not affect ease of use ($\mu_{\#1} = \mu_{\#2} = \mu_{\#3}$)

#1	#2	#3
90	75	85
83	66	75
102	84	93
79	50	62
86	60	70

$T_1 = 440$ $\qquad$ $T_2 = 335$ $\qquad$ $T_3 = 385$ $\quad$ $\sum X = 1160$

$k = 3, \quad n = 5, \quad N = 15$

(1) $\sum X^2 = 92,410.00$
(2) $(\sum X)^2/N = (1,160)^2/15 = 89,706.67$
(3) $\sum (T^2/n) = (440)^2/5 + (335)^2/5 + (385)^2/5 = 90,810.00$

$$
\begin{aligned}
SS_{\text{between groups}} &= \sum (T^2/n) - (\sum X)^2/N \\
&= 90,810.00 - 89,706.67 \\
&= 1,103.33
\end{aligned}
$$

$$
\begin{aligned}
SS_{\text{within groups}} &= \sum X^2 - \sum (T^2/n) \\
&= 92,410.00 - 90,810.00 \\
&= 1,600
\end{aligned}
$$

Source of Variation	Sum of Squares	df	Mean Square	F
Between groups	1103.33	2	551.67	4.14
Within groups	1600.00	12	133.33	

1. $df = (k - 1)/(N - k) = (3 - 1)/(15 - 3) = 2/12$
2. The critical value for F at 0.05 confidence level = 3.88
3. Therefore the result is significant.
4. Interpretation: Keyboard layout does affect ease of use.

An aside on ANOVA and *t*-test

Although they appear to be quite different computation procedures, the ANOVA and *t*-test are closely related. In fact, the *t*-test may be regarded as a special case of the more general analysis of variance procedure. When $k = 2$, the *t*-test is computationally more convenient, but such data could as well be analyzed by ANOVA. If an independent groups *t*-test and a single factor independent groups analysis of variance are performed on the same data, it will be found that $F = t^2$. A discussion of the relationship between the *t* and *F* statistics may be found in Hays, 1973.

9.5 Review Exercises

1. Define or describe the following terms.

   (a) *F*-ratio
   (b) *F* distribution
   (c) *F*-test
   (d) single factor ANOVA
   (e) within groups variation
   (f) between groups variation
   (g) mean square

The following problems present hypothetical or real research situations. In each case:

   (a) identify the independent variable
   (b) identify the dependent variable
   (c) state the null hypothesis being tested
   (d) complete the analysis at 0.05 confidence level
   (e) clearly interpret the result

2. Groups of people aged 4 years, 14 years, and 24 years were tested for generosity. Each subject was given a box lunch consisting of six separately packaged edibles, which he or she then went to eat on a park bench. Soon a same-sex person of equal age sat down beside the subject and commented that he or she had forgotten to bring lunch that day and did not have money to buy any food. The measure taken was the number of edible items the subject gave to the hungry stranger.

4-year-olds	14-year-olds	24-year-olds
3	2	0
2	0	1
4	3	2
3	1	0
3	2	1
3	3	1
5	2	3
3	0	1

3. In the years following World War II, immigrants and refugees from many nations arrived in North America. Fifteen years later, 10 families from each of 3 ethnic backgrounds were surveyed and measured for their success in adopting the North American lifestyle; the measure taken was annual income in thousands of dollars.

Nationality A	Nationality B	Nationality C
10.0	6.6	7.8
12.0	8.1	14.0
8.0	7.6	11.0
7.5	5.0	15.4
9.2	11.9	19.0
6.4	6.0	9.2
9.7	8.4	8.0
11.3	5.1	15.0
8.4	10.8	9.1
9.5	9.5	5.5

4. Four groups of subjects were randomly selected from a population of new Army recruits. One groups was fed a balanced diet containing fats (F), proteins (P), and carbohydrates (C). The diets of the other groups were identical except that one of the three nutrients was absent, with a different deficiency for each group. After three days under these conditions, all subjects were required to run an obstacle course as a test of their physical fitness. The number of minutes each subject required to complete the course was recorded.

FPC group	PC group	PF group	FC group
25	23	11	17
20	24	10	10
21	20	13	18
24	17	16	10
15	20	15	17
20	26	15	13

5. Groups of chimpanzees were given three hours of training on an instrumental response. Members of one group then received an electroshock (ECS), and members of a second group received two electroshocks, after which all subjects were retested. The following data represent percentage of errors on the retest trials.

Control	1 ECS	2 ECS
8	10	11
6	11	16
9	7	9
5	10	15
3	9	10
5		

6. A study by Bates & Horvath (1971) examined rats' ability to learn a discrimination problem while exposed to one of six auditory stimulus conditions. The stimulus conditions were: a selection of Mozart (M), a monotonic amelodic version of the Mozart piece (MAM); a selection of Schoenberg (S); a monotonic amelodic version of the Schoenberg piece (MAS); white noise (WN); and quiet (Q). The Mozart music was selected as representing a rhythmic stimulation; the monotonic amelodic version of Mozart retains the rhythm structure but removes note variation; the Schoenberg music may be termed melodious but nonrhythmic; the monotonic amelodic version of Schoenberg is neither melodious nor rhythmic; and the white noise and quiet groups served as controls for the mere presence of any background auditory stimulation. The data presented are the number of correct responses in a block of 20 trials on the tenth day of training.

M	MAM	S	MAS	WN	Q
18	16	11	8	11	16
17	17	8	12	9	18
16	20	12	13	14	17
16	17	10	11	11	16
20	19	11	11	11	16

7. In an experiment to evaluate whether deprivation of the opportunity to perform normal grooming and self-cleaning responses had an effect on subsequent maternal behavior, Kirby & Horvath (1968) reared a group of female rats with collars that prevented self-licking. A group of normally reared females and a group reared with collars notched so as to allow self-licking served as controls. When all subjects matured and gave birth to a litter of pups, the percentage of each litter to survive to weaning age was noted.

Normals	Notched collar group	Grooming deprivation group
92.3	80.0	50.0
0.0	100.0	100.0
100.0	83.3	100.0
53.8	77.8	44.4
100.0	100.0	92.3

8. A study was conducted in which an "information" booth was set up in the main lounge of a university student center. An attractive young woman was stationed in the information booth and asked to rate the men who passed by in terms of their desirability as potential mates on a 10-point scale such that higher numbers reflected greater desirability. Hidden observers noted that the men passing through the lounge behaved in one of three ways: some approached and spoke to the information girl, some made eye contact but did not approach, and some did neither. Her ratings of nine randomly selected men from each of these behavioral groups are presented.

Approach	Eye contact	Nothing
8	7	6
7	5	6
10	6	6
8	7	5
5	7	7
6	6	4
8	7	6
8	8	6
7	6	5

9. A study was conducted in which a small child handed out leaflets at a main entrance to a shopping plaza. Each leaflet was a coupon good for one free ice cream cone at Lou's Ice Cream Parlor; the problem was that the leaflet contained no information as to where this establishment was located. The shoppers were thus obliged to ask other shoppers for directions, and four types of interactions occurred: a female asking directions from a female (F–F); a female from a male (F–M); a male from a female (M–F); and a male from a male (M–M). Hidden observers recorded the number of minutes that these types of direction-seeking interactions lasted.

F–F	F–M	M–F	M–M
2.0	3.5	2.3	1.1
3.1	1.6	4.4	2.7
1.7	4.7	3.4	2.2
2.5	3.9	2.9	1.8
1.9	3.1	4.0	1.2

10. All reproducing species of animals tend to be consistent in the number of offspring that are produced on any breeding occasion. Presumably, the usual number is the optimal one given such factors as availability of food and parental capacity to produce offspring and/or to feed them. An experi-

ment was conducted in which robins' nests, which usually contain 4 eggs, were altered so that some contained 2, 3, 4, 5, and 6 eggs. Two weeks after hatching, the experimenter rated the health of each young bird on a 10-point scale wherein 10 equaled perfect health and 0 equaled having died. In this way, a mean rating of the young birds' health was derived for each nest.

2 eggs	3 eggs	4 eggs	5 eggs	6 eggs
9.00	7.00	8.75	7.40	6.00
10.00	9.33	7.50	6.00	5.17
8.00	9.00	9.25	7.40	6.33
7.50	9.00	8.50	7.20	4.67

9.6 Single Factor Analysis of Variance: Repeated Measures

In the repeated measures design, a single randomly selected group of subjects is exposed, on different occasions, to the k treatment conditions. Whenever the independent variable permits repeated subject testing, the experimenter should consider using a repeated measures design because it requires fewer subjects and can be more sensitive in detecting subtle independent variable effects. From a procedural viewpoint, however, some difficulty may be created by the need to avoid confounding the independent variable with treatment exposure order. Since there are now three or more treatments to consider, the elimination of systematic effects of exposure order is more complicated than was the case with the repeated measures t-test. Various approaches may be used, including randomized exposure orders for each subject, and other systematic exposure order sequences. A discussion of these matters may be found in D'Amato (1970) and Meyers & Grossen (1978). Suffice to say here that exposure order confounding must be controlled; in our subsequent discussion of repeated measures experiments, we will assume that such control has occurred.

The repeated measures procedure, like all ANOVA designs, subdivides the total variance into components that are attributable to different sources. Compared to the independent groups design, the repeated measures procedure makes an additional subdivision of the total variance, the key feature of which is that the variance due to individual differences between subjects is identified and set aside so as to not be part of the F-ratio. The removal of this source of variability results in an increased sensitivity for detecting independent variable effects. The general computational model for the single factor repeated measures design is as follows.

Subject no.	Treatment 1	Treatment 2	Treatment 3	
1	$X_{1,1}$	$X_{2,1}$	$X_{3,1}$	R_1
2	$X_{1,2}$	$X_{2,2}$	$X_{3,2}$	R_2
3	$X_{1,3}$	$X_{2,3}$	$X_{3,3}$	R_3
4	$X_{1,4}$	$X_{2,4}$	$X_{3,4}$	R_4
5	$X_{1,5}$	$X_{2,5}$	$X_{3,5}$	R_5
	T_1	T_2	T_3	$\sum X$

k = number of treatments (number of levels of the independent variable)
n = number of subjects
N = total number of scores

When the raw data from a repeated measures experiment are presented in tabular form, it is understood that all the scores in any row are the scores obtained from a particular subject. Each subject's scores under the k treatment conditions are summed and symbolized as an R value (row total). The R values form a column at the right and, since each is the sum of one subject's scores, the variability among R values represents between subjects variability. The amount of this variability is termed the *between subjects variance*.

between subjects variance

The objective is to determine whether any significant differences exist among the groups of scores (between the treatment conditions) but in the repeated measures case, the groups of scores have all been obtained from a single group of subjects. The T values are the sums of the scores under the different treatment conditions, but variability among them is now termed within subjects variability. This is because the k scores produced by an individual under the different treatments represent variability within the behavior repertoire of that person. Collectively then, the T values represent the summed total of this within individual, or within subject, variability. The amount of this variability is termed the *within subjects variance*. Note that $\sum X = \sum T = \sum R$.

within subjects variance

The computational procedure involves the calculation of four terms.

(1) $\sum X^2 = X_{1,1}^2 + X_{1,2}^2 + \cdots + X_{3,5}^2$

(2) $(\sum X)^2/N = (X_{1,1} + X_{1,2} + \cdots + X_{3,5})^2/N$

(3) $\sum (T^2/n) = T_1^2/n + T_2^2/n + T_3^2/n = (T_1^2 + T_1^2 + T_3^2)/n$

(4) $\sum R^2/k = (R_1^2 + R_2^2 + R_3^2 + R_4^2 + R_5^2)/k$

The first three terms are identical to those obtained in the independent groups procedure. Note that since in the repeated measures design there is only one value for n, $\sum (T^2/n)$ may be rewritten as $\sum T^2/n$. The new term is $\sum R^2/k$, and is required for the calculation of between subjects variance. The repeated measures procedure first divides the total variance into between subjects and within subjects components; then the within subjects variance is subdivided into a treatment component and a residual, or leftover, term. The Sums of Squares are defined as

$$SS_{\text{between subjects}} = \sum R^2/k - (\sum X)^2/N$$

$$SS_{\text{within subjects}} = \sum X^2 - \sum R^2/k$$

$$SS_{\text{treatment}} = \sum T^2/n - (\sum X)^2/N$$

$$SS_{\text{residual}} = \sum X^2 + (\sum X)^2/N - \sum T^2/n - \sum R^2/k$$

The ANOVA is presented in a standard tabular format.

Source of Variation	Sum of Squares	df	Mean Square	F
Between subjects	$\sum R^2/k - (\sum X)^2/N$	$n-1$		
Within subjects	$\sum X^2 - \sum R^2/k$	$n(k-1)$		
Treatment	$\sum T^2/n - (\sum X)^2/N$	$k-1$	$\dfrac{SS_{\text{treatment}}}{k-1}$	$\dfrac{MS_{\text{treatment}}}{MS_{\text{residual}}}$
Residual	$\sum X^2 + (\sum X)^2/N - \sum T^2/n - \sum R^2/k$	$(n-1)(k-1)$	$\dfrac{SS_{\text{residual}}}{(n-1)(k-1)}$	

Since between subjects differences are not of immediate interest to the experimenter, they represent unwanted variability. The repeated measures ANOVA identifies the amount of the variability in the data that is attributable to differences between subjects and removes it in the form of $SS_{\text{between subjects}}$. Eliminating the between subjects variability enables evaluation of the scores under the different treatments as though the subjects had identical overall response tendencies. The remaining variability is termed within subjects variability and is subdivided into a treatment and a residual component. The amount of variability among the treatment means is termed *treatment variance;* $SS_{\text{treatment}}$ has the same derivation as $SS_{\text{between groups}}$ in the independent groups ANOVA. The remaining within subjects variability is termed *residual variance,* meaning that it is variability not assignable either to overall between treatments differences (variability among the treatment mean values) or to overall between subjects differences (variability among the subjects' mean values). The F-ratio divides the treatment variance ($MS_{\text{treatment}}$) by the residual variance (MS_{residual}). In the presentation of the repeated measures ANOVA, the treatment and residual sources of variability are indented to show that they are subdivisions of the overall within subjects effect.

treatment variance

residual variance

Thus

$$SS_{\text{within subjects}} = SS_{\text{treatment}} + SS_{\text{residual}}$$

and also

$$df_{\text{within subjects}} = df_{\text{treatment}} + df_{\text{residual}}$$
$$n(k - 1) = k - 1 + (n - 1)(k - 1)$$
$$nk - n = k - 1 + nk - k - n + 1$$

The following numerical example will illustrate the repeated measures calculation. Suppose that eight randomly selected subjects served in a study to evaluate consumer preference for four different brands of margarine. Each subject tested and rated each brand on a 10-point preference scale, with larger numbers indicating greater preference. Thus

Independent variable: Type (brand) of margarine

Dependent variable: Consumer preference (defined operationally as taste rating score)

Null hypothesis: The four brands tested do not differ in consumer preference ($\mu_A = \mu_B = \mu_C = \mu_D$).

#1 (Brand A)	#2 (Brand B)	#3 (Brand C)	#4 (Brand D)	
3	3	2	4	$R_1 = 12$
5	7	6	7	$R_2 = 25$
4	4	5	6	$R_3 = 19$
6	5	5	6	$R_4 = 22$
3	4	5	5	$R_5 = 17$
3	3	4	5	$R_6 = 15$
5	6	6	7	$R_7 = 24$
4	4	5	6	$R_8 = 19$
$T_1 = 33$	$T_2 = 36$	$T_3 = 38$	$T_4 = 46$	$\Sigma X = 153$

$$k = 4, \qquad n = 8, \qquad N = 32$$

The first thing that one should notice in a set of repeated measures data is the variability of the R values. In the present case, these can be seen to show fairly large variability; this means that the dependent variable measure is one on which randomly selected individuals tend to show considerable variability. The repeated measures design is most effective in precisely this kind of circumstance. Since between subjects variability stems from individual differences between subjects, it is not a function of the independent variable or a function of sampling error in the context of viewing the treatment condition groups of scores as estimates of population characteristics. The repeated measures design removes this unwanted variability from the analysis.

(1) $\sum X^2 = 785.00$

(2) $(\sum X)^2/N = (153)^2/32$

$\qquad = 731.53$

$\dfrac{T^2}{N} =$

(3) $\sum T^2/n = [(33)^2 + (36)^2 + (38)^2 + (46)^2]/8$

$\qquad = 743.13$

(4) $\sum R^2/k = [(12)^2 + (25)^2 + (19)^2 + (22)^2 + (17)^2$

$\qquad\qquad + (15)^2 + (24)^2 + (19)^2]/4$

$\qquad = 766.25$

$SS_{\text{between subjects}} = \sum R^2/k - (\sum X)^2/N$

$\qquad = 766.25 - 731.53$

$\qquad = 34.72$

$SS_{\text{within subjects}} = \sum X^2 - \sum R^2/k$

$\qquad = 785.00 - 766.25$

$\qquad = 18.75$

$SS_{\text{treatment}} = \sum T^2/n - (\sum X)^2/N$

$\qquad = 743.13 - 731.53$

$\qquad = 11.60$

$SS_{\text{residual}} = \sum X^2 + (\sum X)^2/N - \sum T^2/n - \sum R^2/k$

$\qquad = 785.00 + 731.53 - 743.13 - 766.25$

$\qquad = 7.15$

Source of Variation	Sum of Squares	df	Mean Square	F
Between subjects	34.72	7		
Within subjects	18.75	24		
Treatment	11.60	3	3.87	11.38
Residual	7.15	21	0.34	

1. $df = (k-1)/(n-1)(k-1) = (4-1)/(8-1)(4-1) = 3/21$

2. The critical value for F at 0.05 confidence level $= 3.07$

3. Therefore the result is significant.

4. Interpretation: The four brands of margarine tested differ in consumer preference.

Since the F term is significant, the null hypothesis may be rejected and the result interpreted to mean that the margarine brands differ in consumer preference. Remember that the significant F tells us only that at least two of the brands differ significantly; we do not yet know specifically which comparisons are significantly different, although one certainty is that Brand A differs from Brand D, since these had the lowest and highest rating totals respectively.

I think it is good practice to report $SS_{\text{between subjects}}$ and $SS_{\text{within subjects}}$ in the ANOVA table because, even though they are not used to form the F-ratio, they represent information of potential interest. One can easily obtain an "eyeball" estimate of the relative size of the between subjects and within subjects Mean Squares and this gives an idea of the proportion of the total variance that is attributable to individual differences; this in turn may indicate something about the relative magnitude of the independent variable effect. It is possible to test the null hypothesis that the subjects were not significantly different in their overall response tendencies by forming an F-ratio consisting of $MS_{\text{between subjects}}$ divided by MS_{residual}. The potential insights to be gained by reporting $SS_{\text{between subjects}}$ and $SS_{\text{within subjects}}$ are well worth the little additional effort.

An aside: never discard information

The numerical derivation of the $SS_{\text{treatment}}$ and $SS_{\text{between subjects}}$ terms follows the logic outlined in the previous section dealing with the independent groups design. Thus

$$SS_{\text{treatment}} = n[\textstyle\sum \overline{T}^2 - (\sum \overline{T})^2/k]$$

$$MS_{\text{treatment}} = n[\textstyle\sum \overline{T}^2 - (\sum \overline{T})^2/k]/k - 1$$
$$= ns_{\overline{T}}^2$$

and

$$SS_{\text{between subjects}} = k[\textstyle\sum \overline{R}^2 - (\sum \overline{R})^2/n]$$

$$MS_{\text{between subjects}} = k[\textstyle\sum \overline{R}^2 - (\sum \overline{R})^2/n]/n - 1$$
$$= ks_{\overline{R}}^2$$

It can be shown that

$$SS_{\text{within subjects}} = SS_{s\#1} + SS_{s\#2} + SS_{s\#3} + \cdots + SS_{s\#n}$$

Note: $s\#1$ = Subject no. 1, $s\#2$ = Subject no. 2, etc.

$$MS_{\text{within subjects}} = (s_{s\#1}^2 + s_{s\#2}^2 + s_{s\#3}^2 + \cdots + s_{s\#n}^2)/n$$

Single Factor Repeated Measures ANOVA

Six college freshpersons were tested for their startle response to a mouse, a gartersnake, and a tarantula. Each was tested by being seated at a table containing a trap door through which the experimenter could suddenly liberate the test animal; startle response was measured by means of muscle contraction recording apparatus. Exposure order to the three test objects was randomized. The raw data are shown next.

Independent variable: mouse, gartersnake, and tarantula

Dependent variable: Startle response

Null hypothesis: The type of test object, that is whether a mouse, gartersnake, or tarantula, does not affect startle response ($\mu_{mouse} = \mu_{gartersnake} = \mu_{tarantula}$).

Mouse	Gartersnake	Tarantula	
24	38	40	$R_1 = 102$
56	60	64	$R_2 = 180$
32	42	42	$R_3 = 116$
80	102	100	$R_4 = 282$
42	50	54	$R_5 = 146$
60	68	69	$R_6 = 197$
$T_1 = 294$	$T_2 = 360$	$T_3 = 369$	$\Sigma X = 1023$

$k = 3, \quad n = 6, \quad N = 18$

(1) $\Sigma X^2 = 65,973.00$

(2) $(\Sigma X)^2/N = (1,023)^2/18 = 58,140.50$

(3) $\Sigma T^2/n = [(294)^2 + (360)^2 + (369)^2]/6 = 58,699.50$

(4) $\Sigma R^2/k = [(102)^2 + (180)^2 + (116)^2 + (282)^2 + (146)^2 + (197)^2]/3$
$= 65,303.00$

$$SS_{between\ subjects} = \Sigma R^2/k - (\Sigma X)^2/N$$
$$= 65,303.00 - 58,140.50$$
$$= 7,162.50$$

$$SS_{within\ subjects} = \Sigma X^2 - \Sigma R^2/k$$
$$= 65,973.00 - 65,303.00$$
$$= 670.00$$

$$SS_{treatment} = \Sigma T^2/n - (\Sigma X)^2/N$$
$$= 58,699.50 - 58,140.50$$
$$= 559.00$$

$SS_{residual} = \Sigma X^2 + (\Sigma X)^2/N - \Sigma T^2/n - \Sigma R^2/k$

$\qquad = 65{,}973.00 + 58{,}140.50 - 58{,}699.50 - 65{,}303.00$

$\qquad = 111.00$

Source of Variation	Sum of Squares	df	Mean Square	F
Between subjects	7162.50	5		
Within subjects	670.00	12		
Treatment	559.00	2	279.50	25.18
Residual	111.00	10	11.10	

1. $df = (k - 1)/(n - 1)(k - 1) = (3 - 1)/(6 - 1)(3 - 1) = 2/10$

2. The critical value for F at 0.05 confidence level = 4.10

3. Therefore the result is significant.

4. Interpretation: The type of test object, that is, whether the test object was a mouse, gartersnake, or tarantula, does affect startle response.

The overall within subjects variance ($MS_{\text{within subjects}}$) is equal to the mean of the individual subjects' variances under the k treatment conditions. The $SS_{\text{treatment}}$ is based solely on the treatment means and does not take account of individual subjects' variability: for that reason it is a value different from $SS_{\text{within subjects}}$. The SS_{residual} represents what is left over when the overall variability between the treatments is subtracted from the sum of the individual subjects' variability between the treatments. A small SS_{residual} means that there was consistency among the subjects in responding to the treatment conditions. We have previously shown that the expected value of $ns_{\bar{T}}^2$ ($MS_{\text{treatment}}$) is σ^2. It can be shown that the expected value of MS_{residual} is also σ^2. (This explanation is not given here because it is somewhat involved; the reader may find a lucid presentation in Edwards, (1960).) The F-ratio in the repeated measures ANOVA is thus formed from two independent estimates of σ^2.

9.7 The Randomized Blocks Design

Suppose that in an experiment involving three treatment conditions the subjects were n sets of triplets, and one member of each trio was assigned to each treatment. Although the three groups of scores so generated indisputably come from separate groups of individuals, these scores cannot be regarded as being independent in the same sense that they would be had the groups consisted of independently randomly sampled persons. This situation obviously contains elements of both independent groups and repeated measures designs. Another example might be a matched groups design in which deliberate care was taken to have a person in each experimental group who was matched, for one or several variables, to a control group individual.

　　The correct procedure in such cases is to align the scores of the related/matched individuals, such as the triplets or the matched subjects in the previous examples, so that these related/matched scores are on the same row. Each such row is termed a block. The computational procedure is identical to the repeated measures analysis, with blocks taking the place of individual subject's scores. Such a design is called the randomized blocks design; it is assumed that the individuals in the blocks were randomly assigned to the specific treatment conditions. In the case of using triplets, for example, the members of each triplet trio would be randomly assigned to one of the three treatment groups. In an experiment using four treatment conditions in which there was matching for age, the four oldest subjects would be identified and then randomly assigned to the treatment groups, then the next four oldest, and so on. Whenever the assignment of subjects to the treatment groups produces a deliberately intended equality between the groups, the individuals so involved cannot be regarded as generating independent scores; their data should be blocked and analyzed with the repeated measures procedure. In most cases of behavioral research, the blocks themselves, such as the triplet trios, are regarded as a random sample from a population of such blocks. The reader is referred to Glass & Stanley (1970) for a more thorough discussion of this point.

9.8 Review Exercises

1. Define or describe the following terms.
   - (a) between subjects variance
   - (b) within subjects variance
   - (c) treatment variance
   - (d) residual variance

The following problems represent hypothetical or real research situations. In each case:

   - (a) identify the independent variable
   - (b) identify the dependent variable
   - (c) state the null hypothesis being tested
   - (d) complete the analysis at 0.05 confidence level
   - (e) clearly interpret the result

2. Ray began to paper train a litter of four puppies by systematically rewarding them when they "performed" correctly and shouting at them when they erred. Records were kept for the first three weeks and the following data represent the percentage of times each puppy did the right thing during these periods.

1st week	2nd week	3rd week
50	55	65
58	52	60
46	48	58
51	50	61

3. The following data represent the per share prices of six common stocks at the close of trading on the last trading day of 1978, 1979, and 1980.

1978	1979	1980
14.50	11.25	15.00
6.75	5.00	6.25
8.50	6.25	7.75
17.50	16.25	21.25
9.50	8.00	9.75
12.25	10.25	12.00

4. The young of many species of ungulates acquire a coordinated walking response in a remarkably short time after birth. Though initial attempts to walk are wobbly, they nonetheless make very rapid progress. A study was made of several caribou fawns in which the number of steps taken before losing balance was counted on the first four attempts to walk.

1st	2nd	3rd	4th
2	3	5	7
2	2	4	5
3	4	4	6
1	3	4	4
3	4	5	6
3	5	5	6
3	3	4	6

5. Five sets of triplets were subjects in an experiment in which susceptibility to dizziness was measured after the consumption of six ounces of coffee, bourbon, or zinfandel. One member of each triplet group was randomly assigned to one of the treatment conditions; the measure taken was the number of minutes the person could tolerate being in a centrifuge apparatus.

Coffee	Bourbon	Zinfandel
20	14	16
29	21	24
13	8	10
9	6	9
16	15	15

6. A typewriter manufacturer designed five different keyboard layouts and tested them to see which resulted in the most efficient work. Six persons were randomly selected from the graduating class of Harry's Typing School. Each typist worked for fifteen minutes at each machine (order of use systematically varied) and the number of words typed per minute was recorded.

A	B	C	D	E
55	46	53	43	49
50	50	55	47	50
38	42	51	29	39
44	45	45	43	43
45	47	49	42	46
40	40	42	41	41

7. Eight students were rated for their social maturity by four teachers. The rating was on a 20-point scale, such that higher numbers reflected greater social maturity.

A	B	C	D
15	16	18	18
17	13	12	14
12	12	11	14
14	12	16	13
13	8	14	10
10	11	12	10
19	20	17	18
8	8	10	10

8. In a study of factors determining physical attractiveness, Horvath (1981) presented male subjects with line drawings of female physiques that varied in "figure curvedness," that is, in the ratio of hip width to waist width measurements. Larger values of this ratio reflect a more sharply breaking body line. Each stimulus figure was rated on a 9-point scale wherein higher values reflected greater attractiveness. The following data are the ratings by ten men of the attractiveness of the four hip/waist combinations tested.

Hip/waist

1.36	1.49	1.63	1.71
8	7	4	2
5	6	4	1
6	5	3	4
7	7	5	3
8	7	4	2
7	8	6	1
4	5	5	3
6	5	3	4
6	6	4	3
5	9	7	1

9. In a study of factors determining physical attractiveness, Horvath (1979) presented female subjects with line drawings of male physiques that varied in shoulder width. Each stimulus figure was rated on a 9-point scale wherein higher values reflected greater attractiveness. The following data are the ratings by ten women of the attractiveness of the four shoulder widths tested.

Shoulder width in cm (life size measurements)

39.25	40.75	42.25	43.75
4	6	7	5
4	5	6	6
5	5	7	8
3	4	4	7
7	6	7	8
6	6	7	7
4	4	5	8
4	6	8	8
3	5	5	5
4	4	5	6

10. A golf ball manufacturer tested the influence of wind direction on the performance of five balls, each of which had a unique dimple pattern, identified as pattern A, B, C, D, or E. A driving machine hit each ball four times when a 30 km/hr wind was blowing, such that one hit was with a following wind (F), one was into the wind (I), one was with a left to right crosswind (L–R), and one was with a right to left crosswind (R–L). The measure taken was the number of meters from the point of impact to contact with the ground.

	F	I	L–R	R–L
A	190	175	180	181
B	191	170	184	185
C	190	174	184	182
D	212	201	200	193
E	192	175	187	184

(a) Did wind direction affect performance?

(b) Did the five balls tested differ in overall performance?

11. This problem exercise will dramatize the location of the residual term in the raw data. Imagine that five subjects rated the taste of three brands of strawberry jam on a 10-point scale and generated the following data.

Brand A	Brand B	Brand C
10	5	3
3	7	8
7	5	6
8	6	4
2	7	9

12. The best way to appreciate the similarities and differences between the independent groups and repeated measures analyses is to subject a set of data to both procedures and compare the outcomes. Imagine that the independent variable is the length of time that curlers are left in place, and the dependent variable is the number of washings required to remove the curl.

10 minutes	20 minutes	30 minutes
3	4	5
4	6	5
2	4	4
5	6	6
3	4	4
3	3	4

(a) Analyze these data as an independent groups experiment.
(b) Analyze these data as a repeated measures experiment.

In the following problems, you must determine the appropriate method of analysis. As with previous problem exercises, you should:

(a) identify the independent variable
(b) identify the dependent variable
(c) state the null hypothesis being tested
(d) complete the analysis at 0.05 confidence level
(e) clearly interpret the result

13. Twenty college "freshpersons" were divided into four equal groups. The members of each group were given vitamin E capsules of different dosage; each subject consumed one capsule each day. The number of hours of sleep obtained on seven consecutive nights after beginning the vitamin E intake was recorded and an average determined for each subject. Summary terms from the raw data were

$$\Sigma X^2 = 1155, \quad (\Sigma X)^2/N = 845, \quad \Sigma (T^2/n) = 995, \quad \Sigma R^2/k = 855$$

14. Fifteen people were subjects in an experiment in which they were asked to push a button as soon as they detected a target stimulus. The stimulus was a red light designed to simulate an auto taillight and the test was conducted under three conditions: normal daylight, night illumination level, and night illumination level with fog. The measure taken was the number of milliseconds between light onset and button depression and each subject was tested under all conditions. Summary terms from the raw data were

$$\Sigma X^2 = 5468, \quad (\Sigma X)^2/N = 1000, \quad \Sigma (T^2/n) = 1668, \quad \Sigma R^2/k = 2000$$

15. An experimenter was interested in the basis upon which people judge works of art as appealing or unappealing. He constructed a complex geometrical pattern and made up four versions, such that one was done in shades of grey, a second had some parts in red, a third had some parts in blue, and the fourth had some parts in red and blue. Twenty people served as subjects and the test was an auction situation in that when each pattern was shown, each subject wrote down how much he or she would be willing to pay in numbers of dollars. In order to keep the subjects from realizing that they were seeing the same pattern over and over again, the four test stimuli were interspersed with sixteen others in a series of twenty patterns in all. Summary terms from the raw data were

$$\sum X^2 = 11{,}625, \quad (\sum X)^2/N = 3{,}125, \quad \sum (T^2/n) = 4{,}325, \quad \sum R^2/k = 4{,}725$$

16. At a particular zoo, Louie was in charge of lions and noticed that the lions tended to pace about their cages at different rates depending on the number of people staring at them. He set up an experiment in which he measured the rate of pacing when the lion was being watched by one, two, three, and four people. This procedure was carried out on each of the zoo's six lions. Summary terms from the raw data were

$$\sum X^2 = 2200, \quad (\sum X)^2/N = 700, \quad \sum (T^2/n) = 1150, \quad \sum R^2/k = 1000$$

17. Bob had four daughters (quadruplets) and one Saturday morning he bought each one a shiny new bicycle and taught them to ride as follows. The child took her place on the seat while daddy held the bike steady; he then yelled "Pedal" and let go. On each such trial, he measured the number of feet traveled before the child fell over. Each daughter was given one trial per day for ten consecutive days. Summary terms from the raw data were

$$\sum X^2 = 4125, \quad (\sum X)^2/N = 875, \quad \sum (T^2/n) = 2675, \quad \sum R^2/k = 975$$

18. An experimenter devised chambers that were capable of excluding light and/or sound. Four different conditions could exist inside such a chamber: light and sound, light but no sound, sound but no light, and neither light nor sound. A total of 8 chambers were built and 2 were set up for each of the four conditions. The experimenter then selected 8 pregnant female rats and randomly assigned them to the chambers. In the course of time each female gave birth and the litters were reared in their chambers until weaning age. Upon reaching weaning age, the rat pups, which numbered 33 in all, were tested in a maze-learning task. The number of training trials required by each pup to achieve an error-free run was recorded. Summary terms from the raw data were

$$\sum X^2 = 4000, \quad (\sum X)^2/N = 221, \quad \sum (T^2/n) = 1100, \quad \sum R^2/k = 1000$$

19. Don, Bob, Ray, and Ted each had four racing pigeons. These birds were all from the same genetic stock, but the owners had different opinions on how they should be kept and frequently debated this issue, since each used and swore by a different maintenance system. It was decided to race the birds against each other. The race was over 40 miles and each bird was raced four times. Total time for the four flights was established for each bird. Summary terms from the raw data were

$$\sum X^2 = 4985, \quad (\sum X)^2/N = 2000, \quad \sum(T^2/n) = 3785, \quad \sum R^2/k = 2129$$

20. In a test of dominance, 15 men and 15 women were tested in pairs. The pair of individuals argued opposite viewpoints on an issue until one or the other gave up, with the winner being the more dominant. Each man was so paired with each woman, and vice versa, so that at the end, each subject had a dominance score that indicated the number of persons of the opposite sex he or she was able to dominate. Summary terms from the raw data were

$$\sum X^2 = 2966, \quad (\sum X)^2/N = 2000, \quad \sum(T^2/n) = 2126, \quad \sum R^2/k = 2546$$

21. Forty-one people were subjects in an experiment concerned with the violation of personal space. Each subject was approached by an accomplice of the experimenter who used the pretext of asking for directions. The accomplice moved closer and closer until the subject took a step backwards; the distance at which this happened was recorded in cm. Each subject was approached by the four accomplices (a man, a woman, a six-year-old girl, and a six-year-old boy) in a different random sequence. Summary terms from the raw data were

$$\sum X^2 = 228{,}540, \quad (\sum X)^2/N = 100{,}000,$$
$$\sum(T^2/n) = 107{,}800, \quad \sum R^2/k = 100{,}740$$

22. An experiment was conducted using five different species of finches. Five individuals of each species were tested; the test consisted of allowing the birds to feed at a trough that contained seed of various diameters. High-speed cameras recorded the feeding behavior and later examination of the film enabled a measure of mean seed diameter to be established for each bird. When the data were collected, the experimenter instructed her assistant to perform the analysis and subsequently received the following result.

Source of variation	SS	df	MS	F
Between subjects	200	4		
Within subjects	2948	20		
Treatment	1148	4	287	2.55
Residual	1800	16	112.50	

As you can see, the assistant performed a repeated measures analysis on data that require independent groups analysis. Perform the correct analysis and interpret the result.

23. An experiment was conducted in which three new perfume scents were field-tested. Three pretty waitresses at a busy lunch counter each wore a different scent, and the measure taken was the total number of complimentary remarks about the perfume that each received for the day. This procedure was carried out simultaneously at five lunch counters in the city; the experiment thus involved fifteen waitresses in all. The experimenter gave the data to an assistant with instructions to perform the analysis and subsequently received the following result

Source of variation	SS	df	MS	F
Between subjects	500	2		
Within subjects	360	12		
Treatment	320	4	80	16.00
Residual	40	8	5	

As you can see, the assistant performed a repeated measures analysis on data that require independent groups analysis. Perform the correct analysis and interpret the result.

24. Four children were randomly sampled from each of grades 1, 2, 3, 4, 5, 6, 7, and 8 at a particular school. Each child was given a motor coordination task that took five minutes to complete, and each performed the task four times. A mean performance score was obtained for each child, and the data were given to an assistant for analysis. The assistant returned with the following result.

Source of variation	SS	df	MS	F
Between subjects	210	7		
Within subjects	690	24		
Treatment	420	3	140.00	10.81
Residual	270	21	12.86	

As you can see, the assistant performed a repeated measures analysis on data that require independent groups analysis. Perform the correct analysis and interpret the result.

9.9 Assumptions Underlying Analysis of Variance

Given that the raw scores represent interval/ratio measurement, the assumptions upon which independent groups ANOVA is based are identical to those underlying the t-test, that is: (1) that the subjects were obtained by random sampling procedures and randomly assigned to treatment groups in the case of independent groups experiments, thereby producing independent scores; (2) that the groups of scores represent random samples from normally distributed populations; and (3) that the groups of scores are drawn from populations that have equal variances (this boils down to the expectation that the groups of scores have equal variances). The ANOVA, like the t-test, is robust with respect to the normality and variance assumptions and is not affected by moderate departures from them, particularly when the group n's are equal. Tests to determine whether variances are significantly different are known as tests for homogeneity of variance (see Section 9.3); such tests usually depend on similar assumptions and are, if anything, less robust with respect to their violation than is ANOVA. For this reason, it is not usual practice to apply a test for homogeneity of variance as a preliminary to ANOVA. Thus, these tests are not detailed in this book. However, if the raw scores appear to represent grossly different variances, then one must confirm their homogeneity, or lack thereof, with a suitable test, such as that proposed by Levine (see Glass & Stanley, 1970). If the variances are found to differ significantly, then an alternative form of analysis, such as a nonparametric technique, should be used. The fundamental assumption of independence of scores, insofar as they are expected to be independent for the particular ANOVA design, is crucial, and ANOVA is not robust with respect to its violation.

Repeated measures ANOVA depends on the additional assumption that the variances of the difference scores between all possible treatment pairs are equal. For example, if there are three treatment conditions, a_1, a_2, and a_3, then each pair ($a_1 - a_2$, $a_1 - a_3$, and $a_2 - a_3$) generates a set of n difference scores. The repeated measures ANOVA assumes that the variances of these sets of difference scores are equal in the population. The sense of this assumption may be stated as being that the subjects are not differentially affected by the k treatment conditions. Exercise 9.8–11 illustrates a violation of this assumption in that some subjects showed decreasing scores going from Brand A to C, whereas others showed increasing scores; thus, all subjects did not respond in a similar overall fashion to the treatment conditions. Numerous factors, including subject characteristics, method of counterbalancing treatment exposure order, and fatigue/practice effects, can reduce the degree of consistency of subjects' responses under pairs of treatments, and some amount of differential response to treatments is likely to occur in every real-life case. The repeated measures ANOVA is not robust with respect to this violation, which has the consequence of increasing the probability of a Type I error over that specified for the critical value. Thus, it behooves experimenters to be conservative in choosing confidence levels when testing F-ratios for repeated measures factors; a repeated measures F-ratio that is just barely significant at 0.05 level should be interpreted with caution. The reader is referred to Keppel (1982, pp. 467–469) for a more complete discussion of this issue.

10 Post *F*-Test Comparisons

10.1 Introduction

When an analysis of variance yields a nonsignificant result, the null hypothesis is retained. However, if the result is significant, there remain questions to be answered. A significant F-ratio means only that, among the k treatment conditions, there is at least one pair that differ significantly. It may be that each treatment differs from every other treatment, or that the largest treatment total differs only from the smallest, or any combination of intermediate possibilities. An additional analysis is required to identify which treatment conditions differed significantly from which others; obviously, this is of primary concern to the experimenter. Post F-test analyses are tests of the null hypothesis that $\mu_1 = \mu_2 = \cdots = \mu_k$. Several post F-test analysis techniques have been developed to accomplish this end. These methods vary in their approach to performing the multiple comparisons between the treatment conditions, and consequently in the general confidence with which statisticians regard their use. Performing a multitude of comparisons between the treatments clearly raises the spectre of an increased overall probability of a Type I error. Post F-test procedures must include some accommodation for this danger and the two methods presented in this chapter are among the most effective in this regard. A complete discussion of this matter is beyond the scope of this book and the reader is referred to an excellent presentation by Keppel (1982).

10.2 Tukey's HSD Procedure

Tukey's HSD (Honestly Significant Difference) procedure is perhaps the most generally accurate and useful method when the groups of scores are of equal size (equal n's); this procedure may be used following independent groups or repeated measures designs. There are different computational versions of Tukey's HSD procedure that are used depending upon whether the significance test is between the treatment means or treatment totals. These alternatives are computationally different but functionally equivalent. The method described next represents the Tukey HSD procedure for testing the significance of the difference between treatment totals. It is this writer's view that, since the treatment totals have been derived and used in the ANOVA, this is the most logical and direct approach. (Note: Should the student require it, the procedure for means is presented in: *An aside: HSD between treatment means.*)

The essence of this procedure is the calculation of a critical difference, which is referred to hereafter as *CD*. Any two treatment totals differ significantly when the difference between them equals or exceeds *CD*. The calculation of *CD* involves the use of q, the studentized range statistic. Table J contains the values of q at 0.05 and 0.01 levels of confidence ($q_{0.05}$ and $q_{0.01}$).

error term

Table J is read to obtain the appropriate q value by using the number of treatment conditions (k) and the degrees of freedom of the ANOVA error term as coordinates. The *error term* is the denominator of the F-ratio, $MS_{\text{within groups}}$ in the independent groups analysis and MS_{residual} in the repeated measures analysis. The error term will be referred to as MS_{error}. For example, in an independent groups analysis where $k = 3$ and $n = 5$ and thus $N = 15$, the df of MS_{error} is $N - k = 12$. The appropriate q value at 0.05 level of confidence is $q_{0.05}(k, df\, MS_{\text{error}}) = q_{0.05}(3, 12) = 3.77$. The CD is obtained by multiplying the appropriate q value by the square root of n times the MS_{error} ($\sqrt{nMS_{\text{error}}}$). (Note: If Table J does not contain entries at the $df\, MS_{\text{error}}$ that you seek, the appropriate procedure is to use the value at the next smaller $df\, MS_{\text{error}}$ entry.) For a test at 0.05 level of confidence

$$CD \text{ (critical difference)} = [q_{0.05}(k, df\, MS_{\text{error}})][\sqrt{nMS_{\text{error}}}]$$

and for a test at 0.01 level of confidence,

$$CD = [q_{0.01}(k, df\, MS_{\text{error}})][\sqrt{nMS_{\text{error}}}]$$

When the CD has been determined, the differences between all possible pairs of treatment totals are obtained; those pairs whose difference equals or exceeds the CD, irrespective of sign, are significantly different at the confidence level used.

As a numerical example to illustrate Tukey's HSD procedure for treatment totals, we shall complete the analysis of the margarine preference experiment used to illustrate the repeated measures ANOVA in Section 9.6. Thus

$$k = 4, \qquad n = 8, \qquad N = 32$$
$$T_1 = 33, \qquad T_2 = 36, \qquad T_3 = 38, \qquad T_4 = 46$$
$$MS_{\text{error}} = 0.34, \qquad df\, MS_{\text{error}} = 21$$

From Table J

$$q_{0.05}(k, df\, MS_{\text{error}}) = q_{0.05}(4, 21)$$
$$= 3.96$$

$$\sqrt{nMS_{\text{error}}} = \sqrt{(8)(0.34)}$$
$$= \sqrt{2.72}$$
$$= 1.65$$

$$CD = [q_{0.05}(k, df\, MS_{\text{error}})][\sqrt{nMS_{\text{error}}}]$$
$$= (3.96)(1.65)$$
$$= 6.53$$

Therefore

$$T_1 - T_2 = 33 - 36 = -3: \quad \text{Not significant}$$
$$T_1 - T_3 = 33 - 38 = -5: \quad \text{Not significant}$$
$$T_1 - T_4 = 33 - 46 = -13: \quad \text{Significant}$$
$$T_2 - T_3 = 36 - 38 = -2: \quad \text{Not significant}$$
$$T_2 - T_4 = 36 - 46 = -10: \quad \text{Significant}$$
$$T_3 - T_4 = 38 - 46 = -8: \quad \text{Significant}$$

The previous listing shows that T_4 differed significantly from all other treatments, but that no other pair was significantly different. If we recall that the treatment totals were the preference score totals for the margarine Brands A, B, C, and D respectively, and that the dependent variable was obtained in such a way that larger scores reflected greater preference, then the final interpretation of this experiment is that Brand D is significantly preferred over all other brands tested, and that Brands A, B, and C do not differ in consumer preference.

When ANOVA is performed by computer, the printout ordinarily shows the treatment means, but not usually the treatment totals. If the experimenter wishes to compute CD by hand, which is often more convenient than running this analysis as a separate job, the Tukey HSD Critical Difference between treatment means may be determined by using the following formula.

$$CD = [q(k, df\ MS_{error})][\sqrt{MS_{error}/n}]$$

An aside: HSD between treatment means

The Tukey HSD procedure assumes equal n's in the k treatment conditions, a circumstance that is not always met in independent groups experiments. If the difference in n's is not too great, for example in a design where $k = 4$ and $n = 10$ and one subject was lost from each of two groups, such that $n_1 = 10$, $n_2 = 9$, $n_3 = 9$, and $n_4 = 10$, then it is permissible to use the previous method and substitute the *harmonic mean* of the n's in place of n. The harmonic mean is defined as the number of scores divided by the sum of their reciprocals. Thus

$$\text{Harmonic Mean} = \frac{n}{\Sigma\left(\dfrac{1}{X}\right)}$$

In a case where $n_1 = 10$, $n_2 = 9$, $n_3 = 9$, and $n_4 = 10$, the numbers 10, 9,

9, and 10 would be values of X and n would be 4. Thus

$$\text{Harmonic Mean} = 4/(1/10 + 1/9 + 1/9 + 1/10)$$
$$= 4/(38/90)$$
$$= 4/0.4222$$
$$= 9.47$$

10.3 Scheffé's Test for Treatment Means

Scheffé's test for treatment means is presented here as a way of dealing with situations in which the treatment conditions' n's are dissimilar. It is the most conservative of the post *F*-test comparison procedures. This means that in practice, the probability of a Type I error is usually somewhat below the level of confidence used, and for this reason, the test will yield the fewest significant differences. On the other hand, however, it is quite robust with respect to the assumptions of normality and homogeneity of variance and is therefore useful under a wider range of conditions. The Scheffé procedure requires the calculation of an *F*-ratio for each pair of treatment means being tested. The *F* term so obtained is tested for significance in the usual manner; the null hypothesis is that the two means in question do not differ ($\mu_1 = \mu_2$). Scheffé's test for treatment means is as follows.

$$F = \frac{(\overline{T}_1 - \overline{T}_2)^2}{(MS_{\text{error}})(1/n_1 + 1/n_2)(k - 1)}$$

The *F* term so obtained is tested using the same degrees of freedom as were used to test the *F*-ratio of the overall analysis of variance, that is, $(k - 1)/(N - k)$ for independent groups, and $(k - 1)/(n - 1)(k - 1)$ for repeated measures. Thus the critical value for *F* in the Scheffé tests is identical to that for the overall ANOVA.

To illustrate Scheffé's procedure, we will refer to the experiment that tested problem-solving efficiency as a function of simulated atmospheric pressure that was used to illustrate the independent groups ANOVA in Section 9.4. For the purposes of this demonstration we shall only compare a single pair of treatment means, the sea level (Treatment 1) performance with the 2000 meter (Treatment 3) performance. Thus

$$k = 4, \quad n = 10, \quad N = 40$$
$$T_1 = 152, \quad \overline{T}_1 = T_1/n_1 = 152/10 = 15.2$$
$$T_3 = 133, \quad \overline{T}_3 = T_3/n_3 = 133/10 = 13.3$$
$$MS_{\text{error}} = 5.75$$

Tukey's HSD Post *F*-Test Procedure

Let us complete the computational illustration that occurs at the end of Section 9.4, in which groups of subjects tested the ease of use of three computer keyboard layouts.

$$k = 3, \quad n = 5, \quad N = 15$$
$$T_1 = 440, \quad T_2 = 335, \quad T_3 = 385$$

Source of Variation	Sum of Squares	df	Mean Square	F
Between groups	1103.33	2	551.67	4.14
Within groups	1600.00	12	133.33	

$$
\begin{aligned}
CD &= [q_{0.05}(k, df \, MS_{\text{error}})][\sqrt{nMS_{\text{error}}}\,] \\
&= [q_{0.05}(3, 12)][\sqrt{(5)\,(133.33)}\,] \\
&= [3.77][25.82] \\
&= 97.34
\end{aligned}
$$

$T_1 - T_2 = 440 - 335 = 105$:   Significant

$T_1 - T_3 = 440 - 385 = 55$:   Not significant

$T_2 - T_3 = 335 - 385 = -50$:   Not significant

Interpretation: Keyboard layout #1 differs in ease of use from layout #2 but not from layout #3. Keyboard layout #2 does not differ in ease of use from layout #3.

$$F = \frac{(\overline{T}_1 - \overline{T}_3)^2}{(MS_{error})(1/n_1 + 1/n_3)(k - 1)}$$

$$= \frac{(15.2 - 13.3)^2}{(5.75)(1/10 + 1/10)(3 - 1)}$$

$$= \frac{(1.9)^2}{(5.75)(0.20)(2)}$$

$$= 3.61/2.30$$

$$= 1.57$$

1. $df = (k - 1)/(N - k) = 3/36$
2. The critical value for F at 0.05 level of confidence $= 2.86$
3. Therefore the result is not significant.
4. Interpretation: Problem-solving efficiency at 2000 meters as compared to sea level atmospheric pressure does not differ.

The complete interpretation of any experiment requires the performance of the previous routine for all possible pairs of means differences.

10.4 Review Exercises

1. Define "error term."

The following exercises are keyed to those performed in Sections 9.5 and 9.7; use Tukey's HSD procedure at 0.05 confidence level.

2. In Exercise 9.5–2, which age groups differed in generosity?
3. In Exercise 9.5–4, which diet conditions differed in their effect on physical fitness?
4. In Exercise 9.5–6, which background auditory stimulus conditions differed in their effect on learning the discrimination problem?
5. In Exercise 9.5–8, under which behavior categories of men were the young women's ratings of their desirability different?
6. In Exercise 9.8–2, when did training differentially affect performance?
7. In Exercise 9.8–4, when did walking show improvement as a function of number of attempts?
8. In Exercise 9.8–6, which keyboard layouts differed in work efficiency?
9. In Exercise 9.8–8, which female hip width/waist combinations differed in males' attractiveness ratings?

11 Introduction to Two Factor Analysis of Variance

Chapter Preview

11.1 Introduction

Two factor analysis of variance is a procedure for analyzing the results of an experiment in which two independent variables were manipulated simultaneously. This is not to say that the two independent variables were intentionally confounded, but rather that they were examined in all possible combinations. Think back to the hypothetical experiment used as an illustration in Section 9.4, where four groups of subjects were tested for problem-solving efficiency at four simulated atmospheric pressures. In that example, ten randomly selected persons served in each group and no reference was made to whether all groups were males, females, or mixed. If one were to set up the apparatus for such an experiment, it might be of interest to inquire whether the independent variable of atmospheric pressure, if it affects problem-solving efficiency at all, has a different effect on males as compared to females. One could obtain this additional information with only the minimal additional procedure of selecting the subjects such that in each group, half are of each gender. Such an approach would allow the test of a null hypothesis for each independent variable; that is, atmospheric pressure does not affect problem-solving efficiency ($\mu_{\text{sea level}} = \mu_{1000 \text{ m}} = \mu_{2000 \text{ m}} = \mu_{3000 \text{ m}}$), and, the sexes do not differ in overall problem-solving efficiency ($\mu_{\text{males}} = \mu_{\text{females}}$). While this increase in information would justify whatever procedural inconvenience might be involved in establishing separate male and female groups for each condition, the real added benefit of the two factor design is that it examines the interaction between the two independent variables.

Interaction refers to whether the different levels of one independent variable show a similar or dissimilar effect across the levels of the second independent variable. In the context of the example we have been discussing, the interaction term in the analysis would indicate whether the effect of the different levels of atmospheric pressure was the same or different for males as compared to females. It is conceivable, for example, that females' problem-solving efficiency may improve as atmospheric pressure decreases, whereas males' performance might deteriorate. By providing information on the effect, if any, of the interaction of the two independent variables on the dependent variable, the two factor design yields a much greater return on the experimenter's time and effort than a single factor experiment. In the next section, the nature of interaction will be examined closely and numerical examples will show how to visualize and interpret interaction outcomes. For now, I want to stress that interaction effects are very informative and may supersede in importance the overall effects of the independent variables considered singly.

Actually, all ANOVA designs in which more than one independent variable is manipulated are collectively termed higher-order or *factorial ANOVA designs*. It is not uncommon for experimenters to design studies that manipulate three or four independent variables in all possible combinations. In such designs there are several interaction terms representing different combinations of the independent variables, and the interpretation of these outcomes can be quite complex. In this book, my purpose is to introduce you to factorial ANOVA and we will therefore consider only the two factor independent groups design. If one achieves a good grasp of this, the simplest factorial ANOVA, then understanding the more complex designs will not be difficult.

11.2 Two Factor Analysis of Variance: Independent Groups

The computational approach to the analysis of two factor experiments is a direct extension of that used in single factor designs. Since the situation is somewhat more complicated, we will need to define a few additional notations; however, it will soon be clear that the essence of the analysis process has not changed. We will use the letters A and B to refer to the two independent variables. In the general computational model, presented next, there are two levels of A and two levels of B; this would be termed a 2×2 (two-by-two) design. Thus

Independent variable A

		a_1	a_2
Independent variable B	b_1	$X_{1,1,1}$ $X_{1,1,2}$ $X_{1,1,3}$ $X_{1,1,4}$ $X_{1,1,5}$	$X_{2,1,11}$ $X_{2,1,12}$ $X_{2,1,13}$ $X_{2,1,14}$ $X_{2,1,15}$
	b_2	$X_{1,2,6}$ $X_{1,2,7}$ $X_{1,2,8}$ $X_{1,2,9}$ $X_{1,2,10}$	$X_{2,2,16}$ $X_{2,2,17}$ $X_{2,2,18}$ $X_{2,2,19}$ $X_{2,2,20}$

p = number of levels of independent variable A

q = number of levels of independent variable B

n = number of scores in each group, or cell

N = total number of scores

In the independent groups experiment, there is an independently randomly sampled group of subjects for each combination of A and B treatments.

In a 2×2 design there must be $2 \times 2 = 4$ separate subject groups. The raw scores of these subjects are represented by X's. The triple notation attached to the raw scores indicates level of variable A, level of variable B, and subject number, and serves to identify individual scores; for example, $X_{1,2,8}$ was the raw score of Subject #8 who was tested under independent variable A at level a_1, and under independent variable B at level b_2. The number of scores, or subjects in each group is symbolized by n and equals 5 in this case; the total number of raw scores is symbolized by N and equals 20 in this case; the number of levels of independent variable A is symbolized by p and equals 2 in this case; and the number of levels of independent variable B is symbolized by q and equals 2 in this case.

The next step is to construct the AB Summary Table, which consists of the sums of the raw scores in each group and the overall row and column sums. Thus

AB Summary Table

	a_1	a_2	
b_1	$A_1 B_1$	$A_2 B_1$	B_1
b_2	$A_1 B_2$	$A_2 B_2$	B_2
	A_1	A_2	ΣX

The general rule adopted here in the usage of notation is that lowercase letters refer to variable levels, and uppercase letters refer to actual score sums. Thus, a_1 and a_2 refer to the particular levels of variable A, such as different dosages of a drug, and A_1 and A_2 refer to the dependent variable score totals. The notation $A_1 B_1$ refers to the sum of the raw scores of the group of subjects who served under the $a_1 b_1$ combination of independent variables, and similarly with $A_2 B_1$, etc. The symbol A_1 denotes the sum of all scores obtained under level a_1, and in this case, $A_1 = A_1 B_1 + A_1 B_2$; similarly, $B_1 = A_1 B_1 + A_2 B_1$. As always, ΣX denotes the overall sum of all the raw scores. Thus

$$\Sigma A = A_1 + A_2$$
$$\Sigma B = B_1 + B_2$$
$$\Sigma AB = A_1 B_1 + A_2 B_1 + A_1 B_2 + A_2 B_2$$
$$\Sigma X = \Sigma A = \Sigma B = \Sigma AB$$

In general

$$\Sigma A = A_1 + A_2 + \cdots + A_p$$
$$\Sigma B = B_1 + B_2 + \cdots + B_q$$
$$\Sigma AB = A_1 B_1 + A_2 B_1 + \cdots + A_p B_q$$

The next step is the calculation of five basic terms.

(1) $\sum X^2$

(2) $(\sum X)^2 / N$

(3) $\sum A^2 / nq = \dfrac{A_1^2 + A_2^2}{nq}$

(4) $\sum B^2 / np = \dfrac{B_1^2 + B_2^2}{np}$

(5) $\sum (AB)^2 / n = \dfrac{(A_1 B_1)^2 + (A_1 B_2)^2 + (A_2 B_1)^2 + (A_2 B_2)^2}{n}$

The two factor independent groups ANOVA partitions the total variance in the raw scores into components representing independent variable A, independent variable B, the AB interaction, and a residual component. The four Sums of Squares are defined as follows

$$SS_A = \sum A^2 / nq - (\sum X)^2 / N$$

$$SS_B = \sum B^2 / np - (\sum X)^2 / N$$

$$SS_{AB} = \sum (AB)^2 / n + (\sum X)^2 / N - \sum A^2 / nq - \sum B^2 / np$$

$$SS_{\text{residual}} = \sum X^2 - \sum (AB)^2 / n$$

The two factor independent groups ANOVA is presented in a standard tabular format as shown next.

Source of Variation	Sum of Squares	df	Mean Square	F
A	$\sum A^2 / nq - (\sum X)^2 / N$	$p - 1$	$\dfrac{SS_A}{p - 1}$	$\dfrac{MS_A}{MS_{\text{residual}}}$
B	$\sum B^2 / np - (\sum X)^2 / N$	$q - 1$	$\dfrac{SS_B}{q - 1}$	$\dfrac{MS_B}{MS_{\text{residual}}}$
AB	$\sum (AB)^2 / n + (\sum X)^2 / N - \sum A^2 / nq - \sum B^2 / np$	$(p - 1)(q - 1)$	$\dfrac{SS_{AB}}{(p - 1)(q - 1)}$	$\dfrac{MS_{AB}}{MS_{\text{residual}}}$
Residual	$\sum X^2 - \sum (AB)^2 / n$	$pq(n - 1)$	$\dfrac{SS_{\text{residual}}}{pq(n - 1)}$	

This analysis tests three null hypotheses concerning, respectively, independent variable A ($\mu_{a_1} = \mu_{a_2} = \cdots = \mu_{a_p}$), independent variable B ($\mu_{b_1} = \mu_{b_2} = \cdots = \mu_{b_q}$), and the AB interaction.*

Three F-ratios are derived and tested for significance at the degrees of freedom of their respective numerator and denominator Mean Squares.

Independent variable A: $df = (p - 1)/pq(n - 1)$

Independent variable B: $df = (q - 1)/pq(n - 1)$

AB interaction: $df = (p - 1)(q - 1)/pq(n - 1)$

main effect

The first line in the ANOVA table represents the *main effect* for independent variable A, and is based upon the variability of the A means. A significant F in this line means that independent variable A had an overall effect, taking all levels of B together, on the dependent variable. The second line represents the *main effect* for independent variable B, and is based upon the variability of the B means. A significant F in this line means that independent variable B had an overall effect, taking all levels of A together, on the dependent variable. The third line represents the AB interaction and is based upon the variability of the AB, or cell means. A significant F in this line means that the combination of A and B levels had an effect on the dependent variable. Another way to verbalize an interaction is to say that the effect of variable A differed as a function of the level of variable B, and vice versa. The last line in the ANOVA table represents residual variability, that is, variability in the raw data not accounted for by variability among the column means, row means, or cell means. The Mean Square residual serves as the error term in all three F-ratios.

If none of the F terms is significant, then all null hypotheses are retained; namely, independent variable A does not affect the dependent variable, independent variable B does not affect the dependent variable, and the interaction of A and B does not affect the dependent variable. If either, or both, main effects are significant but the interaction is not significant, then interpretation is also straightforward. Given such an outcome when the significant A or B (or both) effect had been manipulated at more than two levels, it would be necessary to apply a post F-test comparison procedure in order to identify which levels differed significantly; this is known as a main effects test. The

---

*The null hypothesis for the interaction is a bit cumbersome to express in terms of the parameters. An absence of interaction is defined by the condition $\mu_{a_p,b_q} - \mu_{a_p} - \mu_{b_q} + \mu = 0$ for *all* cells. For example, $\mu_{a_1,b_1} - \mu_{a_1} - \mu_{b_1} + \mu = 0$, $\mu_{a_1,b_2} - \mu_{a_1} - \mu_{b_2} + \mu = 0$, and so on. It can be seen that $\mu_{a_1,b_1} - \mu_{a_1,b_2} = \mu_{b_1} - \mu_{b_2}$, which illustrates the sense of an absence of interaction; that is, if a is held constant, then the difference between the parameter means of any pair of cells is entirely a function of the b variable. This is another way of saying that a does not change as a function of b, meaning that a and b do not interact. A similar equation may be derived for any pair of ab cells.

Tukey HSD procedure is recommended and would be applied by determining the Critical Difference (*CD*) between independent variable level totals as follows.

For main effects comparisons between overall totals of variable *A* $(A_1, A_2, \ldots, A_p)$ tested at 0.05 confidence level

$$CD = [q_{0.05}(p, df\ MS_{\text{error}})][\sqrt{nqMS_{\text{error}}}]*$$

For main effects comparisons between overall totals of variable *B* $(B_1, B_2, \ldots, B_q)$ tested at 0.05 confidence level

$$CD = [q_{0.05}(q, df\ MS_{\text{error}})][\sqrt{npMS_{\text{error}}}]*$$

If the *AB* interaction is significant, however, the situation becomes more complicated, and the main effects may not be what they first seemed to be. In order to appreciate an interaction, one must plot the *AB* Summary Table cell totals. This consists of laying out a diagram on which levels of *A* are represented on the abscissa and the ordinate is marked in units sufficient to encompass the range of *AB* cell totals.** This is known as the *AB interaction plot*. The *AB* totals are located as points in the body of the diagram. These points may then be joined by straight lines to show the changes in scores of one variable as a function of level of the other.

AB interaction plot

Figure 11.2–1 shows several significant *F*-ratio outcomes. Figure 11.2–1(a) depicts a case in which all three *F*-ratios are significant. A significant main effect for *A* means that A_1 differed significantly from A_2; this appears visually as a difference in elevation between the mean of A_1 points and the mean of A_2 points. In other words, if you take the midpoint of a line joining A_1B_1 to A_1B_2 and compare it to the midpoint of a line joining A_2B_1 to A_2B_2, you will see that these midpoints differ in vertical elevation. This difference in elevation represents the significant main effect for *A*. Similarly, in Figure 11.2–1(a), the significant main effect for *B* is illustrated by the difference in elevation between the mean of B_1 points, $(A_1B_1 + A_2B_1)/2$, and the mean of B_2 points, $(A_1B_2 + A_2B_2)/2$. The significant *AB* interaction is illustrated by the difference in slope between the two plotted lines; it can be seen that A_1B_2–A_2B_2 slopes upward much more sharply than A_1B_1–A_2B_1.

If you apply this understanding to Figure 11.2–1(b), you will see that it depicts a significant *A* main effect, a significant *B* main effect, but a non-significant *AB* interaction since the plotted lines are parallel. Figure 11.2–1(c) depicts a non-significant *A* effect but a significant *B* effect and a significant

---

*The overall comparison of *A* totals uses the expression $\sqrt{nqMS_{\text{error}}}$ because each *A* total consists of *nq* scores; similarly, the overall comparison of *B* totals uses the expression $\sqrt{npMS_{\text{error}}}$ because each *B* total consists of *np* scores.

**The *AB* interaction may also be depicted by representing levels of *B* on the abscissa; it merely depends on which variable one wishes to perceive as operating across the other.

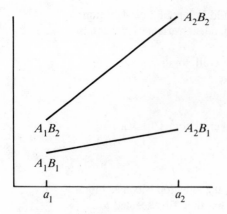

(a) *A* main effect significant,
   B main effect significant,
   AB interaction significant.

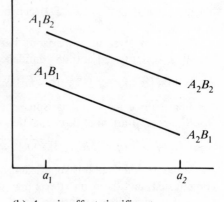

(b) *A* main effect significant,
   B main effect significant,
   AB interaction not significant.

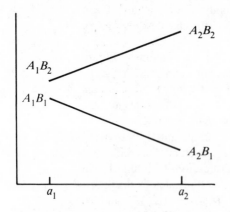

(c) *A* main effect not significant,
   B main effect significant,
   AB interaction significant.

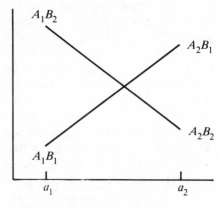

(d) *A* main effect not significant,
   B main effect not significant,
   AB interaction significant.

Figure 11.2–1 2×2 *AB* Summary Table plots showing various main effect and interaction outcomes

AB interaction. This case bears closer examination, however, since it is clear from Figure 11.2–1(c) that there is an effect of variable *A* (A_1 differs from A_2) but the direction of this effect is reversed at B_1 as compared to B_2. The impression gained from the ANOVA table that independent variable *A* has no effect would have been somewhat misleading, and examination of the *AB* interaction is required for a proper understanding of the result.

Figure 11.2–1(d) depicts the case in which both main effects are non-significant but the *AB* interaction is significant. Here again it is obvious that at both levels of *B* the different levels of *A* are affecting the data, and similarly, at both levels of *A* the different levels of *B* are having an effect. The lack of an overall *A* or *B* main effect results from the fact that the *A* main effect is based on the comparison of A_1 and A_2 means, and the *B* main effect is based on the comparison of B_1 and B_2 means.

When a significant *AB* interaction is obtained and the *AB* cell totals are plotted, it cannot be determined merely by inspection whether any given pair of cell totals is significantly different. In an outcome such as that depicted in Figure 11.2–1(a), for example, it is possible that the overall significant main effect for variable *A* is the result of the very strong effect of *A* at b_2; it may be the case that A_1B_1 and A_2B_1 are not significantly different, or in other words, that *A* had no effect at b_1. In order to properly understand the main effect for variable *A*, we must determine whether A_1B_1 differs significantly from A_2B_1; this will tell us whether variable *A* had an effect when variable *B* was held constant at the b_1 level. As a matter of routine we would also compare A_1B_2 with A_2B_2 in order to confirm the impression gained from the plot that variable *A* was effective at level b_2. Such comparisons of *AB* cell totals are known as *simple effects* tests and may be tested using an adaptation of the Tukey HSD procedure in which the Critical Difference between cell totals is determined as follows. For simple effects comparisons between *A* totals at particular *B* levels

simple effects

$$CD = [q_{0.05}(p, df\ MS_{error})][\sqrt{nMS_{error}}]*$$

In order to clearly understand the main effect for variable *B*, we must conduct similar comparisons (simple effect tests) of *B* level totals at particular levels of *A* so that we can determine whether variable *B* had a significant effect at the a_1 level and/or the a_2 level. Significant differences between *B* levels at particular *A* levels are determined as follows. For simple effects comparisons between *B* totals at particular *A* levels

$$CD = [q_{0.05}(q, df\ MS_{error})][\sqrt{nMS_{error}}]*$$

Table 11.2–1 summarizes the decision rules regarding main effects and simple effects tests in the two factor ANOVA.

We will now turn to a numerical illustration of these procedures. There are certain objects in our environment that should be as readily identifiable as possible so that we can respond to them in an appropriate manner, and we have adopted standard colors and/or configurations for such things as school buses, ambulances, and fire trucks. Many readers of this text will be too young to

---

*The derivation of *CD* for simple effects tests is based on the rationale proposed by Winer (1962, 1971). Cicchetti (1972) has suggested a modification in which the $q_{0.05}$ term is selected differently.

Table 11.2–1 Two factor ANOVA decision chart

If	Then
F_A, F_B, and F_{AB} are not significant.	Retain all null hypotheses.
F_{AB} is not significant but F_A and/or F_B is significant.	Perform main effects tests on overall A totals if F_A is significant and $p > 2$. Perform main effects tests on overall B totals if F_B is significant and $q > 2$.
F_{AB} is significant	Perform simple effects tests on A totals at each level of B. Perform simple effects tests on B totals at each level of A.

remember that fire trucks used to be painted red, or "fire engine red" as we used to say. But now they are all greenish-yellowish and, to people over forty, don't seem somehow to be real fire trucks. The decision to change the color of fire trucks was not made to confuse old people, however, but because research had shown that the new color was far easier to detect than red, especially under conditions of poor illumination.

It would be a relatively straightforward matter to set up a laboratory in which illumination level could be adjusted to simulate bright daylight, dim conditions such as heavy overcast or dusk, and night illumination levels. Subjects could be seated before a large screen upon which the experimenter could project spots of any color, any intensity, and for any duration. Each subject might be instructed to fixate on the center of the screen, and then the experimenter could project a spot of color, say 20 times in a random pattern of locations on the screen. Subjects could be instructed to press a button each time they detect a spot of color. By adjusting intensity and exposure duration, it would be possible to find settings at which white light spots resulted in less than 100 percent detection; these settings could then be used in experiments to compare the detectability of other colors. The dependent variable would thus be target detectability defined operationally as the number of times out of 20 that the stimulus was detected. Such a measure would be direct in the sense that larger scores indicate greater detectability. We will imagine this experiment as an illustration of the two factor independent groups ANOVA. (Please note that these data and interpretations are purely hypothetical.)

In our hypothetical experiment the independent variables were $A =$ illumination level where $a_1 =$ sunny, $a_2 =$ overcast, and $a_3 =$ night illumination conditions (in a real case, these would be operationally defined as number of foot candles ambient illumination), and $B =$ color where $b_1 =$ red and $b_2 =$ green-yellow. Since there are three levels of one independent variable and two levels of the other, this would be termed a 3×2 design and would require $3 \times 2 = 6$ independently randomly sampled subject groups or a single random sample with individuals randomly assigned to the six treatment groups. Thus

Independent variable A: illumination level

Independent variable B: color

Dependent variable: target detectability

Null hypotheses: 1. Illumination level does not affect target detectability ($\mu_{\text{sunny}} = \mu_{\text{overcast}} = \mu_{\text{night}}$).

2. Color does not affect target detectability ($\mu_{\text{red}} = \mu_{\text{green-yellow}}$).

3. Illumination level and color do not interact to affect target detectability (See footnote at bottom of page 234).

Assume the raw data were as follows.

Illumination level

Color	a_1 (sunny)	a_2 (overcast)	a_3 (night)
b_1 (red)	16	13	11
	14	11	9
	12	9	7
	14	12	8
	11	8	6
	11	9	5
b_2 (green-yellow)	10	11	12
	12	12	13
	13	14	15
	13	14	14
	12	12	13
	16	17	17

$p = 3,$ $q = 2,$ $n = 6,$ $N = 36$

AB Summary Table

	a_1	a_2	a_3	
b_1	78	62	46	186
b_2	76	80	84	240
	154	142	130	426

(1) $\sum X^2 = 5334.00$

(2) $(\sum X)^2 / N = (426)^2 / 36 = 5041.00$

(3) $\sum A^2/nq = \dfrac{(154)^2 + (142)^2 + (130)^2}{(6)(2)} = 5065.00$

(4) $\sum B^2/np = \dfrac{(186)^2 + (240)^2}{(6)(3)} = 5122.00$

(5) $\sum (AB)^2/n = \dfrac{(78)^2 + (62)^2 + (46)^2 + (76)^2 + (80)^2 + (84)^2}{6}$

$= 5212.67$

$SS_A = \sum A^2/nq - (\sum X)^2/N$

$= 5065.00 - 5041.00$

$= 24.00$

$SS_B = \sum B^2/np - (\sum X)^2/N$

$= 5122.00 - 5041.00$

$= 81.00$

$SS_{AB} = \sum (AB)^2/n + (\sum X)^2/N - \sum A^2/nq - \sum B^2/np$

$= 5212.67 + 5041.00 - 5065.00 - 5122.00$

$= 66.67$

$SS_{\text{residual}} = \sum X^2 - \sum (AB)^2/n$

$= 5334.00 - 5212.67$

$= 121.33$

Source of Variation	Sum of Squares	df	Mean Square	F
A (illumination)	24.00	2	12.00	2.97
B (color)	81.00	1	81.00	20.05
AB	66.67	2	33.34	8.25
Residual	121.33	30	4.04	

Variable A (illumination level):

1. $df = (p - 1)/pq(n - 1) = (3 - 1)/(3)(2)(6 - 1) = 2/30$

2. The critical value for F at 0.05 confidence level = 3.32

3. Therefore the result is not significant.

4. Preliminary interpretation: Illumination level does not affect target detectability.

Variable B (color):

1. $df = (q - 1)/pq(n - 1) = (2 - 1)/(3)(2)(6 - 1) = 1/30$
2. The critical value for F at 0.05 confidence level $= 4.17$
3. Therefore the result is significant.
4. Preliminary interpretation: Color does affect target detectability.

AB (illumination by color) interaction:

1. $df = (p - 1)(q - 1)/pq(n - 1) = (3 - 1)(2 - 1)/(3)(2)(6 - 1)$
   $= 2/30$
2. The critical value for F at 0.05 confidence level $= 3.32$
3. Therefore the result is significant.
4. Preliminary interpretation: Illumination and color interact to affect target
   detectability.

Since the interaction is significant, we must examine these results more closely by plotting the AB Summary Table cell totals. The plot is shown in Figure 11.2–2.

Inspection of the AB Summary Table plot identifies the source of the AB interaction effect as the difference in slope of the b_1 and b_2 lines across the a_1, a_2, a_3 conditions. Keeping in mind that larger scores reflect greater stimulus detectability, it is now obvious that the red (b_1) target showed steadily decreasing detectability as illumination level dropped while the green-yellow

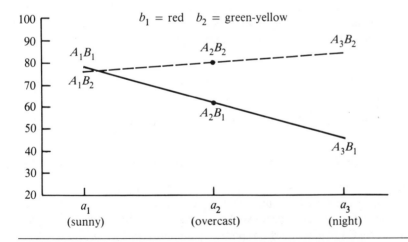

Figure 11.2–2 AB Summary Table plot showing the illumination level by color interaction

(b_2) target showed an apparent increase in detectability. The significant AB interaction term in the ANOVA means that the effect of illumination on detectability is a function of (interacts with) target color.

In order to clearly understand the effect of illumination level, we must compare detectability under the different illumination levels separately for each color. In other words, given a red target, was detectability significantly different under sunny as compared to overcast illumination, under sunny as compared to night, and under overcast as compared to night conditions? The same questions must be answered with reference to the green-yellow target. Such comparisons are known as simple effects tests; the Tukey HSD procedure, described earlier, is recommended and illustrated next.

For simple effects comparisons between A (illumination) totals at particular B (color) levels

$$
\begin{aligned}
CD &= [q_{0.05}(p, df\ MS_{error})][\sqrt{nMS_{error}}] \\
&= [q_{0.05}(3, 30)][\sqrt{(6)(4.04)}] \\
&= (3.49)(4.92) \\
&= 17.17
\end{aligned}
$$

Simple effects comparison of A (illumination) totals at b_1 (red target)

$A_1B_1 - A_2B_1 = 78 - 62 = 16$:   Not significant

$A_1B_1 - A_3B_1 = 78 - 46 = 32$:   Significant

$A_2B_1 - A_3B_1 = 62 - 46 = 16$:   Not significant

These results can be interpreted to mean that the red target is significantly more difficult to detect at night than under sunny conditions ($A_1B_1 - A_3B_1$), but that detectability does not differ between sunny and overcast, or between overcast and night conditions.

Simple effects comparison of A (illumination) totals at b_2 (green-yellow) target

$A_1B_2 - A_2B_2 = 76 - 80 = -4$:   Not significant

$A_1B_2 - A_3B_2 = 76 - 84 = -8$:   Not significant

$A_2B_2 - A_3B_2 = 80 - 84 = -4$:   Not significant

These results indicate that the green-yellow target does not differ in detectability under the three illumination levels. Examination of the simple effects for variable A has made it clear that the overall non-significant main effect for A in the ANOVA table does not portray a complete picture of the effect of this variable when considered at particular B levels. It is for this reason that the interpretations that immediately followed the ANOVA table were termed "preliminary."

To fully understand the effect of B (color) on detectability, we must perform simple effects tests on the two colors at each illumination level so that we can know whether color affects detectability at all or at only some of the illumination levels used. Again the Tukey HSD procedure can be used and proceeds as follows.

For simple effects comparisons between B (color) totals at particular A (illumination) levels

$$
\begin{aligned}
CD &= [q_{0.05}(q, df\ MS_{error})][\sqrt{nMS_{error}}\,] \\
&= [q_{0.05}(2,30)][\sqrt{(6)\,(4.04)}\,] \\
&= (2.89)\,(4.92) \\
&= 14.22
\end{aligned}
$$

Simple effects comparison of B (color) totals at a_1 (sunny illumination)

$A_1 B_1 - A_1 B_2 = 78 - 76 = 2$:   Not significant

This result means that the red and the green-yellow targets do not differ in detectability under sunny illumination.

Simple effects comparison of B (color) totals at a_2 (overcast illumination)

$A_2 B_1 - A_2 B_2 = 62 - 80 = -18$:   Significant

This result means that the red and the green-yellow targets differ in detectability under overcast illumination, and since higher scores reflect greater detectability, we can say that the green-yellow (b_2) target is significantly easier to detect.

Simple effects comparison of B (color) totals at a_3 (night illumination)

$A_3 B_1 - A_3 B_2 = 46 - 84 = -38$:   Significant

This result means that the red and the green-yellow targets differ in detectability under night illumination and, since higher scores reflect greater detectability, we can say that the green-yellow (b_2) target is significantly easier to detect. It is clear from an examination of the simple effects that a main effect may not be what it at first seems to be. As has been shown by this example, a significant main (overall) effect for B does not necessarily mean that B is effective at every level of A.

The final interpretation of this hypothetical experiment would be that the red target is significantly more difficult to detect at night as compared to sunny conditions, whereas this is not the case for the green-yellow target, and that under overcast and night illumination conditions, the green-yellow target is significantly easier to detect than the red target.

For those interested in exploring the derivation of the various Sums of Squares in the two factor independent groups ANOVA, these derivations follow the same rationale shown in Sections 9.4 and 9.6 dealing with the single factor designs, and are presented next.

$$SS_A = qn[\text{Sum of Squares of the } A \text{ means}]$$
$$= qn[\sum \overline{A}^2 - (\sum \overline{A})^2/p]$$

$$SS_B = pn[\text{Sum of Squares of the } B \text{ means}]$$
$$= pn[\sum \overline{B}^2 - (\sum \overline{B})^2/q]$$

$$SS_{AB} = n[\text{Sum of Squares of the } AB \text{ means}]$$
$$- qn[\text{Sum of Squares of the } A \text{ means}]$$
$$+ pn[\text{Sum of Squares of the } B \text{ means}]$$
$$= n[\sum (\overline{AB})^2 - (\sum \overline{AB})^2/pq] - qn[\sum \overline{A}^2 - (\sum \overline{A})^2/p]$$
$$+ pn[\sum \overline{B}^2 - (\sum \overline{B})^2/q]$$

$$SS_{\text{residual}} = \text{Sum of the within groups Sums of Squares}$$
$$= \sum [\sum X^2 - (\sum X)^2/n]$$

11.3 Review Exercises

1. Define or describe the following terms.
   (a) two factor ANOVA
   (b) interaction
   (c) factorial ANOVA designs
   (d) main effect
   (e) AB interaction plot
   (f) simple effect

Note: The following problems represent hypothetical research situations, and in each case you should:
   (a) identify the independent variables
   (b) identify the dependent variable
   (c) state the null hypotheses being tested
   (d) complete the analysis at 0.05 confidence level
   (e) clearly interpret the result

2. An investigator studied the effects on learning of inserting questions into instructional materials. In one condition, the questions were presented at the beginning of the section to be learned, and in the second condition the questions were dispersed throughout. The two types of questions that were used dealt with discrete facts and underlying concepts. Following a single reading of the section, the subjects were given a 50-item test

covering the content of the material. The following data represent number of correct responses.

	Questions at the beginning	Questions dispersed throughout
Facts	22	28
	28	23
	31	32
	24	25
	26	24
	19	28
Concepts	28	28
	21	30
	18	32
	21	26
	26	27
	26	27

3. The following data represent scores on a 30-item vocabulary test that was administered to students of high intelligence (I.Q. score greater than 115) and low intelligence (I.Q. score less than 85) after one month of studying a foreign language under one of the three methods. The raw data represent the number of correct responses on the test.

	Oral	Translation	Sleep learning
High I.Q.	15	20	22
	10	15	18
	12	19	21
	12	16	22
	11	20	17
Low I.Q.	10	15	16
	8	17	18
	9	13	16
	11	16	17
	7	14	13

4. In a study of imprinting, the young of three species of ducks were tested for their imprintability to a soccer ball. Each duckling was confined for twenty minutes with the ball at either ten or sixteen hours post-hatch age. Testing occurred at ninety-six hours post-hatch age and consisted of placing the duckling on the floor one meter from the soccer ball. At the end of twenty seconds, the duckling's distance from the soccer ball was measured in centimeters.

	10 hrs. post-hatch	16 hrs. post-hatch
Mallard	5 2 10 8 9 6 9	3 4 2 6 0 6 0
Canvasback	15 8 12 6 12 11 6	10 9 9 4 6 6 5
Wood	15 20 12 14 14 12 11	18 16 15 14 11 11 13

5. Four different repellants were field tested on dogs and cats to determine which was the most effective in preventing animals from molesting garbage in plastic bags. Each animal was deprived of food for twelve hours and then presented with a bag filled with typical garbage that had been treated with one of the brands of repellant. The measure taken was the percentage of the bag's contents that the animal removed from the bag.

	1	2	3	4
Cats	70 75 65 70	75 75 66 74	20 25 30 25	18 23 25 24
Dogs	19 22 26 23	30 20 27 23	73 69 76 72	71 74 65 70

6. Fifteen children were randomly sampled from grades 1, 4, and 7, and tested for their tendency to persist at an unsolvable problem. Each was told that if he or she could solve the puzzle, he or she would be rewarded with one of three incentives: money, a half-day vacation from school, or

candy. The number of minutes each child persisted in trying to solve the problem was recorded.

	Money	Vacation	Candy
Grade 7	12 10 8 8 12	7 12 10 10 11	2 2 5 5 1
Grade 4	6 10 8 7 9	6 6 11 11 6	7 9 5 9 10
Grade 1	2 6 4 4 4	3 5 5 6 1	13 8 12 9 13

7. An experimenter tested peoples' accuracy in estimating the passage of 20 seconds of time by asking the subjects to push a button when they thought 20 seconds had elapsed, following a start signal. The number of seconds between the occurrence of the start signal and button depression was recorded. The conditions of testing and raw data were as follows.

	Control	60 ml alcohol	20 grains aspirin	50 mg morphine
8:00 a.m.	15 14 14 12	28 26 27 29	14 13 11 17	27 27 30 26
12:00 noon	18 16 16 15	27 24 25 24	18 17 17 13	29 24 21 26
8:00 p.m.	18 22 19 21	25 26 23 21	20 17 21 22	24 26 22 23
12:00 midnight	22 26 20 22	25 24 20 21	23 25 21 21	24 24 22 20

Part IV

Decisions About Relationships

12 Product-Moment Correlation

Chapter Preview

12.1 Introduction to Correlation

Folksy aphorisms like, "absence makes the heart grow fonder," and, "where there is smoke there is fire," reflect a pervasive reality of the natural world, namely, the existence of relationships. Things are said to be related if changes in one are accompanied by changes in the other, as, for example, when the attainability of a thing decreases, its desirability increases. If variation in one variable is accompanied by systematic variation in a second variable, the two *correlation*   may be said to co-vary, or correlate. *Correlation* refers to systematic relationships between variables; such relationships may be either positive cor-*positive correlation*   relations or negative correlations. A *positive correlation* is a relationship between two variables such that as one increases, the other tends also to increase. For example, as the price of beef increases, the amount of chicken *negative correlation*   sold in supermarkets tends to increase. A *negative correlation* is a relationship between two variables such that as one increases, the other tends to decrease. For example, as the price of steak increases, the proportion of people who buy it decreases.

There is a positive correlation between height and weight, that is, taller people tend to be heavier, and vice versa. But there are exceptions; some short people are heavy and some tall people are light. Thus, the correlation between height and weight is not absolutely perfect because a taller person is not always heavier. Further, even though it is generally true that taller people are heavier, it is not the case that people gain a specific number of kilograms or pounds for each additional centimeter or inch of height. We say that as height increases weight tends to increase, thereby reflecting the general but imperfect nature of this correlation. Some relationships are more precise; for example, Newton's second law of motion states that acceleration (A) varies directly with force (F) and inversely with the mass (M) of an object ($A = F/M$). If mass is held constant, then acceleration is a direct function of the force applied, and each additional unit of force will result in a fixed amount of increase in acceleration. Of course, many variables show no systematic tendency to relate to each other. For example, the number of times that I answer the telephone during the day is quite unrelated to the number of times you check your wristwatch.

The point is that two variables may show a degree of relationship, or correlation, that ranges from none at all to some perfect limit. When two variables are unrelated, the value of one is random with respect to the other. When two variables have a perfect relationship, or perfect correlation, each unit of change in one is accompanied by a fixed unit of change in the other. Between these two extremes lies the range of real but less than perfect relationships manifested by many natural events.

In statistics, the procedures that measure the degree of positive or negative relationship between variables are called correlational techniques. Such techniques yield statistics known as *correlation coefficients,* which are quantitative indices of the kind and degree of correlation between variables. Correlation coefficients are derived in such a way that they range in value from -1.00 to $+1.00$. A coefficient of -1.00 indicates a perfect negative correlation, and a coefficient of $+1.00$ indicates a perfect positive correlation; values between these limits reflect varying degrees of relationship. When there is no systematic relationship (value of Y is random with respect to X) the correlation coefficient is 0.00.

correlation coefficient

Correlation coefficients are quantitative expressions of the degree of relationship between variables. However, correlation coefficients are not ratio measurement statistics; a coefficient of $+0.80$ does not represent a relationship that is twice as strong as that represented by $+0.40$. Similarly, a correlation of -0.20 is not one-third as great as one of -0.60. In fact, correlation coefficients are not even interval measurement; a correlation of $+0.50$ is not as much greater than one of $+0.40$ as one of $+0.60$ is greater than one of $+0.50$. In other words, the units in which correlation coefficients are expressed do not reflect the same amount or degree of relationship throughout their range from 0.00 to ±1.00. The correlation coefficient, while it is a quantitative index, provides only a general impression of the closeness of the relationship. This matter will be discussed further in Section 12.6.

When one calculates a correlation coefficient to determine the degree of relationship between two variables, the raw data exist as pairs of observations. For instance, if we wish to determine the correlation between the heights and weights of a number of people, we first obtain these measures on each individual; thus, each subject produces a pair of scores. It is conventional to use the letters X and Y as general designations of the variables so that, for example, the height scores may be labeled as X and the weight scores as Y. In general terms, we compute the correlation between X and Y. The important point is that each X score is naturally paired with a particular Y score, which in this case is the height and weight of a particular individual. It is essential that this pairing of the data not be disturbed or scrambled when the raw scores are subjected to analysis. The usual practice is to present the raw scores in columns; it is understood that scores on any row represent naturally paired observations, as is shown in the following table.

Subject No.	Variable X	Variable Y
1	X_1	Y_1
2	X_2	Y_2
3	X_3	Y_3
.	.	.
.	.	.
.	.	.
N	X_N	Y_N

Since the X and Y data represent two measures taken on some number of individuals, objects, or events, both may be thought of as dependent variables. A correlation coefficient should not be regarded as a measure of the influence of a manipulated condition on some target outcome but merely as an assessment of the degree of relationship between two naturally occurring measures. By naturally occurring, we mean that the experimenter has not done anything to influence the score values obtained. In Chapter 7 we differentiated between treatment type and classification type independent variables, and said that experiments that use classification type independent variables are termed correlational research. The use of this terminology may now be clarified; since a classification type independent variable is a kind of measure of the subject, it is not fundamentally different from a dependent variable. Correlational experiments assess whether there is a relationship between two measures taken on the subjects.

If two variables are shown to be systematically related, this is not evidence that one is causally connected to the other, even if the correlation is perfect. Correlation is simply a measure of the degree to which things co-vary; there is no implication of any causal link between them. We seem to have a strong natural tendency to jump to causal conclusions regarding correlated events and must constantly guard against this error. Ask yourself, if height and weight are positively correlated, is being taller the direct cause of being heavier? Is being heavier the direct cause of being taller? (The question makes equal sense put either way.) Actually, there is a group of factors that jointly determine, or cause, a given person's height (such as genetic and nutritional factors) and a group of factors that cause weight (such as genetic, nutritional, and exercise factors). Height and weight are end results of their respective sets of causal factors and the relationship between them probably results from having some common underlying causal factors, but it is as foolish to think that height causes weight as it is to think that weight causes height. Of course, if two events are causally connected they will show a correlation, but the point that must be reiterated is that a causal link can never be assumed merely from evidence of relationship; there may be a third factor, or any number of factors, acting as the real causal basis for both variables. Having a fever correlates with having a runny nose, but can either be said to cause the other? Obviously in this case, a third factor, namely a viral infection, is the causal basis for both of the observed conditions.

Reynolds (1976) cites a study by Comstock & Partridge (1972), which found a strong negative correlation between church attendance and fatal arteriosclerotic heart disease; the more frequent the church attendance, the less the risk! Since a true "experimental" evaluation of the effect of church attendance on heart disease cannot be done, it is very difficult to establish whether this relationship is causal or artificial. It may be that going to church reduces one's overall level of tension and in that way genuinely contributes to reduced heart disease frequency. Of course, people who attend church differ in many ways from those who don't; any of these differences could be the causal basis for different heart disease probability, in which case the relationship is artificial.

An aside: Feeling sick? Go to church!

Sometimes two events co-vary and it is difficult to conceive of any possible way that they might be connected, as for example if ice cream consumption in Windsor were found to correlate with shark attacks off Melbourne. Such purely coincidental relationships are termed *spurious correlations*. It is said, for example, that since the turn of the century, prices on the New York Stock Exchange show a high correlation with womens' skirt lengths; when skirts are short, prices are high, and vice versa (Morris, 1977; see Figure 12.1–1). The reader is left to conjecture some logical rationale for this apparently spurious relationship.

spurious correlation

12.2 Relationship Between Interval/Ratio Variables

Product-moment correlation is a technique for measuring the degree of relationship between two sets of interval/ratio measures. The *product-moment correlation coefficient* is symbolized by r and can range in value from $+1.00$ (perfect positive relationship) to -1.00 (a perfect negative relationship). The product-moment coefficient is sensitive to the consistency with which Y increases or decreases as X increases, as well as the overall tendency for this to occur.

product-moment correlation
product-moment correlation coefficient

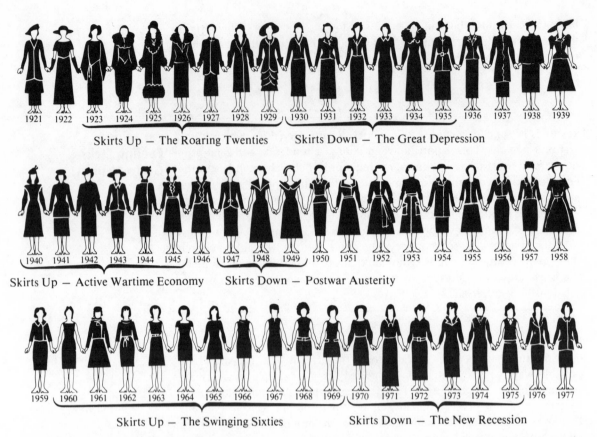

Skirts Up — The Roaring Twenties   Skirts Down — The Great Depression

Skirts Up — Active Wartime Economy   Skirts Down — Postwar Austerity

Skirts Up — The Swinging Sixties   Skirts Down — The New Recession

The skirt length of the modern Western woman acts as an economic barometer. As hemlines rise and fall, so does the economic condition of the country. Short skirts appear at times of high national production and long skirts during the periods of austerity and recession.

Figure 12.1–1 The relationship between skirt length and stock prices. From Morris, D., *Manwatching: A Field Guide to Human Behavior.* Copyright © 1977 by Desmond Morris. Reprinted by permission of Equinox (Oxford) Ltd.

Consider the following data.

X	Y
40	116
38	108
36	100
34	92
32	84

$$r = +1.00$$

The largest value of X is paired with the largest value of Y, the second largest

X with the second largest Y, and so on down to the smallest X paired with the smallest Y. In terms of the alignment of X and Y score magnitudes, these data have the maximum possible correspondence. Notice also that each unit of change in X is accompanied by a consistent amount of change in Y (Y changes by 4 units for each unit change in X). These data represent a perfect positive correlation and the r coefficient is $+1.00$.

Now consider the following data.

X	Y
40	113
38	111
36	100
34	90
32	86

$$r = +0.98$$

Here we have the same set of X scores paired with a different group of Y values. The correspondence between the magnitudes of the X and Y scores is still at the maximum; that is, the largest X is paired with the largest Y, the second largest X with the second largest Y, and so on. But in this case the Y values do not show consistent changes with each unit of change in X, for example, when X goes from 36 to 38, Y changes by 11 units, and when X goes from 38 to 40, Y changes by 2 units. This lack of consistency in the changes in Y that accompany changes in X simply means that the relationship between X and Y is not as perfect as it could be and this is reflected in a lower correlation coefficient ($r = +0.98$).

A more technical way of expressing the requirement for a perfect correlation between X and Y is in terms of z-scores. In order for X and Y to be perfectly correlated, the paired X and Y scores must have identical z-score values in their respective distributions. If each X is expressed as a z-score, and if each Y is expressed as a z-score, and if in every pair the z_x and z_y are identical values, then the correlation is perfect.

Consider the following data in which the X scores are the same as in the previous two illustrations and the Y data is identical to those in the first illustration except that the positions of the scores 92 and 100 have been reversed.

X	Y
40	116
38	108
36	92
34	100
32	84

$$r = +0.90$$

The reversal of the two Y scores disturbs both the alignment of the score magnitudes and the z-score equivalence of the X and Y pairs (the former necessarily results in the latter), and it can be seen that the impact on the correlation coefficient ($r = +0.90$) is more substantial.

In summary, while it is convenient to think of a correlation coefficient as an index of the extent to which changes in X are accompanied by changes in Y, the consistency of such changes is also a relevant factor in determining the value of r.

12.3 The Geometric Appearance of Relationship

bivariate plot

If some number of individuals is measured on two variables, X and Y, we can depict the relationship between X and Y visually by means of a *bivariate plot*, which is also known as a scatter plot, or scatter diagram. A bivariate plot is constructed by marking the abscissa in units representing the X variable, marking the ordinate in units representing the Y variable, and then locating the points of intersection in the body of the graph. To locate the points of intersection one must, for each pair of scores, locate the X value on the abscissa and imagine or draw a vertical line through the body of the graph, and similarly locate the Y value on the ordinate and imagine a horizontal line through the graph. Where these two lines cross is the point of intersection for the pair of scores and identifies the position of that subject in the bivariate plot.

The following hypothetical data represent number of years of formal education (X) and annual income in thousand of dollars (Y) for ten persons.

X (yrs. education)	Y (income $\times$ 1000)
12	14
21	30
15	24
10	11
8	13
16	18
17	12
19	27
13	20
16	25

The bivariate plot for these data is presented in Figure 12.3–1. The first two subjects [(12,14) and (21,30)] have been explicitly located by using straight lines and labeled in the body of the graph, and the remainder of the subjects' positions were similarly plotted.

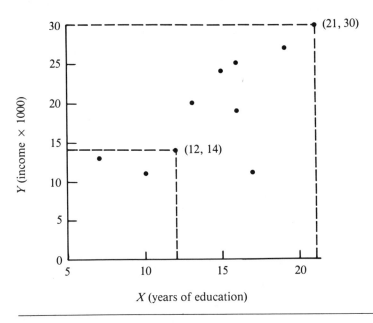

Figure 12.3–1   Bivariate plot of education and income data

If the points in Figure 12.3–1 are bounded by a smooth line, they form an elliptical array in which the long axis slopes upward to the right, as is shown in Figure 12.3–2. An upward sloping array of points in a bivariate plot reflects a positive correlation, that is, Y values tend to increase as X values increase. A negative correlation appears graphically as an array of points that slopes downward to the right, as shown in Figure 12.3–3(a), (b), and (c) on page 261.

Product moment correlation is a measure of the degree of linear relationship between X and Y. A *linear relationship* is a straight line function; thus, product-moment correlation is a suitable measure when the relationship between X and Y can be adequately represented by a straight line. The value of the r coefficient reflects the degree to which the array of points in the bivariate plot forms a straight line. Figure 12.3–3(a) depicts a fairly wide elliptical array and reflects only a moderate correlation ($r = -0.52$). In contrast, Figure 12.3–3(b) depicts a much tighter elliptical array and represents a high degree of relationship ($r = -0.90$). Finally, Figure 12.3–3(c) shows the limiting form of a linear relationship; the bivariate array forms a straight line representing a perfect correlation ($r = -1.00$). Compare also Figure 12.3–3(d), which depicts a high positive correlation ($r = +0.85$), with Figure 12.3–3(e), which represents a perfect positive relationship

linear relationship

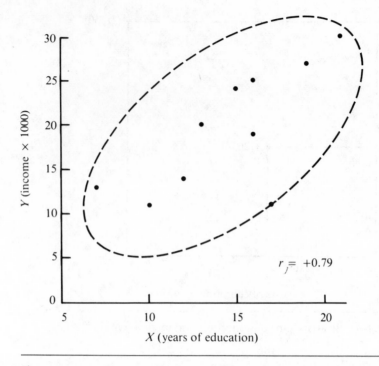

Figure 12.3–2   Bivariate plot bounded by an upward sloping ellipse

($r = +1.00$). When X and Y bear no relationship whatever to each other (the values of Y are random with respect to the values of X), the bivariate plot will show a circular array and the correlation coefficient will be zero, as is depicted in Figure 12.3–3(f), where $r = 0.00$.

It is important to remember that product-moment correlation is a measure of linear relationship and that an r coefficient equal to zero means only that X and Y are not linearly related. Two variables may show a systematic nonlinear (curvilinear) relationship, such as the inverted U function between arousal and performance. At low levels of arousal performance efficiency tends to increase as arousal increases, but a point is reached where further increments in arousal are accompanied by performance decrements. This function is known as the Yerkes-Dodson law, and is depicted in Figure 12.3–4 on page 262. As can be seen, the relationship is quite systematic but the product-moment correlation calculated on these data yields $r = +0.02$. The way to determine whether some nonlinear relation exists between X and Y is to examine the bivariate plot. One must not conclude that an absence of linear relationship represents an absence of any kind of relationship.

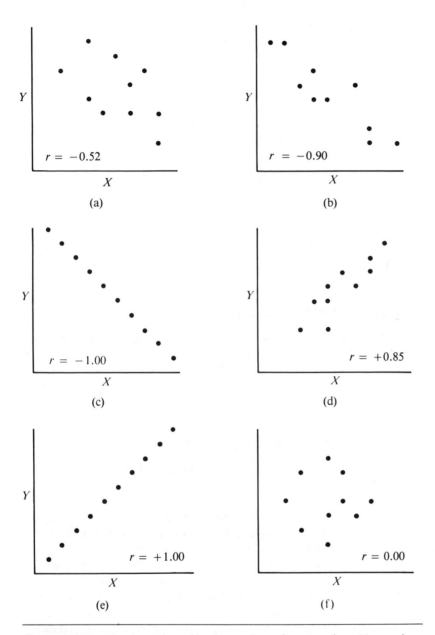

Figure 12.3–3   Bivariate plots showing various degrees of positive and negative correlation

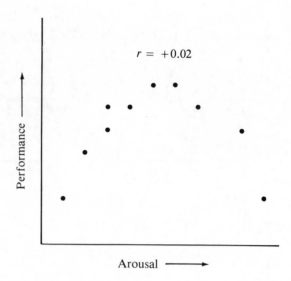

$r = +0.02$

Performance ———▶

Arousal ——▶

Figure 12.3–4 An example of the systematic relationship between arousal and performance, in the shape of an inverted U, known as the Yerkes-Dodson law

12.4 Product-Moment Correlation

This section will illustrate the computation of r with a numerical example and then offer some insight into the manner by which product-moment correlation measures relationship. Although the formula for computing the r coefficient may be presented in several alternative ways, the following method is recommended.

$$r = \frac{N \sum XY - \sum X \sum Y}{\sqrt{[N \sum X^2 - (\sum X)^2][N \sum Y^2 - (\sum Y)^2]}}$$

where X and Y are interval/ratio measures taken on N individuals, objects, or events. Note that we are using upper case N to identify the number of pairs of scores, or number of subjects.

Basically, a correlation coefficient is a descriptive term; it specifies the kind and degree of relationship between variables X and Y for the N individuals who have been directly observed. In real life, we most often use a correlation coefficient as an inferential statistic, and our real purpose is to estimate the relationship between X and Y in the population. This simply means that we test the obtained coefficient for significance to determine whether it is reliable (significant), or likely to be a function of sampling error. The null hypothesis in such a significance test is that the correlation between X and Y in the population is equal to zero ($r_{population} = 0.00$) and may be expressed as, "Variable X is not related to variable Y." In the following numerical illustration, we will assume an inferential purpose, specify a null hypothesis in advance, and interpret the result after conducting the significance test.

Let us consider a purely hypothetical study on the subject of the sexual harassment of working women. Assuming a workable and valid definition of sexual harassment, one could define the degree of sexual harassment as the frequency with which this occurred over some time period. An operational definition might be the number of harassment incidents during the past working year (variable Y). One of the factors that may be related to a woman's likelihood of being harassed is her job status or position in the rank structure of her place of work. Job status could be operationally defined as the annual salary in thousands of dollars (variable X).

Suppose a random sample of ten working women in various occupations reported the following data.

X (Salary)	Y (Harassment frequency)
10	24
27	9
22	22
15	35
12	25
20	15
32	6
26	7
6	41
20	36

The bivariate plot of these data, shown in Figure 12.4–1, indicates a negative linear relationship between annual salary and harassment frequency.

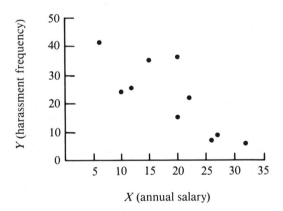

Figure 12.4–1 Bivariate plot of annual salary and sexual harassment frequency data

The calculation of the product-moment correlation between annual salary and harassment frequency, the test of significance for the r coefficient, and interpretation of the result, proceed as follows.

Variable X: Annual salary (in thousands of dollars)*

Variable Y: Number of sexual harassment incidents during the past working year.

Null hypothesis: Annual salary and harassment frequency are not related ($r_{\text{population}} = 0.00$).

X	Y	X^2	Y^2	XY
10	24	100	576	240
27	9	729	81	243
22	22	484	484	484
15	35	225	1225	525
12	25	144	625	300
20	15	400	225	300
32	6	1024	36	192
26	7	676	49	182
6	41	36	1681	246
20	36	400	1296	720
$\sum X = 190$	$\sum Y = 220$	$\sum X^2 = 4218$	$\sum Y^2 = 6278$	$\sum XY = 3432$

$N = 10$

$$r = \frac{N \sum XY - \sum X \sum Y}{\sqrt{[N \sum X^2 - (\sum X)^2][N \sum Y^2 - (\sum Y)^2]}}$$

$$= \frac{(10)(3{,}432) - (190)(220)}{\sqrt{[(10)(4{,}218) - (190)^2][(10)(6{,}278) - (220)^2]}}$$

$$= \frac{-7{,}480}{\sqrt{(6{,}080)(14{,}380)}}$$

$$= \frac{-7{,}480}{9{,}350.422450}$$

$$= -0.799964$$

$$= -0.80$$

The sign and magnitude of the correlation coefficient ($r = -0.80$) confirm the earlier impression that these variables show a fairly strong negative relationship. Before the result can be interpreted, however, the r coefficient must be tested for significance. It is conceivable that by mere chance, two randomly drawn sets of numbers that are randomly paired could show a nonzero correlation. The test of significance establishes whether, at some confidence level, the present outcome should be viewed as the result of such sampling error.

The r coefficient is tested by comparison with a critical value obtained from Table H. The degrees of freedom for the test of significance is $N - 2$,

*Presenting the salary data as the actual income, that is, multiplying X scores by constant $= 1000$, would not change the outcome; the smaller numbers are used for computational convenience.

and the critical value is determined in the usual manner by reading across the appropriate *df* row and down the column headed by the chosen confidence level. The null hypothesis being tested is that X and Y are not related in the population ($r_{\text{population}} = 0.00$), that is, that annual salary and sexual harassment frequency are not related. The null hypothesis is rejected when the calculated r equals or exceeds the critical value obtained from Table H.

1. $df = N - 2 = 10 - 2 = 8$

2. The critical value for r at 0.05 confidence level $= 0.632$

3. Therefore the result is significant.

4. Interpretation: There is a relationship between annual salary and frequency of sexual harassment ($r_{\text{population}} \neq 0.00$). This relationship is such that higher salary is associated with less harassment.

When the result is not significant, it need only be said that variables X and Y are not related, but the clear interpretation of a significant correlation requires an explicit statement of the relationship between the two variables. The existence of a significant correlation implies no casual connection between X and Y. In the previous (hypothetical) case, salary and sexual harassment frequency are associated, but this could not be taken as evidence that either causes the other.

We have shown that the correlation between annual salary and frequency of sexual harassment was $r = -0.80$ for the ten hypothetical women in our computational example. Suppose that when the original data were gathered, only women earning between ten and twenty thousand dollars inclusive had been sampled. In our data there are five such persons; the correlation between annual salary and harassment frequency for these five is $r = +0.04$! Take a look at the bivariate plot of the original data on page 263 and pick out these five women; you can easily see why the correlation was so different from that obtained from the overall group. This example illustrates the effect of the range of scores on the correlation coefficient. When the relationship is linear, unless the correlation is perfect, then restricting the range of values on which the correlation is based results in lowering the correlation coefficient. When the relationship is curvilinear the opposite effect occurs. In a broader sense, do not lose sight of the fact that any correlation coefficient reflects the degree of relationship *within the range of raw scores observed* and should not be extrapolated beyond that range or assumed to reflect the degree of relationship within subparts of that range.

An aside: correlation and score range

The rest of this section will examine the derivation of the r coefficient. The following formulas are alternative ways to calculate r; notice that each is a simple revision of the preceding formula.

$$(1) \quad r = \frac{N \sum XY - \sum X \sum Y}{\sqrt{[N \sum X^2 - (\sum X)^2][N \sum Y^2 - (\sum Y)^2]}}$$

$$(2) \quad r = \frac{\sum XY - \sum X \sum Y/N}{\sqrt{[\sum X^2 - (\sum X)^2/N][\sum Y^2 - (\sum Y)^2/N]}}$$

$$(3) \quad r = \frac{(\sum XY - \sum X \sum Y/N)/N - 1}{\sqrt{[\sum X^2 - (\sum X)^2/N]/N - 1} \times \sqrt{[\sum Y^2 - (\sum Y)^2/N]/N - 1}}$$

You will recognize that in formula (3), the denominator consists of the standard deviation of X times the standard deviation of Y. The numerator is called the covariance of X and Y and may be symbolized as c_{XY}. Thus

$$c_{XY} = \frac{\sum XY - \sum X \sum Y/N}{N - 1}$$

Since

$$\sum XY - \sum X \sum Y/N = \sum[(X - \overline{X})(Y - \overline{Y})]$$

then

$$c_{XY} = \frac{\sum[(X - \overline{X})(Y - \overline{Y})]}{N - 1}$$

Also, since

$$\sum X^2 - (\sum X)^2/N = \sum(X - \overline{X})^2$$

and

$$\sum Y^2 - (\sum Y)^2/N = \sum(Y - \overline{Y})^2$$

Then formula (2) may be rewritten as

$$(4) \quad r = \frac{\sum[(X - \overline{X})(Y - \overline{Y})]}{\sqrt{[\sum(X - \overline{X})^2][\sum(Y - \overline{Y})^2]}}$$

and formula (3) may be rewritten as

$$(5) \quad r = \frac{\sum[(X - \overline{X})(Y - \overline{Y})]/N - 1}{\sqrt{\sum(X - \overline{X})^2/N - 1} \times \sqrt{\sum(Y - \overline{Y})^2/N - 1}}$$

Of particular interest is the covariance of X and Y (c_{XY}), which is the sum of the products of the paired deviations divided by the degrees of freedom. In other words, each X is expressed as a deviation from its mean, and similarly each Y is expressed as a deviation from its mean; the deviation scores of each X and Y pair are multiplied together, the products summed, and that sum is divided by the degrees of freedom. A deviation score can be positive or negative depending on whether the raw score is larger or smaller than its mean.

Product-Moment Correlation

An experiment investigated the relationship between reading speed and memory for detail by having each subject read the same ten-page report and then take an examination on the content of the report. The raw data are shown next.

Variable X: Reading speed (defined operationally as the number of minutes required to read the report).

Variable Y: Memory for detail (defined operationally as the number of items answered correctly on an exam of the content of the report).

Null hypothesis: Reading speed and memory for detail are not related ($r_{population} = 0.00$).

X	Y	X^2	Y^2	XY
10	17	100	289	170
8	17	64	289	136
15	13	225	169	195
12	16	144	256	192
14	15	196	225	210
16	12	256	144	192

$\sum X = 75$ $\sum Y = 90$ $\sum X^2 = 985$ $\sum Y^2 = 1372$ $\sum XY = 1095$

$N = 6$

$$r = \frac{N \sum XY - \sum X \sum Y}{\sqrt{[N \sum X^2 - (\sum X)^2][N \sum Y^2 - (\sum Y)^2]}}$$

$$= \frac{(6)(1095) - (75)(90)}{\sqrt{[(6)(985) - (75)^2][(6)(1372) - (90)^2]}}$$

$$= -0.93$$

1. $df = N - 2 = 4$
2. The critical value for r at 0.05 confidence level = 0.811
3. Therefore the result is significant.
4. Interpretation: Reading speed is related to memory for detail ($r_{population} \neq 0.00$), such that greater reading speed is associated with poorer memory for detail.

Imagine a case where two sets of numbers, X and Y, bear a strong positive relationship to each other. In such a case, a high value of X will have a large and positive deviation from its mean and it will be paired with a large Y also having a large and positive deviation from its mean. The product of these deviations will be a positive and relatively large number. Small values of X will have large but negative deviation scores and will be paired with small Y's that also have large but negative deviation scores; the product of such a pair of deviations will be a relatively large and positive number. Thus, when X and Y have a strong positive relationship, the sum of the products of the deviation scores will be relatively large and positive.

When X and Y have a negative relationship, large positive deviations of X will be paired with large negative deviations of Y and vice versa, so that the sum of the products of the deviation scores will be relatively large and negative. When X and Y bear no systematic relationship to each other, the deviation scores, large and small, positive and negative, will be randomly paired; thus, quantities and signs will tend to cancel and the result will be that the sum of the products of the deviation scores will tend to be zero. The denominator of the covariance term merely corrects for the number of degrees of freedom upon which the sum of the deviation products is based.

The covariance term itself may seem to be a fairly good measure of the kind and degree of relationship between X and Y but a problem with the covariance term is that it is based on raw deviation scores and these are not comparable from one set of data to another without reference to the variability of the raw data. For example, the deviation score $X - \overline{X} = 5$ has a different meaning when $s = 2$ than when $s = 10$. In short, the covariance term must be corrected for differences in variability between the X and Y raw data and to make it comparable to covariance terms obtained from other sets of data. This is accomplished by dividing the covariance by the product of the standard deviations of X and Y. This is exactly what formula (5) consists of, and it may be more conveniently expressed as

$$r = \frac{c_{XY}}{s_X s_Y} = \frac{\text{covariance of } X \text{ and } Y}{(\text{standard deviation of } X)(\text{standard deviation of } Y)}$$

The covariance term can be positive or negative; it will be found that the maximum value of c_{XY} is equal to $s_X s_Y$ and is reached when the correlation between X and Y is perfect. Thus, the value of r can range from -1.00 to $+1.00$.

12.5 Review Exercises

1. Define or describe the following terms.

   (a) correlation
   (b) positive correlation

(c) negative correlation

(d) correlation coefficient

(e) spurious correlation

(f) product-moment correlation

(g) product-moment correlation coefficient

(h) bivariate plot

(i) linear relationship

In each of the following problems:

(a) state the null hypothesis being tested

(b) calculate the product-moment correlation coefficient and test for significance at 0.05 confidence level

(c) clearly interpret the result

2. Ten rats were deprived of food for various numbers of hours (variable X) and then placed at one end of a long straight runway with food placed in a goal box at the other end. Running speed in cm per second (variable Y) was recorded for each rat.

X: 2, 6, 9, 7, 12, 4, 1, 3, 6, 10

Y: 5, 30, 35, 25, 40, 10, 10, 20, 5, 20

3. Ten rats were individually placed in a maze after having been deprived of water for various numbers of hours (variable X). The number of minutes each took to reach the end of the maze (variable Y) was recorded.

X: 2, 3, 18, 1, 16, 8, 9, 4, 6, 12

Y: 18, 12, 2, 15, 4, 7, 5, 10, 9, 4

4. Ten judo experts took part in a tournament. The following data show each contestant's height in inches (variable X), and the number of opponents defeated (variable Y).

X: 71, 72, 75, 73, 76, 70, 66, 67, 67, 66

Y: 1, 4, 3, 4, 5, 6, 7, 8, 8, 10

5. Seven students completed a course evaluation form in which they rated the enjoyability of the course on a 10-point scale (variable X, with high numbers reflecting greater enjoyment). A second item called for a rating of how useful they thought the course material would be in later life (variable Y, with high numbers reflecting greater perceived usefulness).

X: 9, 6, 7, 5, 10, 7, 7

Y: 9, 5, 6, 3, 8, 5, 4

6. Eight persons were required to solve a complex arithmetic problem; the measure taken was termed Arithmetic Proficiency (variable X), and consisted of the time to the nearest tenth of a minute required to complete the problem. Each person was also given a test of Verbal Fluency (vari-

able Y), which consisted of the number of sentences containing a stimulus word that the person could construct in a twenty-minute period.

> X: 5.0, 4.4, 4.1, 3.4, 2.5, 2.1, 2.9, 3.6
> Y: 10, 15, 16, 20, 29, 32, 24, 22

7. At a health spa, people were encouraged to jog as a means of losing weight. Records were kept on nine persons indicating the number of miles jogged (variable X) and the number of pounds lost (variable Y) during a two-week period.

> X: 7, 40, 20, 10, 30, 5, 14, 15, 25
> Y: 6, 25, 12, 8, 16, 3, 9, 10, 15

8. Eleven subjects were asked to record the number of dreams they experienced (variable Y) during a one-week period. Each subject was also asked to record the number of cups of coffee consumed during this period (variable X).

> X: 7, 14, 21, 35, 28, 35, 42, 21, 56, 42, 49
> Y: 0, 4, 2, 5, 5, 6, 9, 4, 14, 8, 14

9. Harry attended hockey games and counted the number of fights that broke out on the ice (variable X) and the number that broke out in the bleachers (variable Y).

> X: 1, 3, 4, 5, 5, 6, 4, 2, 7, 10
> Y: 6, 4, 3, 2, 2, 1, 3, 4, 1, 0

12.6 The Meaning of r

The product-moment correlation coefficient is a means for determining the degree of linear relationship between X and Y and for comparing the degree of relationship between different sets of variables. It is important to understand what r is not. To repeat comments made earlier, the r coefficient is *not* a ratio statistic ($r = 0.80$ is not twice as great a relationship as $r = 0.40$) and the coefficient is *not* an interval statistic (the difference in degree of relationship between $r = 0.70$ and $r = 0.60$ is not the same as the difference between $r = 0.60$ and $r = 0.50$). The r coefficient is *not* a proportion or a percentage: an $r = 0.90$ does not mean 9/10 of a perfect relationship.

The most useful interpretation is not of the r coefficient itself, but rather of r^2; this is known as the variance interpretation of product-moment correlation. The correlation coefficient squared (r^2) is the proportion of the variance of Y that can be predicted from X; it is also the proportion of the variance of X that can be predicted from Y. Some writers say that r^2 is the proportion of the variance of Y that is accounted for by X, but this is intended only to mean predictable from X and does not imply any deterministic connection. Another way to express this is that if you imagine as 100 percent all the information that you would need to make a perfect, error-free, prediction of a Y score, then knowing X provides you with a proportion of that information equal to r^2*. (Please note that all statements are equally true whether one goes from X to Y or from Y to X.)

In the numerical example used in Section 12.4, it was found that the correlation between annual salary and frequency of sexual harassment was $r = -0.80$. We could now say that $r^2 = (-0.80)^2 = 0.6400 = 64$ percent of the variance of frequency of harassment scores may be predicted from annual salary. Conversely, knowing a woman's frequency of harassment provides us with 64 percent of the information we need in order to state her exact salary, or, 64 percent of the variance of salary scores is predictable from harassment frequency. This last statement, that salary is partly predictable from harassment frequency, does not seem logical since it appears to imply that salary depends to some extent on the frequency with which a woman is sexually harassed! Such an implication is obvious nonsense and stems from an implicit assumption of a causal or deterministic connection between salary and harassment frequency.

As we have previously said, the demonstration that X and Y are correlated is in no sense evidence that they are causally connected. Likewise, the variance interpretation of correlation implies no causal link whatever between X and Y, even though the language used may seem to carry that implication. All that has happened is that a degree of relationship between X and Y has been observed and, on the assumption that it holds in the future, one can take advantage of that relationship to predict one variable from the other. It does not matter whether the relation between X and Y is causal (as it could be) or is a function of others factors; as long as this relationship is reliable, it can be used. It is in this sense only that one can say that r^2 is the proportion of the variance of Y that is predictable from X. In Section 13.4, as part of our discussion of linear regression, we will use a numerical illustration to clarify the variance interpretation of the product-moment correlation coefficient.

Examination of Table H shows that, as df increases, the critical value for significance decreases and soon reaches rather low levels; for example, when $df = 100$, an $r = 0.195$ is significant at 0.05 level. If such an outcome occurred in a study using 102 subjects, which is not a great number by any means, it could be reported that a significant relationship existed between variables X and Y when the actual amount of information that one provides about the other is as small as $r^2 = (0.195)^2 = 0.0380 = 4$ percent. Now there is nothing illegal (or immoral) about calling a significant result a significant result, but it is clear that the reader must be more concerned with numbers than with words. Any given degree of relationship becomes less probable by

An aside on "significant" relationships

---

*$r^2$is sometimes referred to as the *coefficient of determination*, but please note that no deterministic (causal) connection between X and Y is assumed or implied.

chance as N increases, so that quite small relationships can be significant if N is large enough. Always square the r coefficient to get a valid notion of how meaningful the relationship being reported is, and under no circumstances accept the statement that X and Y are significantly related without knowing the exact value of r.

12.7 Assumptions Underlying Product-Moment Correlation

Product-moment correlation may be performed on X and Y raw scores when both variables represent interval/ratio measurement; it provides a measure of the degree of linear relationship between X and Y. The calculation of a product-moment correlation is reasonable when the relationship, if any, between X and Y is adequately characterized by a straight line function; if X and Y have some nonlinear relationship, then product-moment correlation is an inappropriate measure. If the correlation coefficient is to be used purely as a descriptive statistic for the data on hand, then no assumptions regarding the nature or distribution of the X and Y data are required. However, if the coefficient is to be used to infer the degree of relationship in the population, then such inference does require certain raw data assumptions. By virtue of the fact that we have routinely tested the correlation coefficient for significance, we have been treating product-moment correlation as an inferential statistic. The underlying assumptions for such inferential use of the product-moment correlation coefficient are described next.

homoscedasticity   A basic underlying assumption is *homoscedasticity,* which means equal variances of the distributions of Y's at the different X's, and equal variances of the distributions of X's at the different Y's. In order to understand homoscedasticity, it will be necessary to imagine a set of data with large N. The examples and exercises in this chapter have involved small N's for the sake of convenience, and thus there were relatively few occurrences of tied X or Y scores (tied scores are multiple occurrences of the same score value) but if a large number of subjects were measured, then tied scores would be more frequent. Suppose that X and Y represent height in cm and weight in kg respectively, and that these measures were obtained on 1000 persons. In a group this large, there would be multiple occurrences of virtually all the possible X and Y scores between the minimum and maximum limits; for example, there would be many people who had height scores of 174 cm. All of the people who had this X score ($X = 174$) would not have the same weight, so that there would be a distribution of weight scores associated with $X = 174$. The same would be true for all other values of X; if the number of subjects is large enough, there will be tied scores (multiple occurrences) at all values of X and there will be a distribution of Y scores associated with each

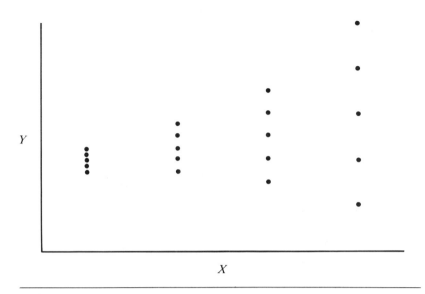

Figure 12.7–1   Scatter plot showing nonhomoscedastic data. Notice that the variability of *Y*'s is not consistent at different values of *X*

measured *X* value. Homoscedasticity means that these distributions of *Y* scores at the different values of *X* have equal variances. In a similar way, there would be many occurrences of any given weight, such as *Y* = 68 kg, but not all the people at this weight would be the same height. Thus there would be a distribution of height scores at this and all other weights; homoscedasticity means that the distributions of *X* scores at the different values of *Y* have equal variances. Figure 12.7–1 illustrates nonhomoscedastic data.

A second underlying assumption is that the distributions of *Y*'s at the different values of *X* are normal in shape, and that the distributions of *X*'s at the different values of *Y* are normal in shape. It is not considered a requirement that the *X* and *Y* raw data be sampled from normal populations; however, the raw data should be symmetrical along the range of measurement. If either set of raw data is badly skewed, then the correlation coefficient will not accurately reflect the degree of relationship between *X* and *Y* toward the ends of the measurement range.

12.8 Testing the Difference Between Two *r* Coefficients

There may be occasions when two independent groups of subjects have been measured on variables *X* and *Y* and it is of interest to determine whether the two groups have significantly different correlations between these variables. The correlation coefficients obtained from Groups 1 and 2 will be identified as r_1 and r_2 respectively. The null hypothesis for this test of significance is that $r_1 = r_2$ ($r_{\text{population } \#1} = r_{\text{population } \#2}$). The procedure involves transforming r_1 and r_2 into z-scores by means of Table I. Thus

r_1 transformed into a z-score is z_{r1}

r_2 transformed into a z-score is z_{r2}

The difference between z_{r1} and z_{r2} is divided by the estimated standard error of the difference [$s_{(z_{r1}-z_{r2})}$] to yield a z-score. Thus

$$z = \frac{z_{r1} - z_{r2}}{s_{(z_{r1}-z_{r2})}}$$

The z-score so obtained may be referred to the normal curve table (Table A) to determine its probability of occurrence. The critical values for significance at 0.05 and 0.01 confidence levels are $z = \pm 1.96$ and $z = \pm 2.58$ respectively.

A more convenient formula for z is

$$z = \frac{z_{r1} - z_{r2}}{\sqrt{1/(N_1 - 3) + 1/(N_2 - 3)}}$$

If both the correlation coefficients are positive, use positive z_r values, and if both coefficients are negative use negative z_r values. If one of the correlation coefficients is positive and the other is negative then the positive coefficient should be labeled as r_1; the signs of the z_r values should correspond to the signs of the correlation coefficients.

Assume that the product-moment correlation between distance from home to school and frequency of being late was calculated on 24 grade one children ($r_1 = +0.85$) and 17 grade two children ($r_2 = +0.43$). The test for whether the two grades differ significantly in the degree of relationship between these variables proceeds as follows.

$r_1 = 0.85 \qquad r_2 = 0.43$

$z_{r1} = 1.256 \qquad z_{r2} = 0.460$

$N_1 = 24 \qquad N_2 = 17$

$$z = \frac{1.256 - 0.460}{\sqrt{1/(24 - 3) + 1/(17 - 3)}}$$

$$= \frac{0.796}{\sqrt{0.119}}$$

$$= \frac{0.796}{0.345}$$

$$= 2.31$$

Since the obtained z-score is greater than 1.96, the difference between r_1 and r_2 is significant at 0.05 level of confidence. Thus, the degree of relationship between distance from home to school and frequency of being late differ significantly (at 0.05 level) between the grade one and grade two children.

12.9 Review Exercises

1. Define or describe the following terms.

   (a) variance interpretation of r
   (b) homoscedasticity

2. When 20 subjects were tested under noisy conditions, it was found that the correlation between the amount of time they were given to complete a task and their number of errors was $r = -0.80$. Another 20 subjects exposed to a similar test under quiet conditions produced a correlation of $r = -0.50$. Was noise level associated with a significant (0.05 level) change in this relationship?

3. At a seaside national park, the correlation between the daily high temperature and the number of visitors was $r = +0.90$ for a 30-day period, while for a wooded national park, the correlation during the same period was $r = +0.69$. Did the two parks differ (0.05 level) in this respect?

4. For 25 cars originally priced over 12,000 dollars, the correlation between miles accumulated on the odometer and the drop in resale value relative to the original price was $r = +0.25$, whereas for 40 cars originally priced under 8,000 dollars, this correlation was $r = +0.60$. Did these two classes of automobile differ (0.05 level) in the relationship between mileage and depreciation?

5. Assume that the correlation between height and weight was $r = +0.78$ for 200 men and $r = +0.61$ for 180 women. Do the sexes differ significantly (at 0.05 level of confidence) in the degree of relationship between these variables?

13 Linear Regression

Chapter Preview

13.1 Prediction of One Variable from Another

Our distant and "primitive" ancestors could predict the passage of the seasons without any knowledge of the earth's transit about the sun and/or the inclination of its axis. To be sure, they created a variety of engaging explanations for the occurrence of the seasons, but the essential fact is that they made accurate predictions based on their observations and experiences without possessing any valid comprehension of the real causes. The accuracy of prediction of a future event does not necessarily depend on one's degree of understanding, but rather on the precision with which its past occurrence has been measured, and on the degree to which the event will behave in the future as it did in the past. In other words, as long as the rules governing a thing's occurrence do not change, if you know the circumstances under which it happened in the past, you can predict its future occurrence without any understanding of the rules, or causes, themselves. The ability to predict could actually precede and lead to a genuine understanding of the phenomenon since the achievement of high prediction accuracy implies an awareness of the relevant circumstances; the identity and relative contribution of these accompanying circumstances might suggest a theory for the causative processes.

It is a tremendous advantage and convenience, in a wide range of real-life situations, to be able to make accurate predictions of future events. In selecting candidates for specialized employment or for admission to educational programs, a great economy could be achieved if it could be predicted in advance which persons would perform well, and which would not. The setting of fair and equitable insurance rates depends on accurate assessment and prediction of accident probabilities for various population subgroups. The success of the launch of a space vehicle or a family picnic depends in part on accurate weather prediction. These few examples only hint at the pervasive impact that accurate prediction of future events can have in everyday life. In this chapter we will examine *linear regression,* which is the process of predicting one variable from another when the two are known to have a significant linear relationship.

linear regression

If two variables have a significant relationship, we can use that relationship as the basis for generating a formula that predicts one variable from a knowledge of the other. The accuracy of such a prediction will depend on the degree of relationship manifested by the data on which the prediction formula is based and on the adequacy with which that original set of data represents the degree of relationship in the population. For example, suppose that we wished to predict a person's weight, based on a knowledge of height. The first step would be to obtain a random sample of subjects from the population of interest and obtain weight and height measures on each subject. Then a product-moment correlation is computed and, if r is significant, we may proceed to develop a formula for predicting weight from height. The prediction formula is known as a regression equation. A formula that predicts weight from height is known as the regression of weight on height. When we have derived such a formula, we need only to know a person's height to generate a prediction of his or her weight.

The accuracy of predictions based on linear regression is directly related to the degree of correlation between the original X and Y data. In Section 12.6 we said that r^2 is the proportion of the variance of Y that can be predicted from X. If X and Y have a perfect correlation, then knowledge of X enables perfect, error-free, prediction of Y. As the correlation between X and Y decreases, X predicts a lessening portion of the variance Y; thus, the prediction of Y based on X cannot be perfect because other factors contribute to the determination of Y values. Finally, if the correlation between X and Y is zero, then a knowledge of X contributes no information about the value of Y and prediction based on X is at chance level, or equivalent to guessing. In such a circumstance the best prediction of Y is the mean of previously observed Ys ($\overline{Y}$).

In this discussion, and in the whole notion of predicting Y from X, it sounds as if some direct and/or causal link is being assumed to exist between X and Y. Nothing of the sort is happening. We are making use of the properties of a known relationship and nothing whatever is being assumed about the reasons for the existence of that relationship. As far as prediction is concerned, those reasons are irrelevant and, to reiterate once again, no causal connection between X and Y is required or assumed. It is a matter of arbitrary convention that, if we wish to predict one variable from another, we label the to-be-predicted variable as Y, and the predictor variable as X; thus, we speak of

regression of
Y *on* X

predicting Y from X, or performing the *regression of* Y *on* X.

Product-moment correlation is a measure of the degree of linear relationship between X and Y. We have said that what is meant by linear is that the relationship between X and Y may be characterized by a straight line function. In visual terms, this means that the bivariate plot of the X and Y data forms an elongated ellipse-like array of points. Such an ellipse-like array can be represented by a straight line drawn through the long axis in such a way that the points are grouped symmetrically about it, as is shown in Figure 13.1–1.

Y

X

Figure 13.1–1 An ellipse-like bivariate array depicts a linear relationship between X and Y and may be represented by a straight line

Since linear regression involves dealing with straight line functions, we must digress momentarily to examine the general equation that defines a straight line. The general definition of a straight line is

$$Y = bX + c$$

where X and Y are variables and b and c are constants.

The equation $Y = bX + c$ expresses Y as a function of X. Any straight line can be represented by this equation when its particular b and c values are determined. Consider the case when $b = 2$ and $c = 3$. Thus

$$Y = 2X + 3$$

If values of X are entered into this equation it can be solved for Y. The result then identifies a point (X, Y) in a bivariate diagram. All of the points derived in this way will be on the straight line $Y = 2X + 3$. In order to plot this line in a bivariate diagram, we need only solve the equation for two values of X, locate the points thus identified, and connect them with a straight line.

$$Y = 2X + 3$$
$$\text{when } X = 0$$
$$Y = (2)(0) + 3$$
$$= 3$$

The point thus identified is $(0, 3)$.

$$\text{when } X = 5$$
$$Y = (2)(5) + 3$$
$$= 10 + 3$$
$$= 13$$

The point thus identified is (5, 13). If these points are located on a bivariate diagram and connected, the line $Y = 2X + 3$ will be depicted, as is shown in Figure 13.1–2.

In the general equation for a straight line, $Y = bX + c$, the definition of the b and c terms can be understood by reference to Figure 13.1–3, which presents several straight line functions on a set of bivariate axes.

Compare the straight lines $Y = 2X + 5$ and $Y = 2X + 3$, which both have $b = 2$ but have different values for c. These lines reveal that the c term is the Y *axis intercept,* or the value at which the line crosses the Y axis (the value of Y when $X = 0$). Observe that the line $Y = 2X - 4$ crosses the Y axis at $Y = -4$.

Y axis intercept

Compare the straight lines $Y = 2X + 3$ and $Y = X + 3$, which both have $c = 3$ but have different values for b. This comparison reveals that the b term is the slope of the line. *Slope* is defined as units of vertical rise divided by units of horizontal run. The line $Y = 2X + 3$ rises two units of Y vertically for each unit of X that it runs horizontally. The line $Y = X + 3$ rises one unit of Y vertically for each unit of X that it runs horizontally. A positive b value indicates that the line slopes upward to the right; a negative b value indicates that the line slopes downward to the right. Consider the line $Y = -2X + 5$; it can be seen that it falls two units of Y for each unit of horizontal run of X.

slope

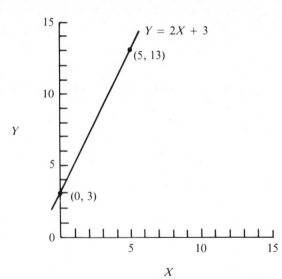

Figure 13.1–2 Bivariate diagram depicting the function $Y = 2X + 3$

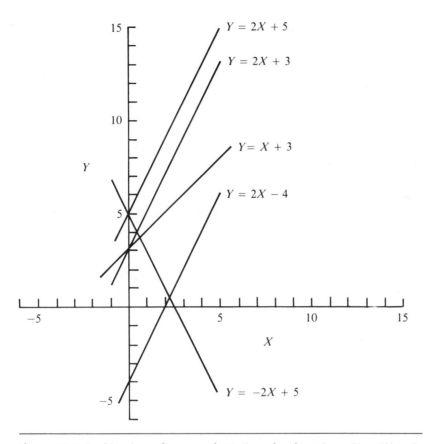

Figure 13.1–3 Bivariate diagram depicting the functions $Y = 2X + 5$, $Y = 2X + 3$, $Y = X + 3$, $Y = 2X - 4$, and $Y = -2X + 5$

In summary then

$Y = bX + c$ (the general expression for a straight line)

$$b = \text{slope} = \frac{\text{units of vertical rise}}{\text{units of horizontal run}}$$

$c = Y$ axis intercept (value of Y when $X = 0$)

Note: b and c may be positive or negative independently of each other.

If the variables X and Y have a significant linear relationship, then we may derive an equation to predict Y from a knowledge of X. Such an equation is written as $\hat{Y} = bX + c$ and is stated in words as follows: predicted Y is equal to b times X plus c.

$\hat{Y} = bX + c$ (predicted Y equals b times X plus c)

In order to obtain the prediction equation $\hat{Y} = bX + c$, we identify the b and c terms for the straight line that best fits the bivariate plot of the original X and Y data. Common sense suggests that the best-fitting straight line is the one that runs closest, on average, to the bivariate plot points. This conception is essentially correct. If one imagines the distances between the bivariate plot points and the straight line as deviations from the points to the line, then some of these deviations will be positive (bivariate points above the line) and some will be negative (bivariate points below the line). The sum of deviations from the line to the points will be zero for any line that is drawn through the central point of the bivariate array, regardless of its slope. We cannot define the best-fitting straight line as the one that minimizes the mean distances (deviations) between itself and the bivariate plot points because there are an infinite number of lines that can be drawn through the central point of the array, all of which have a mean deviation of zero. The problem here is reminiscent of one we encountered in Section 3.10 when we tried to define variability as the mean of raw deviations of scores from their mean; the solution is to operate *best-fitting straight line* in terms of squared deviations. We define the *best-fitting straight line* as that which minimizes the sum of squared deviations between itself and the bivariate points. This is known as the least squares definition of best-fitting, and circumvents the problem created by the fact that raw deviations sum to zero.

In practice, we do not identify the best-fitting straight line by physically measuring the distances between it and the bivariate points; it is done algebraically. Nonetheless, although it would be extremely laborious, one could identify the best-fitting straight line by trial and error using a ruler to plot lines and measure the point-to-line deviations. The suggestion of this method raises a question: Should the distances from the line to the points be measured parallel to the X axis, or parallel to the Y axis? Both approaches could be taken, and the result would be two different best-fitting straight lines. In other words, the straight line that minimizes the sum of squared deviations between the points and itself when measured parallel to the Y axis is not the same as the line that minimizes the sum of squared deviations from the points to itself when measured parallel to the X axis.

If, for a set of X and Y data, there are two different best-fitting straight lines, which will provide the most accurate predictions? The answer is that if you wish to predict Y from a knowledge of X, then you must derive the straight line $\hat{Y} = bX + c$, which is the line that minimizes the sum of squared deviations between itself and the bivariate points when measured parallel to the Y axis and provides the most accurate predictions of Y from X. If you want to predict variable X from a knowledge of Y, then you must derive the straight line $\hat{X} = bY + c$, which is the line that minimizes the sum of squared deviations between itself and the bivariate points when measured parallel to the X axis and provides the most accurate prediction of X from Y. The two regression equations that can be derived from any set of X and Y data are

$$\hat{Y} = b_{YX}X + c_{YX}$$

and

$$\hat{X} = b_{XY}Y + c_{XY}$$

Note that in these equations the b and c terms are given subscripts to identify them as terms in the regression of Y on X, or of X on Y.

When X and Y have a perfect correlation, the two regression equations define the same straight line function because in that case all the bivariate points lie on a single straight line, as is illustrated in Figure 13.1–4(a). As the correlation between the X and Y raw scores departs from perfection, the two regression lines ordinarily become distinct, having different b and c terms, as is illustrated in Figure 13.1–4(b).* Finally, when there is no correlation between X and Y, the two regression lines are at right angles to each other (the best estimate of any Y is $\overline{Y}$, and the best estimate of any X is $\overline{X}$) as is shown in Figure 13.1–4(c). In all cases where there are two regression lines, both pass through the point $(\overline{X}, \overline{Y})$.

Since it is conventional to label the to-be-predicted variable as Y, and the predictor variable as X, and since these labels may be applied arbitrarily, one does not ordinarily have to be concerned with the fact that two different regression lines may be derived from the raw data. It is sufficient for most purposes to be able to derive $\hat{Y} = b_{YX}X + c_{YX}$ and merely attach the X and Y labels to the raw data so as to predict the desired variable.

13.2 The Regression of *Y* on *X*

The prediction of Y from X is illustrated using the hypothetical data on annual salary (variable X) and frequency of sexual harassment incidents (variable Y) that was presented in Section 12.4. Performing the regression of Y on X consists of deriving the equation $\hat{Y} = b_{YX}X + c_{YX}$, which in turn requires the calculation of the b and c terms for the best-fitting regression line. The formulas for the calculation of these terms are given next: Note that b_{YX} indicates the b term for the regression of Y on X, and c_{YX} indicates the c term for the regression of Y on X. Thus

---

*Actually the emergence of distinct regression lines requires that s_1^2 differ from s_2^2, as well as that the correlation be less than perfect. When X and Y have the same variance, which is an extremely unlikely event, the two regression lines are one and the same despite a less than perfect correlation. If the reader attempts to plot the two regression lines when $s_1^2 = s_2^2$ and $r \neq \pm 1.00$, it will appear that they have identical slope (b terms) and pass through a common point $(\overline{X}, \overline{Y})$, but nonetheless converge! This results from misrepresenting the slope of $\hat{X} = b_{XY}Y + c_{XY}$ by projecting it onto coordinates where X is the abscissa. Thus projected, $b_{XY} = 1/b_{YX}$ and $c_{XY} = (-c_{YX})(1/b_{YX})$.

Figure 13.1–4 Regression lines for various degrees of correlation

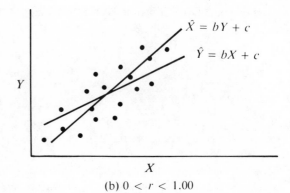

(b) $0 < r < 1.00$

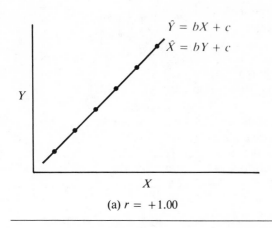

(a) $r = +1.00$

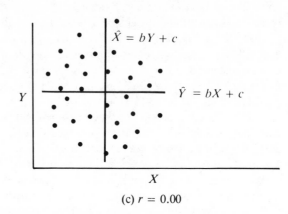

(c) $r = 0.00$

$$b_{YX} = \frac{N \sum XY - \sum X \sum Y}{N \sum X^2 - (\sum X)^2}$$

$$c_{YX} = \frac{\sum Y - b_{YX} \sum X}{N}$$

X	Y	X^2	XY
10	24	100	240
27	9	729	243
22	22	484	484
15	35	225	525
12	25	144	300
20	15	400	300
32	6	1024	192
26	7	676	182
6	41	36	246
20	36	400	720
$\sum X = 190$	$\sum Y = 220$	$\sum X^2 = 4218$	$\sum XY = 3432$

$N = 10$

$$b_{YX} = \frac{N\sum XY - \sum X \sum Y}{N\sum X^2 - (\sum X)^2}$$

$$= \frac{(10)(3432) - (190)(220)}{(10)(4218) - (190)^2}$$

$$= \frac{-7480}{6080}$$

$$= -1.23$$

$$c_{YX} = \frac{\sum Y - b_{YX}\sum X}{N}$$

$$= \frac{220 - (-1.23)(190)}{10}$$

$$= \frac{220 + 233.70}{10}$$

$$= \frac{453.70}{10}$$

$$= 45.37$$

Thus

$$\hat{Y} = b_{YX}X + c_{YX}$$

$$\hat{Y} = -1.23X + 45.37$$

If we now want to predict harassment frequency (Y) based on annual salary (X), we need only substitute the salary score of interest and solve the equation for $\hat{Y}$. Suppose a woman earned 16 thousand dollars per year. Thus when $X = 16$

$$\hat{Y} = (-1.23)(16) + 45.37$$

$$= -19.68 + 45.37$$

$$= 25.69$$

The predicted harassment frequency for a woman earning 16 thousand dollars annually is 25.69 incidents per year.

This prediction fits the raw data in that it was originally observed that a woman earning 15 thousand dollars was harassed 35 times, and the mean of the two women earning 20 thousand dollars was $(15 + 36)/2 = 25.50$, but note that the regression equation predicts a harassment frequency for $X = 16$ closer to that observed (on average) for $X = 20$ than to that observed for $X = 15$. This suggests that the prediction made by $\hat{Y} = -1.23X + 45.37$ is

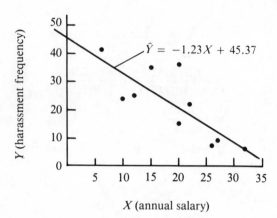

Figure 13.2–1 Bivariate plot of annual salary (X) and harassment frequency (Y) raw data showing the regression of Y on X

not without some error. Let us examine this matter further by predicting the harassment frequency of a woman earning a salary figure that occurred in the original set of data, and let $X = 6$ (Subject no. 9). Thus, when $X = 6$

$$\hat{Y} = (-1.23)(6) + 45.37$$
$$= -7.38 + 45.37$$
$$= 37.99$$

The prediction of a harassment frequency of 37.99 when salary equals 6 is clearly lower than the actually observed score of 41. This discrepancy is a function of the fact that the correlation between X and Y is not perfect ($r = -0.80$). In fact, since $r^2 = 0.64$, fully 36 percent of the variance of the harassment frequency scores is not predictable from annual salary; thus, predictions based on salary can only be approximations.

These predictions represent the most accurate that we can make, given the degree of correlation between X and Y. Figure 13.2–1 depicts the bivariate plot of the raw data and shows the position of the line $\hat{Y} = -1.23X + 45.37$. All predictions generated from the regression equation are points on this line; thus, the amount of error is reflected in the distances between the bivariate points and the line. Obviously, a tighter elliptical array (higher correlation) would result in less prediction error.

Determining What Value of X Predicts a Given Y

The expression $\hat{Y} = bX + c^*$ can be solved for either of its unknowns, $\hat{Y}$ and X. Consider the question: What annual salary would predict the occurrence of 30 harassment incidents per year? This question does not call for a prediction of X from Y, but rather asks what value of X gives rise to the

*Since it is understood that we are concerned with the regression of Y on X we may dispense with subscripts for the b and c terms.

prediction of Y equal to some specified value. It is therefore appropriate to use the function that predicts Y, enter the $\hat{Y}$ value, and solve for X. Thus

$$\hat{Y} = 30$$
$$\hat{Y} = -1.23X + 45.37$$
$$30 = -1.23X + 45.37$$
$$1.23X = 45.37 - 30$$
$$X = 15.37/1.23$$
$$= 12.50$$

An annual salary of 12.50 thousand dollars would predict, or give rise to the expectation of, 30 sexual harassment incidents per year.

The matter being discussed here is a rather subtle point, but it will become clear with some practice. Just remember that the function $\hat{Y} = bX + c$ can be used to answer two types of questions: (1) what is the predicted or expected value of Y given a specific X (enter the value of X and solve for $\hat{Y}$), and (2) what value of X predicts or gives rise to the expectation of a specific $\hat{Y}$ (enter the value of $\hat{Y}$ and solve for X). Exercises 13.3–4 through 13.3–8 will provide practice with both types of question.

13.3 Review Exercises

1. Define or describe the following terms.

    (a) linear regression
    (b) regression of Y on X
    (c) Y axis intercept
    (d) slope
    (e) best-fitting straight line

2. Eight people were given a test of creativity in which higher scores reflected greater creativity. Each was also given a test of mental telepathy in which they were asked to name the number the experimenter was thinking about at that moment; degree of telepathy was defined as the numerical difference between the two numbers, and thus smaller scores represented greater telepathy.

    Creativity: 7, 6, 3, 0, 1, 10, 2, 3
    Telepathy: 6, 7, 10, 30, 21, 4, 17, 11

    What telepathy score would be expected of a person who scores 5, 9, and 3 on the creativity test?

3. Nine members of a family were subjects in an experiment on altruism. The experimenter was a member of this family and, at different times, he told each of nine relatives a standard hard-luck story that ended with a

request to borrow money. The measures taken were nearness of kinship as measured by the proportion of common genes, and the number of dollars loaned.

Kinship: 0.03, 0.06, 0.13, 0.03, 0.50, 0.06, 0.13, 0.50, 0.01
Size of loan: 25,   22,   17,   24,   12,   20,   19,   13,   26

What size loan would be predicted from a kin of 1.00 [identical twin] and 0.00 [brother-in-law]?

4. A researcher wanted to derive a formula that would enable him to predict the number of deer in a given area from the number of tracks seen on the ground. Accordingly, a number of representative areas were fenced off and, within each, measures of track density and population size were obtained.

Track density: 10,   5,   3,   4,   7
Number of deer: 253, 117, 81, 102, 208

(a) Estimate the number of deer in areas where the track density measures were 6, 15, and 20.
(b) What track density measure would predict the presence of 50, 100, and 200 deer?

5. It has been suggested that there is a negative relationship between the number of hitchhikers on the road and the probability of getting a ride. The following data were gathered.

Number of hitchhikers per km: 16, 8, 20,   3, 11,   1
Proportion picked up: 0.30,0.40,0.10,0.70,0.20,0.90

(a) What is the probability of getting a ride when there are 14, 5, and 22 hitchhikers per km?
(b) What number of hitchhikers per km would predict ride probabilities of 0.50, 0.25, and 0.00?

6. Over a period of several years, many students enrolled at a particular flying school. Records were examined for ten student ages to determine the proportion at each age that successfully completed training.

Proportion to graduate:
0.20, 0.40, 0.80, 0.50, 0.20, 0.75, 0.25, 0.75, 0.60, 0.85
Age:
24,   29,   48,   32,   26,   37,   20,   40,   35,   45

(a) What is the predicted graduation probability of persons aged 30, 18, and 50?
(b) What student ages predict graduation probabilities of 0.30, 0.75, and 0.95?

7. One day a group of beavers got to discussing the fact that people were setting more traps in their pond as the years progressed and the number of individuals increased. To further clarify this situation, a council of beavers was held that consisted of delegates from various ponds. Each delegate reported the number of traps and number of individuals in his or her home pond.

    Traps: 2,   5,   8,   6, 15, 30, 19
    Beavers: 12, 20, 35, 29, 50, 82, 61

    (a) How many traps would you expect to find in a pond inhabited by 75, 23, and 40 beavers?
    (b) How many beavers per pond lead to the expectation of 20, 10, and 0 traps?

8. Ten different kinds of caterpillars were measured for their length in cm, and for the number of days from hatching to pupation.

    Length: 1.5, 2.3, 4.4, 7.8, 6.0, 5.2, 6.4, 3.1, 9.4, 4.0
    Days to pupate: 10, 10, 13, 20, 16, 15, 16, 12, 30, 12

    (a) What is the predicted length of caterpillars that took 7, 14, and 28 days to pupate?
    (b) What number of days to pupate would lead you to expect caterpillars of 5, 10 and 20 cm?

9. Consider the following hypothetical figures on total human population (in billions) and total food production (in millions of tons) over the past seven decades.

	1900	1910	1920	1930	1940	1950	1960	1970
Population:	0.25	0.38	0.57	0.86	1.29	1.94	2.91	4.37
Food:	0.50	1.25	2.00	2.75	3.50	4.25	5.00	5.75

    (a) How much food will be produced when the population reaches 10 billion?
    (b) Assuming worldwide famine when food production in millions of tons drops to half the population in billions, in which decade will this occur?

13.4 The F-Test for the Significance of the Regression

The logical basis for predicting Y from X is the demonstration of a significant r_{XY} coefficient. It is possible, however, to proceed directly with the regression of Y on X and then test the regression for significance. This procedure eliminates the need to calculate r_{XY}; the regression will be significant only if r_{XY} is significant. The F-test for the significance of the regression will be illustrated using the data on annual salary (X) and sexual harassment frequency (Y) that has served as the basis of previous discussions.

It was stated in Section 13.2 that, unless the correlation between X and Y is perfect, predictions obtained from the regression equation $\hat{Y} = bX + c$ can be expected to contain some error. Remember that the original Y data represent reality, and that $\hat{Y}$ scores, being estimates, are hypothetical. The Y data constitute the reference; these are the scores that were actually observed, and therefore prediction accuracy means the extent to which predictions ($\hat{Y}$s) match the real data (Y's). *Prediction error* refers to the amount by which the predicted score differs from the actual observation, that is, prediction error $= (Y - \hat{Y})$. Any observed Y score can be thought of as consisting of two parts, a part that could be predicted from X, and the part that could not (prediction error). Thus:

prediction error

Observed score = Predicted score + Prediction error
$$Y = \hat{Y} + (Y - \hat{Y})$$

To avoid confusion in the following presentation, a greater degree of accuracy than we have so far used will be required. When the regression of Y on X is calculated to six decimal places accuracy, it is found to be

$$\hat{Y} = -1.230263X + 45.374997$$

When this equation is solved for all values of X to derive the $\hat{Y}$ and $(Y - \hat{Y})$ scores, we find that

X	Y	$\hat{Y}$	$(Y - \hat{Y})$
10	24	33.072367	−9.072367
27	9	12.157896	−3.157896
22	22	18.309211	+3.690789
15	35	26.921052	+8.078948
12	25	30.611841	−5.611841
20	15	20.769737	−5.769737
32	6	6.006581	−0.006581
26	7	13.388159	−6.388159
6	41	37.993419	+3.006581
20	36	20.769737	+15.230263
$\Sigma X = 190$	$\Sigma Y = 220$	$\Sigma \hat{Y} = 220.000000$	$\Sigma (Y - \hat{Y}) = 0.000000$

It can be readily determined that

$$\Sigma Y^2 = 6278.000000$$
$$\Sigma \hat{Y}^2 = 5760.236606$$
$$\Sigma (Y - \hat{Y})^2 = 517.763158$$

Using these values, we will proceed to calculate the variance of the Y, $\hat{Y}$, and

$(Y - \hat{Y})$ sets of scores. Thus

$$s_Y^2 = \frac{\sum Y^2 - (\sum Y)^2/N}{N - 1}$$

$$= \frac{6278 - (220)^2/10}{10 - 1}$$

$$= 159.777778$$

$$s_{\hat{Y}}^2 = \frac{\sum \hat{Y}^2 - (\sum \hat{Y})^2/N}{N - 1}$$

$$= \frac{5760.236606 - (220)^2/10}{10 - 1}$$

$$= 102.248512$$

$$s_{(Y-\hat{Y})}^2 = \frac{\sum(Y - \hat{Y})^2 - [\sum(Y - \hat{Y})]^2/N}{N - 1}$$

$$= \frac{517.763158 - (0.00)^2/10}{10 - 1}$$

$$= 57.529240$$

Earlier it was pointed out that

$$Y = \hat{Y} + (Y - \hat{Y})$$

It can now be shown that this relationship also holds for the variances of these sets of scores.

$$s_Y^2 = s_{\hat{Y}}^2 + s_{(Y-\hat{Y})}^2$$

$$159.777778 = 102.248512 + 57.529240$$

$$159.777778 = 159.777752 \quad \text{(with allowance for rounding error)}$$

The variance of the observed scores consists of the variance of the predicted scores plus the variance of the prediction errors. Since these variance terms have the same degrees of freedom ($df = N - 1 = 10 - 1 = 9$), it follows that the Sum of Squares of the observed scores equals the Sum of Squares of the predicted scores plus the Sum of Squares of the prediction errors.

$$SS_{\text{observations}} = SS_{\text{predictions}} + SS_{\text{errors}}$$

$$SS_Y = SS_{\hat{Y}} + SS_{(Y-\hat{Y})}$$

$$1438.000000 = 920.236606 + 517.763158$$

$$1438.000000 = 1437.999764 \quad \text{(with allowance for rounding error)}$$

In the discussion of independent groups analysis of variance we saw that the total Sum of Squares of the dependent variable scores (SS_{total}) was divisible into two parts, a part that contained the effect, if any, of the independent variable ($SS_{\text{between groups}}$), and a part that could only be a function of sampling and/or experimental error ($SS_{\text{within groups}}$), which could be expressed as (SS_{error}). Thus

$$SS_{\text{total}} = SS_{\text{between groups}} + SS_{\text{error}}$$

The F-ratio is formed, with regard for degrees of freedom, by dividing the between groups component by the error component, thus allowing an evaluation of their relative contribution to the total. An analogous situation holds with linear regression, wherein the total Sum of Squares (SS_Y) is divisible into a part that is attributable to the regression ($SS_{\hat{Y}}$) and a part representing error ($SS_{(Y-\hat{Y})}$). Thus

SS_{total}

$SS_{regression}$

SS_{error}

SS_Y may be termed SS_{total}

$SS_{\hat{Y}}$ may be termed $SS_{\text{regression}}$

$SS_{(Y-\hat{Y})}$ may be termed SS_{error}

Recall that

$$SS_Y = SS_{\hat{Y}} + SS_{(Y-\hat{Y})}$$

Therefore

$$SS_{\text{total}} = SS_{\text{regression}} + SS_{\text{error}}$$

Just as in ANOVA, we can form an F-ratio from the regression and error components and thus test their relative contribution to the total. The F-ratio for the significance of the linear regression of Y on X is defined as

$$F = \frac{SS_{\text{regression}}}{SS_{\text{error}}/(N-2)} = \frac{SS_{\hat{Y}}}{SS_{(Y-\hat{Y})}/(N-2)}$$

You will recall that an F term is the ratio of two Mean Squares (variances). In the present case it appears that the numerator is a Sum of Squares term; actually there is one degree of freedom associated with the regression so that, technically, the numerator might be written as $SS_{\text{regression}}/1$ or as $SS_{\hat{Y}}/1$.

In the case of our regression of harassment frequency on annual salary ($\hat{Y} = -1.230263X + 45.374997$), the significance test proceeds as follows

$$F = \frac{SS_{\hat{Y}}}{SS_{(Y-\hat{Y})}/(N-2)}$$

$$= \frac{920.236606}{517.763158/(10-2)}$$

$$= \frac{920.236606}{64.720395}$$

$$= 14.22$$

1. $df = 1/(N - 2) = 1/(10 - 2) = 1/8$
2. The critical value for F at 0.05 confidence level $= 5.32$
3. Therefore the result is significant.
4. Interpretation: Annual salary predicts a significant portion of the variance of sexual harassment frequency scores.

The route we have taken to determine the F-ratio for the significance test of the regression is useful for explanatory purposes but is laborious to calculate since it requires the actual derivation of the set of $\hat{Y}$ and $(Y - \hat{Y})$ scores. A simpler and more direct calculation of $SS\hat{y}$ is achieved by the following formula.

$$SS\hat{y} = b_{YX}\left[\Sigma XY - \frac{\Sigma X \Sigma Y}{N}\right]$$

Using the data from our example

$$SS\hat{y} = [-1.230263]\left[3432 - \frac{(190)(220)}{10}\right]$$
$$= [-1.230263][-748]$$
$$= 920.236724$$

$$SS_Y = \Sigma Y^2 - (\Sigma Y)^2/N$$
$$= 6278 - (220)^2/10$$
$$= 1438.000000$$

$$SS_{(Y-\hat{Y})} = SS_Y - SS\hat{y}$$
$$= 1438 - 920.236724$$
$$= 517.763276$$

The slight discrepancies between these values for $SS\hat{y}$ and $SS_{(Y-\hat{Y})}$ and those obtained earlier may be attributed to rounding error. Thus

$$F = \frac{SS\hat{y}}{SS_{(Y-\hat{Y})}/(N - 2)}$$
$$= \frac{920.236724}{517.763276/(10 - 2)}$$
$$= \frac{920.236724}{64.720410}$$
$$= 14.22$$

The same result is achieved, but by way of a much more efficient procedure.

Linear Regression

Suppose that for eight randomly selected U.S. cities, a measure of the number of handguns owned per capita (variable X), and the number of homicides per 100,000 persons over a 12-month period (variable Y) was obtained. The investigator wanted to derive the regression of homicides per 100,000 persons on handguns per capita. The raw data are shown.

X	Y	X^2	Y^2	XY
0.50	5	0.25	25	2.50
0.20	3	0.04	9	0.60
0.95	12	0.90	144	11.40
1.10	15	1.21	225	16.50
0.75	10	0.56	100	7.50
0.64	6	0.41	36	3.84
0.48	10	0.23	100	4.80
0.83	11	0.69	121	9.13
5.45	72	4.29	760	56.27

$$N = 8$$

$$b_{YX} = \frac{(8)(56.27) - (5.45)(72)}{(8)(4.29) - (5.45)^2}$$

$$= 12.50$$

$$c_{YX} = \frac{72 - (12.50)(5.45)}{8}$$

$$= 0.49$$

$$\hat{Y} = 12.50X + 0.49$$

$$SS_{\hat{Y}} = [12.50][56.27 - (5.45)(72)/8]$$
$$= 90.25$$

$$SS_Y = 760 - (72)^2/8$$
$$= 112.00$$

$$SS_{(Y-\hat{Y})} = 112.00 - 90.25$$
$$= 21.75$$

$$F = \frac{90.25}{21.75/6}$$
$$= 24.86$$

1. $df = 1/(N - 2) = 1/6$
2. The critical value for F at 0.05 confidence level $= 5.99$
3. Therefore the result is significant.
4. Interpretation: Per capita handgun ownership predicts a significant portion of the variance of homicides per 100,000 persons.

Question: What is the estimated number of homicides per 100,000 persons when per capita handgun ownership is 1.00?

$$\hat{Y} = (12.50)(1.00) + 0.49$$
$$= 12.99$$

Answer: The predicted frequency of homicides per 100,000 persons is 12.99 when per capita handgun ownership is 1.00.

Question: What per capita handgun ownership predicts a homicide frequency of 10 per 100,000 persons?

$$10 = 12.50X + 0.49$$
$$X = 0.76$$

Answer: A per capita handgun ownership of 0.76 predicts a homicide frequency of 10 per 100,000 persons.

Finally, note that

$$r_{XY}^2 = \frac{s_{\hat{Y}}^2}{s_Y^2} = \frac{SS_{\hat{Y}}}{SS_Y}$$

$$(0.799964)^2 = \frac{102.248512}{159.777778} = \frac{920.236606}{1438}$$

$$0.639942 = 0.639942 = 0.639942$$

The variance interpretation of product-moment correlation is that r^2 equals the proportion of the variance of Y that can be predicted from X. We have demonstrated the validity of the variance interpretation by showing that the variance of the scores predicted from $X\hat{Y}$ is a proportion of the original raw data (Y) variance equal to r^2. We have also seen that it is possible to determine r^2 and apply the variance interpretation to the regression without actually calculating r. We would say in this case that annual salary predicted 0.639942, or 64 percent, of the variance of harassment frequency scores.

13.5 Review Exercises

1. Define or describe the following terms.
    (a) prediction error
    (b) SS_{total}
    (c) SS_{error}
    (d) $SS_{regression}$

2. Test the significance of the regression of telepathy on creativity calculated in Exercise 13.3–2.

3. Test the significance of the regression of altruism on kinship calculated in Exercise 13.3–3.

4. Test the significance of the regression of number of deer on track density calculated in Exercise 13.3–4.

5. Test the significance of the regression of probability of getting a ride on number of hitchhikers per km calculated in Exercise 13.3–5.

6. Test the significance of the regression of graduation probability on age calculated in Exercise 13.3–6.

7. Test the significance of the regression of traps on beavers calculated in Exercise 13.3–7.

8. Test the significance of the regression of caterpillar length on days to pupate calculated in Exercise 13.3–8.

13.6 Assumptions Underlying Linear Regression

It is taken as a given that the X and Y data represent interval/ratio measurement, as is the case for product-moment correlation. The calculation and use of a linear regression function to predict Y from X assumes that the relationship between variables X and Y is linear, that is, adequately represented by a straight line function. If the regression is to be used merely to estimate Y from a knowledge of X within the confines of the range of the original X data, then no assumptions concerning the X and Y raw data are required. However, if we make predictions beyond the range of the original data, that is, infer that the regression function is applicable to the population of scores, then such inferential use of the regression function is based on assumptions of homoscedasticity and normality as described in Section 12.7. It is further assumed that the population means of the distributions of Y's at each value of X lie on the straight line represented by the regression function. Clearly, when we test a regression for significance we are indicating an inferential purpose.

13.7 The Standard Error of Estimate

In Section 13.4 we discussed the relationship between the variances of the observed scores, the predicted scores, and the prediction errors, and saw that

$$s_Y^2 = s_{\hat{Y}}^2 - s_{(Y-\hat{Y})}^2$$

If it can be assumed that the X and Y scores are homoscedastic, normal (meaning that the distribution of X's at each Y value is normal, and likewise the distribution of Y's at each value of X), and that the population means of the distribution of Y's at each value of X lie on a single straight line represented by the regression of Y on X, then the distribution of the prediction errors (the $Y - \hat{Y}$ scores) will be normal, have mean equal to zero [$\Sigma (Y - \hat{Y}) = 0$], and standard deviation equal to $s_{(Y-\hat{Y})}$. The standard deviation of the prediction error scores is known as the *standard error of estimate*. The standard error of estimate may be calculated by several means including the following formulas,

standard error of estimate

$$s_{(Y-\hat{Y})} = \sqrt{s_Y^2 - s_{\hat{Y}}^2}$$

$$s_{(Y-\hat{Y})} = \sqrt{s_Y^2(1 - r^2)}$$

If the F-test for the regression has been performed, the standard error of estimate may be conveniently obtained by the following formula.

$$s_{(Y-\hat{Y})} = \sqrt{\frac{SS_{(Y-\hat{Y})}}{N - 1}}$$

The standard error of estimate may be used to estimate the amount of prediction error in any given instance. As an example, let us again use the data on annual salary and sexual harassment frequency. We know from Section 12.4 that $r = -0.80$, and from Section 13.4 that $s_Y^2 = 159.78$. Thus

$$s_{(Y-\hat{Y})} = \sqrt{(159.78)(1 - 0.64)}$$
$$= 7.58$$

If we multiply the standard error of estimate by $z = 1.96$, we obtain $(1.96)(7.58) = 14.86$. We can say that for any prediction obtained from the regression function $\hat{Y} = -1.23X + 45.37$, the probability is 0.95 that the amount of error in that prediction is less than 14.86. In other words, the true value of Y is at most 14.85 units different from our predicted value. Conversely, the probability is 0.05 that the amount of error is equal to or greater than 14.86.

It is clear that prediction error can be substantial even with a relatively high degree of correlation. It follows that values obtained from regression functions must be regarded in their proper perspective as being estimates and not certainties.

13.8 Introduction to Multiple Linear Regression

Adding a Predictor and Increasing R

In linear regression, we take advantage of the existence of a correlation between X and Y and use X as a basis for predicting future values of Y. Our objective is presumably to make the most accurate possible predictions. It seems reasonable that if we could identify two variables (which we shall term X_1 and X_2), each of which was correlated with Y, then the accuracy of our prediction of Y might be greater if it were based on both X_1 and X_2 than if it were based on either variable alone. In multiple linear regression, Y is predicted from a linear combination of X_1 and X_2. To the extent that X_1 and X_2 each correlate with Y and have little or no correlation with each other (in other words little or no redundancy), then accuracy of predictions of Y will increase. The accuracy of the prediction of Y is reflected in the correlation between the observed and predicted scores ($r_{Y\hat{Y}}$). In the context of multiple linear regression, this correlation is symbolized as R, and is termed the *coefficient of multiple correlation*. Thus

coefficient of multiple correlation

$R = r_{Y\hat{Y}} =$ coefficient of multiple correlation

$R^2 =$ The proportion of the variance of Y that is predicted from the multiple regression.*

The multiple regression of Y on X_1 and X_2 is expressed by the function

$$\hat{Y} = b_1 X_1 + b_2 X_2 + c$$

The derivation of this equation for any set of data requires the calculation of the b_1, b_2, and c terms. The values of these terms maximize R insofar as the degree of correlation between Y and X_1, Y and X_2, and X_1 and X_2 allow.

---

*Note: R^2 is generally used to symbolize the proportion of the variance of Y predicted from the regression, whether the prediction is based on a single or multiple predictors.

Although we will confine our discussion to the multiple regression of Y on two predictors, the prediction of Y may be based on any number of predictor variables. Thus

$$\hat{Y} = b_1 X_1 + b_2 X_2 + \cdots + b_k X_k + c$$

where $k =$ the number of predictor variables.

While fairly complex, the calculation of the regression of Y on two predictor variables is still feasible with a hand-held calculator. If the regression of Y on three or more predictors is called for, then a new level of notation, known as matrix algebra, is required, and the calculations involved are ordinarily handled by computer. The treatment given to multiple linear regression in this chapter is of an introductory nature, as a thorough consideration is beyond the purpose of this book. The intent is to show multiple regression as an extension of single-predictor regression and to describe the calculation, significance test, and interpretation procedure for the two-predictor case. An excellent and thorough presentation of multiple regression may be found in Kerlinger & Pedhazur (1973).

Multiple Regression with Two Predictors

In the discussion of product-moment correlation in Chapter 12 and linear regression in this chapter, we leaned heavily on a hypothetical set of data that represented annual salary and frequency of sexual harassment of working women. It will suit our purposes to resurrect these data once again. There are undoubtedly several factors besides job status, which was defined operationally as annual salary, that might contribute to the occurrence and frequency of the sexual harassment of women; one of these might be the relative number of women and men in the working environment. Let us consider the original data of frequency of sexual harassment incidents during the previous year (Y), and annual salary in thousands of dollars (X_1), and add a measure of the ratio of female to male workers in the work environment (X_2). Suppose these data were as follows:

X_1 (annual salary)	X_2 (female/male ratio)	Y (harassment frequency)
10	5	24
27	4	9
22	3	22
15	2	35
12	9	25
20	6	15
32	9	6
26	8	7
6	1	41
20	3	36

Female/male ratio appears to be negatively related to harassment frequency since decrease in this ratio is accompanied by increase in harassment. It cannot be determined by inspection whether these variables correlate significantly. One might wish to establish this before performing the multiple regression of Y on X_1 and X_2; we already know that r_{X_1Y} is significant. Actually, even knowing r_{X_2Y} would not tell us clearly whether the multiple regression would be useful, since the predictive accuracy of this function is jointly determined by r_{X_1Y}, r_{X_2Y}, and $r_{X_1X_2}$. The simplest procedure is to proceed directly with the multiple regression and then test the significance of the regression. The formulas for the derivation of the b_1, b_2, and c terms are

$$b_1 = \frac{[N\sum X_1 Y - \sum X_1 \sum Y][N\sum X_2^2 - (\sum X_2)^2] - [N\sum X_1 X_2 - \sum X_1 \sum X_2][N\sum X_2 Y - \sum X_2 \sum Y]}{[N\sum X_1^2 - (\sum X_1)^2][N\sum X_2^2 - (\sum X_2)^2] - [N\sum X_1 X_2 - \sum X_1 \sum X_2]^2}$$

$$b_2 = \frac{[N\sum X_2 Y - \sum X_2 \sum Y][N\sum X_1^2 - (\sum X_1)^2] - [N\sum X_1 X_2 - \sum X_1 \sum X_2][N\sum X_1 Y - \sum X_1 \sum Y]}{[N\sum X_1^2 - (\sum X_1)^2][N\sum X_2^2 - (\sum X_2)^2] - [N\sum X_1 X_2 - \sum X_1 \sum X_2]^2}$$

$$c = \frac{\sum Y - b_1 \sum X_1 - b_2 \sum X_2}{N}$$

Using our data, the calculation of $\hat{Y} = b_1 X_1 + b_2 X_2 + c$ proceeds as follows

X_1	X_2	Y	X_1^2	X_2^2	Y^2	$X_1 X_2$	$X_1 Y$	$X_2 Y$
10	5	24	100	25	576	50	240	120
27	4	9	729	16	81	108	243	36
22	3	22	484	9	484	66	484	66
15	2	35	225	4	1225	30	525	70
12	9	25	144	81	625	108	300	225
20	6	15	400	36	225	120	300	90
32	9	6	1024	81	36	288	192	54
26	8	7	676	64	49	208	182	56
6	1	41	36	1	1681	6	246	41
20	3	36	400	9	1296	60	720	108
190	50	220	4218	326	6278	1044	3432	866

$N = 10$

$$b_1 = \frac{[(10)(3,432) - (190)(220)][(10)(326) - (50)^2] - [(10)(1,044) - (190)(50)][(10)(866) - (50)(220)]}{[(10)(4,218) - (190)^2][(10)(326) - (50)^2] - [(10)(1,044) - (190)(50)]^2}$$

$$= \frac{(-7,480)(760) - (940)(-2,340)}{(6,080)(760) - (940)^2}$$

$$= \frac{(-5,684,800) - (-2,199,600)}{(4,620,800) - (883,600)}$$

$$= \frac{-3,485,200}{3,737,200}$$

$$= -0.93$$

$$b_2 = \frac{[(10)(866) - (50)(220)][(10)(4,218) - (190)^2] - [(10)(1,044) - (190)(50)][(10)(3,432) - (190)(220)]}{[(10)(4,218) - (190)^2][(10)(326) - (50)^2] - [(10)(1,044) - (190)(50)]^2}$$

$$= \frac{(-2,340)(6,080) - (940)(-7,480)}{(6,080)(760) - (940)^2}$$

$$= \frac{(-14,227,200) - (-7,031,200)}{(4,620,800) - (883,600)}$$

$$= \frac{-7,196,000}{3,737,200}$$

$$= -1.93$$

$$c = \frac{220 - (-0.93)(190) - (-1.93)(50)}{10}$$

$$= \frac{220 + 176.70 + 96.50}{10}$$

$$= \frac{493.20}{10}$$

$$= 49.32$$

Thus

$$\hat{Y} = -0.93X_1 + (-1.93)X_2 + 49.32$$

or

$$\hat{Y} = -0.93X_1 - 1.93X_2 + 49.32$$

Let us predict the harassment frequency of a woman who earns 19 thousand dollars ($X_1 = 19$) and works in an environment where there are 3 female workers for each male worker ($X_2 = 3$).

$$\hat{Y} = b_1X_1 + b_2X_2 + c$$
$$= (-0.93)(19) + (-1.93)(3) + 49.32$$
$$= -17.67 - 5.79 + 49.32$$
$$= 25.86$$

We predict 25.86 harassment incidents per year for a woman earning 19 thousand dollars per year and working in an environment where the ratio of female to male employees is 3 to 1.

The first and most obvious question to arise concerning the multiple regression of Y on X_1 and X_2 is whether the linear combination of X_1 and X_2 predicts a significant portion of the variance of Y. In essence, the test of significance of the multiple regression is a test of significance of R ($r_{Y\hat{Y}}$); the null hypothesis being tested is that $R = 0$ ($r_{Y\hat{Y}} = 0$). The F-ratio for the significance test of the multiple regression is defined as

$$F = \frac{SS_{\text{regression}}/k}{SS_{\text{error}}/(N - k - 1)}$$

or

$$F = \frac{SS_{\hat{Y}}/k}{SS_{(Y-\hat{Y})}/(N - k - 1)}$$

where k equals the number of predictor variables upon which the regression of Y is performed ($k = 2$ in this case). The degrees of freedom for the F-ratio is $k/(N - k - 1)$.

The F-test for the significance of the multiple linear regression of sexual harassment frequency (Y) on annual salary (X_1) and female to male worker ratio (X_2), proceeds as follows.

$$SS_{\hat{Y}} = b_1\left[\sum X_1 Y - \frac{\sum X_1 \sum Y}{N}\right] + b_2\left[\sum X_2 Y - \frac{\sum X_2 \sum Y}{N}\right]$$

$$= [-0.93]\left[3432 - \frac{(190)(220)}{10}\right]$$

$$+ [-1.93]\left[866 - \frac{(50)(220)}{10}\right]$$

$$= [-0.93][-748] + [-1.93][-234]$$

$$= 695.64 + 451.62$$

$$= 1147.26$$

$$SS_Y = \sum Y^2 - (\sum Y)^2/N$$

$$= 6278 - (220)^2/10$$

$$= 1438$$

$$SS_{(Y-\hat{Y})} = SS_Y = SS_{\hat{Y}}$$

$$= 1438.00 - 1147.26$$

$$= 290.74$$

Thus

$$F = \frac{1147.26/2}{290.74/(10 - 2 - 1)}$$

$$= \frac{573.63}{41.53}$$

$$= 13.81$$

1. $df = k/(N - k - 1) = 2/(10 - 2 - 1) = 2/7$
2. The critical value for F at 0.05 confidence level $= 4.74$
3. Therefore the result is significant.

4. Interpretation: The combination of annual salary and ratio of women to men in the work environment predicts a significant portion of the variance of sexual harassment frequency scores.

Having established that the combination of X_1 and X_2 predicts a significant portion of the variance of Y, we will next want to identify the exact amount of that portion, or R^2.

$$R^2 = \frac{SS_{\text{regression}}}{SS_{\text{total}}}$$

$$= \frac{SS_{\hat{y}}}{SS_Y}$$

$$= \frac{1147.26}{1438}$$

$$= 0.80$$

The combination of annual salary and ratio of women to men coworkers predicts 80 percent of the variance of harassment frequency scores. The coefficient of multiple correlation, R, can be seen to equal $\sqrt{0.80} = 0.89$. It is possible to test the significance of the regression of Y on X_1, and Y on X_2, and establish whether the addition of X_2 resulted in a significant increase in R. Again, the reader is referred to Kerlinger & Pedhazur (1973) for a more thorough discussion.

This brief exposure to multiple regression serves only to hint at its potential applicability. It seems safe to assume that the majority of natural events have more than one contributing factor or accompanying (correlated) variable. Thus multiple regression is a tool that has great potential for widespread use, whether to predict daily temperatures, football scores, or social conformity. Students who pursue advanced study in psychology or other behavioral disciplines will undoubtedly encounter multiple regression techniques again.

13.9 Review Exercises

1. Define or describe the "coefficient of multiple correlation."

The following problems represent hypothetical data. In each case

(a) compute the regression of Y on X_1 and X_2
(b) determine SS_{total}, $SS_{\text{regression}}$, and SS_{error}
(c) test the regression for significance
(d) determine R^2
(e) derive the specific $\hat{Y}$ values called for in each exercise

2. The following data represent accident probability (Y), age in years (X_1), and driving experience expressed as number of tens of thousands of kilometers driven (X_2), for six persons.

X_1	X_2	Y
18	1	.25
20	5	.35
25	6	.30
30	8	.20
40	10	.15
47	10	.05

What is the predicted accident probability for a person

(1) age 21 with 90 thousand kilometers experience?
(2) age 45 with 90 thousand kilometers experience?

3. The following data represent grade point average in the first year of college (Y), grade point average in the final year of high school (X_1), and intelligence test score (X_2), for ten persons.

X_1	X_2	Y
2.50	90	2.00
3.00	130	3.50
4.00	140	3.50
3.50	100	3.00
3.50	120	4.00
2.00	110	2.00
3.50	120	3.00
3.00	100	2.50
2.00	90	1.50
4.00	110	3.00

What is the expected first year college grade point average of a person

(1) with a final year high school grade point average of 3.70 and an intelligence test test score of 95?
(2) with a final year high school grade point average of 2.90 and an intelligence test score of 132?

4. The following data represent mean hours of sleep per night (Y), mean number of cigarettes smokes per day (X_1), and mean number of minutes of physical exercise per day (X_2), for seven persons.

X_1	X_2	Y
5	50	8
10	20	6
0	60	10
25	10	4
3	30	7
10	45	8
30	0	4

How many hours of sleep would be predicted for a person who

(1) smoked 50 cigarettes and exercised 120 minutes per day?

(2) smoked 2 cigarettes and exercised 2 minutes per day?

5. The following data represent the speed in cm/sec at which rats travel down a runway from start to goal box (Y), the number of hours they have been deprived of food (X_1), and their length in cm from nose to base of tail (X_2).

X_1	X_2	Y
2	12	5
6	14	30
9	20	35
7	18	25
12	22	40
4	14	10
1	13	10
3	15	20
6	16	5
10	16	20

How fast would one expect a rat to run that was

(1) 10 cm long and deprived of food for 5 hours?

(2) 21 cm long and deprived of food for 10 hours?

Part V

Some Nonparametric Statistics

14 Chi-Square and Binomial Tests for Nominal Data

Chapter Preview

14.1 Nonparametric Statistical Tests

The statistical procedures covered in previous chapters belong to the class of statistical analyses known as parametric statistical tests. These procedures involve the estimation of a population parameter and, in order for the decision reached to be valid, depend on assumptions regarding parameters (such as that the populations have equal variances) and/or that the raw scores meet certain characteristics (such as being randomly sampled from normal populations). These data assumptions and requirements are referred to as the underlying assumptions of a particular test. To repeat, *parametric statistical tests* involve estimation of or assumptions regarding parameters and assume certain characteristics of the raw data distributions, usually normality of the dependent variable scores or of the sampling distribution of the statistic of interest.

parametric statistical tests

nonparametric statistical tests

Nonparametric statistical tests do not involve parameter estimation or depend on assumptions of normality or any other particular shape of the raw data distribution. For this reason, they are often termed distribution-free statistical tests and, being free of these raw data requirements, may be used when regular parametric tests are inappropriate. This broader applicability is not obtained without cost, however, as nonparametric tests are ordinarily less powerful (more prone to Type II error) than their parametric counterparts. It is not correct to say that nonparametric tests do not depend upon any assumptions; for example, the random selection and random assignment of subjects, which assures both sample representativeness and independence among the raw scores, continues to be a requirement. It may not be lost on the reader that all of the parametric statistical tests thus far discussed use interval/ratio data, and that the nonparametric statistical tests presented in Chapters 14 and 15 all use ordinal or nominal data. By and large this relationship holds up, but note that parametric and nonparametric procedures are not defined by the type of measurement but rather by the considerations discussed earlier.

Nonparametric statistical tests would ordinarily be used when the original data were obtained by nominal or ordinal measurement, or when interval/ratio data were found to violate the assumptions of a particular parametric analysis. In the latter case, the interval/ratio data could be converted to ordinal or nominal form. If, for example, one had a sample of heights from a population known to be heavily skewed, then subjects could be ranked according to height, or arbitrary definitions of "tall" (say, over 183 cm), "medium" (say, 153 to 182 cm), and "short" (say, less than 153 cm) could be set up and the raw scores nominally classified. Two points may be made in this connection: (1) data may only be converted from more complex to less complex measurement types, and (2) the nominalization of interval/ratio data requires that the nominal classes be defined according to some defensible and logical rationale, otherwise any subsequent interpretations may be disputed because of disagreement over the definition of "tall," and so on.

14.2 The Chi-Square Distributions

The Chi-square distributions are a family of sampling distributions that are useful for testing hypotheses about nominal events. Assume a normally distributed population with all the raw scores converted into z-scores; the result would be a normally distributed population of z-scores with mean equal to zero and standard deviation equal to one ($\mu_z = 0.00$, $\sigma_z = 1.00$). Suppose we drew a single z-score at random and squared it, and did this a great many times and entered the z^2 terms into a frequency distribution. This distribution is the Chi-square distribution with one degree of freedom. Individual terms in these distributions are symbolized as χ^2, the Greek letter *chi* squared. Because they are squared z-scores, all χ^2 terms are positive, and may range from zero to infinity. If we drew two z-scores randomly from the original population, squared each and then summed them together, repeated this procedure a great many times and entered the terms into a frequency distribution, it would be the distribution of χ^2 at 2 degrees of freedom. Chi-square is defined as the sum of squared z-scores; by sampling appropriate numbers of z-scores and summing their squares, one could construct the sampling distribution of χ^2 at any number of degrees of freedom. Thus:

$$\chi^2_{(df=n)} = z_1^2 + z_2^2 + \cdots + z_n^2$$

The sampling distribution of χ^2 varies with the number of degrees of freedom, ranging from extremely positively skewed to approximately normal as degrees of freedom increase from one to infinity. Figure 14.2–1 depicts the sampling distribution of χ^2 at *df* equal to 1, 3, 5, and 10.

14.3 Observation and Expectation: The Goodness-of-Fit Test

There are many occasions when we observe a nominal event and have some expectation about the frequencies of the various possible outcomes. When flipping a coin, we normally expect heads and tails to occur with equal frequency. Suppose someone approached you and suggested a game in which she flipped a coin repeatedly and every time it landed head you paid her one dollar, and on every tail outcome, she paid you one dollar. If after 20 flips, the score was 11 heads and 9 tails, you would not consider that anything remarkable had happened; if the score was 13 heads and 7 tails you might conclude that this was not your day. But suppose that after 20 flips, the score was 20 heads and 0 tails. What thoughts might you have about luck, the integrity of this stranger, and two-headed coins?

It is clear that we observe coin flipping with the implicit assumption that the coin is fair. This assumption means that the probability of a head outcome is one-half [$p(\text{H}) = 0.50$], and the probability of a tail outcome is one-half

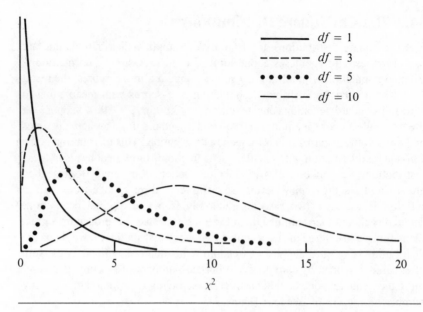

Figure 14.2–1   The sampling distribution of χ^2 at df = 1, 3, 5, and 10

[$p(T) = 0.50$], and this translates into the expectation that heads and tails will each occur with 50 percent frequency. We know that when dealing with small samples of subjects or events we cannot expect an exact match between theoretical expectations and actual trials, but as the discrepancy between what we observe and what we expect becomes greater, we begin to wonder if our expectations are based on valid assumptions. It is not a question of believing our eyes, because the observed frequencies were real events; rather it is the expected frequencies, which are hypothetical after all, and the basis upon which they were derived, that are called into question.

Even a fair coin will occasionally produce a run of 20 consecutive heads, but this is a rare happening. Before we accuse our opponent of cheating, we would want to determine the probability that a fair coin would, purely by chance, produce 20 heads in 20 tosses. If this probability turned out to be unrealistically low, we could reject the assumption that the coin is fair with some confidence. The amount of difference between observed and expected frequencies is a means to evaluate the assumption upon which the expectations were based. Essentially, this operation calls for determining whether the observed frequencies differed significantly from the expected frequencies, with the null hypothesis being that no difference exists. If the difference is found to be significant, the null hypothesis is rejected and this constitutes a rejection of whatever assumption was used to generate the expected frequencies. In our example with the coin flipping game the coin is assumed to be fair, and this leads to the expectation of 10 heads and 10 tails in 20 tosses.

If we compare a given outcome, such as 16 heads and 4 tails, to these expectations and find the difference between observed and expected frequencies to be significant, then we can reject the assumption that the coin is fair.

Assumptions that give rise to expected frequencies of nominal events may be tested by reference to the Chi-square family of sampling distributions. The differences between the observed and expected frequencies are transformed into a Chi-square statistic and tested for significance by reference to Table E. The Chi-square is obtained by squaring the difference between the observed and expected frequencies, dividing by the expected frequency, and summing the resulting terms. There will be as many such terms as there are nominal classes of measurement and the degrees of freedom for the significance test is the number of measurement classes minus one. Thus

$$\chi^2 = \Sigma \left[\frac{(O - E)^2}{E} \right]$$

O = Observed frequencies

E = Expected frequencies

$df = k - 1$ (k is the number of nominal classes of measurement)

The following procedure is called the goodness-of-fit test because it provides a decision criterion by which to judge whether the fit, or equivalence, of observed and expected frequencies is sufficiently good that the assumption giving rise to the expected values may be retained. The procedure involves identifying the assumption being tested, the nominal classes of measurement, and entering the observed and expected frequencies in a standard tabular format. When the χ^2 value has been calculated it is tested for significance by comparing it to a critical value obtained from Table E by reading down the column headed by the selected confidence level and across the row headed by the appropriate number of degrees of freedom. Any calculated χ^2 that equals or exceeds the critical value in Table E is significant. The rule for interpretation is that when the calculated χ^2 is significant, the assumption giving rise to the expected frequencies is rejected; conversely, if the χ^2 is nonsignificant, the assumption giving rise to the expected frequencies is retained.

Let us consider the coin-flipping game described earlier and test the assumption that the coin was fair, given an outcome of 16 heads and 4 tails in 20 tosses. Thus

Assumption being tested: The coin was fair
Nominal measurement classes: Head and Tail ($k = 2$)

	O (observed)	E (expected)	$O - E$	$(O - E)^2$	$(O - E)^2/E$
Head	16	10	6	36	3.60
Tail	4	10	-6	36	3.60
	20	20			$\chi^2 = 7.20$

1. $df = k - 1 = 2 - 1 = 1$

2. The critical value for χ^2 at 0.05 confidence level $= 3.84$

3. Therefore the result is significant.

4. Interpretation: The coin was not fair.*

Suppose that all people could be classified as having blonde, brown, or red hair, and that someone has conjectured that these types occur in the ratio $1:2:1$ in the general population. We could test this proposition by sampling a suitable number of people and classifying them by hair color. If we classified a total of 40 persons, the assumption of a $1:2:1$ distribution ratio would translate into the expectation of 10 blonde, 20 brown-haired, and 10 red-haired individuals. Suppose that we actually observed 14 blonde, 19 brown-haired, and 7 red-haired types. Thus

Assumption being tested: Blonde, brown-haired, and red-haired persons occur in the ratio $1:2:1$ respectively.

Nominal measurement classes: Blonde, brown, and red ($k = 3$)

	O	E	$O - E$	$(O - E)^2$	$(O - E)^2/E$
Blonde	14	10	4	16	1.60
Brown	19	20	−1	1	0.05
Red	7	10	−3	9	0.90
	40	40			$\chi^2 = 2.55$

1. $df = k - 1 = 3 - 1 = 2$

2. The critical value for χ^2 at 0.05 confidence level $= 5.99$

3. Therefore the result is not significant.

4. Interpretation: Blonde, brown-haired, and red-haired persons occur in the ratio $1:2:1$ respectively.**

Note that $\Sigma(O - E) = 0$, as this constitutes a convenient check for possible subtraction errors obtained in calculating the $O - E$ values.

In the goodness-of-fit test the null hypothesis is not the alternative to the assumption underlying the expected frequencies. The null hypothesis is that the observed and expected frequencies do not differ; thus, the null hypothesis predicts that all the $O - E$ terms will equal zero, and consequently that

---

*The assumption that the coin is fair generates the null hypothesis that the proportion of observed and expected frequencies in each measurement class is equal, or $O/N = E/N$ for each nominal class of measurement. This interpretation is based on the rejection of this null hypothesis.

**This interpretation is, in effect, the retention of the null hypothesis and, as always, is based on insufficient evidence to reject rather than evidence to support. (See *An aside: No life on Mars*.)

$\chi^2 = 0$. When the result is significant the null hypothesis is rejected, but since it is the expected and not the observed frequencies that are hypothetical, this requires in turn the rejection of the assumption that gave rise to the expected frequencies. A non-significant result should be viewed as insufficient evidence to reject the assumption that underlies the expected frequencies rather than as direct evidence in support of it.

Consider the hypothesis, "There is no life on Mars." Suppose we sent someone to look for life on Mars and none was found. Does this mean there is no life on Mars? No, only that there was none where our investigator looked or if there was he or she failed to detect it. If a Martian had been found the hypothesis could be rejected with certainty, but even repeated failures to find one do not make it certain that there are none. In the Chi-square test, the assumption giving rise to the expected values may be retained because of insufficient evidence to reject it rather than because of direct evidence for it. This is similar to our retention of null hypotheses in general.

**An aside:
no life on Mars**

Under certain conditions the goodness-of-fit test must include a correction procedure in order to provide accurate decisions. This correction should be applied when both of the following conditions are met: (1) degrees of freedom equals one, and (2) there is one or more expected frequency less than five. The correction takes the form of changing every observed frequency by 0.5 in such a way that the difference between the observed and its expected value is lessened. The corrected observed frequencies may be symbolized by O_c and once they have been derived the procedure follows established practice. Suppose someone showed us an apparently normal deck of playing cards and dealt out the top 12 cards. Our concern is with the occurrence of hearts as opposed to other suits so we would classify each card as a heart or non-heart. If the deck were normal we would expect 3 hearts and 9 non-hearts in the first 12 cards. This example fulfills the conditions of having $df = 1$ and an expected frequency less than 5 (expected hearts = 3). If we actually observed 5 hearts and 7 non-hearts, then the analysis would be as follows.

Assumption being tested: The deck was normal
Nominal measurement classes: Hearts and non-hearts ($k = 2$)

	O	E	O_c	$O_c - E$	$(O_c - E)^2$	$(O_c - E)^2/E$
Hearts	5	3	4.5	1.5	2.25	0.75
Non-hearts	7	9	7.5	−1.5	2.25	0.25
	12	12	12			$\chi^2 = 1.00$

1. $df = k - 1 = 2 - 1 = 1$
2. The critical value for χ^2 at 0.05 confidence level = 3.84
3. Therefore the result is not significant.
4. Interpretation: The deck was normal.

14.4 Review Exercises

1. Define or describe the following terms.

   (a) parametric statistical tests
   (b) nonparametric statistical tests

   In each of the following problem exercises you should:

   (a) identify the assumption being tested
   (b) complete the analysis at 0.05 confidence level
   (c) clearly interpret the result

2. Susan wrote a 70-item true/false test and got 45 items correct. Was she just guessing?

3. In driving through 90 intersections with traffic lights, Cathy encountered 35 red, 30 amber, and 25 green lights. If the lights at any intersection operate independently of those at any other is it the case that the three colors are on for the same length of time?

4. A roulette wheel has 38 slots numbered 00, 0, and 1 through 36. Lori bet the number 29 on 152 consecutive spins and lost every time. She then called a policeman and insisted that the operator be arrested for running a crooked wheel. Does the evidence support this contention?

5. Lou opened an ice cream parlor and decided to serve four flavors: vanilla, chocolate, strawberry, and calorap. Not knowing what proportions to order, he stepped out into the street and asked the first ten people he saw which they would prefer; they answered with 3 vanilla, 1 chocolate, 2 strawberry, and 4 calorap. He ordered a thousand servings based on this breakdown, but the next thousand customers asked for 500 vanilla, 200 chocolate, 200 strawberry, and 100 calorap. Was the sample of ten he originally questioned representative?

6. A properly manufactured parachute has a probability of not opening of 0.0001. The army cites figures for the last 870,000 jumps, which show that 123 failed to open and claims that the parachutes are substandard. Does the evidence support the army's position?

7. At a small rural hospital, records show that the number of children born during the spring, summer, fall, and winter months respectively was 6, 7, 2, and 1. Are births evenly distributed throughout the year?

8. Cheryl tasted the contents of 20 glasses, 40 percent of which held ale and 60 percent of which held beer. After tasting all the drinks, she announced that she had tasted 11 ales and 9 beers. Could she tell the difference?

9. The gyrfalcon occurs in three colors: white, black and grey. If these are color phases in the life of individuals, then populations inhabiting different territories should contain similar proportions of the three types. On the other hand, if these are different genetic variants, then populations in different regions should exhibit different proportions as a function of different selection pressures. The Iceland population is known to be white, black, and grey in the ratio $1:2:4$. Thirty-five individuals observed in the Keewatin district were determined to consist of 18 white, 7 black, and 10 grey. Which view do these data support?

14.5 Relationship Between Nominal Variables: The Test of Independence

In nominal measurement, the classes of outcome must be mutually exclusive for any given variable, but this does not prevent a subject from being classified on two different variable dimensions at the same time. For example, people may be classified as male or female, which is a nominal measurement on the variable of gender, and as being timid or aggressive, which is a nominal measurement of a behavior tendency. In this example the two variables may each occur as one of two outcomes, so that we could encounter $2 \times 2 = 4$ different types of people, namely, timid men, aggressive men, timid women, and aggressive women. Suppose we performed these classifications of gender and aggressiveness on 25 women and 25 men and that this resulted in the identification of 14 women as aggressive and 11 as timid, and 16 men as aggressive and 9 as timid. These data could be organized into a table, known as a *contingency table,* as is shown next.

contingency table

	Male	Female	
Timid	9	11	20
Aggressive	16	14	30
	25	25	50

The column sums indicate the total numbers of men and women, the row sums indicate the total numbers of timid and aggressive types, and the overall sum in the lower right corner indicates the total number of subjects. A question of interest is whether the ratio, or distribution, of timid and aggressive types is the same or different among men as compared to women. Also, is the ratio of men and women among the timid group the same or different as compared to the aggressive group? These are merely two ways of asking the same more general question: Is the variable of gender independent of the variable of aggressiveness? To say that gender and aggressiveness are independent is to say that these two variables in no way co-vary, so that the ratio of timid to aggressive types should be the same for the two sexes, and the ratio of males to females should be the same in the timid and aggressive groups. The alternative possibility that gender and aggressiveness are related would mean that the outcome on one variable is systematically associated with the outcome on the other. If this were true, then the ratio of aggressive to timid types would be different for men as compared to women, and the ratio of men to women would be different among timid as compared to aggressive groups.

The test of independence enables us to decide whether nominal variables are independent or related. This procedure involves generating an expected value for each cell of the contingency table and then proceeding to calculate a Chi-square from the observed and expected values. The key issue in this process is the rationale behind the generation of the expected values. Let us consider the upper left cell of the contingency table, that representing timid males. Of the 50 persons measured in this hypothetical study, 20 were classified as being timid; therefore, the probability that any randomly selected person from this group will be timid is $p(T) = 20/50 = 0.40$. Twenty-five persons were men, so the probability that any randomly selected person will be a male is $p(M) = 25/50 = 0.50$. If gender and aggressiveness are independent of each other, then the probability that any randomly selected individual will be a timid male is

$$p(T) = 20/50 = 0.40$$
$$p(M) = 25/50 = 0.50$$

$$p(T \cap M) = p(T) \times p(M)$$
$$= 0.40 \times 0.50$$
$$= 0.20$$

Since there were $N = 50$ subjects altogether, the expected frequency of timid men may be determined as $0.20 \times 50 = 10$. We have thus generated an expected frequency of timid men that can be compared to the actually observed frequency. A similar procedure can be used to generate an expected frequency for each cell of the contingency table. A more convenient computational formula is

Expected frequency = (row sum $\times$ column sum)/total sum

Thus

Expected frequency of timid men = $(20 \times 25)/50 = 10$
Expected frequency of timid women = $(20 \times 25)/50 = 10$
Expected frequency of aggressive men = $(30 \times 25)/50 = 15$
Expected frequency of aggressive women = $(30 \times 25)/50 = 15$

The expected frequencies so obtained are entered in a box in the upper corner of each cell of the contingency table, as is shown below.

	Male	Female	
Timid	10 / 9	10 / 11	20
Aggressive	15 / 16	15 / 14	30
	25	25	50

The expected frequencies in each row must sum to the row sum, the expected frequencies in each column must sum to the column sum, and finally, the sum of all the expected frequencies must equal the total sum. The important point in connection with the expected frequencies is that they are generated on the assumption that the variables are independent. This assumption of no relationship constitutes the null hypothesis in the test of independence. A comparison of the observed with the expected frequencies by means of calculating a χ^2 and testing it for significance is thus a test of the null hypothesis that gender and aggressiveness are independent. The degrees of freedom for the significance test consist of the number of contingency table rows minus one times the number of contingency table columns minus one. The remainder of this procedure is as follows

Variables: Gender and aggressiveness

Null hypothesis: Gender and aggressiveness are independent

O	E	$O - E$	$(O - E)^2$	$(O - E)^2/E$
9	10	−1	1	0.10
11	10	+1	1	0.10
16	15	+1	1	0.07
14	15	−1	1	0.07
50	50			$\chi^2 = 0.34$

1. $df = (R - 1)(C - 1) = (2 - 1)(2 - 1) = 1$
   Note: R = number of rows in the contingency table
   $\quad\quad\quad C$ = number of columns in the contingency table

2. The critical value for χ^2 at 0.05 confidence level = 3.84

3. Therefore the result is not significant.

4. Interpretation: Gender and aggressiveness are independent.

The general rule for interpreting a Chi-square result applies, and thus a significant result rejects the hypothesis underlying the expected values. In the text of independence, the hypothesis underlying the expected frequencies is that the variables are independent (not related) and thus the interpretation of the non-significant result is a retention of the null hypothesis that gender and aggressiveness are independent.

An additional numerical example should clear up any uncertainties about this procedure. Suppose an individual built a bird feeder and counted the different types of birds that fed there at dawn, noon, and sunset. Over a period of time the number of cardinals, bluejays, and chickadees respectively was 11,

	Dawn	Noon	Sunset	
Cardinals	15 / 11	20 / 18	15 / 21	50
Bluejays	9 / 9	12 / 14	9 / 7	30
Chickadees	6 / 10	8 / 8	6 / 2	20
	30	40	30	100

9, and 10 at dawn; 18, 14, and 8 at noon; and 21, 7, and 2 at sunset. The two variables in this example are the type of bird and the time of feeding. We shall test the null hypothesis that these variables are independent. Note that it does not matter which variable is placed on the horizontal axis and which is placed on the vertical axis.

Variables: Type of bird and time of feeding

Null hypothesis: Type of bird and time of feeding are independent (one could also say that there is no relationship between type of bird and time of feeding).

O	E	$O - E$	$(O - E)^2$	$(O - E)^2/E$
11	15	−4	16	1.07
18	20	−2	4	0.20
21	15	+6	36	2.40
9	9	0	0	0.00
14	12	+2	4	0.33
7	9	−2	4	0.44
10	6	+4	16	2.67
8	8	0	0	0.00
2	6	−4	16	2.67
100	100			$\chi^2 = 9.78$

1. $df = (R - 1)(C - 1) = (3 - 1)(3 - 1) = 4$
2. The critical value for χ^2 at 0.05 confidence level = 9.49
3. Therefore the result is significant.
4. Interpretation: There is a relationship between feeding time and the types of birds that appear to feed.

In a test of independence, a significant result tells only that the two variables are in some way systematically related to each other and we learn nothing more than that. We can, in the previous example, inspect the raw data and see that cardinals tend to feed later in the day and that chickadees tend to feed early, but the test of independence cannot tell us whether these trends differ significantly, or, for example, whether the frequencies of the different types of birds are significantly different at any given feeding time. We learn only that there is some systematic, or non-random, relationship between feeding time and the tendency of different types of birds to feed. This is, nonetheless, valuable and interesting information.

In the discussion of the goodness-of-fit test in Section 14.3, it was pointed out that when there is one degree of freedom and any expected value less than five, a correction must be applied to the observed frequencies in order to preserve the decision-making accuracy of the Chi-square test. The same requirement has traditionally been applied to the test of independence, and the correction procedure is identical. Each observed frequency is changed by 0.5 so as to make it numerically more similar to its expected value. Take care that all observed values are corrected and that the O_c terms thus obtained sum to the proper row, column, and overall totals. With the observed frequencies thus corrected, the test of independence proceeds in the normal fashion.

Some authors have suggested that the criterion of a single expected frequency less than five when $df = 1$ is perhaps too conservative; whether this should be taken to mean that the test of independence does not require correction for small frequencies at all is unclear. Relative to uncorrected data, the correction has the effect of making a significant result more difficult to achieve, that is, reducing the probability of a Type I error. It can be argued that if any error is likely, then a conservative error is preferable to the alternative. In any event, cautious interpretation is recommended when dealing with small frequencies.

14.6 Review Exercises

1. Define or describe the term "contingency table."

   In each of the following problem exercises you should:
   (a) identify the variables being measured
   (b) state the null hypothesis being tested
   (c) complete the analysis at 0.05 confidence level
   (d) clearly interpret the result

2. A sample of 20 students was classified as to whether they generally did or did not attend class. At the end of the semester each student either passed or failed; of the 10 who passed, 9 were attenders and 1 a non-attender, while only one attender failed. Is attendance related to failure?

3. An experimenter found three black phase gyrfalcon nests with 2 eggs and five with 3 eggs. He also found seven white phase gyrfalcon nests with 2 eggs and five with 1 egg. Is clutch size related to color phase?

4. People were classed as being aggressive, even-tempered, or timid, and as being good, poor, or terrible golfers. It was found that the number of aggressive individuals who were good, poor, and terrible golfers respectively was 180, 190, and 130. The numbers were 120, 120, and 60 for even-tempered golfers, and 100, 90, and 10 for timid golfers.

5. In an experiment dealing with interpersonal attraction, subjects were asked to indicate which of the following characteristics, i.e., cleanliness, sense of humor, physical attractiveness, or intelligence, they regarded as

the most important factor in determining their initial reaction to a person of the opposite sex. The number of male subjects who indicated the four categories respectively was 65, 150, 35, and 50; the number of females respectively was 35, 150, 15, and 100.

6. The question of whether Quebec should secede from Canada was put to a sample of five hundred francophones and five hundred anglophones. The number of francophones who voted Yes, No, and Undecided, was 300, 100, and 100. The number of anglophones who voted Yes, No, and Undecided, was 200, 150, and 150.

7. Rose had ten cats and fifteen dogs and was interested in knowing whether the cats and dogs differed in mouse-catching ability. She arranged a test and scored each animal as being "good" or "poor" as a mouse-catcher. Six of the cats and four of the dogs were scored as "good."

8. The following data are taken from a study in which people were asked to indicate what changes they would make to themselves in order to become more beautiful. Among the female subjects, the most frequently mentioned changes involved weight (loss), hair, and complexion. Broken down into age groups of 19 years and under, 20 to 25 years inclusive, and 26 years and over, the number of women who wished for changes in weight, hair, and complexion, respectively, was 49, 52, and 64 for the 19 and under group; 26, 18, and 16 for the 20 to 25 group; and 15, 20, and 10 for the 26 and over group.

9. The following data are taken from a study in which people were asked to indicate what changes they would make to themselves in order to become more beautiful. Of the total of 85 men who responded, 28 indicated a concern over complexion, while of the 205 women who responded, 89 indicated concern over complexion.

10. A survey was taken regarding leisure activities of people in different age groups. The age groups were: below 25 years, 25 to 40 years, and over 40 years, and the leisure activities were hiking, fishing, golf, and tennis. The number of under-25 persons who engaged in the four activities respectively was 0, 0, 2, and 18; for the 25 to 40 group the numbers were 0, 7, 15, and 18; and for the over 40 group the numbers were 5, 3, 8, and 24.

11. For 100 consecutive days Virginia noted the daily high temperature and relative humidity. The temperature was classed as being either hot or cold, and the relative humidity was classed as being very humid, humid, dry, or very dry. The number of hot days on which it was very humid, humid, dry, and very dry, respectively, was 25, 17, 11, and 7, while for cold days the numbers were 15, 13, 9, and 3.

14.7 The Binomial Test

The binomial test does not make use of the Chi-square distributions but is included in this chapter because it is appropriate for two-outcome nominal events. Although some events, such as a coin toss have *only* two outcomes, the majority of real-life situations are more complex; nonetheless, it is usually possible to classify all outcomes as favorable or unfavorable and thereby create two nominal measurement classes. For example, an investigator interested in the occurrence of red-haired persons would classify any subject as being red-haired or not-red-haired. In Section 5.8 we introduced the binomial expansion and saw how it could be used to determine the probability of r favorable events, or outcomes, in n total trials if the probability of the favorable event (p) could be specified. The binomial expansion is written as

$$\left(\frac{n}{r}\right)p^r q^{n-r}$$

where n = total trials or opportunities

r = frequency of the favorable event

p = probability of the favorable event

q = probability of the unfavorable event ($q = 1 - p$)

Since our introduction to the binomial expansion, we have come to understand that rejecting or retaining an hypothesis depends ultimately on the probability that we would obtain the observed result if the hypothesis in question were true. Using the binomial expansion to calculate the probability of occurrence of some specified frequency of the favorable event requires specification of p, the probability of the favorable event. If an hypothesis concerning the probability of the favorable event is used to generate a value for p, and if the resulting probability is below some criterion, such as 0.05 confidence level, then this constitutes evidence to reject the hypothesis that gave rise to the p value used; this procedure is known as the binomial test.

Suppose we have an hypothesis that female students are twice as likely to wear jeans as they are any alternative. This hypothesis would generate $p(\text{Jeans}) = p = 0.67$, and $p(\text{Alternatives}) = q = 0.33$. If a random sample of 20 female students were obtained and 9 were found to be wearing jeans, the binomial test of the original hypothesis would proceed as follows

$$\binom{20}{9}(0.67)^9(0.33)^{11} = (167,960)\,(0.027207)\,(0.000005)$$

$$= 0.022848$$

$$= 0.02$$

Since the result is less than 0.05 we can reject the hypothesis (at 0.05 confidence level) that female students are twice as likely to wear jeans as they are any alternative.

As shown in the previous example, the binomial test is quite straightforward. It is widely applied in circumstances wherein the outcome, or the subjects' behavior, may occur as one of several mutually exclusive possibilities. The hypothesis that all outcome or response possibilities are equally probable may serve as the basis for generating the value of p for any given outcome or response alternative. The binomial test has the added nicety of calculating the exact probability of your observed outcome, as opposed to merely providing a rejection or retention decision.

14.8 Review Exercises

1. In an experiment to determine if rats show any turning preference, eight rats were tested in a T-maze wherein they ran down a straight section and then had to make either a left or right turn. Seven turned left. Do rats show a turning preference?

2. In an experiment on odor identification, subjects were blindfolded and asked to sniff four nightshirts and identify which of the four they had worn the previous night. Six persons were tested and four selected their own nightshirt. Does this evidence suggest that people can discriminate?

3. Lyn wrote a 15-item true/false examination and got 10 correct. Test the hypothesis that she guessed at every answer.

4. At a youth camp, the counselor sent a frog-catching team to the swamp to catch frogs; he assumed that the team was equally likely to catch male as female frogs. The team returned with nine males and five females. Test the hypothesis that the counselor's assumption was correct.

5. It is claimed that buyers of a Warsaw Lottery ticket have a 20 percent chance of winning. Barbara bought 12 tickets and didn't win anything. Test the hypothesis that the claim is valid.

6. It is claimed that baseball batters are equally likely to take their first swing at any of the first three pitches. A random sample of ten batters was observed and it was found that six swung at the second pitch. Test the original claim.

15 Selected Tests for Ordinal Data

Chapter Preview

15.1 Correlation Between Ranked Variables: Kendall's Tau

Occasionally, the variable of interest cannot be easily defined operationally in a way that yields interval/ratio data but is a variable that lends itself readily to ordinal measurement. There might also be occasions when the data are ranked and analyzed as ordinal measures in the interests of obtaining a rapid and convenient evaluation of the results even if an interval/ratio measurement is possible. In cases where the raw data do not meet the assumptions required for a parametric analysis, then interval/ratio data may be converted into ordinal data and analyzed in that form. This section will describe Kendall's *tau* coefficient of rank correlation; this procedure does not require homoscedasticity or normality in the raw data as underlying assumptions.

When any set of individuals, objects, or events is subjected to ordinal measurement, the resulting data consist of the rank values 1 through *n*. In order that there be no ambiguity, it is essential that the rule by which ranking is done be made clear. For example, if ten persons are to be ranked on the variable of beauty, this can be done according to the rule that the rank of 1 goes to the most beautiful, or according to the rule that the rank of 1 goes to the least beautiful. This little detail concerning how the ranks were assigned must be made explicit before one can interpret even a single set of ordinal data, much less the correlation between two sets of ranks.

M. Kendall (1970) has derived an interesting and serviceable coefficient of rank correlation, which is symbolized as τ, Greek letter *tau*. In the derivation of this coefficient, degree of relationship between the X and Y ranks means the extent to which pairs of subjects show consistency in the relative magnitude of their Y ranks as compared with their X ranks. Given that there are N^* subjects that have been ranked on variables X and Y, any pair of subjects may be said to be in agreement, or in inversion, with respect to each other. Let us assume that nine people have been ranked on variables X and Y, and that the raw data were as shown on page 328.

Any pair of subjects is in *agreement* when they have the same rank magnitude relationship (larger or smaller) on variable Y that they have on variable X. Consider subjects 1 and 2; subject 1 has a smaller rank on variable X than does subject 2 and subject 1 also has a smaller rank on variable Y than does subject 2. Thus, subjects 1 and 2 are said to be in agreement. Consider subjects 1 and 6; it can be seen that this pair is also in agreement because subject 1 has a larger rank on variable X than subject 6 and also a larger rank on variable Y than subject 6.

agreement

---

*In the discussion of correlation in Chapter 12, upper case N was used to refer to the number of pairs of scores, or the number of subjects. To be consistent with this practice, upper case N is used in this section whenever reference is being made to the number of subjects on whom two ordinal measures have been obtained.

Subject no.	X	Y
1	6	5
2	9	8
3	7	7
4	1	1
5	3	2
6	5	4
7	8	6
8	2	9
9	4	3

inversion

A pair of subjects is in *inversion* when they have a dissimilar rank magnitude relationship on variable Y as compared to variable X. Consider subjects 8 and 9; subject 8 has a smaller rank on variable X than subject 9, but subject 8 has a larger rank on variable Y than subject 9. Thus, subjects 8 and 9 are said to be in inversion. Again, consider subjects 3 and 8; subject 3 has a larger rank on variable X than subject 8, but a smaller rank on variable Y than subject 8. Subjects 3 and 8 are also in inversion.

tau

For any set of N subjects, there are $N(N - 1)/2$ possible pairs that can be considered. Kendall's *tau* coefficient of rank correlation is defined as the total number of agreements minus the total number of inversions, divided by the number of possible pairs. Thus

$$\tau = \frac{\text{(total agreements)} - \text{(total inversions)}}{N(N - 1)/2}$$

When there is a perfect positive relationship between the X and Y ranks, all possible pairs of subjects will be in agreement, and $\tau = +1.00$. When there is a perfect negative relationship between the X and Y ranks, all possible pairs of subjects will be in inversion, and $\tau = -1.00$. The coefficient τ may be understood as the probability of being in agreement minus the probability of being in inversion. Put another way, τ is the difference between the probability of being in agreement and the probability of being in inversion for any randomly selected pair of subjects.

In the following illustration, we shall symbolize the total number of agreements as A and the total number of inversions as I. The formula for *tau* is

$$\tau = \frac{A - I}{N(N - 1)/2}$$

where

$$A = \text{total agreements}$$
$$I = \text{total inversions}$$
$$N(N - 1)/2 = \text{total number of possible pairs of subjects}$$

We shall use the data previously shown and assume that variable X was beauty, with 1st rank as most beautiful, and variable Y was talent, with 1st rank as most talented. We shall determine the nature and degree of relationship, if any, between beauty and talent and test the null hypothesis that beauty and talent are not related. The first step is to arrange the raw data so that the ranks are ordered from 1 to N on variable X. It is an arbitrary convention that the data should be ordered on the X variable; note that the original pairings of X and Y ranks must be preserved. Thus

X (beauty)	Y (talent)
1	1
2	9
3	2
4	3
5	4
6	5
7	7
8	6
9	8

In practice, we do not actually identify all possible pairs of subjects to determine agreements and inversions; rather, a more convenient method is used. (In fact, the following procedure is one of several methods that can be used.) First we establish the headings "agreements" and "inversions" to the right of the X and Y rank columns. We next determine the number of agreements as follows. Beginning with the first (top) Y rank, count the number of subsequent Y ranks that are larger and enter that number in the first row under the agreements heading. In our example, the first Y rank is 1 and all 8 subsequent Y ranks are larger, so that we enter an 8 in the first row under the agreements heading. The second Y rank is 9 and none of the 7 subsequent Y ranks is larger, so we enter a 0 in the second row. The third Y rank is 2 and all 6 subsequent Y ranks are larger, so we enter a 6 in the third row, and so on.

X (beauty)	Y (talent)	Agreements	Inversions
1	1	8	0
2	9	0	7
3	2	6	0
4	3	5	0
5	4	4	0
6	5	3	0
7	7	1	1
8	6	1	0
9	8	0	0
		$A = 28$	$I = 8$

The number of inversions is determined in a similar fashion. Beginning with the first Y rank, count the number of subsequent ranks that are smaller and enter that number in the appropriate row under the inversions heading. The first Y rank is 1 and none of the subsequent Y ranks is smaller, so we enter a 0 in the first row under the inversions heading. The next Y rank is 9 and all 7 subsequent Y ranks are smaller, so we enter a 7 in the second row under the inversions heading, and so on.

In order to obtain A, the entries in the agreements column are summed, and I is obtained by summing the entries in the inversions column. Since $N = 9$, *tau* is calculated as follows

$$\tau = \frac{A - I}{N(N - 1)/2}$$

$$= \frac{28 - 8}{9(9 - 1)/2}$$

$$= \frac{20}{36}$$

$$= +0.56$$

[Note: $A + I = N(N - 1)/2$]

The *tau* coefficient must be tested for significance to establish whether the observed result should be regarded as a chance event. The null hypothesis is that there is no relationship between the X and Y ranks in the population and consequently predicts that $\tau = 0$. The obtained value of τ is compared to a critical value found in Table F by reading across the row headed by the appropriate N and down the column of the confidence level chosen. The correlation is significant when the calculated τ equals or exceeds the critical value in Table F. Thus

1. $N = 9$

2. The critical value for τ at 0.05 confidence level $= 0.556$.

3. Therefore the result is significant.

4. Interpretation: There is a relationship between beauty and talent such that greater beauty is associated with more talent.

In the interpretation of a correlation, one must clearly indicate the form of the relationship between the two variables. The sign of the coefficient can be misleading; it tells only that the two sets of numbers were positively or negatively related. Since the assignment of ranks involves an arbitrary rule, such as the 1st rank is the most beautiful or the 1st rank is the least beautiful, it is possible that a positive coefficient could reflect a negative relationship between the variables themselves, or vice versa. For example, in the present case, if beauty had been ranked with 1st rank to most beautiful and talent ranked with 1st rank to least talented, then the τ coefficient would have been negative even though it would still be the case that greater beauty is associated with greater talent. To avoid confusion and miscommunication, the best procedure is to test the coefficient for significance of the basis of its magnitude and then, by reference to the raw data, make the form of the relationship explicit in the interpretation statement.

We have examined the product-moment correlation for determining the degree of relationship between interval/ratio variables, and Kendall's *tau* for use with ordinal data. The Chi-square test of independence can be thought of as a measure of relationship between nominal variables but only in the crude sense of determining whether or not a relationship exists. These procedures by no means exhaust the possibilities for calculating coefficients of relationships between variables. There are procedures for estimating relationship between interval/ratio and dichotomous variables (point-biserial coefficient), between two dichotomous variables (phi coefficient or tetrachoric coefficient), and other cases. An excellent review of this subject is provided by Glass and Hopkins (1984).

An aside: other correlation coefficients

Kendall's Tau with Tied Ranks

Occasionally, it may be desirable to obtain the correlation between two variables, one of which is expressed as interval/ratio data and the other as ordinal data. In such cases, the interval/ratio data must be converted into ranks so that a rank correlation coefficient, such as Kendall's tau, may be computed. The conversion of interval/ratio data into ranks is straightforward unless there are tied scores (multiple occurrences of the same numerical value). In such cases, the tied scores are all given the rank that is the mean of the rank positions they occupy. Remember that if there are n scores, then the rank positions 1 through n must be assigned; thus, between these limits, tied scores are given the mean of the ranks they would have received had they not been tied. A couple of examples will serve to illustrate this procedure.

Interval/ratio scores ($n = 6$)	Ranks
10	1
8	2.5
8	2.5
5	4
3	5
2	6

Interval/ratio scores ($n = 15$)	Ranks
24	1.5
24	1.5
21	3
19	4
18	6
18	6
18	6
14	8
12	9
9	10
7	12.5
7	12.5
7	12.5
7	12.5
6	15

When tied ranks have occurred as a consequence of converting interval/ratio data into ordinal data or as a direct result of ordinal measurement, one must use a modification of Kendall's *tau* that is designed to correct for the occurrence to tied ranks.

Kendall's *tau* when X and/or Y have tied ranks

$$\tau = \frac{A - I}{\sqrt{N(N - 1)/2] - K_x}\sqrt{[N(N - 1)/2] - K_y}}$$

$$K_x = (0.50)[\Sigma f_i(f_i - 1)]$$

where f_i is the number of tied observations in each group of ties on X.

$$K_y = (0.50)[\Sigma f_i(f_i - 1)]$$

where f_i is the number of tied observations in each group of ties on Y.

15.2　Review Exercises

1. Define or describe the following terms.

   (a) agreement
   (b) inversion
   (c) tau

In each of the following problem exercises you should:

   (a) state the null hypothesis being tested
   (b) complete the analysis at 0.05 confidence level
   (c) clearly interpret the result.

Kendall's Tau

An instructor drew a random sample of ten persons from her class list and ranked them on the nearness to the front of the classroom where they normally sat (variable X) with first rank to nearest to the front. At the end of the semester, she ranked them in terms of their final grade (variable Y) with first rank to highest grade. The raw data are shown next.

Variable X: Seat position relative to the front of the classroom.

Variable Y: Performance in the course

Null hypothesis: Seat position relative to the front of the classroom is not related to performance in the course.

X (seat position)	Y (performance)	A	I
1	2	8	1
2	4	6	2
3	1	7	0
4	5	5	1
5	3	5	0
6	6	4	0
7	8	2	1
8	10	0	2
9	9	0	1
10	7	0	0
		$A = 37$	$I = 8$

$N = 10$

$$\tau = \frac{37 - 8}{(10)\,(9)/2}$$

$$= +0.64$$

1. $N = 10$
2. The critical value for τ at 0.05 confidence level = 0.511
3. Therefore the result is significant.
4. Interpretation: Seat position is related to course performance such that sitting nearer to the front of the classroom is associated with a higher final grade.

2. A teacher's ranking of students' intellectual potential (1st rank to greatest potential) was compared to performance on a standard I.Q. test (1st rank to highest score).

    Teacher's ranking: 1, 6, 7, 2, 4, 8, 9, 5, 3, 10
    Test score rank: 2, 5, 8, 1, 3, 7, 10, 6, 4, 9

3. In a family with seven children, the birth order position of each child was paired with a ranking on aggressiveness (1st rank to most aggressive). The raw data were as follows

    Birth order: 1, 2, 4, 5, 7, 3, 6
    Aggressiveness: 1, 5, 4, 3, 7, 6, 2

4. Nine people were ranked on tenacity (1st rank to most tenacious) and on self-confidence (1st rank to most confident).

    Tenacity: 2, 3, 8, 1, 5, 7, 4, 9, 6
    Self-confidence: 3, 4, 9, 2, 6, 8, 5, 1, 7

5. An experimenter ranked seven people on their need for affiliation (1st rank to greatest need). Each was also ranked on the age difference between himself or herself and the nearest age sibling (1st rank to smallest age difference).

    Need for affiliation: 1, 2, 5, 3, 4, 7, 6
    Age difference to nearest sibling: 3, 1, 7, 2, 4, 6, 5

6. Seven bees were ranked on size (1st rank to largest) and on the potency of their venom (1st rank to least potent).

    Size: 1, 3, 2, 6, 5, 4, 7
    Potency: 7, 6, 4, 2, 3, 5, 1

7. Roy tested ten stereo speakers by connecting them in turn to the same receiver and, playing the same recording, ranking the speakers with 1st rank going to the best sounding speaker. The speakers were also ranked according to price, with 1st rank going to the most expensive speaker.

    Sound: 2, 5, 3, 6, 1, 8, 9, 4, 7, 10
    Price: 3, 5, 1, 9, 4, 10, 6, 2, 7, 8

8. Eight partially bald men were ranked on their sex appeal, with first rank going to most sexy. Each was also ranked on the degree of baldness, with 1st rank going to most hairy.

    Sex appeal: 5, 1, 3, 7, 8, 6, 4, 2
    Hairiness: 4, 7, 6, 1, 3, 2, 5, 8

9. Two hundred women were given a list of ten physical features. Each was asked to identify which of these she would change on herself in order to be more attractive, and to rank the changes in order of importance. When all the data had been collected, the ten features were ranked in terms of

frequency of mention (1st rank to most frequently mentioned). By taking the mean of individual subject's ranks it was also possible to rank the ten features in terms of importance (1st rank to most important).

Frequency of mention: 3, 2, 6, 4, 1, 10, 8, 9, 5, 7
Importance: 3, 7, 8, 5, 1, 6, 9, 10, 2, 4

10. Ten people were ranked on wit (1st rank to most witty) and on generosity (1st rank to least generous).

Wit: 1, 4, 3, 6, 9, 10, 5, 2, 7, 8
Generosity: 2, 3, 1, 9, 8, 10, 5, 4, 6, 7

15.3 The Mann-Whitney *U*-Test

The Mann-Whitney U-test is a procedure that tests whether two independent groups differ significantly when the raw data are ordinal measurement. This test has proven to be a powerful and reliable decision-making device that does not depend on or require assumptions of normality of distributions or homogeneity of variances. Though it is conceivable that a dependent variable might be directly obtained as ordinal data, a more likely use of the Mann-Whitney U-test is as an alternative to the independent groups t-test when the raw data do not meet the t-test's underlying assumptions. In such cases, the dependent variable scores may be ranked and analyzed by the Mann-Whitney U-test.

The Mann-Whitney U-test procedure is based on the ranks obtained when the two groups of scores are considered as one and derives the statistics U_A and U_B, which are defined as

$$U_A = n_A n_B + (n_A)(n_A + 1)/2 - \Sigma R_A$$

$$U_B = n_A n_B + (n_B)(n_B + 1)/2 - \Sigma R_B$$

where

n_A = number of scores in Group A

n_B = number of scores in Group B

ΣR_A = sum of ranks of Group A scores

ΣR_B = sum of ranks of Group B scores

The smaller of U_A or U_B ($U_{smaller}$) is tested for significance by reference to Table C. The result is significant if $U_{smaller}$ is equal to or smaller than the critical value obtained from Table C. The null hypothesis is that the distributions of the dependent variable in the populations represented by the two groups are identical. A significant $U_{smaller}$ can be interpreted to mean that population A differs from population B under the circumstances of the experiment.

Assume that two randomly selected groups served in a reaction time experiment in which each subject was instructed to push a button as quickly as possible after onset of a stimulus light. Members of the experimental group were tested 15 minutes after ingesting 20 grains of acetylsalicylic acid (A.S.A.) whereas control subjects ingested an inert placebo. Assume the dependent variable was measured in hundredths of a second, and that the raw data were as shown.

Independent variable: ingestion of 20 grains of A.S.A.

Dependent variable: reaction time

Null hypothesis: Ingestion of 20 grains of A.S.A. does not affect reaction time ($\mu_{A\ ranks} = \mu_{B\ ranks}$).

Group A (control)	Group B (A.S.A.)
45	150
20	50
70	80
65	230
60	30
70	310
50	110
40	

Since these groups of scores can be shown to have significantly different variances (see Section 9.3), the decision is to convert them to ranks and analyze using the Mann-Whitney U-test. The first step is to arrange all the scores in ascending or descending order and convert to ranks. Note that it is not necessary for n_A to equal n_B. Thus

Score: 20, 30, 40, 45, 50, 50, 60, 65, 70, 70, 80, 110, 150, 230, 310

Rank: 1, 2, 3, 4, 5.5, 5.5, 7, 8, 9.5, 9.5, 11, 12, 13, 14, 15

Group: A B A A   A   B A A   A   A B   B   B   B   B

Note: A = control group

B = A.S.A. group

$\sum R_A = 1 + 3 + 4 + 5.5 + 7 + 8 + 9.5 + 9.5$

$= 47.50$

$\sum R_B = 2 + 5.5 + 11 + 12 + 13 + 14 + 15$

$= 72.50$

$U_A = (8)(7) + (8)(8 + 1)/2 - 47.50$

$= 56 + 36 - 47.50$

$= 44.50$

$$U_B = (8)(7) + (7)(7 + 1)/2 - 72.50$$
$$= 56 + 28 - 72.50$$
$$= 11.50$$

Therefore $U_{smaller} = 11.50$

The statistic $U_{smaller}$ may be tested for significance by reference to Table C; $U_{smaller}$ is significant when it is equal to or smaller than the critical value in Table C. The Mann-Whitney U-test can handle cases where the two groups have different n's, and Table C is set up with the headings "smaller n" and "larger n". Simply read down the appropriate column and across the appropriate row to locate the critical value. If $n_A = n_B$, then use the row and column headed by the appropriate value.

1. $n_A = 8$, $n_B = 7$
2. The critical value for $U_{smaller}$ at 0.05 confidence level $= 10$.
3. Therefore the result is not significant.
4. Interpretation: Ingestion of 20 grains of A.S.A. does not affect reaction time.

Table C provides critical values for $U_{smaller}$ only for cases where neither n_A nor n_B exceeds 20. If either group of scores is larger than 20, a z-score may be derived and tested for significance by reference to the normal distribution; critical values are 1.96 and 2.58 for 0.05 and 0.01 confidence levels respectively. The z-score is derived as follows

$$z = \frac{U_{smaller} - (n_A n_B / 2)}{\sqrt{(n_A)(n_B)(n_A + n_B + 1)/12}}$$

15.4 Review Exercise

An instructive way to practice the Mann-Whitney U-test computation and at the same time compare its decisions regarding the null hypothesis to those made by the independent groups t-test, might be to use the problems in Section 8.8. Although the problems in Section 8.8 do not require this treatment because of violation of t-test assumptions, you should convert the data into ranks and analyze using the Mann-Whitney U-test. The answers given in Appendix III refer to their opposite numbered problems in Section 8.8.

15.5 The Wilcoxon Matched-Pairs Signed-Ranks Test

The Wilcoxon matched-pairs signed-ranks test may be viewed as an alternative to the repeated measures/correlated samples t-test and can be used when interval/ratio data obtained in an experiment do not meet the assumptions required by the t-test. The Wilcoxon test does not assume homogeneity of variances or normality of distributions. This procedure consists of obtaining the difference between each pair of scores: these differences may be either positive or negative. The difference scores are then ranked according to their absolute value, with signs ignored, and the rule that rank of 1 is assigned to the smallest difference. Then the sign of each difference is attached to the rank of that difference. The sum of the positive ranks is symbolized by T^+, and the sum of the negative ranks is symbolized by T^-. The statistic of interest is T, which is the smaller of T^+ and T^-. The statistic T is tested for significance by reference to Table G and is termed significant if it is equal to or smaller than the critical value obtained from Table G. The Wilcoxon matched-pairs signed-ranks procedure tests the null hypothesis that the populations represented by the two groups of scores are identical. A significant result may be interpreted to mean that the groups of scores differed significantly at the confidence level used.

Suppose that eight people were subjects in a test of two motion-sickness drugs. Each person was tested in a mechanical chair that rocked, spun, and dipped; the number of minutes each subject could tolerate this treatment until becoming nauseated was recorded. The dependent variable measure was obtained for each person on two occasions, that is, after having taken Brand A and Brand B motion-sickness drugs.

Independent variable: Brand A compared to Brand B motion-sickness drugs.

Dependent variable: Number of minutes before becoming nauseated in the test condition.

Null hypothesis: Brand A does not differ from Brand B in effect on motion-sickness ($\mu_A = \mu_B$).

S#	Brand A	Brand B	Difference	Rank	Signed-rank
1	12	5	+7	5	+5
2	11	16	−5	2.5	−2.5
3	15	20	−5	2.5	−2.5
4	14	8	+6	4	+4
5	11	11	0	*	*
6	17	39	−22	7	−7
7	16	32	−16	6	−6
8	10	14	−4	1	−1

Note: Difference scores that equal zero pose a special problem. If there is an even number of zeros, then half are arbitrarily assigned negative signs; if there is an odd number, then one is randomly discarded and half of the remaining ones, if any, are assigned negative signs.

$$T^+ = 5 + 4$$
$$= 9$$

$$T^- = 2.5 + 2.5 + 7 + 6 + 1$$
$$= 19$$

Therefore $T = 9$ [T is the smaller of T^+ and T^-]

1. $N = 7$ [Notice that this critical value is obtained at $N = 7$ since one Difference score was discarded.]
2. The critical value for T at 0.05 confidence level $= 2$.
3. Therefore the result is not significant.
4. Interpretation: Brand A does not differ from Brand B in effect on motion sickness.

Table G provides critical values of T for N's up to 20. If N exceeds 20, a z-score may be derived and tested for significance by reference to the normal distribution; critical values are 1.96 and 2.58 for 0.05 and 0.01 confidence levels respectively. The z-score is derived as follows

$$z = \frac{T - (N)(N + 1)/4}{\sqrt{(N)(N + 1)(2N + 1)/24}}$$

15.6 Review Exercise

It is recommended that computational practice with the Wilcoxon matched-pairs signed-ranks test be obtained by reanalysis of the problems in Section 8.10. This will enable a comparison of the decisions reached by this procedure with those of the repeated measures/correlated samples t-test. Although the problems in Section 8.10 do not require conversion to ordinal data because of violation of t-test assumptions, you should make the conversion and analyze using the Wilcoxon test. The answers given in Appendix III refer to their opposite numbered problems in Section 8.10.

Part VI

Overview

16 How to Get There From Here

Chapter Preview

16.1   How Do I Analyze This?

Now that you have completed a course in statistics, you are likely to be viewed as an expert by those of your friends who have not had this beneficial and memorable experience. It may even happen that one of them is involved in a class project and, having collected the data, appeals to you for advice on what statistics should be done. (Don't be surprised if they say, "I can't do math.") Because I am a statistics instructor, I am regularly approached by students who are in this predicament. Let us imagine that we are the "expert" in this situation and consider how we might determine the correct analysis for the data in question.

The various statistical procedures we have studied provide different kinds of information, are appropriate to specific situations, and are applicable to particular types of data. There are three questions that immediately come to mind. "What, specifically, do you want to find out?" "What or whom have you observed, and under what circumstances?" and, "What kind of measures or observations have you taken?" Actually, these questions are a sequence that progressively narrows and clarifies the experimenter's particular situation. If we set up a chart with headings corresponding to these questions, that is, information sought, experimental context, and type of data, and itemized the various possibilities under each heading, a left to right reading of this chart would direct us to the proper analysis. Such a chart, which is presented as Table 16.1–1 and limited to the statistical procedures contained in this text, makes up the latter part of this section.

Table 16.1–1 does not, of course, have to be read from left to right. One may begin with any clue, such as the type of data gathered, and narrow the range of possibilities accordingly. It should be possible, however, to determine the correct analysis for any set of data analyzable by a procedure contained in this book. A more encompassing directory for the appropriate analysis for given data and/or circumstances may be found in Andrews et al. (1981). In a way, the summary chart presented in Table 16.1–1 is regrettable because it tends to imply a degree of separation and categorization of the various statistical techniques that is not altogether valid. Compartmentalization is a convenient and sometimes efficient way of thinking but is inevitably an over-simplification and can become a misleading habit. Readers of this book will not, of course, succumb to such a simple temptation.

16.2 The Joy of Planning Ahead

The previous section provided a guide to help solve the problem of not knowing how to analyze data after having collected it. The joy of planning ahead is to never be in that predicament. Whenever you set out to do research or gather data on any question, you should decide on the statistical treatment to be applied to the data before a single observation is taken. In fact, you

Table 16.1-1 Guide to analysis procedures*

Information sought	Experimental context	Data	Analysis (text section)
Estimate value of unknown population mean based on data from a sample.	Scores obtained from random sample.	Interval/ratio	Confidence interval for population mean (8.3).
Determine whether a sample mean differs significantly from a known population mean.	Scores obtained from random sample.	Interval/ratio	Test for difference between $\bar{X}$ and μ (8.5)
Determine whether an independent variable condition affects, or is related to, some dependent variable measure.	Scores obtained from two independently selected subject groups.	Interval/ratio Ordinal	Independent groups t-test (8.7). Mann-Whitney U-test (15.3).
	Scores obtained from a single group observed on two occasions, or from two groups equated by some matching procedure.	Interval/ratio Ordinal	Repeated measures/correlated samples t-test (8.9). Wilcoxon matched-pairs signed-ranks test (15.5).
Determine whether two variances differ significantly.	Variances obtained from two independent samples.	Interval/ratio	Homogeneity of variance test (9.3).
Determine whether an independent variable condition affects, or is related to, some dependent variable measure.	Scores obtained from three or more independently selected subject groups.	Interval/ratio	Single factor independent groups ANOVA (9.4).
	Scores obtained from a single group observed repeatedly, or from three or more groups equated by some matching procedure.	Interval/ratio	Single factor repeated measures ANOVA (9.6).
Determine whether two independent variable conditions, singly or in combination, affect or relate to a dependent variable measure.	Each combination of independent variable conditions is applied to a separate group of subjects.	Interval/ratio	Two factor independent groups ANOVA (11.2).
Determine whether a significant relationship exists between two variables.	Measures of two variables taken on a single group of subjects.	Interval/ratio Ordinal Nominal	Product-moment correlation (12.4). Kendall's tau (15.1). Chi-square test of independence (14.5).
Prediction of one variable from knowledge of another.	A single group of subjects is measured on the predictor, and to-be-predicted, variables.	Interval/ratio	Linear regression (13.2).
Prediction of one variable from knowledge of two others.	A single group of subjects is measured on two predictors and the to-be-predicted variables.	Interval/ratio	Multiple linear regression (13.8).
Determine whether observed data differs significantly from results expected on the basis of some assumption.	Some number of subjects or events is classified into mutually exclusive and exhaustive categories.	Nominal	Chi-square goodness-of-fit test (14.3).
Determine probability of r favorable events in n total trials as a test of the hypothesis underlying the probability of the favorable event (p).	All outcomes are classified as favorable or unfavorable.	Nominal	Binomial test (14.7).

*The association of types of measurement with particular statistical analyses is simplified here. The reader is referred to the discussion of nonparametric statistical tests in Section 14.1. (An abbreviated version of this table appears on the inside back cover of this text.)

should organize and set up your experiment in such a way as to tailor the data to fit a predetermined analysis. Sounds ridiculous, you say, putting the cart before the horse, infringing on your personal freedom to be creative in research. Nothing of the sort, creativity in research is finding out things that were not known before. Collecting data that cannot be analyzed is a complete waste.

When you begin a research project, you will have in mind a broad conception of your objective. You might want to know if this condition affects that behavior, or if this group differs on some variable from that group, or if this variable and that one show any significant degree of relationship. The important part of research planning consists of arranging the circumstances under which you gather the data. How can you judge the effect of this condition on that behavior if there is no control group for comparison? How can you interpret the difference between a control group and an experimental group if the independent variable is confounded by procedural differences? How can the relationship between two variables be determined if the measures are not taken on the same group of subjects? There are usually only a few ways to do something correctly but an infinity of ways of doing it incorrectly; thus, if you plunge on blindly, the odds favor disaster much more than success. After some experience has been gained, experimenters naturally avoid the most obvious mistakes, but the beginning experimenter cannot be blamed for his or her lack of research design skills. It may seem to be backward, but it is good advice to the novice to proceed from the analysis format to the experiment design. Given a general conception of the research objective, an examination of statistical analysis procedures will indicate the circumstances in which they may be used, and then these circumstances can be the structural guide for the to-be-performed research.

The ability to perform a suitable and interpretable statistical analysis depends on a careful gathering of data. You must consider such things as the operational definitions of your variables, the representativeness of your subject sample(s), and the clarity and controllability of instructions to subjects. A simple mistake like failing to balance treatment exposure order in a repeated measures design results in uninterpretable data. Almost any set of numbers can be plugged into some statistical analysis, but what sense can the outcome make if underlying assumptions and proper experimental practice are violated left and right? A good researcher is one who finds ways to isolate and clarify the question being asked so that there is a clear route to gathering and analyzing the evidence. These skills are learned by experience, and it is expected that the novice researcher will make mistakes and indeed, this is perhaps the best form of instruction. However, the skills you have acquired in working through this book represent a pool of useful knowledge; if you think in terms of applying this knowledge to the whole process of research, rather than just as the last bit of procedure, you will be well rewarded.

It is an inescapable reality, and a somewhat demoralizing admission for a statistics instructor, that skills learned in statistics courses tend to be quickly forgotten, unless they are kept fresh by regular practice. In your subsequent courses you will be called upon to collect and analyze research data and you may well feel that the knowledge has all been lost. This is not so, and you will be able to relearn surprisingly quickly. Keep this book and the other statistics texts you will use in more advanced courses; they are familiar friends that, within the limits of their content, will guide you to your analysis objectives. Seek advice by all means, but don't lose the confidence of mastery that you now enjoy. Good luck!

Apropos of the comments in this last section, a statistics professor of mine once told a story of a student who had collected data, was uncertain as to the correct analysis, and came seeking advice. My professor listened to a description of the research, recognized it as a factorial ANOVA design, and showed the student the model for the analysis in Winer's *Statistical Principles in Experimental Design* (1962). Some weeks later the student returned bearing a small mountain of paperwork; starting with the analysis that had been pointed out to him, he had performed *every* subsequent analysis contained in that book, utterly mindless of the appropriateness or lack thereof! Surely there is nothing blissful about such ignorance.

An aside: Let not this be you!

Appendix I:
Tables

349

Table A: Areas under the normal curve

z	Area between μ and z	Area beyond z	z	Area between μ and z	Area beyond z	z	Area between μ and z	Area beyond z
0.00	.0000	.5000	0.40	.1554	.3446	0.80	.2881	.2119
0.01	.0040	.4960	0.41	.1591	.3409	0.81	.2910	.2090
0.02	.0080	.4920	0.42	.1628	.3372	0.82	.2939	.2061
0.03	.0120	.4880	0.43	.1664	.3336	0.83	.2967	.2033
0.04	.0160	.4840	0.44	.1700	.3300	0.84	.2995	.2005
0.05	.0199	.4801	0.45	.1736	.3264	0.85	.3023	.1977
0.06	.0239	.4761	0.46	.1772	.3228	0.86	.3051	.1949
0.07	.0279	.4721	0.47	.1808	.3192	0.87	.3078	.1922
0.08	.0319	.4681	0.48	.1844	.3156	0.88	.3106	.1894
0.09	.0359	.4641	0.49	.1879	.3121	0.89	.3133	.1867
0.10	.0398	.4602	0.50	.1915	.3085	0.90	.3159	.1841
0.11	.0438	.4562	0.51	.1950	.3050	0.91	.3186	.1814
0.12	.0478	.4522	0.52	.1985	.3015	0.92	.3212	.1788
0.13	.0517	.4483	0.53	.2019	.2981	0.93	.3238	.1762
0.14	.0557	.4443	0.54	.2054	.2946	0.94	.3264	.1736
0.15	.0596	.4404	0.55	.2088	.2912	0.95	.3289	.1711
0.16	.0636	.4364	0.56	.2123	.2877	0.96	.3315	.1685
0.17	.0675	.4325	0.57	.2157	.2843	0.97	.3340	.1660
0.18	.0714	.4286	0.58	.2190	.2810	0.98	.3365	.1635
0.19	.0753	.4247	0.59	.2224	.2776	0.99	.3389	.1611
0.20	.0793	.4207	0.60	.2257	.2743	1.00	.3413	.1587
0.21	.0832	.4168	0.61	.2291	.2709	1.01	.3438	.1562
0.22	.0871	.4129	0.62	.2324	.2676	1.02	.3461	.1539
0.23	.0910	.4090	0.63	.2357	.2643	1.03	.3485	.1515
0.24	.0948	.4052	0.64	.2389	.2611	1.04	.3508	.1492
0.25	.0987	.4013	0.65	.2422	.2578	1.05	.3531	.1469
0.26	.1026	.3974	0.66	.2454	.2546	1.06	.3554	.1446
0.27	.1064	.3936	0.67	.2486	.2514	1.07	.3577	.1423
0.28	.1103	.3897	0.68	.2517	.2483	1.08	.3599	.1401
0.29	.1141	.3859	0.69	.2549	.2451	1.09	.3621	.1379
0.30	.1179	.3821	0.70	.2580	.2420	1.10	.3643	.1357
0.31	.1217	.3783	0.71	.2611	.2389	1.11	.3665	.1335
0.32	.1255	.3745	0.72	.2642	.2358	1.12	.3686	.1314
0.33	.1293	.3707	0.73	.2673	.2327	1.13	.3708	.1292
0.34	.1331	.3669	0.74	.2704	.2296	1.14	.3729	.1271
0.35	.1368	.3632	0.75	.2734	.2266	1.15	.3749	.1252
0.36	.1406	.3594	0.76	.2764	.2236	1.16	.3770	.1230
0.37	.1443	.3557	0.77	.2794	.2206	1.17	.3790	.1210
0.38	.1480	.3520	0.78	.2823	.2177	1.18	.3810	.1190
0.39	.1517	.3483	0.79	.2852	.2148	1.19	.3830	.1170

Table A continued

z	Area between μ and z	Area beyond z	z	Area between μ and z	Area beyond z	z	Area between μ and z	Area beyond z
1.20	.3849	.1151	1.60	.4452	.0548	2.00	.4772	.0228
1.21	.3869	.1131	1.61	.4463	.0537	2.01	.4778	.0222
1.22	.3888	.1112	1.62	.4474	.0526	2.02	.4783	.0217
1.23	.3907	.1093	1.63	.4484	.0516	2.03	.4788	.0212
1.24	.3925	.1075	1.64	.4495	.0505	2.04	.4793	.0207
1.25	.3944	.1056	1.65	.4505	.0495	2.05	.4798	.0202
1.26	.3962	.1038	1.66	.4515	.0485	2.06	.4803	.0197
1.27	.3980	.1020	1.67	.4525	.0475	2.07	.4808	.0192
1.28	.3997	.1003	1.68	.4535	.0465	2.08	.4812	.0188
1.29	.4015	.0985	1.69	.4545	.0455	2.09	.4817	.0183
1.30	.4032	.0968	1.70	.4554	.0446	2.10	.4821	.0179
1.31	.4049	.0951	1.71	.4564	.0436	2.11	.4826	.0174
1.32	.4066	.0934	1.72	.4573	.0427	2.12	.4830	.0170
1.33	.4082	.0918	1.73	.4582	.0418	2.13	.4834	.0166
1.34	.4099	.0901	1.74	.4591	.0409	2.14	.4838	.0162
1.35	.4115	.0885	1.75	.4599	.0401	2.15	.4842	.0158
1.36	.4131	.0869	1.76	.4608	.0392	2.16	.4846	.0154
1.37	.4147	.0853	1.77	.4616	.0384	2.17	.4850	.0150
1.38	.4162	.0838	1.78	.4625	.0375	2.18	.4854	.0146
1.39	.4177	.0823	1.79	.4633	.0367	2.19	.4857	.0143
1.40	.4192	.0808	1.80	.4641	.0359	2.20	.4861	.0139
1.41	.4207	.0793	1.81	.4649	.0351	2.21	.4864	.0136
1.42	.4222	.0778	1.82	.4656	.0344	2.22	.4868	.0132
1.43	.4236	.0764	1.83	.4664	.0336	2.23	.4871	.0129
1.44	.4251	.0749	1.84	.4671	.0329	2.24	.4875	.0125
1.45	.4265	.0735	1.85	.4678	.0322	2.25	.4878	.0122
1.46	.4279	.0721	1.86	.4686	.0314	2.26	.4881	.0119
1.47	.4292	.0708	1.87	.4693	.0307	2.27	.4884	.0116
1.48	.4306	.0694	1.88	.4699	.0301	2.28	.4887	.0113
1.49	.4319	.0681	1.89	.4706	.0294	2.29	.4890	.0110
1.50	.4332	.0668	1.90	.4713	.0287	2.30	.4893	.0107
1.51	.4345	.0655	1.91	.4719	.0281	2.31	.4896	.0104
1.52	.4357	.0643	1.92	.4726	.0274	2.32	.4898	.0102
1.53	.4370	.0630	1.93	.4732	.0268	2.33	.4901	.0099
1.54	.4382	.0618	1.94	.4738	.0262	2.34	.4904	.0096
1.55	.4394	.0606	1.95	.4744	.0256	2.35	.4906	.0094
1.56	.4406	.0594	1.96	.4750	.0250	2.36	.4909	.0091
1.57	.4418	.0582	1.97	.4756	.0244	2.37	.4911	.0089
1.58	.4429	.0571	1.98	.4761	.0239	2.38	.4913	.0087
1.59	.4441	.0559	1.99	.4767	.0233	2.39	.4916	.0084

Table A continued

z	Area between μ and z	Area beyond z	z	Area between μ and z	Area beyond z	z	Area between μ and z	Area beyond z
2.40	.4918	.0082	2.70	.4965	.0035	3.00	.4987	.0013
2.41	.4920	.0080	2.71	.4966	.0034			
2.42	.4922	.0078	2.72	.4967	.0033	3.05	.4989	.0011
2.43	.4925	.0075	2.73	.4968	.0032			
2.44	.4927	.0073	2.74	.4969	.0031	3.10	.4990	.0010
2.45	.4929	.0071	2.75	.4970	.0030			
2.46	.4931	.0069	2.76	.4971	.0029	3.15	.4992	.0008
2.47	.4932	.0068	2.77	.4972	.0028			
2.48	.4934	.0066	2.78	.4973	.0027	3.20	.4993	.0007
2.49	.4936	.0064	2.79	.4974	.0026			
2.50	.4938	.0062	2.80	.4974	.0026	3.25	.4994	.0006
2.51	.4940	.0060	2.81	.4975	.0025			
2.52	.4941	.0059	2.82	.4976	.0024	3.30	.4995	.0005
2.53	.4943	.0057	2.83	.4977	.0023			
2.54	.4945	.0055	2.84	.4977	.0023	3.35	.4996	.0004
2.55	.4946	.0054	2.85	.4978	.0022			
2.56	.4948	.0052	2.86	.4979	.0021	3.40	.4997	.0003
2.57	.4949	.0051	2.87	.4979	.0021			
2.58	.4951	.0049	2.88	.4980	.0020	3.50	.4998	.0002
2.59	.4952	.0048	2.89	.4981	.0019			
2.60	.4953	.0047	2.90	.4981	.0019	4.00	.49997	.00003
2.61	.4955	.0045	2.91	.4982	.0018			
2.62	.4956	.0044	2.92	.4982	.0018			
2.63	.4957	.0043	2.93	.4983	.0017			
2.64	.4959	.0041	2.94	.4984	.0016			
2.65	.4960	.0040	2.95	.4984	.0016			
2.66	.4961	.0039	2.96	.4985	.0015			
2.67	.4962	.0038	2.97	.4985	.0015			
2.68	.4963	.0037	2.98	.4986	.0014			
2.69	.4964	.0036	2.99	.4986	.0014			

Table A is taken from Table IIi of Fisher and Yates: *Statistical Tables for Biological, Agricultural and Medical Research*, published by Longman Group Ltd. London (previously published by Oliver and Boyd Ltd. Edinburgh) and by permission of the authors and publishers.

Table B: Critical values for *t*

df	Confidence level for one-tailed test			
	.05	.025	.01	.005
	Confidence level for two-tailed test			
	.10	.05	.02	.01
1	6.314	12.706	31.821	63.657
2	2.920	4.303	6.965	9.925
3	2.353	3.182	4.541	5.841
4	2.132	2.776	3.747	4.604
5	2.015	2.571	3.365	4.032
6	1.943	2.447	3.143	3.707
7	1.895	2.365	2.998	3.499
8	1.860	2.306	2.896	3.355
9	1.833	2.262	2.821	3.250
10	1.812	2.228	2.764	3.169
11	1.796	2.201	2.718	3.106
12	1.782	2.179	2.681	3.055
13	1.771	2.160	2.650	3.012
14	1.761	2.145	2.624	2.977
15	1.753	2.131	2.602	2.947
16	1.746	2.120	2.583	2.921
17	1.740	2.110	2.567	2.898
18	1.734	2.101	2.552	2.878
19	1.729	2.093	2.539	2.861
20	1.725	2.086	2.528	2.845
21	1.721	2.080	2.518	2.831
22	1.717	2.074	2.508	2.819
23	1.714	2.069	2.500	2.807
24	1.711	2.064	2.492	2.797
25	1.708	2.060	2.485	2.787
26	1.706	2.056	2.479	2.779
27	1.703	2.052	2.473	2.771
28	1.701	2.048	2.467	2.763
29	1.699	2.045	2.462	2.756
30	1.697	2.042	2.457	2.750
35	1.687	2.030	2.438	2.724
40	1.684	2.021	2.423	2.704
45	1.679	2.014	2.412	2.690
50	1.676	2.009	2.403	2.678
60	1.671	2.000	2.390	2.660
90	1.662	1.987	2.369	2.632
120	1.658	1.980	2.358	2.617
∞	1.645	1.960	2.326	2.576

Table B is taken from Table III: Distribution of *t*, of Fisher and Yates: *Statistical Tables for Biological, Agricultural and Medical Research,* published by Longman Group Ltd. London (previously published by Oliver & Boyd Ltd. Edinburgh) and by permission of the authors and publishers.

Table C: Critical values for $U_{smaller}$

Two-tailed test at .05 confidence level

smaller n

larger n	3	4	5	6	7	8	9	10	11	12	13	14	15	16	17	18	19	20
3	–																	
4	–	0																
5	0	1	2															
6	1	2	3	5														
7	1	3	5	6	8													
8	2	4	6	8	10	13												
9	2	4	7	10	12	15	17											
10	3	5	8	11	14	17	20	23										
11	3	6	9	13	16	19	23	26	30									
12	4	7	11	14	18	22	26	29	33	37								
13	4	8	12	16	20	24	28	33	37	41	45							
14	5	9	13	17	22	26	31	36	40	45	50	55						
15	5	10	14	19	24	29	34	39	44	49	54	59	64					
16	6	11	15	21	26	31	37	42	47	53	59	64	70	75				
17	6	11	17	22	28	34	39	45	51	57	63	69	75	81	87			
18	7	12	18	24	30	36	42	48	55	61	67	74	80	86	93	99		
19	7	13	19	25	32	38	45	52	58	65	72	78	85	92	99	106	113	
20	8	14	20	27	34	41	48	55	62	69	76	83	90	98	105	112	119	127

Two-tailed test at .01 confidence level

smaller n

larger n	3	4	5	6	7	8	9	10	11	12	13	14	15	16	17	18	19	20
3	–																	
4	–	–																
5	–	–	0															
6	–	0	1	2														
7	–	0	1	3	4													
8	–	1	2	4	6	7												
9	0	1	3	5	7	9	11											
10	0	2	4	6	9	11	13	16										
11	0	2	5	7	10	13	16	18	21									
12	1	3	6	9	12	15	18	21	24	27								
13	1	3	7	10	13	17	20	24	27	31	34							
14	1	4	7	11	15	18	22	26	30	34	38	42						
15	2	5	8	12	16	20	24	29	33	37	42	46	51					
16	2	5	9	13	18	22	27	31	36	41	45	50	55	60				
17	2	6	10	15	19	24	29	34	39	44	49	54	60	65	70			
18	2	6	11	16	21	26	31	37	42	47	53	58	64	70	75	81		
19	3	7	12	17	22	28	33	39	45	51	57	63	69	74	81	87	93	
20	3	8	13	18	24	30	36	42	48	54	60	67	73	79	86	92	99	105

This table is adapted from L. C. Freeman, *Elementary Applied Statistics,* John Wiley and Sons, 1965, by permission of the publisher.

Table D: Critical Values for *F*

| | | α | \multicolumn{9}{c}{Degrees of freedom for numerator variance (mean square)} |
			1	2	3	4	5	6	7	8	9
	2	.05	18.51	19.00	19.16	19.25	19.30	19.33	19.36	19.37	19.38
		.01	98.49	99.01	99.17	99.25	99.30	99.33	99.34	99.36	99.38
	3	.05	10.13	9.55	9.28	9.12	9.01	8.94	8.88	8.84	8.81
		.01	34.12	30.81	29.46	28.71	28.24	27.91	27.67	27.49	27.34
	4	.05	7.71	6.94	6.59	6.39	6.26	6.16	6.09	6.04	6.00
		.01	21.20	18.00	16.69	15.98	15.52	15.21	14.98	14.80	14.66
	5	.05	6.61	5.79	5.41	5.19	5.05	4.95	4.88	4.82	4.78
		.01	16.26	13.27	12.06	11.39	10.97	10.67	10.45	10.27	10.15
	6	.05	5.99	5.14	4.76	4.53	4.39	4.28	4.21	4.15	4.10
		.01	13.74	10.92	9.78	9.15	8.75	8.47	8.26	8.10	7.98
	7	.05	5.59	4.74	4.35	4.12	3.97	3.87	3.79	3.73	3.68
		.01	12.25	9.55	8.45	7.85	7.46	7.19	7.00	6.84	6.71
	8	.05	5.32	4.46	4.07	3.84	3.69	3.58	3.50	3.44	3.39
		.01	11.26	8.65	7.59	7.01	6.63	6.37	6.19	6.03	5.91
	9	.05	5.12	4.26	3.86	3.63	3.48	3.37	3.29	3.23	3.18
		.01	10.56	8.02	6.99	6.42	6.06	5.80	5.62	5.47	5.35
	10	.05	4.96	4.10	3.71	3.48	3.33	3.22	3.14	3.07	3.02
		.01	10.04	7.56	6.55	5.99	5.64	5.39	5.21	5.06	4.95
	11	.05	4.84	3.98	3.59	3.36	3.20	3.09	3.01	2.95	2.90
		.01	9.65	7.20	6.22	5.67	5.32	5.07	4.88	4.74	4.63
	12	.05	4.75	3.88	3.49	3.26	3.11	3.00	2.92	2.85	2.80
		.01	9.33	6.93	5.95	5.41	5.06	4.82	4.65	4.50	4.39
	13	.05	4.67	3.80	3.41	3.18	3.02	2.92	2.84	2.77	2.72
		.01	9.07	6.70	5.74	5.20	4.86	4.62	4.44	4.30	4.19
	14	.05	4.60	3.74	3.34	3.11	2.96	2.85	2.77	2.70	2.65
		.01	8.86	6.51	5.56	5.03	4.69	4.46	4.28	4.14	4.03
	15	.05	4.54	3.68	3.29	3.06	2.90	2.79	2.70	2.64	2.59
		.01	8.68	6.36	5.42	4.89	4.56	4.32	4.14	4.00	3.89
	16	.05	4.49	3.63	3.24	3.01	2.85	2.74	2.66	2.59	2.54
		.01	8.53	6.23	5.29	4.77	4.44	4.20	4.03	3.89	3.78
	17	.05	4.45	3.59	3.20	2.96	2.81	2.70	2.62	2.55	2.50
		.01	8.40	6.11	5.18	4.67	4.34	4.10	3.93	3.79	3.68
	18	.05	4.41	3.55	3.16	2.93	2.77	2.66	2.58	2.51	2.46
		.01	8.28	6.01	5.09	4.58	4.25	4.01	3.85	3.71	3.60
	19	.05	4.38	3.52	3.13	2.90	2.74	2.63	2.55	2.48	2.43
		.01	8.18	5.93	5.01	4.50	4.17	3.94	3.77	3.63	3.62

Degrees of freedom for denominator variance (mean square)

Table D continued

| | | α | \multicolumn{9}{c}{Degrees of freedom for numerator variance (mean square)} |
			1	2	3	4	5	6	7	8	9
	20	.05	4.35	3.49	3.10	2.87	2.71	2.60	2.52	2.45	2.40
		.01	8.10	5.85	4.94	4.43	4.10	3.87	3.71	3.56	3.45
	21	.05	4.32	3.47	3.07	2.84	2.68	2.57	2.49	2.42	2.37
		.01	8.02	5.78	4.87	4.37	4.04	3.81	3.65	3.51	3.40
	22	.05	4.30	3.44	3.05	2.82	2.66	2.55	2.47	2.40	2.35
		.01	7.94	5.72	4.82	4.31	3.99	3.76	3.59	3.45	3.35
	23	.05	4.28	3.42	3.03	2.80	2.64	2.53	2.45	2.38	2.32
		.01	7.88	5.66	4.76	4.26	3.94	3.71	3.54	3.41	3.30
	24	.05	4.26	3.40	3.01	2.78	2.62	2.51	2.43	2.36	2.30
		.01	7.82	5.61	4.72	4.22	3.90	3.67	3.50	3.36	3.25
	25	.05	4.24	3.38	2.99	2.76	2.60	2.49	2.41	2.34	2.28
		.01	7.77	5.57	4.68	4.18	3.86	3.63	3.46	3.32	3.21
	26	.05	4.22	3.37	2.89	2.74	2.59	2.47	2.39	2.32	2.27
		.01	7.72	5.53	4.64	4.14	3.82	3.59	3.42	3.29	3.17
	27	.05	4.21	3.35	2.96	2.73	2.57	2.46	2.37	2.30	2.25
		.01	7.68	5.49	4.60	4.11	3.79	3.56	3.39	3.26	3.14
	28	.05	4.20	3.34	2.95	2.71	2.56	2.44	2.36	2.29	2.24
		.01	7.64	5.45	4.57	4.07	3.76	3.53	3.36	3.23	3.11
	29	.05	4.18	3.33	2.93	2.70	2.54	2.43	2.35	2.28	2.22
		.01	7.60	5.52	4.54	4.04	3.73	3.50	3.32	3.20	3.08
	30	.05	4.17	3.32	2.92	2.69	2.53	2.42	2.34	2.27	2.21
		.01	7.56	5.39	4.51	4.02	3.70	3.47	3.30	3.17	3.06
	32	.05	4.15	3.30	2.90	2.67	2.51	2.40	2.32	2.25	2.19
		.01	7.50	5.34	4.46	3.97	3.66	3.42	3.25	3.12	3.01
	36	.05	4.11	3.26	2.86	2.63	2.48	2.36	2.28	2.21	2.15
		.01	7.39	5.25	4.38	3.89	3.58	3.35	3.18	3.04	2.94
	40	.05	4.08	3.23	2.84	2.61	2.45	2.34	2.25	2.18	2.12
		.01	7.31	5.18	4.31	3.83	3.51	3.29	3.12	2.99	2.88
	46	.05	4.05	3.20	2.81	2.57	2.42	2.30	2.22	2.14	2.09
		.01	7.21	5.10	4.24	3.76	3.44	3.22	3.05	2.92	2.82
	60	.05	4.00	3.15	2.76	2.52	2.37	2.25	2.17	2.10	2.04
		.01	7.08	4.98	4.13	3.65	3.34	3.12	2.95	2.82	2.72
	100	.05	3.94	3.09	2.70	2.46	2.30	2.19	2.10	2.03	1.97
		.01	6.90	4.82	3.98	3.51	3.20	2.99	2.82	2.69	2.59
	∞	.05	3.84	2.99	2.60	2.37	2.21	2.09	2.01	1.94	1.88
		.01	6.64	4.60	3.78	3.32	3.02	2.80	2.64	2.51	2.41

Degrees of freedom for denominator variance (mean square) is the vertical axis label.

Table E: Critical values for χ^2

df	Confidence level		
	.05	.01	.001
1	3.841	6.635	10.827
2	5.991	9.210	13.815
3	7.815	11.345	16.266
4	9.488	13.277	18.467
5	11.070	15.086	20.515
6	12.592	16.812	22.457
7	14.067	18.475	24.322
8	15.507	20.090	26.125
9	16.919	21.666	27.877
10	18.307	23.209	29.588
11	19.675	24.725	31.264
12	21.026	26.217	32.909
13	22.362	27.688	34.528
14	23.685	29.141	36.123
15	24.996	30.578	37.696
16	26.292	32.000	39.252
17	27.587	33.409	40.790
18	28.869	34.805	42.312
19	30.144	36.191	43.820
20	31.410	37.566	45.315
21	32.671	38.932	46.797
22	33.924	40.289	48.268
23	35.172	41.638	49.728
24	36.415	42.980	51.179
25	37.652	44.314	52.620
26	38.885	45.642	54.052
27	40.113	46.963	55.476
28	41.337	48.278	56.893
29	42.557	49.588	58.302
30	43.773	50.892	59.703
40	55.759	63.691	73.402
50	67.505	76.154	86.661
60	79.082	88.379	99.607

Table E is taken from Table IV: Distribution of χ^2, of Fisher & Yates: *Statistical Tables for Biological, Agricultural and Medical Research*, published by Longman Group Ltd. London (previously published by Oliver & Boyd Ltd. Edinburgh) and by permission of the authors and publishers.

Table F: Critical values for τ (tau)

N	Confidence level for one-tailed test			
	.05	.025	.01	.005
	Confidence level for two-tailed test			
	.10	.05	.02	.01
4	1.000			
5	.800	1.000		
6	.733	.867	1.000	
7	.619	.714	.810	.905
8	.571	.643	.714	.786
9	.500	.556	.667	.722
10	.422	.511	.600	.644
11	.418	.491	.564	.636
12	.364	.455	.515	.576
13	.359	.436	.513	.564
14	.341	.407	.473	.538
15	.333	.390	.467	.505
16	.317	.367	.433	.483
17	.294	.353	.426	.471
18	.294	.346	.412	.451
19	.275	.333	.392	.439
20	.274	.326	.379	.421
25	.240	.280	.333	.373
30	.214	.255	.301	.333
35	.197	.234	.277	.308
40	.182	.218	.256	.285

This table was compiled by the author; a correction for continuity is included when $N < 10$. Note that when $N(N-1)/2$ is an even number, then only even $A - I$ terms are possible; similarly, when $N(N-1)/2$ is an odd number, then only odd $A - I$ terms are possible. The entries in this table represent the ratio of the minimum $A - I$ term that is possible and has the confidence level or lower probability of occurrence over $N(N-1)/2$.

Table G: Critical values for T

	Confidence level for one-tailed test			
	.05	.025	.01	.005
	Confidence level for two-tailed test			
N	.10	.05	.02	.01
5	0			
6	2	0		
7	3	2	0	
8	5	3	1	0
9	8	5	3	1
10	10	8	5	3
11	13	10	7	5
12	17	13	9	7
13	21	17	12	9
14	25	21	15	12
15	30	25	19	15
16	35	29	23	19
17	41	34	27	23
18	47	40	32	27
19	53	46	37	32
20	60	52	43	37

From Wilcoxon, F., and Wilcox, R. A., *Some Rapid Approximate Statistical Procedures,* Lederle Laboratories, 1964, as adapted in Runyon, R. P., and Haber, A., *Fundamentals of Behavioral Statistics,* © 1980. Addison-Wesley, Reading, MA. p. 395. Reprinted with permission of the American Cyanamid Company and Addison-Wesley Publishing Company.

Table H: Critical values for *r*

df	Confidence level for one-tailed test			
	.05	.025	.01	.005
	Confidence level for two-tailed test			
	.10	.05	.02	.01
2	.900	.950	.980	.990
3	.805	.878	.934	.959
4	.729	.811	.882	.917
5	.669	.754	.833	.874
6	.622	.707	.789	.834
7	.582	.666	.750	.798
8	.549	.632	.716	.765
9	.521	.602	.685	.735
10	.497	.576	.658	.708
11	.476	.553	.634	.684
12	.458	.532	.612	.661
13	.441	.514	.592	.641
14	.426	.497	.574	.623
15	.412	.482	.558	.606
16	.400	.468	.542	.590
17	.389	.456	.528	.575
18	.378	.444	.516	.561
19	.369	.433	.503	.549
20	.360	.423	.492	.537
21	.352	.413	.482	.526
22	.344	.404	.472	.515
23	.337	.396	.462	.505
24	.330	.388	.453	.496
25	.323	.381	.445	.487
26	.317	.374	.437	.479
27	.311	.367	.430	.471
28	.306	.361	.423	.463
29	.301	.355	.416	.486
30	.296	.349	.409	.449
35	.275	.325	.381	.418
40	.257	.304	.358	.393
45	.243	.288	.338	.372
50	.231	.273	.322	.354
60	.211	.250	.295	.325
80	.183	.217	.256	.283
100	.164	.195	.230	.254

Table H is taken from Table VII: The Correlation Coefficient, of Fisher & Yates: *Statistical Tables for Biological, Agricultural and Medical Research,* published by Longman Group Ltd. London (previously published by Oliver & Boyd Ltd. Edinburgh) and by permission of the authors and publishers.

Table I: Transformation of r to z_r

r	z_r	r	z_r	r	z_r	r	z_r	r	z_r
.000	.000	.200	.200	.400	.424	.600	.693	.800	1.099
.005	.005	.205	.208	.405	.430	.605	.701	.805	1.113
.010	.010	.210	.213	.410	.436	.610	.709	.810	1.127
.015	.015	.215	.218	.415	.442	.615	.717	.815	1.142
.020	.020	.220	.224	.420	.448	.620	.725	.820	1.157
.025	.025	.225	.229	.425	.454	.625	.733	.825	1.172
.030	.030	.230	.234	.430	.460	.630	.741	.830	1.188
.035	.035	.235	.239	.435	.466	.635	.750	.835	1.204
.040	.040	.240	.245	.440	.472	.640	.758	.840	1.221
.045	.045	.245	.250	.445	.478	.645	.767	.845	1.238
.050	.050	.250	.255	.450	.485	.650	.775	.850	1.256
.055	.055	.255	.261	.455	.491	.655	.784	.855	1.274
.060	.060	.260	.266	.460	.497	.660	.793	.860	1.293
.065	.065	.265	.271	.465	.504	.665	.802	.865	1.313
.070	.070	.270	.277	.470	.510	.670	.811	.870	1.333
.075	.075	.275	.282	.475	.517	.675	.820	.875	1.354
.080	.080	.280	.288	.480	.523	.680	.829	.880	1.376
.085	.085	.285	.293	.485	.530	.685	.838	.885	1.398
.090	.090	.290	.299	.490	.536	.690	.848	.890	1.422
.095	.095	.295	.304	.495	.543	.695	.858	.895	1.447
.100	.100	.300	.310	.500	.549	.700	.867	.900	1.472
.105	.105	.305	.315	.505	.556	.705	.877	.905	1.499
.110	.110	.310	.321	.510	.563	.710	.887	.910	1.528
.115	.116	.315	.326	.515	.570	.715	.897	.915	1.557
.120	.121	.320	.332	.520	.576	.720	.908	.920	1.589
.125	.126	.325	.337	.525	.583	.725	.918	.925	1.623
.130	.131	.330	.343	.530	.590	.730	.929	.930	1.658
.135	.136	.335	.348	.535	.597	.735	.940	.935	1.697
.140	.141	.340	.354	.540	.604	.740	.950	.940	1.738
.145	.146	.345	.360	.545	.611	.745	.962	.945	1.783
.150	.151	.350	.365	.550	.618	.750	.973	.950	1.832
.155	.156	.355	.371	.555	.626	.755	.984	.955	1.886
.160	.161	.360	.377	.560	.633	.760	.996	.960	1.946
.165	.167	.365	.383	.565	.640	.765	1.008	.965	2.014
.170	.172	.370	.388	.570	.648	.770	1.020	.970	2.092
.175	.177	.375	.394	.575	.655	.775	1.033	.975	2.185
.180	.182	.380	.400	.580	.662	.780	1.045	.980	2.298
.185	.187	.385	.406	.585	.670	.785	1.058	.985	2.443
.190	.192	.390	.412	.590	.678	.790	1.071	.990	2.647
.195	.198	.395	.418	.595	.685	.795	1.085	.995	2.994

Table J: Values of the studentized range (q)

| Error df | α | \multicolumn{9}{c}{Number of treatment groups} |
		2	3	4	5	6	7	8	9	10
5	.05	3.64	4.60	5.22	5.67	6.03	6.33	6.58	6.80	6.99
	.01	5.70	6.98	7.80	8.42	8.91	9.32	9.67	9.97	10.24
6	.05	3.46	4.34	4.90	5.30	5.63	5.90	6.12	6.32	6.49
	.01	5.24	6.33	7.03	7.56	7.97	8.32	8.61	8.87	9.10
7	.05	3.34	4.16	4.68	5.06	5.36	5.61	5.82	6.00	6.16
	.01	4.95	5.92	6.54	7.01	7.37	7.68	7.94	8.17	8.37
8	.05	3.26	4.04	4.53	4.89	5.17	5.40	5.60	5.77	5.92
	.01	4.75	5.64	6.20	6.62	6.96	7.24	7.47	7.68	7.86
9	.05	3.20	3.95	4.41	4.76	5.02	5.24	5.43	5.59	5.74
	.01	4.60	5.43	5.96	6.35	6.66	6.91	7.13	7.33	7.49
10	.05	3.15	3.88	4.33	4.65	4.91	5.12	5.30	5.46	5.60
	.01	4.48	5.27	5.77	6.14	6.43	6.67	6.87	7.05	7.21
11	.05	3.11	3.82	4.26	4.57	4.82	5.03	5.20	5.35	5.49
	.01	4.39	5.15	5.62	5.97	6.25	6.48	6.67	6.84	6.99
12	.05	3.08	3.77	4.20	4.51	4.75	4.95	5.12	5.27	5.39
	.01	4.32	5.05	5.50	5.84	6.10	6.32	6.51	6.67	6.81
13	.05	3.06	3.73	4.15	4.45	4.69	4.88	5.05	5.19	5.32
	.01	4.26	4.96	5.40	5.73	5.98	6.19	6.37	6.53	6.67
14	.05	3.03	3.70	4.11	4.41	4.64	4.83	4.99	5.13	5.25
	.01	4.21	4.89	5.32	5.63	5.88	6.08	6.26	6.41	6.54
15	.05	3.01	3.67	4.08	4.37	4.59	4.78	4.94	5.08	5.20
	.01	4.17	4.84	5.25	5.56	5.80	5.99	6.16	6.31	6.44
16	.05	3.00	3.65	4.05	4.33	4.56	4.74	4.90	5.03	5.15
	.01	4.13	4.79	5.19	5.49	5.72	5.92	6.08	6.22	6.35
17	.05	2.98	3.63	4.02	4.30	4.52	4.70	4.86	4.99	5.11
	.01	4.10	4.74	5.14	5.43	5.66	5.85	6.01	6.15	6.27
18	.05	2.97	3.61	4.00	4.28	4.49	4.67	4.82	4.96	5.07
	.01	4.07	4.70	5.09	5.38	5.60	5.79	5.94	6.08	6.20
19	.05	2.96	3.59	3.98	4.25	4.47	4.65	4.79	4.92	5.04
	.01	4.05	4.67	5.05	5.33	5.55	5.73	5.89	6.02	6.14
20	.05	2.95	3.58	3.96	4.23	4.45	4.62	4.77	4.90	5.01
	.01	4.02	4.64	5.02	5.29	5.51	5.69	5.84	5.97	6.09
24	.05	2.92	3.53	3.90	4.17	4.37	4.54	4.68	4.81	4.92
	.01	3.96	4.55	4.91	5.17	5.37	5.54	5.69	5.81	5.92
30	.05	2.89	3.49	3.85	4.10	4.30	4.46	4.60	4.72	4.82
	.01	3.89	4.45	4.80	5.05	5.24	5.40	5.54	5.65	5.76
40	.05	2.86	3.44	3.79	4.04	4.23	4.39	4.52	4.63	4.73
	.01	3.82	4.37	4.70	4.93	5.11	5.26	5.39	5.50	5.60
60	.05	2.83	3.40	3.74	3.98	4.16	4.31	4.44	4.55	4.65
	.01	3.76	4.28	4.59	4.82	4.99	5.13	5.25	5.36	5.45
∞	.05	2.77	3.31	3.63	3.86	4.03	4.17	4.29	4.39	4.47
	.01	3.64	4.12	4.40	4.60	4.76	4.88	4.99	5.08	5.16

Table K: 2000 random digits

8077181924	4262225811	1633601019	5947296388	1135791492
6063331250	8150400497	6693359971	2108449000	9945531705
3474659760	3295786101	4312831413	3686635925	5312502294
9031678606	2224356872	4875714606	5726179269	0727198420
4355472676	7308516508	3651146142	0738738059	5818876221
1459977139	4422139295	7571999750	2161785543	1124101476
5902107457	6572679873	4705228837	2381957915	4473338479
5524457108	8080656408	2824364722	7869574932	3870325401
3152129234	8651711004	1727759735	8951346649	5920711891
7238864953	3190536523	6374702207	4313669381	7797985308
0346352670	0572295580	6630203546	9143608686	7763990855
3836888049	0136280897	7867392644	5768421811	9134302191
1337339085	6024184823	3751795818	2501469902	4279127716
0532405901	2292138797	9309762720	7218357945	1802703113
0859393982	6225862538	8590194732	8491006105	4555638373
2510205395	0752885809	5487064694	6106458660	2266376515
2581224144	3250486823	4874050374	3692782186	8845656487
0062053395	5603772438	5041979162	0548493605	5742771189
6991572128	3644521963	3719791395	2198678107	6049110156
5869866210	1574617174	4139281473	4780386283	5289865516
8339931941	3736189050	9411587508	6480773176	2272913616
9124294459	4792198908	9680558855	6567903484	6962876321
7224819898	0050747587	4900485859	1647679374	0294737569
3389635376	0885152108	9931682488	5120875494	9211620777
6531082437	6900638112	7278454999	3619792876	4792588443
3533830800	4970101063	9170813401	4811647963	4572851601
0897856020	2529022141	4454967091	9847382312	5487420508
2122968090	7165122949	2715976035	8948302317	0577627466
9964939782	2937626424	6670263667	0067610587	5194002010
0310108971	8995476902	5974204877	6595123404	3232996164
3150088919	6139550292	4290804006	5354242233	0322090118
4237668043	0575349144	9027634523	4480034839	9954841635
8897691864	8143801052	5185632672	8636854732	1893106855
2990523640	7605255179	4463729610	3030647790	0661695256
3089574460	5874894194	5180870858	0191765563	7403152334
2336731184	4708199595	4422663824	2742433083	5642162801
0282058594	8824731684	9439218201	4438495594	1317695878
2581756298	1320831672	3924718605	5336148443	6328283798
0424092964	9752154243	2779262716	5236778695	8411845417
3971840970	1837251058	4436480360	9356636705	8035340873

This table was compiled by August T. Horvath.

Table L: Squares and Square Roots

N	N^2	$\sqrt{N}$	$\sqrt{10N}$	N	N^2	$\sqrt{N}$	$\sqrt{10N}$
1	1	1.0000	3.1623	51	2601	7.1414	22.5832
2	4	1.4142	4.4721	52	2704	7.2111	22.8035
3	9	1.7321	5.4772	53	2809	7.2801	23.0217
4	16	2.0000	6.3246	54	2916	7.3485	23.2379
5	25	2.2361	7.0711	55	3025	7.4162	23.4521
6	36	2.4495	7.7460	56	3136	7.4833	23.6643
7	49	2.6458	8.3666	57	3249	7.5498	23.8747
8	64	2.8284	8.9443	58	3364	7.6158	24.0832
9	81	3.0000	9.4868	59	3481	7.6811	24.2899
10	100	3.1623	10.0000	60	3600	7.7460	24.4949
11	121	3.3166	10.4881	61	3721	7.8102	24.6982
12	144	3.4641	10.9545	62	3844	7.8740	24.8998
13	169	3.6056	11.4018	63	3969	7.9373	25.0998
14	196	3.7417	11.8322	64	4096	8.0000	25.2982
15	225	3.8730	12.2474	65	4225	8.0623	25.4951
16	256	4.0000	12.6491	66	4356	8.1240	25.6905
17	289	4.1231	13.0384	67	4489	8.1854	25.8844
18	324	4.2426	13.4164	68	4624	8.2462	26.0768
19	361	4.3589	13.7840	69	4761	8.3066	26.2679
20	400	4.4721	14.1421	70	4900	8.3666	26.4575
21	441	4.5826	14.4914	71	5041	8.4261	26.6458
22	484	4.6904	14.8324	72	5184	8.4853	26.8328
23	529	4.7958	15.1658	73	5329	8.5440	27.0185
24	576	4.8990	15.4919	74	5476	8.6023	27.2029
25	625	5.0000	15.8114	75	5625	8.6603	27.3861
26	676	5.0990	16.1245	76	5776	8.7178	27.5681
27	729	5.1962	16.4317	77	5929	8.7750	27.7489
28	784	5.2915	16.7332	78	6084	8.8318	27.9285
29	841	5.3852	17.0294	79	6241	8.8882	28.1069
30	900	5.4772	17.3205	80	6400	8.9443	28.2843
31	961	5.5678	17.6068	81	6561	9.0000	28.4605
32	1024	5.6569	17.8885	82	6724	9.0554	28.6356
33	1089	5.7446	18.1659	83	6889	9.1104	28.8097
34	1156	5.8310	18.4391	84	7056	9.1652	28.9828
35	1225	5.9161	18.7083	85	7225	9.2195	29.1548
36	1296	6.0000	18.9737	86	7396	9.2736	29.3258
37	1369	6.0828	19.2354	87	7569	9.3274	29.4958
38	1444	6.1644	19.4936	88	7744	9.3808	29.6648
39	1521	6.2450	19.7484	89	7921	9.4340	29.8329
40	1600	6.3246	20.0000	90	8100	9.4868	30.0000
41	1681	6.4031	20.2485	91	8281	9.5394	30.1662
42	1764	6.4807	20.4939	92	8464	9.5917	30.3315
43	1849	6.5574	20.7364	93	8649	9.6437	30.4959
44	1936	6.6332	20.9762	94	8836	9.6954	30.6594
45	2025	6.7082	21.2132	95	9025	9.7468	30.8221
46	2116	6.7823	21.4476	96	9216	9.7980	30.9839
47	2209	6.8557	21.6795	97	9409	9.8489	31.1448
48	2304	6.9282	21.9089	98	9604	9.8995	31.3049
49	2401	7.0000	22.1359	99	9801	9.9499	31.4643
50	2500	7.0711	22.3607	100	10000	10.0000	31.6228
N	N^2	$\sqrt{N}$	$\sqrt{10N}$	N	N^2	$\sqrt{N}$	$\sqrt{10N}$

Table L continued

N	N^2	$\sqrt{N}$	$\sqrt{10N}$	N	N^2	$\sqrt{N}$	$\sqrt{10N}$
101	10 201	10.0499	31.7805	151	22 801	12.2882	38.8587
102	10 404	10.0995	31.9374	152	23 104	12.3288	38.9872
103	10 609	10.1489	32.0936	153	23 409	12.3693	39.1152
104	10 816	10.1980	32.2490	154	23 716	12.4097	39.2428
105	11 025	10.2470	32.4037	155	24 025	12.4499	39.3700
106	11 236	10.2956	32.5576	156	24 336	12.4900	39.4968
107	11 449	10.3441	32.7109	157	24 649	12.5300	39.6232
108	11 664	10.3923	32.8634	158	24 964	12.5698	39.7492
109	11 881	10.4403	33.0151	159	25 281	12.6095	39.8748
110	12 100	10.4881	33.1662	160	25 600	12.6491	40.0000
111	12 321	10.5357	33.3167	161	25 921	12.6886	40.1248
112	12 544	10.5830	33.4664	162	26 244	12.7279	40.2492
113	12 769	10.6301	33.6155	163	26 569	12.7671	40.3733
114	12 996	10.6771	33.7639	164	26 896	12.8062	40.4969
115	13 225	10.7238	33.9117	165	27 225	12.8452	40.6202
116	13 456	10.7703	34.0588	166	27 556	12.8841	40.7431
117	13 689	10.8167	34.2053	167	27 889	12.9228	40.8656
118	13 924	10.8628	34.3511	168	28 224	12.9615	40.9878
119	14 161	10.9087	34.4964	169	28 561	13.0000	41.1096
120	14 400	10.9545	34.6410	170	28 900	13.0384	41.2311
121	14 641	11.0000	34.7851	171	29 241	13.0767	41.3521
122	14 884	11.0454	34.9285	172	29 584	13.1149	41.4729
123	15 129	11.0905	35.0714	173	29 929	13.1529	41.5933
124	15 376	11.1355	35.2136	174	30 276	13.1909	41.7133
125	15 625	11.1803	35.3553	175	30 625	13.2288	41.8330
126	15 876	11.2250	35.4965	176	30 976	13.2665	41.9523
127	16 129	11.2694	35.6371	177	31 329	13.3041	42.0714
128	16 384	11.3137	35.7771	178	31 684	13.3417	42.1900
129	16 641	11.3578	35.9166	179	32 041	13.3791	42.3084
130	16 900	11.4018	36.0555	180	32 400	13.4164	42.4264
131	17 161	11.4455	36.1939	181	32 761	13.4536	42.5441
132	17 424	11.4891	36.3318	182	33 124	13.4907	42.6615
133	17 689	11.5326	36.4692	183	33 489	13.5277	42.7785
134	17 956	11.5758	36.6060	184	33 856	13.5647	42.8952
135	18 225	11.6190	36.7423	185	34 225	13.6015	43.0116
136	18 496	11.6619	36.8782	186	34 596	13.6382	43.1277
137	18 769	11.7047	37.0135	187	34 969	13.6748	43.2435
138	19 044	11.7473	37.1484	188	35 344	13.7113	43.3590
139	19 321	11.7898	37.2827	189	35 721	13.7477	43.4741
140	19 600	11.8322	37.4166	190	36 100	13.7840	43.5890
141	19 881	11.8743	37.5500	191	36 481	13.8203	43.7036
142	20 164	11.9164	37.6829	192	36 864	13.8564	43.8178
143	20 449	11.9583	37.8153	193	37 249	13.8924	43.9318
144	20 736	12.0000	37.9473	194	37 636	13.9284	44.0454
145	21 025	12.0416	38.0789	195	38 025	13.9642	44.1588
146	21 316	12.0830	38.2099	196	38 416	14.0000	44.2719
147	21 609	12.1244	38.3406	197	38 809	14.0357	44.3847
148	21 904	12.1655	38.4708	198	39 204	14.0712	44.4972
149	22 201	12.2066	38.6005	199	39 601	14.1067	44.6094
150	22 500	12.2474	38.7298	200	40 000	14.1421	44.7214
N	N^2	$\sqrt{N}$	$\sqrt{10N}$	N	N^2	$\sqrt{N}$	$\sqrt{10N}$

Table L continued

N	N²	√N	√10N	N	N²	√N	√10N
201	40 401	14.1774	44.8330	251	63 001	15.8430	50.0999
202	40 804	14.2127	44.9444	252	63 504	15.8745	50.1996
203	41 209	14.2478	45.0555	253	64 009	15.9060	50.2991
204	41 616	14.2829	45.1664	254	64 516	15.9374	50.3984
205	42 025	14.3178	45.2769	255	65 025	15.9687	50.4975
206	42 436	14.3527	45.3872	256	65 536	16.0000	50.5964
207	42 849	14.3875	45.4973	257	66 049	16.0312	50.6952
208	43 264	14.4222	45.6070	258	66 564	16.0624	50.7937
209	43 681	14.4568	45.7165	259	67 081	16.0935	50.8920
210	44 100	14.4914	45.8258	260	67 600	16.1245	50.9902
211	44 521	14.5258	45.9347	261	68 121	16.1555	51.0882
212	44 944	14.5602	46.0435	262	68 644	16.1864	51.1859
213	45 369	14.5945	46.1519	263	69 169	16.2173	51.2835
214	45 796	14.6287	46.2601	264	69 696	16.2481	51.3809
215	46 225	14.6629	46.3681	265	70 225	16.2788	51.4781
216	46 656	14.6969	46.4758	266	70 756	16.3095	51.5752
217	47 089	14.7309	46.5833	267	71 289	16.3401	51.6720
218	47 524	14.7648	46.6905	268	71 824	16.3707	51.7687
219	47 961	14.7986	46.7974	269	72 361	16.4012	51.8652
220	48 400	14.8324	46.9042	270	72 900	16.4317	51.9615
221	48 841	14.8661	47.0106	271	73 441	16.4621	52.0577
222	49 284	14.8997	47.1169	272	73 984	16.4924	52.1536
223	49 729	14.9332	47.2229	273	74 529	16.5227	52.2494
224	50 176	14.9666	47.3286	274	75 076	16.5529	52.3450
225	50 625	15.0000	47.4342	275	75 625	16.5831	52.4404
226	51 076	15.0333	47.5395	276	76 176	16.6133	52.5357
227	51 529	15.0665	47.6445	277	76 729	16.6433	52.6308
228	51 984	15.0997	47.7493	278	77 284	16.6733	52.7257
229	52 441	15.1327	47.8539	279	77 841	16.7033	52.8204
230	52 900	15.1658	47.9583	280	78 400	16.7332	52.9150
231	53 361	15.1987	48.0625	281	78 961	16.7631	53.0094
232	53 824	15.2315	48.1664	282	79 524	16.7929	53.1037
233	54 289	15.2643	48.2701	283	80 089	16.8226	53.1977
234	54 756	15.2971	48.3736	284	80 656	16.8523	53.2917
235	55 225	15.3297	48.4768	285	81 225	16.8819	53.3854
236	55 696	15.3623	48.5798	286	81 796	16.9115	53.4790
237	56 169	15.3948	48.6826	287	82 369	16.9411	53.5724
238	56 644	15.4272	48.7852	288	82 944	16.9706	53.6656
239	57 121	15.4596	48.8876	289	83 521	17.0000	53.7587
240	57 600	15.4919	48.9898	290	84 100	17.0294	53.8517
241	58 081	15.5242	49.0918	291	84 681	17.0587	53.9444
242	58 564	15.5563	49.1935	292	85 264	17.0880	54.0370
243	59 049	15.5885	49.2950	293	85 849	17.1172	54.1295
244	59 536	15.6205	49.3964	294	86 436	17.1464	54.2218
245	60 025	15.6525	49.4975	295	87 025	17.1756	54.3139
246	60 516	15.6844	49.5984	296	87 616	17.2047	54.4059
247	61 009	15.7162	49.6991	297	88 209	17.2337	54.4977
248	61 504	15.7480	49.7996	298	88 804	17.2627	54.5894
249	62 001	15.7797	49.8999	299	89 401	17.2916	54.6809
250	62 500	15.8114	50.0000	300	90 000	17.3205	54.7723
N	N²	√N	√10N	N	N²	√N	√10N

Table L continued

N	N²	√N	√10N	N	N²	√N	√10N
301	90 601	17.3494	54.8635	351	123 201	18.7350	59.2453
302	91 204	17.3781	54.9545	352	123 904	18.7617	59.3296
303	91 809	17.4069	55.0454	353	124 609	18.7883	59.4138
304	92 416	17.4356	55.1362	354	125 316	18.8149	59.4979
305	93 025	17.4642	55.2268	355	126 025	18.8414	59.5819
306	93 636	17.4929	55.3173	356	126 736	18.8680	59.6657
307	94 249	17.5214	55.4076	357	127 449	18.8944	59.7495
308	94 864	17.5499	55.4978	358	128 164	18.9209	59.8331
309	95 481	17.5784	55.5878	359	128 881	18.9473	59.9166
310	96 100	17.6068	55.6776	360	129 600	18.9737	60.0000
311	96 721	17.6352	55.7674	361	130 321	19.0000	60.0833
312	97 344	17.6635	55.8570	362	131 044	19.0263	60.1664
313	97 969	17.6918	55.9464	363	131 769	19.0526	60.2495
314	98 596	17.7200	56.0357	364	132 496	19.0788	60.3324
315	99 225	17.7482	56.1249	365	133 225	19.1050	60.4152
316	99 856	17.7764	56.2139	366	133 956	19.1311	60.4979
317	100 489	17.8045	56.3027	367	134 689	19.1572	60.5805
318	101 124	17.8326	56.3915	368	135 424	19.1833	60.6630
319	101 761	17.8606	56.4801	369	136 161	19.2094	60.7454
320	102 400	17.8885	56.5685	370	136 900	19.2354	60.8276
321	103 041	17.9165	56.6569	371	137 641	19.2614	60.9098
322	103 684	17.9444	56.7450	372	138 384	19.2873	60.9918
323	104 329	17.9722	56.8331	373	139 129	19.3132	61.0737
324	104 976	18.0000	56.9210	374	139 876	19.3391	61.1555
325	105 625	18.0278	57.0088	375	140 625	19.3649	61.2372
326	106 276	18.0555	57.0964	376	141 376	19.3907	61.3188
327	106 929	18.0831	57.1839	377	142 129	19.4165	61.4003
328	107 584	18.1108	57.2713	378	142 884	19.4422	61.4817
329	108 241	18.1384	57.3585	379	143 641	19.4679	61.5630
330	108 900	18.1659	57.4456	380	144 400	19.4936	61.6441
331	109 561	18.1934	57.5326	381	145 161	19.5192	61.7252
332	110 224	18.2209	57.6194	382	145 924	19.5448	61.8062
333	110 889	18.2483	57.7062	383	146 689	19.5704	61.8870
334	111 556	18.2757	57.7927	384	147 456	19.5959	61.9677
335	112 225	18.3030	57.8792	385	148 225	19.6214	62.0484
336	112 896	18.3303	57.9655	386	148 996	19.6469	62.1289
337	113 569	18.3576	58.0517	387	149 769	19.6723	62.2093
338	114 244	18.3848	58.1378	388	150 544	19.6977	62.2896
339	114 921	18.4120	58.2237	389	151 321	19.7231	62.3699
340	115 600	18.4391	58.3095	390	152 100	19.7484	62.4500
341	116 281	18.4662	58.3952	391	152 881	19.7737	62.5300
342	116 964	18.4932	58.4808	392	153 664	19.7990	62.6099
343	117 649	18.5203	58.5662	393	154 449	19.8242	62.6897
344	118 336	18.5472	58.6515	394	155 236	19.8494	62.7694
345	119 025	18.5742	58.7367	395	156 025	19.8746	62.8490
346	119 716	18.6011	58.8218	396	156 816	19.8997	62.9285
347	120 409	18.6279	58.9067	397	157 609	19.9249	63.0079
348	121 104	18.6548	58.9915	398	158 404	19.9499	63.0872
349	121 801	18.6815	59.0762	399	159 201	19.9750	63.1664
350	122 500	18.7083	59.1608	400	160 000	20.0000	63.2456
N	N²	√N	√10N	N	N²	√N	√10N

Table L continued

N	N²	√N	√10N	N	N²	√N	√10N
401	160 801	20.0250	63.3246	451	203 401	21.2368	67.1565
402	161 604	20.0499	63.4035	452	204 304	21.2603	67.2309
403	162 409	20.0749	63.4823	453	205 209	21.2838	67.3053
404	163 216	20.0998	63.5610	454	206 116	21.3073	67.3795
405	164 025	20.1246	63.6396	455	207 025	21.3307	67.4537
406	164 836	20.1494	63.7181	456	207 936	21.3542	67.5278
407	165 649	20.1742	63.7966	457	208 849	21.3776	67.6018
408	166 464	20.1990	63.8749	458	209 764	21 4009	67.6757
409	167 281	20.2238	63.9531	459	210 681	21.4243	67.7495
410	168 100	20.2485	64.0313	460	211 600	21.4476	67.8233
411	168 921	20.2731	64.1093	461	212 521	21.4709	67.8970
412	169 744	20.2978	64.1872	462	213 444	21.4942	67.9706
413	170 569	20.3224	64.2651	463	214 369	21.5174	68.0441
414	171 396	20.3470	64.3428	464	215 296	21.5407	68.1175
415	172 225	20.3715	64.4205	465	216 225	21.5639	68.1909
416	173 056	20.3961	64.4981	466	217 156	21.5870	68.2642
417	173 889	20.4206	64.5755	467	218 089	21.6102	68.3374
418	174 724	20.4450	64.6529	468	219 024	21.6333	68.4105
419	175 561	20.4695	64.7302	469	219 961	21.6564	68.4836
420	176 400	20.4939	64.8074	470	220 900	21.6795	68.5565
421	177 241	20.5183	64.8845	471	221 841	21.7025	68.6294
422	178 084	20.5426	64.9615	472	222 784	21.7256	68.7023
423	178 929	20.5670	65.0385	473	223 729	21.7486	68.7750
424	179 776	20.5913	65.1153	474	224 676	21.7715	68.8477
425	180 625	20.6155	65.1920	475	225 625	21.7945	68.9202
426	181 476	20.6398	65.2687	476	226 576	21.8174	68.9928
427	182 329	20.6640	65.3452	477	227 529	21.8403	69.0652
428	183 184	20.6882	65.4217	478	228 484	21.8632	69.1375
429	184 041	20.7123	65.4981	479	229 441	21.8861	69.2098
430	184 900	20.7364	65.5744	480	230 400	21.9089	69.2820
431	185 761	20.7605	65.6506	481	231 361	21.9317	69.3542
432	186 624	20.7846	65.7267	482	232 324	21.9545	69.4262
433	187 489	20.8087	65.8027	483	233 289	21.9773	69.4982
434	188 356	20.8327	65.8787	484	234 256	22.0000	69.5701
435	189 225	20.8567	65.9545	485	235 225	22.0227	69.6419
436	190 096	20.8806	66.0303	486	236 196	22.0454	69.7137
437	190 969	20.9045	66.1060	487	237 169	22.0681	69.7854
438	191 844	20.9285	66.1816	488	238 144	22.0907	69.8570
439	192 721	20.9523	66.2571	489	239 121	22.1133	69.9285
440	193 600	20.9762	66.3325	490	240 100	22.1359	70.0000
441	194 481	21.0000	66.4078	491	241 081	22.1585	70.0714
442	195 364	21.0238	66.4831	492	242 064	22.1811	70.1427
443	196 249	21.0476	66.5582	493	243 049	22.2036	70.2140
444	197 136	21.0713	66.6333	494	244 036	22.2261	70.2851
445	198 025	21.0950	66.7083	495	245 025	22.2486	70.3562
446	198 916	21.1187	66.7832	496	246 016	22.2711	70.4273
447	199 809	21.1424	66.8581	497	247 009	22.2935	70.4982
448	200 704	21.1660	66.9328	498	248 004	22.3159	70.5691
449	201 601	21.1896	67.0075	499	249 001	22.3383	70.6399
450	202 500	21.2132	67.0820	500	250 000	22.3607	70.7107
N	N²	√N	√10N	N	N²	√N	√10N

Table L continued

N	N^2	$\sqrt{N}$	$\sqrt{10N}$	N	N^2	$\sqrt{N}$	$\sqrt{10N}$
501	251 001	22.3830	70.7814	551	303 601	23.4734	74.2294
502	252 004	22.4054	70.8520	552	304 704	23.4947	74.2967
503	253 009	22.4277	70.9225	553	305 809	23.5159	74.3640
504	254 016	22.4500	70.9930	554	306 916	23.5372	74.4312
505	255 025	22.4722	71.0634	555	308 025	23.5584	74.4983
506	256 036	22.4944	71.1337	556	309 136	23.5797	74.5654
507	257 049	22.5167	71.2039	557	310 249	23.6008	74.6324
508	258 064	22.5388	71.2741	558	311 364	23.6220	74.6994
509	259 081	22.5610	71.3442	559	312 481	23.6432	74.7663
510	260 100	22.5832	71.4143	560	313 600	23.6643	74.8331
511	261 121	22.6053	71.4843	561	314 721	23.6854	74.8999
512	262 144	22.6274	71.5542	562	315 844	23.7065	74.9667
513	263 169	22.6495	71.6240	563	316 969	23.7276	75.0333
514	264 196	22.6716	71.6938	564	318 096	23.7487	75.0999
515	265 225	22.6936	71.7635	565	319 225	23.7697	75.1665
516	266 256	22.7156	71.8331	566	320 356	23.7908	75.2330
517	267 289	22.7376	71.9027	567	321 489	23.8118	75.2994
518	268 324	22.7596	71.9722	568	322 624	23.8327	75.3658
519	269 361	22.7816	72.0417	569	323 761	23.8537	75.4321
520	270 400	22.8035	72.1110	570	324 900	23.8747	75.4983
521	271 441	22.8254	72.1803	571	326 041	23.8956	75.5645
522	272 484	22.8473	72.2496	572	327 184	23.9165	75.6307
523	273 529	22.8692	72.3187	573	328 329	23.9374	75.6968
524	274 576	22.8911	72.3879	574	329 476	23.9583	75.7628
525	275 625	22.9129	72.4569	575	330 625	23.9792	75.8288
526	276 676	22.9347	72.5259	576	331 776	24.0000	75.8947
527	277 729	22.9565	72.5948	577	332 929	24.0208	75.9605
528	278 784	22.9783	72.6636	578	334 084	24.0416	76.0263
529	279 841	23.0000	72.7324	579	335 241	24.0624	76.0921
530	280 900	23.0217	72.8011	580	336 400	24.0832	76.1577
531	281 961	23.0434	72.8698	581	337 561	24.1039	76.2234
532	283 024	23.0651	72.9383	582	338 724	24.1247	76.2889
533	284 089	23.0868	73.0069	583	339 889	24.1454	76.3544
534	285 156	23.1084	73.0753	584	341 056	24.1661	76.4199
535	286 225	23.1301	73.1437	585	342 225	24.1868	76.4853
536	287 296	23.1517	73.2120	586	343 396	24.2074	76.5506
537	288 369	23.1733	73.2803	587	344 569	24.2281	76.6159
538	289 444	23.1948	73.3485	588	345 744	24.2487	76.6812
539	290 521	23.2164	73.4166	589	346 921	24.2693	76.7463
540	291 600	23.2379	73.4847	590	348 100	24.2899	76.8115
541	292 681	23.2594	73.5527	591	349 281	24.3105	76.8765
542	293 764	23.2809	73.6207	592	350 464	24.3311	76.9415
543	294 849	23.3024	73.6885	593	351 649	24.3516	77.0065
544	295 936	23.3238	73.7564	594	352 836	24.3721	77.0714
545	297 025	23.3452	73.8241	595	354 025	24.3926	77.1362
546	298 116	23.3666	73.8918	596	355 216	24.4131	77.2010
547	299 209	23.3880	73.9594	597	356 409	24.4336	77.2658
548	300 304	23.4094	74.0270	598	357 604	24.4540	77.3305
549	301 401	23.4307	74.0945	599	358 801	24.4745	77.3951
550	302 500	23.4521	74.1620	600	360 000	24.4949	77.4597
N	N^2	$\sqrt{N}$	$\sqrt{10N}$	N	N^2	$\sqrt{N}$	$\sqrt{10N}$

Table L continued

N	N^2	$\sqrt{N}$	$\sqrt{10N}$	N	N^2	$\sqrt{N}$	$\sqrt{10N}$
601	361 201	24.5153	77.5242	651	423 801	25.5147	80.6846
602	362 404	24.5357	77.5887	652	425 104	25.5343	80.7465
603	363 609	24.5561	77.6531	653	426 409	25.5539	80.8084
604	364 816	24.5764	77.7174	654	427 716	25.5734	80.8703
605	366 025	24.5967	77.7818	655	429 025	25.5930	80.9321
606	367 236	24.6171	77.8460	656	430 336	25.6125	80.9938
607	368 449	24.6374	77.9102	657	431 649	25.6320	81.0555
608	369 664	24.6577	77.9743	658	432 964	25.6515	81.1172
609	370 881	24.6779	78.0385	659	434 281	25.6710	81.1788
610	372 100	24.6982	78.1025	660	435 600	25.6905	81.2404
611	373 321	24.7184	78.1665	661	436 921	25.7099	81.3019
612	374 544	24.7386	78.2304	662	438 244	25.7294	81.3634
613	375 769	24.7588	78.2943	663	439 569	25.7488	81.4248
614	376 996	24.7790	78.3582	664	440 896	25.7682	81.4862
615	378 225	24.7992	78.4219	665	442 225	25.7876	81.5475
616	379 456	24.8194	78.4857	666	443 556	25.8070	81.6088
617	380 689	24.8395	78.5493	667	444 889	25.8263	81.6701
618	381 924	24.8596	78.6130	668	446 224	25.8457	81.7313
619	383 161	24.8797	78.6766	669	447 561	25.8650	81.7924
620	384 400	24.8998	78.7401	670	448 900	25.8844	81.8535
621	385 641	24.9199	78.8036	671	450 241	25.9037	81.9146
622	386 884	24.9399	78.8670	672	451 584	25.9230	81.9756
623	388 129	24.9600	78.9303	673	452 929	25.9422	82.0366
624	389 376	24.9800	78.9937	674	454 276	25.9615	82.0975
625	390 625	25.0000	79.0569	675	455 625	25.9808	82.1584
626	391 876	25.0200	79.1202	676	456 976	26.0000	82.2192
627	393 129	25.0400	79.1833	677	458 329	26.0192	82.2800
628	394 384	25.0599	79.2464	678	459 684	26.0384	82.3408
629	395 641	25.0799	79.3095	679	461 041	26.0576	82.4015
630	396 900	25.0998	79.3725	680	462 400	26.0768	82.4621
631	398 161	25.1197	79.4355	681	463 761	26.0960	82.5227
632	399 424	25.1396	79.4984	682	465 124	26.1151	82.5833
633	400 689	25.1595	79.5613	683	466 489	26.1343	82.6438
634	401 956	25.1794	79.6241	684	467 856	26.1534	82.7043
635	403 225	25.1992	79.6869	685	469 225	26.1725	82.7647
636	404 496	25.2190	79.7496	686	470 596	26.1916	82.8251
637	405 769	25.2389	79.8123	687	471 969	26.2107	82.8855
638	407 044	25.2587	79.8749	688	473 344	26.2298	82.9458
639	408 321	25.2785	79.9375	689	474 721	26.2488	83.0060
640	409 600	25.2982	80.0000	690	476 100	26.2679	83.0662
641	410 881	25.3180	80.0625	691	477 481	26.2869	83.1264
642	412 164	25.3377	80.1249	692	478 864	26.3059	83.1865
643	413 449	25.3575	80.1873	693	480 249	26.3249	83.2466
644	414 736	25.3772	80.2496	694	481 636	26.3439	83.3067
645	416 025	25.3969	80.3119	695	483 025	26.3629	83.3667
646	417 316	25.4165	80.3741	696	484 416	26.3818	83.4266
647	418 609	25.4362	80.4363	697	485 809	26.4008	83.4865
648	419 904	25.4558	80.4984	698	487 204	26.4197	83.5464
649	421 201	25.4755	80.5605	699	488 601	26.4386	83.6062
650	422 500	25.4951	80.6226	700	490 000	26.4575	83.6660
N	N^2	$\sqrt{N}$	$\sqrt{10N}$	N	N^2	$\sqrt{N}$	$\sqrt{10N}$

Table L continued

N	N^2	$\sqrt{N}$	$\sqrt{10N}$	N	N^2	$\sqrt{N}$	$\sqrt{10N}$
701	491 401	26.4764	83.7257	751	564 001	27.4044	86.6603
702	492 804	26.4953	83.7854	752	565 504	27.4226	86.7179
703	494 209	26.5141	83.8451	753	567 009	27.4408	86.7756
704	495 616	26.5330	83.9047	754	568 516	27.4591	86.8332
705	497 025	26.5518	83.9643	755	570 025	27.4773	86.8907
706	498 436	26.5707	84.0238	756	571 536	27.4955	86.9483
707	499 849	26.5895	84.0833	757	573 049	27.5136	87.0057
708	501 264	26.6083	84.1427	758	574 564	27.5318	87.0632
709	502 681	26.6271	84.2021	759	576 081	27.5500	87.1206
710	504 100	26.6458	84.2615	760	577 600	27.5681	87.1780
711	505 521	26.6646	84.3208	761	579 121	27.5862	87.2353
712	506 944	26.6833	84.3801	762	580 644	27.6044	87.2926
713	508 369	26.7021	84.4393	763	582 169	27.6225	87.3499
714	509 796	26.7208	84.4985	764	583 696	27.6405	87.4071
715	511 225	26.7395	84.5577	765	585 225	27.6586	87.4643
716	512 656	26.7582	84.6168	766	586 756	27.6767	87.5214
717	514 089	26.7769	84.6759	767	588 289	27.6948	87.5785
718	515 524	26.7955	84.7349	768	589 824	27.7128	87.6356
719	516 961	26.8142	84.7939	769	591 361	27.7309	87.6926
720	518 400	26.8328	84.8528	770	592 900	27.7489	87.7496
721	519 841	26.8514	84.9117	771	594 441	27.7669	87.8066
722	521 284	26.8701	84.9706	772	595 984	27.7849	87.8635
723	522 729	26.8887	85.0294	773	597 529	27.8029	87.9204
724	524 176	26.9072	85.0882	774	599 076	27.8209	87.9773
725	525 625	26.9258	85.1469	775	600 625	27.8388	88.0341
726	527 076	26.9444	85.2056	776	602 176	27.8568	88.0909
727	528 529	26.9629	85.2643	777	603 729	27.8747	88.1476
728	529 984	26.9815	85.3229	778	605 284	27.8927	88.2043
729	531 441	27.0000	85.3815	779	606 841	27.9106	88.2610
730	532 900	27.0185	85.4400	780	608 400	27.9285	88.3176
731	534 361	27.0370	85.4985	781	609 961	27.9464	88.3742
732	535 824	27.0555	85.5570	782	611 524	27.9643	88.4308
733	537 289	27.0740	85.6154	783	613 089	27.9821	88.4873
734	538 756	27.0924	85.6738	784	614 656	28.0000	88.5438
735	540 225	27.1109	85.7321	785	616 225	28.0179	88.6002
736	541 696	27.1293	85.7904	786	617 796	28.0357	88.6566
737	543 169	27.1478	85.8487	787	619 369	28.0535	88.7130
738	544 644	27.1662	85.9069	788	620 944	28.0713	88.7694
739	546 121	27.1846	85.9651	789	622 521	28.0891	88.8257
740	547 600	27.2029	86.0233	790	624 100	28.1069	88.8819
741	549 081	27.2213	86.0814	791	625 681	28.1247	88.9382
742	550 564	27.2397	86.1394	792	627 264	28.1425	88.9944
743	552 049	27.2580	86.1975	793	628 849	28.1603	89.0506
744	553 536	27.2764	86.2554	794	630 436	28.1780	89.1067
745	555 025	27.2947	86.3134	795	632 025	28.1957	89.1628
746	556 516	27.3130	86.3713	796	633 616	28.2135	89.2188
747	558 009	27.3313	86.4292	797	635 209	28.2312	89.2749
748	559 504	27.3496	86.4870	798	636 804	28.2489	89.3308
749	561 001	27.3679	86.5448	799	638 401	28.2666	89.3868
750	562 500	27.3861	86.6025	800	640 000	28.2843	89.4427
N	N^2	$\sqrt{N}$	$\sqrt{10N}$	N	N^2	$\sqrt{N}$	$\sqrt{10N}$

Table L continued

N	N^2	$\sqrt{N}$	$\sqrt{10N}$	N	N^2	$\sqrt{N}$	$\sqrt{10N}$
801	641 601	28.3019	89.4986	851	724 201	29.1719	92.2497
802	643 204	28.3196	89.5545	852	725 904	29.1890	92.3038
803	644 809	28.3373	89.6103	853	727 609	29.2062	92.3580
804	646 416	28.3549	89.6660	854	729 316	29.2233	92.4121
805	648 025	28.3725	89.7218	855	731 025	29.2404	92.4662
806	649 636	28.3901	89.7775	856	732 736	29.2575	92.5203
807	651 249	28.4077	89.8332	857	734 449	29.2746	92.5743
808	652 864	28.4253	89.8888	858	736 164	29.2916	92.6283
809	654 481	28.4429	89.9444	859	737 881	29.3087	92.6823
810	656 100	28.4605	90.0000	860	739 600	29.3258	92.7362
811	657 721	28.4781	90.0555	861	741 321	29.3428	92.7901
812	659 344	28.4956	90.1110	862	743 044	29.3598	92.8440
813	660 969	28.5132	90.1665	863	744 769	29.3769	92.8978
814	662 596	28.5307	90.2220	864	746 496	29.3939	92.9516
815	664 225	28.5482	90.2774	865	748 225	29.4109	93.0054
816	665 856	28.5657	90.3327	866	749 956	29.4279	93.0591
817	667 489	28.5832	90.3880	867	751 689	29.4449	93.1128
818	669 124	28.6007	90.4434	868	753 424	29.4618	93.1665
819	670 761	28.6182	90.4986	869	755 161	29.4788	93.2202
820	672 400	28.6356	90.5538	870	756 900	29.4958	93.2738
821	674 041	28.6531	90.6091	871	758 641	29.5127	93.3274
822	675 684	28.6705	90.6642	872	760 384	29.5296	93.3809
823	677 329	28.6880	90.7193	873	762 129	29.5466	93.4345
824	678 976	28.7054	90.7744	874	763 876	29.5635	93.4880
825	680 625	28.7228	90.8295	875	765 625	29.5804	93.5414
826	682 276	28.7402	90.8845	876	767 376	29.5973	93.5949
827	683 929	28.7576	90.9395	877	769 129	29.6142	93.6483
828	685 584	28.7750	90.9945	878	770 884	29.6311	93.7017
829	687 241	28.7924	91.0494	879	772 641	29.6479	93.7550
830	688 900	28.8097	91.1043	880	774 400	29.6648	93.8083
831	690 561	28.8271	91.1592	881	776 161	29.6816	93.8616
832	692 224	28.8444	91.2140	882	777 924	29.6985	93.9149
833	693 889	28.8617	91.2688	883	779 689	29.7153	93.9681
834	695 556	28.8791	91.3236	884	781 456	29.7321	94.0213
835	697 225	28.8964	91.3783	885	783 225	29.7490	94.0744
836	698 896	28.9137	91.4330	886	784 996	29.7657	94.1276
837	700 569	28.9310	91.4877	887	786 769	29.7825	94.1807
838	702 244	28.9482	91.5423	888	788 544	29.7993	94.2337
839	703 921	28.9655	91.5969	889	790 321	29.8161	94.2868
840	705 600	28.9828	91.6515	890	792 100	29.8329	94.3398
841	707 281	29.0000	91.7061	891	793 881	29.8496	94.3928
842	708 964	29.0172	91.7606	892	795 664	29.8664	94.4458
843	710 649	29.0345	91.8150	893	797 449	29.8831	94.4987
844	712 336	29.0517	91.8695	894	799 236	29.8998	94.5516
845	714 025	29.0689	91.9239	895	801 025	29.9165	94.6044
846	715 716	29.0861	91.9783	896	802 816	29.9333	94.6573
847	717 409	29.1033	92.0326	897	804 609	29.9500	94.7101
848	719 104	29.1204	92.0869	898	806 404	29.9666	94.7629
849	720 801	29.1376	92.1412	899	808 201	29.9833	94.8156
850	722 500	29.1548	92.1955	900	810 000	30.0000	94.8683
N	N^2	$\sqrt{N}$	$\sqrt{10N}$	N	N^2	$\sqrt{N}$	$\sqrt{10N}$

Table L continued

N	N²	√N̄	√10N̄	N	N²	√N̄	√10N̄
901	811 801	30.0167	94.9210	951	904 401	30.8383	97.5192
902	813 604	30.0333	94.9737	952	906 304	30.8545	97.5705
903	815 409	30.0500	95.0263	953	908 209	30.8707	97.6217
904	817 216	30.0666	95.0789	954	910 116	30.8869	97.6729
905	819 025	30.0832	95.1315	955	912 025	30.9031	97.7241
906	820 836	30.0998	95.1840	956	913 936	30.9193	97.7753
907	822 649	30.1164	95.2366	957	915 849	30.9354	97.8264
908	824 464	30.1330	95.2890	958	917 764	30.9516	97.8775
909	826 281	30.1496	95.3415	959	919 681	30.9677	97.9285
910	828 100	30.1662	95.3939	960	921 600	30.9839	97.9796
911	829 921	30.1828	95.4463	961	923 521	31.0000	98.0306
912	831 744	30.1993	95.4987	962	925 444	31.0161	98.0816
913	833 569	30.2159	95.5510	963	927 369	31.0322	98.1326
914	835 396	30.2324	95.6034	964	929 296	31.0484	98.1835
915	837 225	30.2490	95.6556	965	931 225	31.0645	98.2344
916	839 056	30.2655	95.7079	966	933 156	31.0805	98.2853
917	840 889	30.2820	95.7601	967	935 089	31.0966	98.3362
918	842 724	30.2985	95.8123	968	937 024	31.1127	98.3870
919	844 561	30.3150	95.8645	969	938 961	31.1288	98.4378
920	846 400	30.3315	95.9166	970	940 900	31.1448	98.4886
921	848 241	30.3480	95.9688	971	942 841	31.1609	98.5393
922	850 084	30.3645	96.0208	972	944 784	31.1769	98.5901
923	851 929	30.3809	96.0729	973	946 729	31.1929	98.6408
924	853 776	30.3974	96.1249	974	948 676	31.2090	98.6914
925	855 625	30.4138	96.1769	975	950 625	31.2250	98.7421
926	857 476	30.4303	96.2289	976	952 576	31.2410	98.7927
927	859 329	30.4467	96.2808	977	954 529	31.2570	98.8433
928	861 184	30.4631	96.3328	978	956 484	31.2730	98.8939
929	863 041	30.4795	96.3846	979	958 441	31.2890	98.9444
930	864 900	30.4959	96.4365	980	960 400	31.3049	98.9949
931	866 761	30.5123	96.4883	981	962 361	31.3209	99.0454
932	868 624	30.5287	96.5401	982	964 324	31.3369	99.0959
933	870 489	30.5450	96.5919	983	966 289	31.3528	99.1464
934	872 356	30.5614	96.6437	984	968 256	31.3688	99.1968
935	874 225	30.5778	96.6954	985	970 225	31.3847	99.2472
936	876 096	30.5941	96.7471	986	972 196	31.4006	99.2975
937	877 969	30.6105	96.7988	987	974 169	31.4166	99.3479
938	879 844	30.6268	96.8504	988	976 144	31.4325	99.3982
939	881 721	30.6431	96.9020	989	978 121	31.4484	99.4485
940	883 600	30.6594	96.9536	990	980 100	31.4643	99.4987
941	885 481	30.6757	97.0052	991	982 081	31.4802	99.5490
942	887 364	30.6920	97.0567	992	984 064	31.4960	99.5992
943	889 249	30.7083	97.1082	993	986 049	31.5119	99.6494
944	891 136	30.7246	97.1597	994	988 036	31.5278	99.6996
945	893 025	30.7408	97.2111	995	990 025	31.5436	99.7497
946	894 916	30.7571	97.2625	996	992 016	31.5595	99.7998
947	896 809	30.7734	97.3139	997	994 009	31.5753	99.8499
948	898 704	30.7896	97.3653	998	996 004	31.5911	99.8999
949	900 601	30.8058	97.4166	999	998 001	31.6070	99.9500
950	902 500	30.8221	97.4679	1000	1000 000	31.6228	100.0000
N	N²	√N̄	√10N̄	N	N²	√N̄	√10N̄

Appendix II: Some Basic Arithmetic and Algebra: A Review

This appendix reviews some arithmetic and algebraic operations that are useful in statistics. It is in no sense a complete discussion of these matters, but is intended to serve merely as a refresher for operations that you learned in high school but may not have used since then.

Some algebraic symbols

$\neq$ means not equal to: $5 \neq 7$, five is not equal to seven
$$X \neq Y, X \text{ is not equal to } Y$$
$>$ means greater than: $10 > 9$, ten is greater than nine
$$A > B, A \text{ is greater than } B$$
$\geq$ means equal to or greater than: $5 \geq 4$, five is equal to or greater than four
$$Y \geq X, Y \text{ is equal to or greater than } X$$
$<$ means less than: $20 < 26$, twenty is less than twenty-six
$$B < A, B \text{ is less than } A$$
$\leq$ means equal to or less than: $3 \leq 4$, three is equal to or less than four
$$X \leq Y, X \text{ is equal to or less than } Y$$
$\pm$ means plus or minus: ± 2.58 is the range of values from -2.58 to $+2.58$
$$\pm t \text{ is the range of values from } -t \text{ to } +t$$

Addition

The statement, "five plus seven equals twelve," is expressed as

$$5 + 7 = 12$$

The resultant value (12 in this case) is known as the *sum;* therefore, addition may be termed summation.

Subtraction

The statement, "ten minus six equals four," is expressed as

$$10 - 6 = 4$$

The resultant value (4 in this case) is known as the *difference*.

Multiplication

The statement, "five times nine equals forty-five," may be expressed in any of the following ways

$$5 \cdot 9 = 45, \qquad 5 \times 9 = 45, \qquad \text{or} \qquad (5)(9) = 45$$

The resultant value (45 in this case) is known as the *product*.

Note: When numbers are represented by letters, such as X and Y, then X times Y is expressed as XY.

Division

The statement, "twenty-eight divided by four equals seven," may be expressed in any of the following ways

$$28 \div 4 = 7, \qquad \frac{28}{4} = 7, \qquad \text{or} \qquad 28/4 = 7$$

The resultant value (7 in this case) is known as the *quotient*.

Mixed operations

When addition, subtraction, multiplication, and division occur within a single statement, then multiplication and/or division should be performed before addition and/or subtraction. Thus

$$5 \times 2 + 6 - 1 + 8/4 = 10 + 6 - 1 + 2 = 17$$

The best practice is to enclose the operations in parentheses; then the operations within parentheses are completed before you perform the operations between parentheses. Thus

$$(5 \times 2) + (6 \times 3) - (10/5) = 10 + 18 - 2 = 26$$

and

$$(3 + 2)(4 + 8) = (5)(12) = 60$$

and

$$[(6)(4)] + [(4 + 10)/7] = 24 + [14/7] = 24 + 2 = 26$$

Note: Exponents have higher priority than multiplication or division; see the section on exponents elsewhere in this appendix.

Decimal fractions

When adding or subtracting decimal fractions, be sure to align the numbers so that the decimal points are in a vertical line. If one number has fewer terms after the decimal point than the other, simply add zeros until they are equal in this respect. Thus

$$4.6725 + 103.721 + 25.7 = 134.0935$$

is performed as follows

$$
\begin{array}{r}
4.6725 \\
103.7210 \\
\underline{25.7000} \\
134.0935
\end{array}
$$

Similarly,

$$103.721 - 25.7 = 78.021$$

is performed as follows

$$
\begin{array}{r}
103.721 \\
\underline{-25.700} \\
78.021
\end{array}
$$

When multiplying decimal fractions, remember that the product contains as many terms after the decimal point as the sum of terms after the decimal point of the numbers being multiplied. Thus

$$(4.6725)(25.7) = 120.08325$$

is performed as follows

$$
\begin{array}{r}
4.6725 \\
\underline{\times 25.7} \\
3.27075 \\
23.3625 \\
\underline{93.450} \\
120.08325
\end{array}
$$

When dividing decimal fractions, the easiest procedure is to make the divisor (denominator) into a whole number by moving the decimal point to the right; then move the decimal point in the dividend (numerator) the same number of spaces to the right. Thus

$$120.08325/25.7 = 4.6725$$

is performed as follows

$$
\begin{array}{r}
4.6725 \\
257\,)\overline{1200.8325} \\
\underline{1028} \\
1728 \\
\underline{1542} \\
1863 \\
\underline{1799} \\
642 \\
\underline{514} \\
1285 \\
\underline{1285} \\
0000
\end{array}
$$

Proper fractions

The addition and subtraction of proper fractions requires that they have a common (equal value) denominator. If this is not initially the case, then one or both must be converted so that a common denominator exists. The simplest way to identify the common denominator is to multiply the two (or more) existing denominator values. Thus, for the fractions $1/5$ and $1/6$, the common denominator is $5 \times 6 = 30$. Remember that in converting fractions to achieve a common denominator, the numerator terms must also be multiplied. Thus

$$\frac{1}{5} + \frac{1}{6} = \left(\frac{6}{6}\right)\left(\frac{1}{5}\right) + \left(\frac{5}{5}\right)\left(\frac{1}{6}\right) = \frac{6}{30} + \frac{5}{30} = \frac{11}{30}$$

and

$$\frac{1}{3} - \frac{1}{4} = \left(\frac{4}{4}\right)\left(\frac{1}{3}\right) - \left(\frac{3}{3}\right)\left(\frac{1}{4}\right) = \frac{4}{12} - \frac{3}{12} = \frac{1}{12}$$

When multiplying a proper fraction by a whole number, the whole number multiplies only the numerator term. Thus

$$5 \times \frac{2}{17} = \frac{10}{17} \qquad \text{or} \qquad (5)(2/17) = 10/17$$

When multiplying two proper fractions, simply multiply numerator times numerator, and denominator times denominator. Thus

$$\frac{4}{9} \times \frac{4}{7} = \frac{16}{63} \qquad \text{or} \qquad (4/9)(4/7) = 16/63$$

When dividing a proper fraction by a whole number, the whole number multiplies the denominator term. Thus

$$(1/3)/2 = 1/(3 \times 2) = 1/6$$

When dividing one proper fraction by another, simply invert the divisor (denominator) fraction and then multiply. Thus

$$\frac{4/9}{4/7} = (4/9)(7/4) = 28/36 = 7/9$$

The last step in the previous expression, in which 28/36 was reduced to 7/9, is called canceling. It means that the numerator and denominator are divided by some number, which in this case is 4; thus we would say that 4 has been canceled out of the fraction (numerator and denominator are both divided by 4). Consider that

$$\frac{28}{36} = \frac{7 \times 4}{9 \times 4} = \frac{7}{9}$$

Factoring

Factoring consists of reducing an expression to the simplest terms whose product equals the original expression. Thus

$$nX + nY = n(X + Y)$$

and

$$12 - 21 = 3(4 - 7)$$

Signs

Numbers can be positive (values greater than zero) or negative (values less than zero). Adding a negative number is actually a subtraction. Thus

$$5 + (-3) = 5 - 3 = 2$$

Note that the minus sign takes precedence.

Subtracting a negative number is actually an addition. Thus

$$5 - (-3) = 5 + 3 = 8$$

Note that the occurrence of two consecutive minus signs represents an addition. Note also

$$(-10) + (-16) = -10 - 16 = -26$$

and

$$(-10) - (-16) = -10 + 16 = 6$$

When a positive number is multiplied by a negative number the product is negative; if both numbers are negative the product is positive. In general, if there is an odd number of negative signs the product is negative, and if there is an even number of negative signs the product is positive. Thus

$$(5)(-7) = -35$$

and

$$(-6)(-9) = 54$$

and

$$(-5)(-4)(-11) = -220$$

and

$$(-2)(6)(-7)(-10)(-3) = 2520$$

When dividing, if both the dividend (numerator) and divisor (denominator) are negative the quotient is positive; if either one is negative the quotient is negative. Thus

$$-50/-10 = 5$$

and

$$40/-5 = -8$$

and

$$-24/6 = -4$$

Exponents

In the expression 5^2, the number 5 is the *base,* and the superscript number 2 is the *exponent*. This expression means, in words, the base number multiplied by itself a number of times equal to the exponent number. Thus:

$$5^2 = (5)(5) = 25$$

and

$$6^3 = (6)(6)(6) = 216$$

Note that

(1) When the exponent is a 2 this is termed "squared," so that 4^2 may be described as 4 squared.

(2) A term with exponent 1 is equal to the base value, thus $6^1 = 6$ and $X^1 = X$.

(3) A term with exponent 0 is always equal to 1, thus $7^0 = 1$ and $X^0 = 1$.

Numbers with exponents cannot be added or subtracted until the bases have been multiplied out.

$$2^6 + 2^3 = 64 + 8 = 72$$

When the bases are identical, multiplication may be performed by adding the exponents.

$$(2^6)(2^3) = 2^{6+3} = 2^9 = 512$$

When the bases are identical, division may be performed by subtracting the exponents.

$$2^6/2^3 = 2^{6-3} = 2^3 = 8$$

In mixed operations, exponents have higher priority than multiplication or division.

$$(5)(2)^2 = (5)(4) = 20$$
$$(54)/(3)^3 = 54/27 = 2$$

Transposing

In an algebraic equation, when a term crosses the equals sign its sign changes; that is, positive numbers become negative, and negative numbers become positive. Thus

$$4 + 3 = 7$$
$$4 = 7 - 3$$
$$3 = 7 - 4$$
$$4 + 3 - 7 = 0$$

Consider the expression

$$\frac{A}{B} = C$$

If we multiply both terms by B, then

$$\frac{BA}{B} = BC$$

Now cancel the B's in the proper fraction and we have

$$A = BC$$

A term that divides the values on one side of the equals sign multiplies the values on the other. Thus

$$\frac{10}{2} = 5$$

$$10 = (2)(5)$$

Also, if $A = BC$, then $B = A/C$ Thus

$$10 = (2)(5)$$
$$2 = 10/5$$

Rounding

When one number (the divisor) is divided into another (the dividend), the result (the quotient) is not always a whole number; it may be a fractional value. For example, $21/8 = 2.625$, and in this form the value 2.625 is said to be accurate to three decimal places, which means that there are three numbers to the right of the decimal point. The greater the number of decimal places, the more accurate the value; for example, $22/7 = 3.142857143$, in which case the answer is accurate to nine decimal places. For many purposes, including those for which this book is intended, it is sufficient to perform calculations that are accurate to two decimal places. When a value occurs that does not work out evenly at two decimal places, it may be rounded off so as to be accurate to only two decimal places. If the value to be rounded off occurs as a number with three decimal places, you round it to two decimal places as follows. If the third number to the right of the decimal point is 6 or larger, then increase the second number to the right of the decimal point by 1. For example, $2.627 = 2.63, 4.379 = 4.38, 10.706 = 10.71$, and $9.496 = 9.50$. If the third number to the right of the decimal point is 4 or smaller, then simply drop it without changing any numbers. For example, $2.624 = 2.62, 4.371 = 4.37$, and $7.093 = 7.09$. If the third number to the right of the decimal point is exactly 5, then round the second number to the next even value; if it is an even number, leave it as is and if it is an odd number, increase by 1. For example, $17.345 = 17.34$ and $9.115 = 9.12$. If the value to be rounded off occurs as a number with four decimal places, then if the third and fourth numbers to the right of the decimal point are 51 or larger, you increase the second number to the right of the decimal point by 1. For example, $6.5462 = 6.55, 7.8851 = 7.89, 10.2192 = 10.22$, and $16.4958 = 16.50$. If the third and fourth numbers to the right of the decimal point are 49 or smaller, you simply drop them without changing any numbers. For example, $3.1428 = 3.14, 6.7539 = 6.75$, and $10.1849 = 10.18$. If the third and fourth numbers to the right of the decimal point are exactly 50, then round the second number to the next even value; that is, leave it as is if it is even and increase by 1 if it is odd. For example, $5.6450 = 5.64$ and $7.9350 = 7.94$. The previous procedure may be extended and generalized to round off numbers with five or more decimal places. [Note: The rounding procedure described here is the convention adopted by most mathematicians. A simpler, and generally sufficient procedure is to increase the to-be-rounded digit by one when the next digit is 5 or larger regardless of whether the to-be-rounded digit is odd or even. Many calculators and computers round in this fashion; as a result, you may encounter some discrepancies with the method described previously.]

Roots

The square root of a number is that value which, when multiplied by itself, equals the number in question. The square root of 4 is 2 since $2 \times 2 = 4$. Square root is expressed by the symbol $\sqrt{}$ placed before and over the number, so that the square root of 25 is $\sqrt{25} = 5$. The cube root of a number is that value which, when multiplied by itself three times, equals the number in question. The cube root of 27 is 3 since $3 \times 3 \times 3 = 27$, and is symbolized as $\sqrt[3]{27}$. The fourth root of a number is symbolized as $\sqrt[4]{\text{number}}$ and is the value which, when multiplied by itself four times, equals the number; for example, $\sqrt[4]{625} = 5$, and so on with the fifth, sixth, to nth roots.

Appendix III: Answers to Problem Review Exercises

It is presumed that users of this text will work out the problem exercises with a hand-held calculator. In most cases the answers in this appendix have been calculated with an accuracy of two decimal places, and whenever intermediate terms were derived part-way through a calculation, they were ordinarily rounded to two decimal places before proceeding. Sometimes it is more convenient to leave intermediate terms in the calculator register and simply proceed directly with the next step; in such instances the reader may find that his or her final answer is not exactly as presented here.

Chapter 3

Section 3.5

3.5–2: (a) 95.47, 84.59, 0.30
         (b) 19.30, 24.68, 30.98

3.5–3: (a) 3.33, 61.81, 92.71
         (b) 3.47, 3.90, 6.59

Section 3.7

3.7–1: (a) 240 (b) 150 (c) 4065 (d) 36,000 (e) 390 (f) 90
         (g) 8618 (h) 2982 (i) 57,600 (j) 22,500 (k) 2,130,857
         (l) 25,698,876 (m) 1,296,000,000

3.7–2: (a) True (b) True (c) False (d) False (e) False (f) False
         (g) False (h) True

3.7–3: True

Section 3.9

3.9–2: (a) 10 (b) 13 (c) 14.94

3.9–3: (a) 20.50 (b) 18.83 (c) 17.93

3.9–4: (a) 6 (b) 6.30 (c) 6.36

3.9–5: 2.31

3.9–6: (a) 11.36 (b) 3.36 (c) 25.43 (d) 3.18

3.9–7:   63.31

3.9–8:   168.60

3.9–9:   (a) 128.43   (b) 141

3.9–10: 22.12

3.9–11: 3.97

Section 3.11

3.11–2: (a) $s^2 = 3.37$, $s = 1.84$
         (b) $s^2 = 6.67$, $s = 2.58$
         (c) $s^2 = 17.87$, $s = 4.23$
         (d) $s^2 = 16.00$, $s = 4.00$

3.11–3: (a) $s^2 = 9.17$, $s = 3.03$
         (b) $s^2 = 21.12$, $s = 4.60$
         (c) $s^2 = 8.84$, $s = 2.97$
         (d) $s^2 = 5.25$, $s = 2.29$

3.11–4: (a) $s^2 = 16.00$, $s = 4.00$
         (b) $s^2 = 400.00$, $s = 20.00$

3.11–5: (a) $s^2 = 16.00$, $s = 4.00$
         (b) $s^2 = 1.00$, $s = 1.00$

3.11–6: $s^2 = 8.62$, $s = 2.94$

3.11–7: $s^2 = 615.89$, $s = 24.82$

3.11–8: ^{0}C: $\overline{X} = 0.86$, $s = 5.30$
         ^{0}F: $\overline{X} = 33.54$, $s = 9.55$

3.11–9: ^{0}F: $\overline{X} = 81.43$, $s = 3.87$
         ^{0}C: $\overline{X} = 27.46$, $s = 2.15$

Chapter 4

Section 4.4

4.4–2:   (a) 0.3159   (b) 0.4951   (c) 0.4987   (d) 0.3665   (e) 0.0199
         (f) 0.4750

4.4–3:   (a) 0.0359   (b) 0.0125   (c) 0.0793   (d) 0.1611   (e) 0.9750
         (f) 0.9968   (g) 0.9535   (h) 0.7794

4.4–4:   (a) 0.3830   (b) 0.9500   (c) 0.9902   (d) 0.8064   (e) 0.9544
         (f) 0.6578

4.4–5:   (a) 0.8185   (b) 0.8002   (c) 0.6714   (d) 0.8844   (e) 0.0356
         (f) 0.2857   (g) 0.1146   (h) 0.0082

4.4–6:   (a) 0.52   (b) 0.84   (c) 1.65   (d) 0.23   (e) 1.96   (f) 2.58

4.4–7:   (a) +0.67   (b) −0.31   (c) 0.00   (d) −1.65   (e) −0.67
         (f) +0.31   (g) +1.28   (h) −2.33

4.4–8:   (a) ±0.67   (b) ±1.65   (c) ±1.41   (d) ±0.48   (e) ±1.96
         (f) ±2.58

Section 4.6

4.6–1:

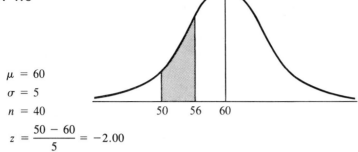

$\mu = 60$

$\sigma = 5$

$n = 40$

$$z = \frac{50 - 60}{5} = -2.00$$

Area between μ and $z = 0.4772$

$$z = \frac{56 - 60}{5} = -0.80$$

Area between μ and $z = 0.2881$

Since $0.4772 - 0.2881 = 0.1891$, then 0.1891 of the students got from 50 to 55 inclusive. Since $n = 40$, then $(40)(0.1891) = 7.56$ and therefore 7.56 students got a lower mark than Dave but still passed (that is, got from 50 to 55 inclusive).

4.6–2: 18.29 minutes

4.6–3: 5.48 left-handers

4.6–4: (a) 47.50 persons
(b) $167.39

4.6–5: (a) 22.80 men plus 370.70 women
(b) anything less than 79.40
(c) anything larger than 105.05

4.6–6:   F = 0 − 59.75
P = 59.76 − 74.72
P+ = 74.73 − 100

4.6–7: 161.70 − 162.30 cm inclusive

4.6–8: (a) 130.76
(b) 6,000,000 − 9,000 = 5,991,000

4.6–9: (a) 264.30
(b) 226.60

4.6–10: (a) 21.19 men plus 10.56 women
(b) more than 24.32 miles
(c) 12.10 women

4.6–11: (a) 401.30
(b) 308.50

4.6–12: (a) 2.70
(b) 322.20 small plus 19.20 large
(c) more than 275.92

4.6–13: (a) more than 26.80
         (b) 201.12
         (c) lemon: more than 25.24
              poor: 21.35 − 25.24
              acceptable: 14.98 − 21.34
              good: less than 14.98

Chapter 5

Section 5.3

5.3–2: (a) 1/6 + 1/6 = 2/6 = 0.3333
        (b) 1/6 + 1/6 + 1/6 = 3/6 = 0.5000
        (c) 1 − 1/6 = 5/6 = 0.8333
        (d) 1 − (1/6 + 1/6 + 1/6) = 3/6 = 0.5000

5.3–3: (a) 13/52 + 13/52 + 13/52 = 3/4 = 0.7500
        (b) 4/52 + 4/52 = 8/52 = 0.1538
        (c) 4/52 + 2/52 = 6/52 = 0.1154
        (d) 4/52 + 4/52 + 4/52 + 4/52 + 4/52 = 20/52 = 0.3846
        (e) 6/52 + 20/52 = 26/52 = 0.5000

5.3–4: (a) 12/62 + 4/62 = 16/62 = 0.2581
        (b) 6/62 + 10/62 + 1/62 = 17/62 = 0.2742
        (c) 3/62 + 8/62 + 18/62 = 29/62 = 0.4677
        (d) 1 − 6/62 = 56/62 = 0.9032
        (e) 1 − (4/62 + 18/62) = 40/62 = 0.6452

5.3–5: (a) 0.15 + 0.25 = 0.40
        (b) 0.20 + 0.15 + 0.10 = 0.45
        (c) 1 − 0.10 = 0.90
        (d) 1 − (0.15 + 0.20) = 0.65
        (e) 1 − (0.30 + 0.25) = 0.45

5.3–6: (a) 1/9 + 3/9 = 4/9 = 0.4444
        (b) 1/9 + 1/9 + 2/9 = 4/9 = 0.4444
        (c) 2/9 + 2/9 + 3/9 = 7/9 = 0.7778
        (d) 1 − 3/9 = 6/9 = 0.6667
        (e) 1 − (1/9 + 1/9 + 2/9) = 5/9 = 0.5556

5.3–7: (a) 0.25 + 0.20 + 0.10 = 0.55
        (b) 0.20 + 0.10 + 0.08 = 0.38
        (c) 1 − 0.25 = 0.75
        (d) 0.10 + 0.10 + 0.10 + 0.20 + 0.25 = 0.75
        (e) 0.25 + 0.20 + 0.08 + 0.01 = 0.54

5.3–8: (a) 1/76 = 0.0132
        (b) 22/76 + 16/76 = 38/76 = 0.5000
        (c) 7/76 + 10/76 + 20/76 = 37/76 = 0.4868
        (d) 1 − 10/76 = 66/76 = 0.8684
        (e) 1 − (22/76 + 20/76 + 1/76) = 33/76 = 0.4342

5.3–9: (a) $14/331 = 0.0423$

(b) $5/331 + 3/331 + 4/331 + 3/331 + 3/331 + 5/331 =$
$23/331 = 0.0695$

(c) $58/331 + 40/331 + 35/331 + 16/331 + 14/331 + 10/331 =$
$173/331 = 0.5227$

(d) $100/331 + 18/331 = 118/331 = 0.3565$

(e) $179/331 = 0.5408$

Section 5.5

5.5–2: (a) $1/2 \times 1/2 \times 1/2 \times 1/2 = 1/16 = 0.0625$

(b) $1/2 \times 1/2 \times 1/2 \times 1/2 = 1/16 = 0.0625$

(c) $1/2 \times 1/2 \times 1/2 \times 1/2 \times 1/2 \times 1/2 = 1/64 = 0.0156$

(d) $1/2 \times 1/2 \times 1/2 \times 1/2 \times 1/2 \times 1/2 \times 1/2 \times 1/2 = 1/256 =$
0.0039

5.5–3: (a) $1/6 \times 1/6 \times 1/6 = 1/216 = 0.0046$

(b) $1/6 \times 1/6 \times 1/6 = 1/216 = 0.0046$

(c) $3/6 \times 3/6 \times 3/6 = 27/216 = 0.1250$

(d) $5/6 \times 5/6 \times 5/6 = 125/216 = 0.5787$

5.5–4: (a) $0.50 \times 0.40 = 0.20$

(b) $0.50 \times (1 - 0.30) = 0.35$

(c) $0.25 \times 0.50 \times (1 - 0.40) = 0.0750$

(d) $0.25 \times 0.50 \times 0.15 \times 0.30 \times 0.40 = 0.0023$

5.5–5: (a) $0.25 \times 0.50 \times 0.10 = 0.0125$

(b) $0.20 \times (0.75 + 0.15) = 0.18$

(c) $(0.30 + 0.20)(0.75 + 0.15) = 0.45$

(d) $1 - (0.30 \times 0.75 \times 0.75) = 0.8313$

5.5–6: (a) $1/20 \times 6/20 = 6/400 = 0.0150$

(b) $(8/20 \times 5/20) + (5/20 \times 8/20) = 80/400 = 0.20$

(c) $5/20 \times 5/20 = 25/400 = 0.0625$

(d) $(8/20 + 1/20)(6/20 + 5/20) = 99/400 = 0.2475$

(e) $(6/20 + 8/20)(6/20 + 1/20) + (6/20 + 1/20) \cdot$
$(6/20 + 8/20) = 196/400 = 0.49$

(f) $(8/20 + 6/20 + 1/20)^2 = 225/400 = 0.5625$

5.5–7: (a) $4/52 \times 4/52 \times 4/52 \times 4/52 = 256/7311616 = 0.000035$

(b) $12/52 \times 12/52 \times 12/52 \times 12/52 = 20736/7311616 = 0.0028$

(c) $1/4 \times 1/4 \times 1/4 \times 1/4 = 1/256 = 0.0039$

(d) $1/4 \times 1/4 \times 1/4 \times 1/4 = 1/256 = 0.0039$

(e) HHHS + HHSH + HSHH + SHHH =
$1/256 + 1/256 + 1/256 + 1/256 =$
$4/256 = 0.0156$

(f) QQKK + QKQK + QKKQ + KKQQ + KQKQ + KQQK =
$(1/13)^4 + (1/13)^4 + (1/13)^4 + (1/13)^4 +$
$(1/13)^4 + (1/13)^4 = 6/28561 = 0.00021$

5.5–8: (a) $(6/15)^5 = 7776/759375 = 0.0102$

(b) $1/15 \times 3/15 \times 4/15 \times 6/15 \times 1/15 = 72/759375 = 0.00009$

(c) $(1/15)^4 \times 1/15 = 1/759375 = 0.0000013$

(d) LLLLC + LLLCL + LLCLL + LCLLL + CLLLL =
$(1/759375) (5) = 5/759375 = 0.0000066$

(e) $4/15 \times 4/15 \times 1/15 \times 1/15 \times 1/15 = 16/759375 = 0.000021$

(f) GGLLL + GLGLL + GLLGL + GLLLG + LGGLL +
LGLGL + LGLLG + LLGGL + LLGLG + LLLGG =
$(16/759375) (10) = 160/759375 = 0.00021$

5.5–9: (a) $(1 - 2/11)(1 - 2/11) = 81/121 = 0.6694$

(b) $1/11 \times 2/11 = 2/121 = 0.0165$

(c) $(5/11 \times 3/11) + (3/11 \times 5/11) = 30/121 = 0.2479$

(d) $1/11 \times (3/11 + 5/11) = 8/121 = 0.0661$

(e) $[(5/11 + 1/11)(2/11 + 3/11)] +$
$[(2/11 + 3/11)(5/11 + 1/11)] = 60/121 = 0.4959$

5.5–10: (a) $(2/20 \times 2/20) + (4/20 \times 4/20) = 20/400 = 0.05$

(b) $(5/20 \times 9/20) + (9/20 \times 5/20) = 90/400 = 0.2250$

(c) $[(5/20 \times 9/20) + (9/20 \times 5/20)] + (5/20 \times 5/20) =$
$115/400 = 0.2875$

(d) $[(2/20 \times 4/20) + (4/20 \times 2/20)] + [(2/20 \times 9/20) +$
$(9/20 \times 2/20)] + [(2/20 \times 5/20) + (5/20 \times 2/20)] =$
$72/400 = 0.18$

(e) $[(5/20 \times 4/20) + (4/20 \times 5/20)] + [(2/20 \times 9/20) +$
$(9/20 \times 2/20)] + [(9/20 \times 4/20) + (4/20 \times 9/20)] =$
$148/400 = 0.37$

5.5–11: (a) $(0.58)^4 = 0.1132$

(b) $(0.21 \times 0.21) + (0.05 \times 0.05) = 0.0466$

(c) [CBB + BCB + BBC] + [STT + TST + TTS] =
$[(0.21 \times 0.05 \times 0.05) + (0.05 \times 0.21 \times 0.05) +$
$(0.05 \times 0.05 \times 0.21)] + [(0.15 \times 0.01 \times 0.01) +$
$(0.01 \times 0.15 \times 0.01) + (0.01 \times 0.01 \times 0.15)] =$
$(0.000525) (3) + (0.000015) (3) = 0.00162$

(d) TTBB + TBTB + TBBT + BBTT + BTBT + BTTB =
$(0.00000025) (6) = 0.0000015$

5.5–12: (a) $(9/20 + 6/20)^3 = 3375/8000 = 0.4219$

(b) $(1/20 + 4/20 + 9/20)^3 = 2744/8000 = 0.3430$

(c) $[(1/20 + 4/20)(9/20 + 6/20)(9/20 + 6/20)] +$
$[(9/20 + 6/20)(1/20 + 4/20)(9/20 + 6/20)] +$
$[(9/20 + 6/20)(9/20 + 6/20)(1/20 + 4/20)] =$
$(1125/8000) (3) = 3375/8000 = 0.4219$

(d) $[(1/20 + 4/20)(9/20 + 6/20)(1/20 + 6/20)] +$
$[(1/20 + 4/20)(1/20 + 6/20)(9/20 + 6/20)] +$
$[(9/20 + 6/20)(1/20 + 4/20)(1/20 + 6/20)] +$
$[(9/20 + 6/20)(1/20 + 6/20)(1/20 + 4/20)] +$
$[(1/20 + 6/20)(1/20 + 4/20)(9/20 + 6/20)] +$
$[(1/20 + 6/20)(9/20 + 6/20)(1/20 + 4/20)] +$
$= (525/8000) (6) = 3150/8000 = 0.3938$

Section 5.7

5.7–1:   (a) 0.0418
           (b) 0.1307
           (c) 0.0509

5.7–2:   (a) 0.0228
           (b) 0.3357
           (c) 0.0500

5.7–3:   (a) 0.3085
           (b) 0.0564
           (c) 0.3632

5.7–4:   (a) 0.7257
           (b) 0.2742
           (c) 0.3336

5.7–5:   (a) 0.1210
           (b) 0.1056
           (c) $(0.2316)^2 = 0.0536$

5.7–6:   (a) $(0.0475)^2 = 0.0023$
           (b) $(0.4706)^2 = 0.2215$
           (c) $(0.6293)^2 = 0.3960$

Section 5.9

5.9–4:   (a) $p = p(\text{Female}) = 0.50$
$$q = p(\text{Male}) = 0.50$$
$$n = 20$$
Frequency of interest = 15
$$\mu_b = np = (20)(0.5) = 10$$
$$\sigma_b = \sqrt{npq} = \sqrt{(20)(0.5)(0.5)} = 2.24$$
$$X_{\text{EL}} = 15.50$$
$$z = (15.50 - 10)/2.24 = 2.46$$

Area beyond $z = 0.0069$, therefore the probability that more than 15 will be female is 0.0069.

       (b) $p = p(\text{Female}) = 0.50$
$$q = p(\text{Male}) = 0.50$$
$$n = 20$$
Frequency of interest = 6
$$\mu_b = np = 10$$
$$\sigma_b = \sqrt{npq} = 2.24$$
$$X_{\text{EL}} = 5.50$$
$$z = (5.50 - 10)/2.24 = -2.01$$

Area beyond $z = 0.0222$, therefore the probability that less than 6 will be male is 0.0222.

5.9–5:   (a) $z = 3.09$, probability = 0.0010
           (b) $z = -1.55$, probability = 0.0606

5.9–6:   (a) $z = 3.20$, probability $= 0.0007$
          (b) $z = -1.20$, probability $= 0.1151$

5.9–7:   (a) $z = 1.27$, probability $= 0.1020$
          (b) $z = -2.12$, probability $= 0.0170$

Chapter 8

Section 8.4

8.4–1:   (a) $n = 36$

$\overline{X} = 170$

$s = 13$

$s_{\overline{x}} = s/\sqrt{n} = 13/\sqrt{36} = 2.17$

(b) $df = n - 1 = 36 - 1 = 35$

$t_{0.05}$ (from Table B) $= \pm 2.030$

Upper Limit of Confidence
Interval $= 170 + (2.030)(2.17) = 174.41$
Lower Limit of Confidence
Interval $= 170 - (2.030)(2.17) = 165.59$
Thus $p[165.59 \le \mu \le 174.41] = 0.95$
Therefore the 0.95 Confidence Interval for rats' population mean weight is 165.59 gm to 174.41 gm.

(c) $df = n - 1 = 35$

$t_{0.01}$ (from Table B) $= \pm 2.724$

Upper Limit of Confidence
Interval $= 170 + (2.724)(2.17) = 175.91$
Lower Limit of Confidence
Interval $= 170 - (2.724)(2.17) = 164.09$
Thus $p[164.09 \le \mu \le 175.91] = 0.99$
Therefore the 0.99 Confidence Interval for rats' population mean weight is 164.09 gm to 175.91 gm.

8.4–2: $10.89 - 13.11$

8.4–3: $18.34 - 23.66$

8.4–4: $48.48 - 51.52$

8.4–5:   No

8.4–6:   Yes

8.4–7: $7.53 - 8.47$

8.4–8:   8.61

8.4–9:   92.99

Section 8.6

8.6–1:   Null hypothesis: Steel workers' annual mean income does not differ from the population annual mean income $(\mu_{\text{steel workers}} = \mu_{\text{population}})$.

$\mu = 15000$

$\overline{X} = 17000$

$s = 5000$

$n = 36$

$s_{\overline{x}} = 5000/\sqrt{36} = 833.33$

$t = \dfrac{17000 - 15000}{833.33} = 2.40$

1. $df = n - 1 = 36 - 1 = 35$
2. The critical value for t at 0.05 confidence level $= 2.030$
3. Therefore the result is significant.
4. Interpretation: Steel workers' annual mean income does differ from the population annual mean income.

8.6–2: $t = -0.50$

8.6–3: $t = -4.02$

8.6–4: $t = 3.85$

8.6–5: $z_{\overline{x}} = 1.33$

8.6–6: $z_{\overline{x}} = 2.32$

Section 8.8

8.8–1: (a) Independent variable: Siamese as compared to Manx cats
(b) Dependent variable: ability to catch mice
(c) Null hypothesis: Siamese and Manx cats do not differ in ability to catch mice ($\mu_{\text{Siamese}} = \mu_{\text{Manx}}$).
(d) Siamese $= X_1$; Manx $= X_2$

$n_1 = 8$ $n_2 = 8$

$\Sigma X_1 = 48$ $\Sigma X_2 = 32$

$\overline{X}_1 = 6.00$ $\overline{X}_2 = 4.00$

$\Sigma X_1^2 = 300$ $\Sigma X_2^2 = 132$

$s^2 = \dfrac{300 - (48)^2/8 + 132 - (32)^2/8}{8 + 8 - 2} = 1.14$

$t = \dfrac{6.00 - 4.00}{\sqrt{1.14/8 + 1.14/8}} = 3.77$

1. $df = 8 + 8 - 2 = 14$
2. The critical value for t at 0.05 confidence level $= 2.145$
3. Therefore the result is significant.

(e) Interpretation: Siamese cats differ from Manx cats in ability to catch mice.

8.8–2: $t = 0.91$

8.8–3: $t = 2.29$

8.8–4: $t = 2.31$

8.8–5: $t = 2.83$

8.8–6: $t = 0.50$

8.8–7: $t = 1.32$

8.8–8: $t = 2.24$

Section 8.10

8.10–1:   (a) Independent variable: colored as compared to grey toys

         (b) Dependent variable: children's preference

         (c) Null hypothesis: children do not show any preference between colored as compared to grey toys $(\mu_{colored} = \mu_{grey})$.

         (d) colored $= X_1$; grey $= X_2$

$$N = 10$$

$$\Sigma D = 39$$

$$\Sigma D^2 = 247$$

$$t = \frac{39}{\sqrt{\dfrac{(10)(247) - (39)^2}{10 - 1}}} = 3.80$$

        1. $df = 10 - 1 = 9$

        2. The critical value for t at 0.05 confidence level $= 2.262$

        3. Therefore the result is significant.

         (e) Interpretation: Children do show a preference between colored as compared to grey toys.

8.10–2: $t = 4.86$

8.10–3: $t = 0.16$

8.10–4: $t = 3.49$

8.10–5: $t = 5.24$

8.10–6: $t = 6.33$

8.10–7: $t = 2.52$

8.10–8: $t = 4.58$

8.10–9:   independent groups; $t = 1.67$
repeated measures/correlated samples; $t = 3.16$

8.10–10:   independent groups; $t = 2.00$

8.10–11:   repeated measures; $t = 3.31$

8.10–12:   repeated measures; $t = 4.00$

8.10–13:   independent groups; $t = 3.00$

8.10–14:   correlated samples; $t = 3.57$

8.10–15:   independent groups; $t = 2.33$

8.10–16: repeated measures; $t = 6.32$

8.10–17: correlated samples; $t = 2.00$

8.10–18: repeated measures; $t = 4.00$

Chapter 9

Section 9.5

9.5–2: (a) Independent variable: age

(b) Dependent variable: generosity

(c) Null hypothesis: age is not related to generosity
$$(\mu_4 = \mu_{14} = \mu_{24}).$$

(d) $k = 3; n = 8; N = 24$

(1) $\Sigma X^2 = 138.00$

(2) $(\Sigma X)^2/N = 96.00$

(3) $\Sigma(T^2/n) = 115.75$

Source of variation	Sum of squares	df	Mean square	F
Between groups	19.75	2	9.88	9.32
Within groups	22.25	21	1.06	

1. $df = 2/21$

2. The critical value for F at 0.05 confidence level $= 3.47$

3. Therefore the result is significant.

(e) Interpretation: age is related to generosity.

9.5–3: $F = 31.30/8.82 = 3.55$

9.5–4: $F = 113.89/10.62 = 10.72$

9.5–5: $F = 53.00/5.54 = 9.57$

9.5–6: $F = 62.53/2.55 = 24.52$

9.5–7: $F = 454.43/918.15 = 0.49$

9.5–8: $F = 7.12/1.19 = 5.98$

9.5–9: $F = 3.25/0.70 = 4.64$

9.5–10: $F = 7.41/0.79 = 9.38$

Section 9.8

9.8–2: (a) Independent variable: number of weeks of training

(b) Dependent variable: performance (percentage of correct responses)

(c) Null hypothesis: number of weeks of training does not affect performance ($\mu_1 = \mu_2 = \mu_3$).

(d) $k = 3; n = 4; N = 12$

(1) $\Sigma X^2 = 36024.00$

(2) $(\Sigma X)^2/N = 35643.00$

(3) $\Sigma T^2/n = 35896.50$

(4) $\Sigma R^2/k = 35716.00$

Source of variation	Sum of squares	df	Mean square	F
Between subjects	73.00	3		
Within subjects	308.00	8		
Treatment	253.50	2	126.75	13.96
Residual	54.50	6	9.08	

1. $df = 2/6$

2. The critical value for F at 0.05 confidence level $= 5.14$

3. Therefore the result is significant.

(e) Interpretation: number of weeks of training does affect performance.

9.8–3: $F = 10.50/0.93 = 11.29$

9.8–4: $F = 13.81/0.37 = 37.32$

9.8–5: $F = 26.60/2.18 = 12.20$

9.8–6: $F = 52.42/10.24 = 5.12$

9.8–7: $F = 2.37/2.94 = 0.81$

9.8–8: $F = 35.53/1.76 = 20.19$

9.8–9: $F = 11.27/0.75 = 15.03$

9.8–10: (a) $F = 218.33/14.00 = 15.60$
(b) $F = 286.00/14.00 = 20.43$

9.8–11: $F = 0.00/9.50 = 0.00$

9.8–12: (a) $F = 3.17/1.08 = 2.94$
(b) $F = 3.17/0.23 = 13.78$

9.8–13: independent groups; $F = 5.00$

9.8–14: repeated measures; $F = 3.34$

9.8–15: repeated measures; $F = 4.00$

9.8–16: repeated measures; $F = 3.00$

9.8–17: repeated measures; $F = 4.00$

9.8–18: independent groups; $F = 2.93$

9.8–19: independent groups; $F = 5.95$

9.8–20: independent groups; $F = 4.20$

9.8–21: repeated measures; $F = 2.60$

9.8–22: $F = 287/100 = 2.87$
9.8–23: $F = 160/45 = 3.56$
9.8–24: $F = 60/20 = 3.00$

Chapter 10

Section 10.4

10.4–2: $k = 3; n = 8; N = 24$
  $T_1 = 26; T_2 = 13; T_3 = 9$
  $MS_{error} = 1.06; df MS_{error} = 21$
  $CD = [q_{0.05}(3, 21)][\sqrt{nMS_{error}}]$
    $= [3.58][2.91]$
    $= 10.42$
  $T_1 - T_2 = 26 - 13 = 13$: Significant
  $T_1 - T_3 = 26 - 9 = 17$: Significant
  $T_2 - T_3 = 13 - 9 = 4$: Not Significant

  Since $T_1 = 4$-year-olds, $T_2 = 14$-year-olds, and $T_3 = 24$-year-olds, we can say that 4-year-olds differ in generosity from 14-year-olds and from 24-year-olds, and that 14-year-olds do not differ in generosity from 24-year-olds.

10.4–3: $CD = 31.60$
10.4–4: $CD = 15.60$
10.4–5: $CD = 11.54$
10.4–6: $CD = 26.17$
10.4–7: $CD = 6.44$
10.4–8: $CD = 33.16$
10.4–9: $CD = 16.38$

Chapter 11

Section 11.3

11.3–2: (a) Independent variable A: location of questions
      Independent variable B: type of question
    (b) Dependent variable: degree (or amount) of learning
    (c) Null hypotheses: (1) location of questions does not affect degree of learning ($\mu_{beginning} = \mu_{throughout}$).
              (2) type of question does not affect degree of learning ($\mu_{fact} = \mu_{concept}$).
              (3) location of questions and type of question do not interact to affect degree of learning.

(d) $p = 2;\ q = 2;\ n = 6;\ N = 24$

(1) $\sum X^2 = 16348.00$

(2) $(\sum X)^2/N = 16016.67$

(3) $\sum A^2/nq = 16083.33$

(4) $\sum B^2/np = 16016.67$

(5) $\sum (AB)^2/n = 16100.00$

Source of variation	Sum of Squares	df	Mean Square	F
A	66.66	1	66.66	5.38
B	0.00	1	0.00	0.00
AB	16.67	1	16.67	1.34
Residual	248.00	20	12.40	

1. df for all F ratios $= 1/20$

2. The critical value for F at 0.05 confidence level $= 4.35$

3. Therefore: Variable A is significant.
   Variable B is not significant.
   The AB interaction is not significant.

(e) Interpretation: (1) location of questions does affect degree of learning.

(2) type of question does not affect degree of learning.

(3) location of questions and type of question do not interact to affect degree of learning.

Since the AB interaction was not significant no simple effects tests are called for, and since there were only two levels of variable A no main effects test is called for.

11.3–3: $F_A = 157.50/3.83 = 41.12$
$F_B = 83.33/3.83 = 21.76$
$F_{AB} = 0.84/3.83 = 0.22$
Main Effects Tukey HSD Critical Difference for overall A totals $= 21.85$

11.3–4: $F_A = 57.16/7.83 = 7.30$
$F_B = 288.17/7.83 = 36.80$
$F_{AB} = 15.17/7.83 = 1.94$
Main Effects Tukey HSD Critical Difference for overall B totals $= 36.54$

11.3–5: $F_A = 16.67/14.00 = 1.19$
$F_B = 0.00/14.00 = 0.00$
$F_{AB} = 6016.67/14.00 = 429.76$

Simple Effects Tukey HSD Critical Difference for As at levels of $B = 29.17$
Simple Effects Tukey HSD Critical Difference for Bs at levels of $A = 21.84$

11.3–6: $F_A = 0.00/4.06 = 0.00$
  $F_B = 11.67/4.06 = 2.87$
  $F_{AB} = 81.67/4.06 = 20.12$
  Simple Effects Tukey HSD Critical Difference for As at levels of $B = 15.74$
  Simple Effects Tukey HSD Critical Difference for Bs at levels of $A = 15.74$

11.3–7: $F_A = 229.69/4.22 = 54.43$
  $F_B = 14.06/4.22 = 3.33$
  $F_{AB} = 47.74/4.22 = 11.31$
  Simple Effects Tukey HSD Critical Difference for As at levels of $B = 15.58$
  Simple Effects Tukey HSD Critical Difference for Bs at levels of $A = 15.58$

Chapter 12

Section 12.5

12.5–2: (a) Variable X: hours of food deprivation
   Variable Y: running speed
   Null hypothesis: hours of food deprivation and running speed are not related ($r_{\text{population}} = 0$).

 (b) $N = 10$
   $\Sigma X = 60; \Sigma Y = 200; \Sigma XY = 1500; \Sigma X^2 = 476; \Sigma Y^2 = 5400$

$$r = \frac{(10)(1500) - (60)(200)}{\sqrt{[(10)(476) - (60)^2][(10)(5400) - (200)^2]}}$$
$$= +0.74$$

   1. $df = 10 - 2 = 8$

   2. The critical value for r at 0.05 confidence level $= 0.632$

   3. Therefore the result is significant.

 (c) Interpretation: There is a relationship between hours of food deprivation and running speed such that longer deprivation is associated with faster running speed.

12.5–3: $r = -0.90$

12.5–4: $r = -0.74$

12.5–5: $r = +0.90$

12.5–6: $r = -0.99$

12.5–7: $r = +0.99$

12.5–8: $r = +0.93$

12.5–9: $r = -0.95$

Section 12.9

12.9–2: $r_1 = -0.80; n_1 = 20; z_{r1} = 1.099$

$r_2 = -0.50; n_2 = 20; z_{r2} = 0.549$

$$z = \frac{1.099 - 0.549}{\sqrt{1/(20 - 3) + 1/(20 - 3)}} = 1.60$$

1. The critical value for z at 0.05 confidence level = 1.96
2. Therefore the result is not significant.
3. Interpretation: The degree of relationship between the amount of time to complete the task and the number of errors made does not differ under noisy as compared to quiet conditions.

12.9–3: $z = 2.29$

12.9–4: $z = 1.63$

12.9–5: $z = 3.20$

Note: Section 12.9 answers were calculated using four decimal places accuracy in the intermediate terms.

Chapter 13

Section 13.3

13.3–2: creativity = X; telepathy = Y

$N = 8; \Sigma X = 32; \Sigma Y = 106; \Sigma X^2 = 208; \Sigma XY = 242$

$$b_{YX} = \frac{(8)(242) - (32)(106)}{(8)(208) - (32)^2} = -2.275$$

$$c_{YX} = \frac{106 - (-2.275)(32)}{8} = 22.350$$

Therefore: $\hat{Y} = -2.275X + 22.350$

when creativity = 5, predicted telepathy = 10.98

when creativity = 9, predicted telepathy = 1.88

when creativity = 3, predicted telepathy = 15.53

13.3-3: $\hat{Y} = -23.43X + 23.55$
   when $X = 0$, $\hat{Y} = 23.55$
   when $X = 1.00$, $\hat{Y} = 0.12$

13.3-4: $\hat{Y} = 26.24X + 0.0080$
   (a) when $X = 6$, $\hat{Y} = 157.45$
     when $X = 15$, $\hat{Y} = 393.61$
     when $X = 20$, $\hat{Y} = 524.81$
   (b) $X = 1.91$ predicts $\hat{Y} = 50$
     $X = 3.81$ predicts $\hat{Y} = 100$
     $X = 7.62$ predicts $\hat{Y} = 200$

13.3-5: $\hat{Y} = -0.0383X + 0.8100$
   (a) when $X = 14$, $\hat{Y} = 0.27$
     when $X = 5$, $\hat{Y} = 0.62$
     when $X = 22$, $\hat{Y} = 0.03$
   (b) $X = 8.09$ predicts $\hat{Y} = 0.50$
     $X = 14.62$ predicts $\hat{Y} = 0.25$
     $X = 21.15$ predicts $\hat{Y} = 0.00$

13.3-6: $\hat{Y} = 0.0265X - 0.3604$
   (a) when $X = 30$, $\hat{Y} = 0.43$
     when $X = 18$, $\hat{Y} = 0.12$
     when $X = 50$, $\hat{Y} = 0.96$
   (b) $X = 24.92$ predicts $\hat{Y} = 0.30$
     $X = 41.90$ predicts $\hat{Y} = 0.75$
     $X = 49.45$ predicts $\hat{Y} = 0.95$

13.3-7: $\hat{Y} = 0.3968X - 4.2386$
   (a) when $X = 75$, $\hat{Y} = 25.52$
     when $X = 23$, $\hat{Y} = 4.89$
     when $X = 40$, $\hat{Y} = 11.63$
   (b) $X = 61.09$ predicts $\hat{Y} = 20$
     $X = 35.88$ predicts $\hat{Y} = 10$
     $X = 10.68$ predicts $\hat{Y} = 0.00$

13.3-8: $\hat{Y} = 0.3823X - 0.8774$
   (a) when $X = 7$, $\hat{Y} = 1.80$
     when $X = 14$, $\hat{Y} = 4.47$
     when $X = 28$, $\hat{Y} = 9.83$
   (b) $X = 15.40$ predicts $\hat{Y} = 5$
     $X = 28.45$ predicts $\hat{Y} = 10$
     $X = 54.61$ predicts $\hat{Y} = 20$

13.3-9: $\hat{Y} = 1.189X + 1.256$
   (a) when $X = 10$, $\hat{Y} = 13.15$

(b)	1980	1990	2000	2010
Population	6.56	9.84	14.76	22.14
Food	6.25	7.00	7.75	8.50

Note: The secret to this answer is to realize that population increases geometrically while food production increases arithmetically. If you plot the original X and Y data, along with the extension shown here, you will see that X and Y do not have a linear relationship and therefore a linear regression was inappropriate in the first place.

Section 13.5

13.5–2:   Null hypothesis: Creativity does not predict a significant portion of the variance of telepathy.

$N = 8; \Sigma X = 32; \Sigma Y = 106; \Sigma XY = 242; \Sigma X^2 = 208;$
$\Sigma Y^2 = 1952$

$\hat{Y} = -2.275X + 22.350$

$$SS_{\hat{Y}} = [-2.275]\left[242 - \frac{(32)(106)}{8}\right] = 414.05$$

$SS_Y = 1952 - (106)^2/8 = 547.50$

$SS_{(Y-\hat{Y})} = 547.50 - 414.05 = 133.45$

$$F = \frac{414.05}{133.45/6} = 18.62$$

  1. $df = 1/6$

  2.   The critical value for F at 0.05 confidence level = 5.99

  3.   Therefore the result is significant.

  4.   Interpretation: Creativity does predict a significant portion of the variance of telepathy.

13.5–3: $F = 169.63/4.85 = 34.98$

13.5–4: $F = 21207.17/298.54 = 71.04$

13.5–5: $F = 0.3972/0.0190 = 20.91$

13.5–6: $F = 0.5279/0.0079 = 66.82$

13.5–7: $F = 570.48/2.48 = 230.03$

13.5–8: $F = 47.12/0.95 = 49.60$

Section 13.9

13.9–2:   (a)   RAW SCORES; $N = 6$

X_1	X_2	Y
18	1	.25
20	5	.35
25	6	.3
30	8	.2
40	10	.15
47	10	.05

$$\sum X_1 = 180$$
$$\sum X_2 = 40$$
$$\sum Y = 1.3$$
$$\sum X_1^2 = 6058$$
$$\sum X_2^2 = 326$$
$$\sum Y^2 = .34$$
$$\sum X_1 X_2 = 1378$$
$$\sum X_1 Y = 33.35$$
$$\sum X_2 Y = 7.4$$
$$\hat{Y} = -0.0149194X_1 + 0.0234097X_2 + 0.508182$$

(b) $SS_{total} = 0.0583334$

$SS_{regression} = 0.054642$

$SS_{error} = 0.00369142$

(c) $F = 0.027321/0.00123047 = 22.2037$

$df = 2/3$

(d) $R^2 = 0.936719$

(e) 1. When $X_1 = 21$ and $X_2 = 9$, $\hat{Y} = 0.4054999$

2. When $X_1 = 45$ and $X_2 = 9$, $\hat{Y} = 0.0474343$

13.9–3: (a) RAW SCORES; $N = 10$

X_1	X_2	Y
2.5	90	2
3	130	3.5
4	140	3.5
3.5	100	3
3.5	120	4
2	110	2
3.5	120	3
3	100	2.5
2	90	1.5
4	110	3

$$\sum X_1 = 31$$
$$\sum X_2 = 1110$$
$$\sum Y = 28$$
$$\sum X_1^2 = 101$$
$$\sum X_2^2 = 125700$$
$$\sum Y^2 = 84$$
$$\sum X_1 X_2 = 3505$$
$$\sum X_1 Y = 91$$

$$\sum X_2 Y = 3200$$

$$\hat{Y} = 0.563849X_1 + 0.0224553X_2 - 1.44047$$

(b) $SS_{total} = 5.6$

$SS_{regression} = 4.43405$

$SS_{error} = 1.16595$

(c) $F = 2.21703/0.166564 = 13.3104$

$df = 2/7$

(d) $R^2 = 0.791795$

(e) 1. When $X_1 = 3.70$ and $X_2 = 95$, $\hat{Y} = 2.7790248$

2. When $X_1 = 2.90$ and $X_2 = 132$, $\hat{Y} = 3.1587917$

13.9–4: (a) RAW SCORES; $N = 7$

X_1	X_2	Y
5	50	8
10	20	6
0	60	10
25	10	4
3	30	7
10	45	8
30	0	4

$\sum X_1 = 83$

$\sum X_2 = 215$

$\sum Y = 47$

$\sum X_1^2 = 1759$

$\sum X_2^2 = 9525$

$\sum Y^2 = 345$

$\sum X_1 X_2 = 1240$

$\sum X_1 Y = 421$

$\sum X_2 Y = 1730$

$\hat{Y} = -0.0420997X_1 + 0.0791763X_2 + 4.78162$

(b) $SS_{total} = 29.4286$

$SS_{regression} = 28.416$

$SS_{error} = 1.01261$

(c) $F = 14.208/0.253152 = 56.1242$

$df = 2/4$

(d) $R^2 = 0.965591$

(e) 1. When $X_1 = 50$ and $X_2 = 120$, $\hat{Y} = 12.177791$

2. When $X_1 = 2$ and $X_2 = 2$, $\hat{Y} = 4.8557732$

13.9–5: (a) RAW SCORES; $N = 10$

X_1	X_2	Y
2	12	5
6	14	30
9	20	35
7	18	25
12	22	40
4	14	10
1	13	10
3	15	20
6	16	5
10	16	20

$\sum X_1 = 60$

$\sum X_2 = 160$

$\sum Y = 200$

$\sum X_1^2 = 476$

$\sum X_2^2 = 2650$

$\sum Y^2 = 5400$

$\sum X_1 X_2 = 1048$

$\sum X_1 Y = 1500$

$\sum X_2 Y = 3480$

$\hat{Y} = 0.875371 X_1 + 2.25519 X_2 - 21.3353$

(b) $SS_{total} = 1400$

$SS_{regression} = 894.065$

$SS_{error} = 505.935$

(c) $F = 447.033/72.2764 = 6.18505$

$df = 2/7$

(d) $R^2 = 0.638618$

(e) 1. When $X_1 = 5$ and $X_2 = 10$, $\hat{Y} = 5.593455$

2. When $X_1 = 10$ and $X_2 = 21$, $\hat{Y} = 34.7774$

Chapter 14

Section 14.4

14.4–2: Assumption being tested: Susan guessed at all items.
Nominal measurement classes: correct and incorrect ($k = 2$)

	O	E	$O - E$	$(O - E)^2$	$(O - E)^2/E$
Correct	45	35	10	100	2.86
Incorrect	25	35	−10	100	2.86
	70	70			$\chi^2 = 5.72$

1. $df = 2 - 1 = 1$
2. The critical value for χ^2 at 0.05 confidence level = 3.84
3. Therefore the result is significant.
4. Interpretation: Susan did not guess at all items.

14.4–3: $\chi^2 = 1.66$
14.4–4: $\chi^2 = 3.14$
14.4–5: $\chi^2 = 458.33$
14.4–6: $\chi^2 = 14.90$
14.4–7: $\chi^2 = 6.50$
14.4–8: $\chi^2 = 1.88$
14.4–9: $\chi^2 = 39.70$

Section 14.6

14.6–2: (a) Variables: Attendance in class and success in the course.
  (b) Null hypothesis: Attendance in class and success in the course are not related (i.e., are independent).

  (c)

	Pass	Fail	
Attend	5 / 9	5 / 1	10
Not attend	5 / 1	5 / 9	10
	10	10	20

$\chi^2 = 12.80$

1. $df = (2 - 1)(2 - 1) = 1$
2. The critical value for χ^2 at 0.05 confidence level = 3.84
3. Therefore the result is significant.

  (d) Interpretation: There is a relationship between attendance in class and success in the course.

14.6–3: $\chi^2 = 11.25$
14.6–4: $\chi^2 = 40.25$
14.6–5: $\chi^2 = 33.66$
14.6–6: $\chi^2 = 40.00$
14.6–7: $\chi^2 = 1.57$
14.6–8: $\chi^2 = 8.42$
14.6–9: $\chi^2 = 2.73$

14.6–10: $\chi^2 = 21.20$

14.6–11: $\chi^2 = 0.87$

Section 14.8

14.8–1: Null hypothesis: Rats do not show a left-right turning preference in a T-maze.

Thus: $p(\text{Left}) = 0.50$

$p(\text{Alternative}) = 0.50$

$n = 8; r = 7$

probability $= \binom{8}{7}(0.50)^7(0.50)^1 = 0.03$

Since the probability of occurrence of the observed events, given the null hypothesis, is less than 0.05 we may reject the null hypothesis and interpret the result to mean that the rats do show a turning preference in the T-maze.

14.8–2: probability $= 0.03$

14.8–3: probability $= 0.09$

14.8–4: probability $= 0.12$

14.8–5: probability $= 0.07$

14.8–6: probability $= 0.055$

Chapter 15

Section 15.2

15.2–2: (a) Null hypothesis: There is no relationship between teacher's ranking of intellectual potential and I.Q. test performance ranks ($\tau_{\text{population}} = 0$).

(b) $N = 10$

Teacher's ranks	I.Q. test ranks	A	I
1	2	8	1
2	1	8	0
3	4	6	1
4	3	6	0
5	6	4	1
6	5	4	0
7	8	2	1
8	7	2	0
9	10	0	1
10	9	0	0
		$A = 40$	$I = 5$

$$\tau = \frac{40 - 5}{(10)(10 - 1)/2} = +0.778$$

1. $N = 10$

2. The critical value for τ at 0.05 confidence level = 0.511

3. Therefore the result is significant.

(c) Interpretation: Teacher's ranking of intellectual potential is related to I.Q. test performance ranks such that higher teacher's ranks are associated with higher I.Q. test performance ranks.

15.2–3: $\tau = +0.143$

15.2–4: $\tau = +0.556$

15.2–5: $\tau = +0.619$

15.2–6: $\tau = -0.810$

15.2–7: $\tau = +0.511$

15.2–8: $\tau = -0.786$

15.2–9: $\tau = +0.467$

15.2–10: $\tau = +0.733$

Section 15.4

15.4–1: This solution represents the Mann-Whitney U-test applied to the data of Exercise 8.8–1.

Independent variable: Siamese as compared to Manx cats

Dependent variable: ability to catch mice

Null hypothesis: Siamese and Manx cats do not differ in ability to catch mice.

Score: 3,   3,   4, 4, 4, 4, 4,   5,   5,   5,   5,   6,   6,   7,   7,   8

Rank: 1.5, 1.5, 5, 5, 5, 5, 5, 9.5, 9.5, 9.5, 9.5, 12.5, 12.5, 14.5, 14.5, 16

Group: B   B   B B B B A B   B   A   A   A   A   A   A   A

$n_A = 8; \sum R_A = 94; n_B = 8; \sum R_B = 42$

$U_{smaller} = (8)(8) + (8)(8 + 1)/2 - 94 = 6.00$

1. $n_A = 8, n_B = 8$

2. The critical value for $U_{smaller}$ at 0.05 confidence level = 13

3. Therefore the result is significant.

4. Interpretation: Siamese cats differ from Manx cats in ability to catch mice.

15.4–2: $U_{smaller} = 14$ (8.8–2)

15.4–3: $U_{smaller} = 31$ (8.8–3)

15.4–4: $U_{smaller} = 38.5$ (8.8–4)

15.4–5: $U_{smaller} = 7$ (8.8–5)

15.4–6: $U_{smaller} = 34.5$ (8.8–6)

15.4–7: $U_{smaller} = 67$ (8.8–7)

15.4–8: $U_{smaller} = 17$ (8.8–8)

Section 15.6

15.6–1: This solution represents the Wilcoxon matched-pairs signed-ranks test applied to the data of Exercise 8.10–1.

Independent variable: Colored as compared to grey toys

Dependent variable: children's preference

Null hypothesis: Children do not show any preference between colored as compared to grey toys.

Colored	Grey	Difference	Rank	Signed-rank
20	10	+10	9	+9
15	15	0	*	*
16	12	+4	4	+4
15	10	+5	5.5	+5.5
18	12	+6	7.5	+7.5
10	8	+2	2.5	+2.5
20	15	+5	5.5	+5.5
16	10	+6	7.5	+7.5
16	14	+2	2.5	+2.5
10	11	−1	1	−1

$T^- = 1; T^+ = 44$

Therefore $T = 1$

1. $N = 9$

2. The critical value for T at 0.05 confidence level $= 5$

3. Therefore the result is significant.

4. Interpretation: Children do show a preference between colored as compared to grey toys.

15.6–2: $T = 0$ (8.10–2)

15.6–3: $T = 36$ (8.10–3)

15.6–4: $T = 2$ (8.10–4)

15.6–5: $T = 0$ (8.10–5)

15.6–6: $T = 0$ (8.10–6)

15.6–7: $T = 1.5$ (8.10–7)

15.6–8: $T = 0$ (8.10–8)

Answers to Exercises in Appendix V

1: (a) $4/52 + 4/52 = 8/52 = 0.1538$
    (b) $4/52 + 13/52 − (4/52 \times 13/52) = 832/2704 = 0.3077$
    (c) $4/52 + 26/52 − (4/52 \times 26/52) = 1456/2704 = 0.5385$
    (d) $13/52 + 12/52 − (13/52 \times 12/52) = 1144/2704 = 0.4231$

2: (a) $0.20 \times 0.31 = 0.0620$
    (b) $0.20 + 0.31 − (0.20 \times 0.31) = 0.4480$
    (c) $0.15 + 0.45 − (0.15 \times 0.45) = 0.5325$

(d) $0.70 + 0.31 - (0.70 \times 0.31) = 0.7930$
(e) $0.50 \times 0.10 \times [0.15 + 0.20 - (0.15 \times 0.20)] = 0.0160$
(f) $0.15 \times [0.31 + 0.20 - (0.31 \times 0.20)] \times 0.70 = 0.0473$

3:      $0.40 + 0.20 - 0.10 = 0.50$

4:      (a) $0.55 + 0.45 - 0.13 = 0.87$
         (b) $0.55 + 0.45 - (0.55 \times 0.45) = 0.75$

5:      (a) $4/52 \times 4/51 = 16/2652 = 0.0060$
         (b) $13/52 \times 13/51 = 169/2652 = 0.00038$
         (c) $12/52 \times 11/51 = 132/2652 = 0.0498$
         (d) $1/52 \times 1/51 \times 1/50 \times 1/49 \times 1/48 = 1/311875200 = 0.0000000032$
         (e) $4/52 \times 4/51 \times 4/50 \times 4/49 \times 4/48 = 1024/311875200 = 0.0000033$
         (f) $4/52 \times 1/51 \times 1/50 \times 1/49 \times 1/48 = 4/311875200 = 0.000000013$

6:      (a) $0.05 \times 0.44 = 0.0220$
         (b) $0.21 \times 0.1048 = 0.0220$

7:      (a) $0.02 \times 0.19 = 0.0038$
         (b) $0.02 \times 0.19 = 0.0038$

8:      $p(\text{SA}) = (0.64 \times 0.20)/0.32 = 0.4000$
     Thus $p(\text{SA} \cap \text{BE}) = 0.40 \times 0.32 = 0.1280$

9:      $p(\text{dying if drive}) = 0.01 \times 0.30 = 0.003$
     $p(\text{dying if fly}) = 0.001 \times 0.99 = 0.00099$
     $p(\text{dying if hitchhike}) = (0.05 \times 0.50) + (0.02 \times 0.50) + (0.01 \times 0.50) = 0.04$
     Therefore you should fly.

10:      $p(\text{dying if stay put}) = (0.15 \times 0.90) + (0.02 \times 0.99) + 0.25 = 0.4048$
     $p(\text{dying if go}) = (0.40 \times 0.90) + (0.10 \times 0.99) = 0.4590$
     Therefore he should stay put.

11:      (a) $2/10 \times 1/9 = 2/90 = 0.0222$
         (b) $7/10 \times 1/7 = 7/70 = 0.1000$

12:      (a) $1/5 \times 1/4 \times 1/3 \times 1/2 \times 1/1 = 1/120 = 0.0083$
         (b) $4/20 + 5/20 - (4/20 \times 5/20) = 8/20 = 0.4000$

13:      $[0.40 + 0.10 - (0.40 \times 0.10)][0.40 + 0.10 - (0.40 \times 0.10)] = (0.46)^2 = 0.2116$

14:      (a) $45/100 + 2/100 = 47/100 = 0.47$
         (b) $(5/100 \times 10/99) + (10/100 \times 5/99) = 100/9900 = 0.0101$

15:      (a) $[0.80 + 0.25 - (0.80 \times 0.25)]^4 = 0.5220$
         (b) $(0.25 \times 0.40 \times 0.40 \times 0.40)(4) = 0.0640$

16:      (a) $13/25 + 2/25 - (13/25 \times 2/25) = 349/625 = 0.5584$
         (b) $7/25 \times 6/24 \times 5/23 \times 4/22 = 840/303600 = 0.0028$

(c) $17/25 \times 16/24 \times 15/23 \times 14/22 = 57120/303600 = 0.1881$
(All eight blacks finish if the four which drop out are non-blacks.)

(d) $(4/25 \times 12/25)(2/24 \times 11/24) = 1056/360000 = 0.0029$

(e) $[(13/25 \times 8/25)(12/24 \times 7/24)] +$
$[(13/25 \times 7/25)(12/24 \times 8/24)] = 17472/360000 = 0.0485$

17: (a) $3/33 \times 2/32 \times 1/31 = 6/32736 = 0.00018$

(b) $(9/33 \times 10/32) + (10/33 \times 9/32) = 180/1056 = 0.1705$

(c) $32/33 \times 31/32 \times 30/31 = 29760/32736 = 0.9091$
(The bourbon reaches your table if the three that are spilled are non-bourbon.)

(d) $(1/33 \times 4/32 \times 10/31) + (1/33 \times 10/32 \times 4/31) +$
$(4/33 \times 1/32 \times 10/31) + (4/33 \times 10/31 \times 1/31) +$
$(10/33 \times 1/32 \times 4/31) + (10/33 \times 4/32 \times 1/31) =$
$(40/32736)(6) = 240/32736 = 0.0073$

Appendix IV:
Analysis Programs in
BASIC Computer Language

This appendix contains programs in BASIC computer language that may be used to perform many of the calculations in this text. Each program is presented in an explicit format and is accompanied by an instructional example. Students new to BASIC programming should not have any difficulty seeing how the programs set up and execute the steps of the computations. Readers who are proficient in BASIC may wish to enhance the efficiency and features of these programs. The programs in this appendix are written in Microsoft BASIC but use commands which are common to virtually all varieties of BASIC; thus these programs should run on any brand of microcomputer with minimal if any need for transformation. The display output of these programs assumes a 40 column display. If your computer has an 80 column display you may wish to revise some of the PRINT statements appropriately.

Program 1: Descriptive Statistics

```
10 REM DESCRIPTIVE STATISTICS
20 CLS
30 PRINT "ENTER N:";
40 INPUT N
50 CLS
60 PRINT "N =";N
70 PRINT
80 PRINT "ENTER RAW SCORES; HIT RETURN AFTER EACH"
90 PRINT
100 FOR A=1 TO N
110 INPUT X
120 LET EX=EX+X
130 LET X2=X*X
140 LET EX2=EX2+X2
150 NEXT A
160 PRINT
170 PRINT "CHECK YOUR RAW DATA FOR ACCURACY"
180 PRINT
```

410

```
190 PRINT "TO CONTINUE PUSH ANY KEY THEN RETURN"
200 PRINT
210 INPUT A$
220 IF A$="" THEN 210
230 CLS
240 PRINT "N =";N
250 PRINT
260 PRINT "SUM X =";EX
270 PRINT "MEAN =";EX/N
280 PRINT "SUM X SQUARED =";EX2
290 LET EXQ2=EX*EX
300 LET SS=EX2-EXQ2/N
310 PRINT "SUM OF SQUARES =";SS
320 PRINT
330 PRINT "POPULATION VARIANCE =";SS/N
340 PRINT "POPULATION S.D. =";SQR (SS/N)
350 PRINT "SAMPLE VARIANCE =";SS/(N-1)
360 PRINT "SAMPLE S.D. =";SQR (SS/(N-1))
370 END
```

Instructions

When the program is loaded, type RUN and push RETURN. The screen will display

ENTER N:?

Enter the value of n. Using the data presented in Section 3.7 as an example, if we enter 8 and push RETURN the screen will display

N = 8

ENTER RAW SCORES; HIT RETURN AFTER EACH

?

Now enter each raw score in turn and push RETURN after each entry. When RETURN is pushed for the eighth time the screen will display

N = 8

ENTER RAW SCORES; HIT RETURN AFTER EACH

?   20
?   23
?   18
?   31
?   27
?   26
?   21
?   30

CHECK YOUR RAW DATA FOR ACCURACY

TO CONTINUE PUSH ANY KEY THEN RETURN

?

Now push any key and then RETURN and the screen will display

N = 8
SUM X = 196
MEAN = 24.5
SUM X SQUARED = 4960
SUM OF SQUARES = 158 .
POPULATION VARIANCE = 19.75
POPULATION S. D. = 4.4441
SAMPLE VARIANCE = 22.5714
SAMPLE S. D. = 4.75094

Note: In the program EX is used for ΣX, EX2 for ΣX^2, and EXQ2 for $(\Sigma X)^2$. All of the programs in this appendix provide an opportunity to check that the raw data have been entered accurately; however, there is no provision to revise the scores. If you find that you have entered scores incorrectly then you must rerun the program from the beginning.

Program 2: The 0.95 Confidence Interval for the Population Mean Given a Sample Mean, Standard Deviation, and N

```
10 REM 0.95 CONFIDENCE INTERVAL
20 CLS
30 PRINT "ENTER N:";
40 INPUT N
50 CLS
60 PRINT "ENTER SAMPLE MEAN:";
70 INPUT X
80 CLS
90 PRINT "ENTER STANDARD DEVIATION:";
100 INPUT S
110 CLS
120 PRINT "N =";N
130 PRINT
140 PRINT "SAMPLE MEAN =";X
150 PRINT
160 PRINT "STANDARD DEVIATION =";S
170 PRINT
180 IF N=2 THEN LET T=12.706
190 IF N=3 THEN LET T=4.303
200 IF N=4 THEN LET T=3.182
210 IF N=5 THEN LET T=2.776
220 IF N=6 THEN LET T=2.571
230 IF N=7 THEN LET T=2.447
240 IF N=8 THEN LET T=2.365
```

```
250 IF N=9 THEN LET T=2.306
260 IF N=10 THEN LET T=2.262
270 IF N=11 THEN LET T=2.228
280 IF N=12 THEN LET T=2.201
290 IF N=13 THEN LET T=2.179
300 IF N=14 THEN LET T=2.16
310 IF N=15 THEN LET T=2.145
320 IF N=16 THEN LET T=2.131
330 IF N=17 THEN LET T=2.12
340 IF N=18 THEN LET T=2.11
350 IF N=19 THEN LET T=2.101
360 IF N=20 THEN LET T=2.093
370 IF N=21 THEN LET T=2.086
380 IF N=22 THEN LET T=2.08
390 IF N=23 THEN LET T=2.074
400 IF N=24 THEN LET T=2.069
410 IF N=25 THEN LET T=2.064
420 IF N=26 THEN LET T=2.06
430 IF N=27 THEN LET T=2.056
440 IF N=28 THEN LET T=2.052
450 IF N=29 THEN LET T=2.048
460 IF N=30 THEN LET T=2.045
470 IF N>=31 AND N<=35 THEN LET T=2.042
480 IF N>=36 AND N<=40 THEN LET T=2.03
490 IF N>=41 AND N<=45 THEN LET T=2.021
500 IF N>=46 AND N<=50 THEN LET T=2.014
510 IF N>=51 AND N<=60 THEN LET T=2.009
520 IF N>=61 AND N<=90 THEN LET T=2
530 IF N>=91 AND N<=150 THEN LET T=1.987
540 IF N>150 THEN LET T=1.96
550 LET SX=S/SQR(N)
560 LET UL=X+T*SX
570 LET LL=X-T*SX
580 PRINT "ESTIMATED STANDARD ERROR"
590 PRINT "OF THE MEAN =";SX
600 PRINT
610 PRINT "THE 0.95 CONFIDENCE INTERVAL FOR"
620 PRINT "THE POPULATION MEAN IS:"
630 PRINT
640 PRINT "";LL;" <= MU <= ";"";UL
650 END
```

Instructions

When the program is loaded, type RUN and push RETURN. The screen will display

ENTER N:?

Using Exercise 8.4–3 to illustrate, enter the sample size (16) and push RETURN and the screen will display

ENTER SAMPLE MEAN:?

Enter the sample mean (21) and push RETURN and the screen will display

ENTER STANDARD DEVIATION:?

Enter the standard deviation (5) and push RETURN and the screen will display

N = 16

SAMPLE MEAN = 21

STANDARD DEVIATION = 5

ESTIMATED STANDARD ERROR
OF THE MEAN = 1.25

THE 0.95 CONFIDENCE INTERVAL FOR
THE POPULATION MEAN IS:

$18.3363 <= MU <= 23.6638$

Note: $z = 1.960$ is used in place of a t value when n is larger than 150.

Program 3: *t*-Test for Population vs. Sample Mean

```
10 REM MU-XBAR T-TEST
20 CLS
30 PRINT "ENTER POPULATION MEAN:";
40 INPUT M
50 CLS
60 PRINT "ENTER SAMPLE N:";
70 INPUT N
80 CLS
90 PRINT "ENTER SAMPLE MEAN:";
100 INPUT X
110 CLS
120 PRINT "ENTER SAMPLE STANDARD DEVIATION:";
130 INPUT S
140 CLS
150 PRINT "POPULATION MEAN =";M
160 PRINT
170 PRINT "SAMPLE N =";N
180 PRINT "SAMPLE MEAN =";X
190 PRINT "SAMPLE STANDARD DEVIATION =";S
200 PRINT
210 LET SE=S/SQR(N)
220 LET T=(X-M)/SE
230 LET DF=N-1
240 PRINT "ESTIMATED STANDARD ERROR"
250 PRINT "OF THE MEAN =";SE
260 PRINT
270 PRINT "T = ";T
280 PRINT
290 PRINT "DEGREES OF FREEDOM =";DF
300 END
```

Instructions

When the program is loaded, type RUN and push RETURN. The screen will display

ENTER POPULATION MEAN:?

Exercise 8.6–1 is used to illustrate. Enter the population mean (15000) and push RETURN and the screen will display

ENTER SAMPLE N:?

Enter the sample size (36) and push RETURN and the screen will display

ENTER SAMPLE MEAN:?

Enter the sample mean (17000) and push RETURN and the screen will display

ENTER SAMPLE STANDARD DEVIATION:?

Enter the sample standard deviation (5000) and push RETURN and the screen will display

POPULATION MEAN = 15000

SAMPLE N = 36
SAMPLE MEAN = 17000
SAMPLE STANDARD DEVIATION = 5000

ESTIMATED STANDARD ERROR
OF THE MEAN = 833.333

T = 2.4

DEGREES OF FREEDOM = 35

Note: If the population standard deviation is known, it may be entered in place of the sample standard deviation. The value thus obtained will actually be a z-score rather than a t.

Program 4: Independent Groups t-Test

```
10 REM INDEPENDENT GROUPS T-TEST
20 CLS
30 PRINT "ENTER N1:";
40 INPUT N1
50 CLS
60 PRINT "N1 =";N1
70 PRINT
80 PRINT "ENTER X1 SCORES; PUSH RETURN AFTER EACH"
90 PRINT
100 FOR Y=1 TO N1
110 INPUT A
120 LET EA=EA+A
130 LET A2=A*A
```

```
140 LET EA2=EA2+A2
150 LET EAQ2=EA*EA
160 NEXT Y
170 PRINT
180 PRINT "CHECK X1 DATA FOR ACCURACY"
190 PRINT
200 PRINT "TO CONTINUE PUSH ANY KEY THEN RETURN"
210 PRINT
220 INPUT A$
230 IF A$="" THEN 220
240 CLS
250 PRINT "ENTER N2:";
260 INPUT N2
270 CLS
280 PRINT "N2 =";N2
290 PRINT
300 PRINT "ENTER X2 SCORES; PUSH RETURN AFTER EACH"
310 PRINT
320 FOR Z=1 TO N2
330 INPUT B
340 LET EB=EB+B
350 LET B2=B*B
360 LET EB2=EB2+B2
370 LET EBQ2=EB*EB
380 NEXT Z
390 PRINT
400 PRINT "CHECK X2 DATA FOR ACCURACY"
410 PRINT
420 PRINT "TO CONTINUE PUSH ANY KEY THEN RETURN"
430 PRINT
440 INPUT A$
450 IF A$="" THEN 440
460 CLS
470 PRINT "N1 =";N1
480 PRINT "SUM X1 =";EA
490 PRINT "MEAN X1 =";EA/N1
500 PRINT "SUM X1 SQUARED =";EA2
510 PRINT "(SUM X1) SQUARED =";EAQ2
520 PRINT
530 PRINT "N2 =";N2
540 PRINT "SUM X2 =";EB
550 PRINT "MEAN X2 =";EB/N2
560 PRINT "SUM X2 SQUARED =";EB2
570 PRINT "(SUM X2) SQUARED =";EBQ2
580 PRINT
590 LET DF=N1+N2-2
600 LET PV=((EA2-EAQ2/N1)+(EB2-EBQ2/N2))/DF
610 LET T=(EA/N1-EB/N2)/SQR(PV/N1+PV/N2)
620 PRINT "POOLED VARIANCE =";PV
630 PRINT
640 PRINT "T = ";T
650 PRINT
660 PRINT "DEGREES OF FREEDOM =";DF
670 END
```

Instructions

When the program is loaded, type RUN and push RETURN. The screen will display

ENTER N1:?

Exercise 8.8–1 will be used to illustrate. Enter the value of n_1 (8) and push RETURN and the screen will display

N1 = 8

ENTER X1 SCORES; PUSH RETURN AFTER EACH
?

Enter the X_1 raw scores, pushing RETURN after each. When RETURN has been pushed for the eighth time the screen will display

N1 = 8

ENTER X1 SCORES; PUSH RETURN AFTER EACH

?   4
?   8
?   5
?   7
?   6
?   6
?   5
?   7

CHECK X1 DATA FOR ACCURACY

TO CONTINUE PUSH ANY KEY THEN RETURN
?

Now push any key then RETURN and the screen will display

ENTER N2:?

Enter the value of n_2 (8) and push RETURN and the screen will display

N2 = 8

ENTER X2 SCORES; PUSH RETURN AFTER EACH
?

Enter the X_2 raw scores pushing RETURN after each. When RETURN has been pushed for the eighth time the screen will display

N2 = 8

ENTER X2 SCORES; PUSH RETURN AFTER EACH

?   4
?   3

? 4
? 5
? 4
? 3
? 4
? 5

CHECK X2 DATA FOR ACCURACY

TO CONTINUE PUSH ANY KEY THEN RETURN

?

Now push any key then RETURN and the screen will display

N1 = 8
SUM X1 = 48
MEAN X1 = 6
SUM X1 SQUARED = 300
(SUM X1) SQUARED = 2304

N2 = 8
SUM X2 = 32
MEAN X2 = 4
SUM X2 SQUARED = 132
(SUM X2) SQUARED = 1024

POOLED VARIANCE = 1.14286

T = 3.74166

DEGREES OF FREEDOM = 14

Program 5: Repeated Measures/Correlated Samples *t*-Test

```
10 REM REPEATED/CORRELATED T-TEST
20 CLS
30 PRINT "ENTER N:";
40 INPUT N
50 CLS
60 PRINT "ENTER X1 AND X2 SCORES IN PAIRS"
70 PRINT
80 PRINT "N =";N; TAB(17)"X1"; TAB(25)"X2"; TAB(33)"D"
90 FOR Z=1 TO N
100 INPUT A,B
110 LET D=A-B
120 LET ED=ED+D
130 LET D2=D*D
140 LET ED2=ED2+D2
150 LET EDQ2=ED*ED
160 PRINT TAB(16)"";A; TAB(24)"";B; TAB(32)"";D
170 NEXT Z
180 PRINT
190 PRINT "CHECK RAW DATA FOR ACCURACY"
```

```
200 PRINT
210 PRINT "TO CONTINUE PUSH ANY KEY THEN RETURN"
220 PRINT
230 INPUT A$
240 IF A$="" THEN 230
250 CLS
260 LET DF=N-1
270 LET DD=SQR((N*ED2-EDQ2)/DF)
280 LET T=ED/DD
290 PRINT "N =";N
300 PRINT "SUM D = ";ED
310 PRINT "SUM D SQUARED =";ED2
320 PRINT "(SUM D) SQUARED =";EDQ2
330 PRINT
340 PRINT "T = ";T
350 PRINT
360 PRINT "DEGREES OF FREEDOM =";DF
370 END
```

Instructions

When the program is loaded, type RUN and push RETURN. The screen will display

ENTER N:?

Exercise 8.10–1 will be used to illustrate. Enter the value of N (10) and push RETURN and the screen will display

ENTER X1 AND X2 SCORES IN PAIRS

N = 10   X1   X2   D
?

Enter the raw data as follows. Enter the first X_1 score, a comma, the first X_2 score, and then push RETURN. Enter the second X_1 score, a comma, the second X_2 score, then push RETURN and continue in this manner until all pairs of raw scores have been entered. When RETURN is pushed for the tenth time the screen will display

ENTER X1 and X2 SCORES IN PAIRS

N = 10	X1	X2	D
? 20,10			
	20	10	10
? 15,15			
	15	15	0
? 16,12			
	16	12	4
? 15,10			
	15	10	5
? 18,12			
	18	12	6

?	10,8			
		10	8	2
?	20,15			
		20	15	5
?	16,10			
		16	10	6
?	16,14			
		16	14	2
?	10,11			
		10	11	−1

CHECK RAW DATA FOR ACCURACY

TO CONTINUE PUSH ANY KEY THEN RETURN

?

This program lists the raw scores so that you may check them for accuracy, but since the screen has a limited capacity to display data, you may find that the top of the display output begins to scroll off the top of your screen before you are finished entering all the raw scores. In such cases simply pause and check the data entered before proceeding to enter the remainder of the raw scores. When the data have all been entered push any key then RETURN and the screen will display

N = 10
SUM D = 39
SUM D SQUARED = 247
(SUM D) SQUARED = 1521

T = 3.79798

DEGREES OF FREEDOM = 9

Program 6: Independent Groups Analysis of Variance

This program may be used when k (the number of groups) is between 3 and 6 inclusive; the groups may have different ns.

```
10 REM INDEPENDENT GROUPS ANOVA
20 CLS
30 PRINT "ENTER K:";
40 INPUT K
50 CLS
60 PRINT "ENTER N1:";
70 INPUT N1
80 CLS
90 PRINT "N1 =";N1
100 PRINT
110 PRINT "ENTER X1 SCORES; PUSH RETURN AFTER EACH"
120 PRINT
130 FOR U=1 TO N1
```

```
140 INPUT A
150 LET EA=EA+A
160 LET A2=A*A
170 LET EA2=EA2+A2
180 LET EAQ2=EA*EA
190 NEXT U
200 GOSUB 1280
210 PRINT "ENTER N2:";
220 INPUT N2
230 CLS
240 PRINT "N2 =";N2
250 PRINT
260 PRINT "ENTER X2 SCORES; PUSH RETURN AFTER EACH"
270 PRINT
280 FOR V=1 TO N2
290 INPUT B
300 LET EB=EB+B
310 LET B2=B*B
320 LET EB2=EB2+B2
330 LET EBQ2=EB*EB
340 NEXT V
350 GOSUB 1280
360 PRINT "ENTER N3:";
370 INPUT N3
380 CLS
390 PRINT "N3 =";N3
400 PRINT
410 PRINT "ENTER X3 SCORES; PUSH RETURN AFTER EACH"
420 PRINT
430 FOR W=1 TO N3
440 INPUT C
450 LET EC=EC+C
460 LET C2=C*C
470 LET EC2=EC2+C2
480 LET ECQ2=EC*EC
490 NEXT W
500 GOSUB 1280
510 IF K=3 THEN 1000
520 PRINT "ENTER N4:";
530 INPUT N4
540 CLS
550 PRINT "N4 =";N4
560 PRINT
570 PRINT "ENTER X4 SCORES; PUSH RETURN AFTER EACH"
580 PRINT
590 FOR X=1 TO N4
600 INPUT D
610 LET ED=ED+D
620 LET D2=D*D
630 LET ED2=ED2+D2
640 LET EDQ2=ED*ED
650 NEXT X
660 GOSUB 1280
670 IF K=4 THEN 1020
```

```
680 PRINT "ENTER N5:";
690 INPUT N5
700 CLS
710 PRINT "N5 =";N5
720 PRINT
730 PRINT "ENTER X5 SCORES; PUSH RETURN AFTER EACH"
740 PRINT
750 FOR Y=1 TO N5
760 INPUT E
770 LET EE=EE+E
780 LET E2=E*E
790 LET EE2=EE2+E2
800 LET EEQ2=EE*EE
810 NEXT Y
820 GOSUB 1280
830 IF K=5 THEN 1050
840 PRINT "ENTER N6:";
850 INPUT N6
860 CLS
870 PRINT "N6 =";N6
880 PRINT
890 PRINT "ENTER X6 SCORES; PUSH RETURN AFTER EACH"
900 PRINT
910 FOR Z=1 TO N6
920 INPUT G
930 LET EG=EG+G
940 LET G2=G*G
950 LET EG2=EG2+G2
960 LET EGQ2=EG*EG
970 NEXT Z
980 GOSUB 1280
990 IF K=6 THEN 1080
1000 PRINT "T1 =";EA;" T2 =";EB;" T3 =";EC
1010 GOTO 1100
1020 PRINT "T1 =";EA;" T2 =";EB;" T3 =";EC
1030 PRINT "T4 =";ED
1040 GOTO 1100
1050 PRINT "T1 =";EA;" T2 =";EB;" T3 =";EC
1060 PRINT "T4 =";ED;" T5 =";EE
1070 GOTO 1100
1080 PRINT "T1 =";EA;" T2 =";EB;" T3 =";EC
1090 PRINT "T4 =";ED;" T5 =";EE;" T6 =";EG
1100 LET SSB=ET2N-EXQ2/N
1110 LET SSW=EX2-ET2N
1120 LET DFB=K-1
1130 LET DFW=N-K
1140 LET MSB=SSB/DFB
1150 LET MSW=SSW/DFW
1160 LET F=MSB/MSW
1170 PRINT
1180 PRINT "SOURCE OF VARIATION"; TAB(25)"SUM OF SQUARES"
1190 PRINT
1200 PRINT "BETWEEN GROUPS"; TAB(25)"";SSB
1210 PRINT "WITHIN GROUPS"; TAB(25)"";SSW
1220 PRINT
```

```
1230 PRINT " DF"; TAB(10)"MEAN SQUARE"; TAB(28)"F"
1240 PRINT
1250 PRINT "";DFB; TAB(10)"";MSB; TAB(25)"";F
1260 PRINT "";DFW; TAB(10)"";MSW
1270 END
1280 PRINT
1290 PRINT "CHECK RAW DATA FOR ACCURACY"
1300 PRINT
1310 PRINT "TO CONTINUE PUSH AND KEY THEN RETURN"
1320 PRINT
1330 INPUT A$
1340 IF A$="" THEN 1330
1350 CLS
1360 LET EX=EA+EB+EC+ED+EE+EG
1370 LET EX2=EA2+EB2+EC2+ED2+EE2+EG2
1380 LET EXQ2=EX*EX
1390 LET N=N1+N2+N3+N4+N5+N6
1400 LET ET2N=EAQ2/N1+EBQ2/N2+ECQ2/N3+EDQ2/N4+EEQ2/N5+EGQ2/N6
1410 RETURN
```

Instructions

When the program is loaded, type RUN and push RETURN. The screen will display

ENTER K:?

Exercise 9.5–2 will be used to illustrate. Enter the value of k (3) and push RETURN and the screen will display

ENTER N1:?

Enter the value of n_1 (8) and push RETURN and the screen will display

N1 = 8

ENTER X1 SCORES; PUSH RETURN AFTER EACH

?

Enter the X_1 raw scores pushing RETURN after each. When RETURN has been pushed for the eighth time the screen will display

N1 = 8

ENTER X1 SCORES; PUSH RETURN AFTER EACH

? 3
? 2
? 4
? 3
? 3
? 3
? 5
? 3

CHECK RAW DATA FOR ACCURACY

TO CONTINUE PUSH ANY KEY THEN RETURN

?

Push any key then RETURN and the screen will display

ENTER N2:?

Proceed to enter the X_2 and X_3 raw data following the procedure established for the X_1 scores. When the raw data have all been entered and RETURN is pushed after the last groups of scores, the screen will display

T1 = 26   T2 = 13   T3 = 9

SOURCE OF VARIATION	SUM OF SQUARES
BETWEEN GROUPS	19.75
WITHIN GROUPS	22.25

DF	MEAN SQUARE	F
2	9.875	9.32023
21	1.05952	

This program prints the treatment totals so that if the F term is significant you may readily perform the Tukey HSD procedure.

Program 7: Repeated Measures Analysis of Variance

This program may be used when k (the number of treatments) is between three and five inclusive.

```
10 REM REPEATED MEASURES ANOVA
20 CLS
30 PRINT "ENTER K:";
40 INPUT K
50 CLS
60 PRINT "ENTER N:";
70 INPUT N
80 CLS
90 PRINT "K =";K;" N =";N;" ENTER RAW DATA"
100 PRINT
110 IF K=4 THEN 180
120 IF K=5 THEN 240
130 PRINT "   X1,X2,X3"
140 PRINT
150 GOSUB 550
160 PRINT "T1 =";EA;" T2 =";EB;" T3 =";EC
170 GOTO 290
180 PRINT "   X1,X2,X3,X4"
190 PRINT
200 GOSUB 550
210 PRINT "TI =";EA;" T2 =";EB;" T3 =";EC
```

```
220 PRINT "T4 =";ED
230 GOTO 290
240 PRINT "   X1,X2,X3,X4,X5"
250 PRINT
260 GOSUB 550
270 PRINT "T1 =";EA;" T2 =";EB;" T3 =";EC
280 PRINT "T4 =";ED;" T5 =";EE
290 LET SSB=ER2K-EXQ2N
300 LET SSW=EX2-ER2K
310 LET SST=ET2N-EXQ2N
320 LET SSR=EX2+EXQ2N-ET2N-ER2K
330 LET DFB=N-1
340 LET DFW=N*(K-1)
350 LET DFT=K-1
360 LET DFR=(N-1)*(K-1)
370 LET MST=SST/DFT
380 LET MSR=SSR/DFR
390 LET F=MST/MSR
400 PRINT
410 PRINT "SOURCE OF VARIATION"; TAB(25)"SUM OF SQUARES"
420 PRINT
430 PRINT "BETWEEN SUBJECTS"; TAB(25)"";SSB
440 PRINT "WITHIN SUBJECTS"; TAB(25)"";SSW
450 PRINT "   TREATMENT"; TAB(25)"";SST
460 PRINT "   RESIDUAL"; TAB(25)"";SSR
470 PRINT
480 PRINT " DF"; TAB(10)"MEAN SQUARE"; TAB(28)"F"
490 PRINT
500 PRINT "";DFB
510 PRINT "";DFW
520 PRINT "";DFT; TAB(10)"";MST; TAB(25)"";F
530 PRINT "";DFR; TAB(10)"";MSR
540 END
550 FOR Z=1 TO N
560 IF K=4 THEN 600
570 IF K=5 THEN 620
580 INPUT A,B,C
590 GOTO 630
600 INPUT A,B,C,D
610 GOTO 630
620 INPUT A,B,C,D,E
630 LET EA=EA+A
640 LET A2=A*A
650 LET EA2=EA2+A2
660 LET EAQ2=EA*EA
670 LET EB=EB+B
680 LET B2=B*B
690 LET EB2=EB2+B2
700 LET EBQ2=EB*EB
710 LET EC=EC+C
720 LET C2=C*C
730 LET EC2=EC2+C2
740 LET ECQ2=EC*EC
750 LET ED=ED+D
```

```
760 LET D2=D*D
770 LET ED2=ED2+D2
780 LET EDQ2=ED*ED
790 LET EE=EE+E
800 LET E2=E*E
810 LET EE2=EE2+E2
820 LET EEQ2=EE*EE
830 LET R=A+B+C+D+E
840 LET R2=R*R
850 LET ER2=ER2+R2
860 NEXT Z
870 PRINT
880 PRINT "CHECK RAW DATA FOR ACCURACY"
890 PRINT
900 PRINT "TO CONTINUE PUSH ANY KEY THEN RETURN"
910 PRINT
920 INPUT A$
930 IF A$="" THEN 920
940 CLS
950 LET EX=EA+EB+EC+ED+EE
960 LET EX2=EA2+EB2+EC2+ED2+EE2
970 LET EXQ2N=(EX*EX)/(N*K)
980 LET ET2N=(EAQ2+EBQ2+ECQ2+EDQ2+EEQ2)/N
990 LET ER2K=ER2/K
1000 RETURN
```

Instructions

When the program is loaded, type RUN and push RETURN. The screen will display

ENTER K:?

Exercise 9.8–2 will be used to illustrate. Enter the value of k (3) and push RETURN and the screen will display

ENTER N:?

Enter the value of n (4) and push RETURN and the screen will display

K = 3   N = 4   ENTER RAW DATA

   X1,X2,X3

?

Now enter the first X_1 score, a comma, the first X_2 score, a comma, the first X_3 score and push RETURN. Then enter the second X_1 score, a comma, the second X_2 score, a comma, the second X_3 score and push RETURN. Continue in this manner until all data have been entered. When RETURN is pushed after the nth row of data has been entered the screen will display

K = 3   N = 4   ENTER RAW DATA

   X1,X2,X3

? 50,55,65
? 58,52,60
? 46,48,58
? 51,50,61

CHECK RAW DATA FOR ACCURACY

TO CONTINUE PUSH ANY KEY THEN RETURN

?

Now push any key then RETURN and the screen will display

T1 = 205   T2 = 205   T3 = 244

SOURCE OF VARIATION	SUM OF SQUARES
BETWEEN SUBJECTS	73
WITHIN SUBJECTS	308
TREATMENT	253.5
RESIDUAL	54.5

DF	MEAN SQUARE	F
3		
8		
2	126.75	13.9541
6	9.08333	

This program prints the treatment totals so that if the F term is significant you may readily perform the Tukey HSD procedure. Note: Your computer may not display the numerical values aligned with respect to the decimal point as shown here; this is not cause for alarm.

Program 8: Two–Factor Independent Groups Analysis of Variance

This program may be used for any design in which p and q are 4 or less.

```
10 REM TWO FACTOR IND GPS ANOVA
20 CLS
30 PRINT "ENTER P:";
40 INPUT P
50 CLS
60 PRINT "ENTER Q:";
70 INPUT Q
80 CLS
90 PRINT "ENTER N:";
100 INPUT N
110 CLS
120 PRINT "ENTER A1B1 CELL SCORES"
130 PRINT
140 FOR Z=1 TO N
150 INPUT A
```

```
160 LET EA=EA+A
170 LET A2=A*A
180 LET EA2=EA2+A2
190 LET EAQ2=EA*EA
200 NEXT Z
210 GOSUB 3610
220 PRINT "ENTER A2B1 CELL SCORES"
230 PRINT
240 FOR Z=1 TO N
250 INPUT B
260 LET EB=EB+B
270 LET B2=B*B
280 LET EB2=EB2+B2
290 LET EBQ2=EB*EB
300 NEXT Z
310 GOSUB 3610
320 IF P=2 THEN 540
330 PRINT "ENTER A3B1 CELL SCORES"
340 PRINT
350 FOR Z=1 TO N
360 INPUT C
370 LET EC=EC+C
380 LET C2=C*C
390 LET EC2=EC2+C2
400 LET ECQ2=EC*EC
410 NEXT Z
420 GOSUB 3610
430 IF P=3 THEN 540
440 PRINT "ENTER A4B1 CELL SCORES"
450 PRINT
460 FOR Z=1 TO N
470 INPUT D
480 LET ED=ED+D
490 LET D2=D*D
500 LET ED2=ED2+D2
510 LET EDQ2=ED*ED
520 NEXT Z
530 GOSUB 3610
540 PRINT "ENTER A1B2 CELL SCORES"
550 PRINT
560 FOR Z=1 TO N
570 INPUT E
580 LET EE=EE+E
590 LET E2=E*E
600 LET EE2=EE2+E2
610 LET EEQ2=EE*EE
620 NEXT Z
630 GOSUB 3610
640 PRINT "ENTER A2B2 CELL SCORES"
650 PRINT
660 FOR Z=1 TO N
670 INPUT G
680 LET EG=EG+G
```

```
690 LET G2=G*G
700 LET EG2=EG2+G2
710 LET EGQ2=EG*EG
720 NEXT Z
730 GOSUB 3610
740 IF P=2 AND Q=2 THEN 1880
750 IF P=2 THEN 990
760 PRINT "ENTER A3B2 CELL SCORES"
770 PRINT
780 FOR Z=1 TO N
790 INPUT H
800 LET EH=EH+H
810 LET H2=H*H
820 LET EH2=EH2+H2
830 LET EHQ2=EH*EH
840 NEXT Z
850 GOSUB 3610
860 IF P=3 AND Q=2 THEN 2010
870 IF P=3 THEN 990
880 PRINT "ENTER A4B2 CELL SCORES"
890 PRINT
900 FOR Z=1 TO N
910 INPUT I
920 LET EI=EI+I
930 LET I2=I*I
940 LET EI2=EI2+I2
950 LET EIQ2=EI*EI
960 NEXT Z
970 GOSUB 3610
980 IF P=4 AND Q=2 THEN 2150
990 PRINT "ENTER A1B3 CELL SCORES"
1000 PRINT
1010 FOR Z=1 TO N
1020 INPUT J
1030 LET EJ=EJ+J
1040 LET J2=J*J
1050 LET EJ2=EJ2+J2
1060 LET EJQ2=EJ*EJ
1070 NEXT Z
1080 GOSUB 3610
1090 PRINT "ENTER A2B3 CELL SCORES"
1100 PRINT
1110 FOR Z=1 TO N
1120 INPUT K
1130 LET EK=EK+K
1140 LET K2=K*K
1150 LET EK2=EK2+K2
1160 LET EKQ2=EK*EK
1170 NEXT Z
1180 GOSUB 3610
1190 IF P=2 AND Q=3 THEN 2300
1200 IF P=2 THEN 1440
1210 PRINT "ENTER A3B3 CELL SCORES"
```

```
1220 PRINT
1230 FOR Z=1 TO N
1240 INPUT L
1250 LET EL=EL+L
1260 LET L2=L*L
1270 LET EL2=EL2+L2
1280 LET ELQ2=EL*EL
1290 NEXT Z
1300 GOSUB 3610
1310 IF P=3 AND Q=3 THEN 2450
1320 IF P=3 THEN 1440
1330 PRINT "ENTER A4B3 CELL SCORES"
1340 PRINT
1350 FOR Z=1 TO N
1360 INPUT M
1370 LET EM=EM+M
1380 LET M2=M*M
1390 LET EM2=EM2+M2
1400 LET EMQ2=EM*EM
1410 NEXT Z
1420 GOSUB 3610
1430 IF P=4 AND Q=3 THEN 2610
1440 PRINT "ENTER A1B4 CELL SCORES"
1450 PRINT
1460 FOR Z=1 TO N
1470 INPUT O
1480 LET EO=EO+O
1490 LET O2=O*O
1500 LET EO2=EO2+O2
1510 LET EOQ2=EO*EO
1520 NEXT Z
1530 GOSUB 3610
1540 PRINT "ENTER A2B4 CELL SCORES"
1550 PRINT
1560 FOR Z=1 TO N
1570 INPUT R
1580 LET ER=ER+R
1590 LET R2=R*R
1600 LET ER2=ER2+R2
1610 LET ERQ2=ER*ER
1620 NEXT Z
1630 GOSUB 3610
1640 IF P=2 AND Q=4 THEN 2780
1650 PRINT "ENTER A3B4 CELL SCORES"
1660 PRINT
1670 FOR Z=1 TO N
1680 INPUT S
1690 LET ES=ES+S
1700 LET S2=S*S
1710 LET ES2=ES2+S2
1720 LET ESQ2=ES*ES
1730 NEXT Z
1740 GOSUB 3610
```

```
1750 IF P=3 AND Q=4 THEN 2950
1760 PRINT "ENTER A4B4 CELL SCORES"
1770 PRINT
1780 FOR Z=1 TO N
1790 INPUT T
1800 LET ET=ET+T
1810 LET T2=T*T
1820 LET ET2=ET2+T2
1830 LET ETQ2=ET*ET
1840 NEXT Z
1850 GOSUB 3610
1860 IF P=4 AND Q=4 THEN 3130
1870 REM 2 X 2 DESIGN
1880 LET EX=EA+EB+EE+EG
1890 LET EX2=EA2+EB2+EE2+EG2
1900 LET AA1=EA+EE
1910 LET AA2=EB+EG
1920 LET EA2NQ=(AA1*AA1+AA2*AA2)/(N*Q)
1930 LET BB1=EA+EB
1940 LET BB2=EE+EG
1950 LET EB2NP=(BB1*BB1+BB2*BB2)/(N*P)
1960 LET EAB2N=(EAQ2+EBQ2+EEQ2+EGQ2)/N
1970 PRINT "A1B1 =";EA;" A2B1 =";EB
1980 PRINT "A1B2 =";EE;" A2B2 =";EG
1990 GOTO 3300
2000 REM 3 X 2 DESIGN
2010 LET EX=EA+EB+EC+EE+EG+EH
2020 LET EX2=EA2+EB2+EC2+EE2+EG2+EH2
2030 LET AA1=EA+EE
2040 LET AA2=EB+EG
2050 LET AA3=EC+EH
2060 LET EA2NQ=(AA1*AA1+AA2*AA2+AA3*AA3)/(N*Q)
2070 LET BB1=EA+EB+EC
2080 LET BB2=EE+EG+EH
2090 LET EB2NP=(BB1*BB1+BB2*BB2)/(N*P)
2100 LET EAB2N=(EAQ2+EBQ2+ECQ2+EEQ2+EGQ2+EHQ2)/N
2110 PRINT "A1B1 =";EA;" A2B1 =";EB;" A3B1 =";EC
2120 PRINT "A1B2 =";EE;" A2B2 =";EG;" A3B2 =";EH
2130 GOTO 3300
2140 REM 4 X 2 DESIGN
2150 LET EX=EA+EB+EC+ED+EE+EG+EH+EI
2160 LET EX2=EA2+EB2+EC2+ED2+EE2+EG2+EH2+EI2
2170 LET AA1=EA+EE
2180 LET AA2=EB+EG
2190 LET AA3=EC+EH
2200 LET AA4=ED+EI
2210 LET EA2NQ=(AA1*AA1+AA2*AA2+AA3*AA3+AA4*AA4)/(N*Q)
2220 LET BB1=EA+EB+EC+ED
2230 LET BB2=EE+EG+EH+EI
2240 LET EB2NP=(BB1*BB1+BB2*BB2)/(N*P)
2250 LET EAB2N=(EAQ2+EBQ2+ECQ2+EDQ2+EEQ2+EGQ2+EHQ2+EIQ2)/N
2260 PRINT "A1B1=";EA;"A2B1=";EB;"A3B1=";EC;"A4B1=";ED
2270 PRINT "A1B2=";EE;"A2B2=";EG;"A3B2=";EH;"A4B2=";EI
```

```
2280 GOTO 3300
2290 REM 2 X 3 DESIGN
2300 LET EX=EA+EB+EE+EG+EJ+EK
2310 LET EX2=EA2+EB2+EE2+EG2+EJ2+EK2
2320 LET AA1=EA+EE+EJ
2330 LET AA2=EB+EG+EK
2340 LET EA2NQ=(AA1*AA1+AA2*AA2)/(N*Q)
2350 LET BB1=EA+EB
2360 LET BB2=EE+EG
2370 LET BB3=EJ+EK
2380 LET EB2NP=(BB1*BB1+BB2*BB2+BB3*BB3)/(N*P)
2390 LET EAB2N=(EAQ2+EBQ2+EEQ2+EGQ2+EJQ2+EKQ2)/N
2400 PRINT "A1B1 =";EA;" A2B1 =";EB
2410 PRINT "A1B2 =";EE;" A2B2 =";EG
2420 PRINT "A1B3 =";EJ;" A2B3 =";EK
2430 GOTO 3300
2440 REM 3 X 3 DESIGN
2450 LET EX=EA+EB+EC+EE+EG+EH+EJ+EK+EL
2460 LET EX2=EA2+EB2+EC2+EE2+EG2+EH2+EJ2+EK2+EL2
2470 LET AA1=EA+EE+EJ
2480 LET AA2=EB+EG+EK
2490 LET AA3=EC+EH+EL
2500 LET EA2NQ=(AA1*AA1+AA2*AA2+AA3*AA3)/(N*Q)
2510 LET BB1=EA+EB+EC
2520 LET BB2=EE+EG+EH
2530 LET BB3=EJ+EK+EL
2540 LET EB2NP=(BB1*BB1+BB2*BB2+BB3*BB3)/(N*P)
2550 LET EAB2N=(EAQ2+EBQ2+ECQ2+EEQ2+EGQ2+EHQ2+EJQ2+EKQ2+ELQ2)/N
2560 PRINT "A1B1 =";EA;" A2B1 =";EB;" A3B1 =";EC
2570 PRINT "A1B2 =";EE;" A2B2 =";EG;" A3B2 =";EH
2580 PRINT "A1B3 =";EJ;" A2B3 =";EK;" A3B3 =";EL
2590 GOTO 3300
2600 REM 4 X 3 DESIGN
2610 LET EX=EA+EB+EC+ED+EE+EG+EH+EI+EJ+EK+EL+EM
2620 LET EX2=EA2+EB2+EC2+ED2+EE2+EG2+EH2+EI2+EJ2+EK2+EL2+EM2
2630 LET AA1=EA+EE+EJ
2640 LET AA2=EB+EG+EK
2650 LET AA3=EC+EH+EL
2660 LET AA4=ED+EI+EM
2670 LET EA2NQ=(AA1*AA1+AA2*AA2+AA3*AA3+AA4*AA4)/(N*Q)
2680 LET BB1=EA+EB+EC+ED
2690 LET BB2=EE+EG+EH+EI
2700 LET BB3=EJ+EK+EL+EM
2710 LET EB2NP=(BB1*BB1+BB2*BB2+BB3*BB3)/(N*P)
2720 LET EAB2N=(EAQ2+EBQ2+ECQ2+EDQ2+EEQ2+EGQ2+EHQ2+EIQ2+EJQ2+EKQ2+ELQ2+EMQ
2)/N
2730 PRINT "A1B1=";EA;"A2B1=";EB;"A3B1=";EC;"A4B1=";ED
2740 PRINT "A1B2=";EE;"A2B2=";EG;"A3B2=";EH;"A4B2=";EI
2750 PRINT "A1B3=";EJ;"A2B3=";EK;"A3B3=";EL;"A4B3=";EM
2760 GOTO 3300
2770 REM 2 X 4 DESIGN
2780 LET EX=EA+EB+EE+EG+EJ+EK+EO+ER
2790 LET EX2=EA2+EB2+EE2+EG2+EJ2+EK2+EO2+ER2
```

```
2800 LET AA1=EA+EE+EJ+EO
2810 LET AA2=EB+EG+EK+ER
2820 LET EA2NQ=(AA1*AA1+AA2*AA2)/(N*Q)
2830 LET BB1=EA+EB
2840 LET BB2=EE+EG
2850 LET BB3=EJ+EK
2860 LET BB4=EO+ER
2870 LET EB2NP=(BB1*BB1+BB2*BB2+BB3*BB3+BB4*BB4)/(N*P)
2880 LET EAB2N=(EAQ2+EBQ2+EEQ2+EGQ2+EJQ2+EKQ2+EOQ2+ERQ2)/N
2890 PRINT "A1B1 =";EA;" A2B1 =";EB
2900 PRINT "A1B2 =";EE;" A2B2 =";EG
2910 PRINT "A1B3 =";EJ;" A2B3 =";EK
2920 PRINT "A1B4 =";EO;" A2B4 =";ER
2930 GOTO 3300
2940 REM 3 X 4 DESIGN
2950 LET EX=EA+EB+EC+EE+EG+EH+EJ+EK+EL+EO+ER+ES
2960 LET EX2=EA2+EB2+EC2+EE2+EG2+EH2+EJ2+EK2+EL2+EO2+ER2+ES2
2970 LET AA1=EA+EE+EJ+EO
2980 LET AA2=EB+EG+EK+ER
2990 LET AA3=EC+EH+EL+ES
3000 LET EA2NQ=(AA1*AA1+AA2*AA2+AA3*AA3)/(N*Q)
3010 LET BB1=EA+EB+EC
3020 LET BB2=EE+EG+EH
3030 LET BB3=EJ+EK+EL
3040 LET BB4=EO+ER+ES
3050 LET EB2NP=(BB1*BB1+BB2*BB2+BB3*BB3+BB4*BB4)/(N*P)
3060 LET EAB2N=(EAQ2+EBQ2+ECQ2+EEQ2+EGQ2+EHQ2+EJQ2+EKQ2+ELQ2+EOQ2+ERQ2+ESQ
2)/N
3070 PRINT "A1B1 =";EA;" A2B1 =";EB;" A3B1 =";EC
3080 PRINT "A1B2 =";EE;" A2B2 =";EG;" A3B2 =";EH
3090 PRINT "A1B3 =";EJ;" A2B3 =";EK;" A3B3 =";EL
3100 PRINT "A1B4 =";EO;" A2B4 =";ER;" A3B4 =";ES
3110 GOTO 3300
3120 REM 4 X 4 DESIGN
3130 LET EX=EA+EB+EC+ED+EE+EG+EH+EI+EJ+EK+EL+EM+EO+ER+ES+ET
3140 LET EX2=EA2+EB2+EC2+ED2+EE2+EG2+EH2+EI2+EJ2+EK2+EL2+EM2+EO2+ER2+ES2+E
T2
3150 LET AA1=EA+EE+EJ+EO
3160 LET AA2=EB+EG+EK+ER
3170 LET AA3=EC+EH+EL+ES
3180 LET AA4=ED+EI+EM+ET
3190 LET EA2NQ=(AA1*AA1+AA2*AA2+AA3*AA3+AA4*AA4)/(N*Q)
3200 LET BB1=EA+EB+EC+ED
3210 LET BB2=EE+EG+EH+EI
3220 LET BB3=EJ+EK+EL+EM
3230 LET BB4=EO+ER+ES+ET
3240 LET EB2NP=(BB1*BB1+BB2*BB2+BB3*BB3+BB4*BB4)/(N*P)
3250 LET EAB2N=(EAQ2+EBQ2+ECQ2+EDQ2+EEQ2+EGQ2+EHQ2+EIQ2+EJQ2+EKQ2+ELQ2
+EMQ2+EOQ2+ERQ2+ESQ2+ETQ2)/N
3260 PRINT "A1B1=";EA;"A2B1=";EB;"A3B1=";EC;"A4B1=";ED
3270 PRINT "A1B2=";EE;"A2B2=";EG;"A3B2=";EH;"A4B2=";EI
3280 PRINT "A1B3=";EJ;"A2B3=";EK;"A3B3=";EL;"A4B3=";EM
3290 PRINT "A1B4=";EO;"A2B4=";ER;"A3B4=";ES;"A4B4=";ET
```

```
3300 LET EXQ2NPQ=(EX*EX)/(N*P*Q)
3310 LET SSA=EA2NQ-EXQ2NPQ
3320 LET SSB=EB2NP-EXQ2NPQ
3330 LET SSAB=EAB2N+EXQ2NPQ-EA2NQ-EB2NP
3340 LET SSR=EX2-EAB2N
3350 LET DFA=P-1
3360 LET DFB=Q-1
3370 LET DFAB=(P-1)*(Q-1)
3380 LET DFR=P*Q*(N-1)
3390 LET MSA=SSA/DFA
3400 LET MSB=SSB/DFB
3410 LET MSAB=SSAB/DFAB
3420 LET MSR=SSR/DFR
3430 LET FA=MSA/MSR
3440 LET FB=MSB/MSR
3450 LET FAB=MSAB/MSR
3460 PRINT
3470 PRINT "SOURCE OF VARIATION"; TAB(25)"SUM OF SQUARES"
3480 PRINT
3490 PRINT "A"; TAB(25)"";SSA
3500 PRINT "B"; TAB(25)"";SSB
3510 PRINT "AB"; TAB(25)"";SSAB
3520 PRINT "RESIDUAL"; TAB(25)"";SSR
3530 PRINT
3540 PRINT " DF"; TAB(10)"MEAN SQUARE"; TAB(28)"F"
3550 PRINT
3560 PRINT "";DFA; TAB(10)"";MSA; TAB(25)"";FA
3570 PRINT "";DFB; TAB(10)"";MSB; TAB(25)"";FB
3580 PRINT "";DFAB; TAB(10)"";MSAB; TAB(25)"";FAB
3590 PRINT "";DFR; TAB(10)"";MSR
3600 END
3610 PRINT
3620 PRINT "CHECK RAW DATA FOR ACCURACY"
3630 PRINT
3640 PRINT "TO CONTINUE PUSH ANY KEY THEN RETURN"
3650 PRINT
3660 INPUT A$
3670 IF A$="" THEN 3660
3680 CLS
3690 RETURN
```

Instructions

When the program is loaded, type RUN and push RETURN. The screen will display

ENTER P:?

Exercise 11.3–2 will be used to illustrate. Enter the value of p (2) and push RETURN and the screen will display

ENTER Q:?

Enter the value of q (2) and push RETURN and the screen will display

ENTER N:?

Enter the value of n (6) and push RETURN and the screen will display

ENTER A1B1 CELL SCORES
?

Enter the first raw score in the a_1b_1 cell and push RETURN, then the second raw score in the a_1b_1 cell and push RETURN, and so on. When RETURN has been pushed for the sixth time the screen will display

ENTER A1B1 CELL SCORES

?   22
?   28
?   31
?   24
?   26
?   19

CHECK RAW DATA FOR ACCURACY

TO CONTINUE PUSH ANY KEY THEN RETURN
?

Push any key then RETURN and the screen will display

ENTER A2B1 CELL SCORES

Enter the raw scores in the a_2b_1 cell according to the previous routine. When this has been completed the screen will prompt you to enter the raw data in the a_1b_2 cell. This program will prompt you to enter the cell scores for all cells in the design defined by your p and q entries. When the raw scores for the last cell have been entered and RETURN pushed the screen will display:

A1B1 = 150   A2B1 = 160
A1B2 = 140   A2B2 = 170

SOURCE OF VARIATION	SUM OF SQUARES
A	66.666
B	0
AB	16.668
RESIDUAL	248

DF	MEAN SQUARE	F
1	66.666	5.37629
1	0	0
1	16.668	1.34419
20	12.4	

This program displays the *AB* cell totals so that the interaction may be plotted and simple effects tests may be performed conveniently. If main effects tests are required then the overall *A* and *B* totals can be readily obtained by summing appropriate *AB* cell totals.

Program 9: Product-Moment Correlation and Linear Regression

This program computes the product-moment r between variables X and Y, the regression of Y on X, and the F-ratio for the significance test of the regression.

```
10 REM CORRELATION/REGRESSION
20 CLS
30 PRINT "ENTER N:";
40 INPUT N
50 CLS
60 PRINT "ENTER X AND Y SCORES IN PAIRS"
70 PRINT
80 PRINT "N =";N; TAB(17)"X"; TAB(25)"Y"
90 FOR Z=1 TO N
100 INPUT X,Y
110 PRINT TAB(16)"";X; TAB(24)"";Y
120 LET EX=EX+X
130 LET X2=X*X
140 LET EX2=EX2+X2
150 LET EXQ2=EX*EX
160 LET EY=EY+Y
170 LET Y2=Y*Y
180 LET EY2=EY2+Y2
190 LET EYQ2=EY*EY
200 LET XY=X*Y
210 LET EXY=EXY+XY
220 NEXT Z
230 PRINT
240 PRINT "CHECK RAW DATA FOR ACCURACY"
250 PRINT
260 PRINT "TO CONTINUE PUSH ANY KEY THEN RETURN"
270 PRINT
280 INPUT A$
290 IF A$="" THEN 280
300 CLS
310 LET CV=N*EXY-EX*EY
320 LET NSSX=N*EX2-EXQ2
330 LET NSSY=N*EY2-EYQ2
340 LET R=CV/SQR(NSSX*NSSY)
350 LET DF=N-2
360 LET B=CV/NSSX
370 LET C=(EY-B*EX)/N
380 LET SST=EY2-EYQ2/N
390 LET SSR=B*(EXY-(EX*EY)/N)
400 LET SSE=SST-SSR
410 LET F=SSR/(SSE/DF)
```

```
420 PRINT "N =";N
430 PRINT "SUM X =";EX
440 PRINT "SUM X SQUARED =";EX2
450 PRINT "SUM Y =";EY
460 PRINT "SUM Y SQUARED =";EY2
470 PRINT "SUM XY =";EXY
480 PRINT
490 PRINT "PRODUCT-MOMENT R = ";R
500 PRINT "DEGREES OF FREEDOM =";DF
510 PRINT "R SQUARED =";R*R
520 PRINT
530 PRINT "THE REGRESSION OF Y ON X IS:"
540 PRINT
550 IF C<0 THEN 580
560 PRINT "Y^ = ";B;"X   + ";C
570 GOTO 600
580 LET C=-C
590 PRINT "Y^ = ";B;"X   - ";C
600 PRINT
610 PRINT "SS REGRESSION =";SSR
620 PRINT "SS ERROR =";SSE
630 PRINT
640 PRINT "F =";F;" :  DF = 1 /";DF
650 END
```

Instructions

When the program is loaded, type RUN and push RETURN. The screen will display

ENTER N:?

Exercise 12.5–2 will be used to illustrate. Enter the value of N (10) and push RETURN and the screen will display

ENTER X AND Y SCORES IN PAIRS

N = 10   X   Y
?

Enter the raw data as follows. Enter the first X score, a comma, the first Y score and then push RETURN. Continue to enter pairs of X and Y scores in this manner. When RETURN has been pushed for the tenth time the screen will display

ENTER X AND Y SCORES IN PAIRS

N = 10   X   Y
? 2,5

              2   5

? 6,30

              6   30

```
?  9,35
                        9       35
?  7,25
                        7       25
?  12,40
                        12      40
?  4,10
                        4       10
?  1,10
                        1       10
?  3,20
                        3       20
?  6,5
                        6       5
?  10,20
                        10      20
```

CHECK RAW DATA FOR ACCURACY

TO CONTINUE PUSH ANY KEY THEN RETURN

?

Push any key then RETURN and the screen will display

N = 10
SUM X = 60
SUM X SQUARED = 476
SUM Y = 200
SUM Y SQUARED = 5400
SUM XY = 1500

PRODUCT-MOMENT R = .744438
DEGREES of FREEDOM = 8
R SQUARED = .554187

THE REGRESSION OF Y ON X IS:
$\hat{Y}$ = 2.58621 X + 4.48276

SS REGRESSION = 775.862
SS ERROR = 624.138

F = 9.94475 : DF = 1/8

Note: The screen displays $\hat{Y}$ as $\hat{Y}$.

Program 10: Multiple Regression with Two Predictor Variables

```
10 REM MULTIPLE RESGESSION
20 CLS
30 PRINT "ENTER N:";
```

```
40 INPUT N
50 CLS
60 PRINT "ENTER X1, X2, AND Y SCORES IN TRIOS"
70 PRINT
80 PRINT "N =";N; TAB(17)"X1"; TAB(24)"X2"; TAB(31)"Y"
90 FOR Z=1 TO N
100 INPUT X1,X2,Y
110 PRINT TAB(16)"";X1; TAB(23)"";X2; TAB(30)"";Y
120 LET EX1=EX1+X1
130 LET EX2=EX2+X2
140 LET EY=EY+Y
150 LET X12=X1*X1
160 LET X22=X2*X2
170 LET Y2=Y*Y
180 LET X1X2=X1*X2
190 LET X1Y=X1*Y
200 LET X2Y=X2*Y
210 LET EX12=EX12+X12
220 LET EX22=EX22+X22
230 LET EY2=EY2+Y2
240 LET EX1X2=EX1X2+X1X2
250 LET EX1Y=EX1Y+X1Y
260 LET EX2Y=EX2Y+X2Y
270 NEXT Z
280 PRINT
290 PRINT "CHECK RAW DATA FOR ACCURACY"
300 PRINT
310 PRINT "TO CONTINUE PUSH ANY KEY THEN RETURN"
320 PRINT
330 INPUT A$
340 IF A$="" THEN 330
350 CLS
360 LET NX1Y=N*EX1Y-EX1*EY
370 LET NX2=N*EX22-EX2*EX2
380 LET NX1X2=N*EX1X2-EX1*EX2
390 LET NX2Y=N*EX2Y-EX2*EY
400 LET NX1=N*EX12-EX1*EX1
410 LET B1=(NX1Y*NX2-NX1X2*NX2Y)/(NX1*NX2-NX1X2*NX1X2)
420 LET B2=(NX2Y*NX1-NX1X2*NX1Y)/(NX1*NX2-NX1X2*NX1X2)
430 LET C=(EY-B1*EX1-B2*EX2)/N
440 LET SSY=EY2-EY*EY/N
450 LET SSR=B1*(EX1Y-EX1*EY/N)+B2*(EX2Y-EX2*EY/N)
460 LET SSE=SSY-SSR
470 LET MSR=SSR/2
480 LET MSE=SSE/(N-3)
490 LET F=MSR/MSE
500 LET R2=SSR/SSY
510 PRINT "B1 = ";B1
520 PRINT "B2 = ";B2
530 PRINT "C = ";C
540 PRINT
550 PRINT "THE REGRESSION OF Y ON X1 AND X2 IS:"
560 PRINT
570 PRINT "Y^ = ";B1;"X1";
```

```
580 IF B2<0 THEN 610
590 PRINT "   + ";B2;"X2";
600 GOTO 630
610 LET B2=-B2
620 PRINT "   - ";B2;"X2";
630 IF C<0 THEN 660
640 PRINT "   + ";C
650 GOTO 680
660 LET C=-C
670 PRINT "   - ";C
680 PRINT
690 PRINT "F =";F
700 PRINT
710 PRINT "DEGREES OF FREEDOM = 2 /";N-3
720 PRINT
730 PRINT "R SQUARED =";R2
740 END
```

Instructions

When the program is loaded, type RUN and push RETURN. The screen will display

ENTER N:?

Exercise 13.9–2 will be used to illustrate. Enter the value of N (5) and push RETURN and the screen will display

ENTER X1, X2, AND Y SCORES IN TRIOS
N = 5   X1   X2   Y
?

Enter the raw data as follows. Enter the first X_1 score, a comma, the first X_2 score, a comma, the first Y score and then push RETURN. Continue to enter trios of X_1, X_2, and Y scores in this manner. When RETURN has been pushed for the fifth time the screen will display

ENTER X1, X2, AND Y SCORES IN TRIOS
N = 5   X1   X2   Y
? 18,1,.25
               18   1   .25
? 20,5,.35
               20   5   .35
? 25,6,.3
               25   6   .3
? 30,8,.2
               30   8   .2
? 40,10,.15
               40   10   .15

CHECK RAW DATA FOR ACCURACY

TO CONTINUE PUSH ANY KEY THEN RETURN

?

Push any key then RETURN and the screen will display

B1 = −.0169285

B2 = .0274377

C = .535672

THE REGRESSION OF Y ON X1 AND X2 IS:

$\hat{Y}$ = −.0169285 + .0274377 + .535672

F = 6.41067

DEGREES OF FREEDOM = 2/2

R SQUARED = .865059

Note: The screen displays $\hat{Y}$ as $\hat{Y}$.

Appendix V:
The General Rules
for $A \cup B$ and $A \cap B$

In Section 5.2 we discussed the addition rule for the probability of occurrence of any of several mutually exclusive events, and in Section 5.4 we considered the multiplication rule for the probability of occurrence of two or more independent events. These are special cases; real-life events need not be mutually exclusive or independent. This appendix completes the discussion of addition and multiplication of probabilities by examining the general case rules.

When A and B are mutually exclusive, the joint occurrence $(A \cap B)$ is impossible. An event can be one or the other but never both, and we determine the probability of occurrence of A or B by adding $p(A)$ and $p(B)$. This method is not satisfactory when A and B are not mutually exclusive, that is, when the two outcomes can occur together. In such cases, if we added the proportion of all outcomes that manifest property A, or $p(A)$, to the proportion of all outcomes that manifest property B, or $p(B)$, the outcomes in which both properties occurred together would be counted twice, once with the A's and once with the B's. This error is easily corrected by subtracting $A \cap B$; thus, the general rule for determining the probability of occurrence of A or B when A and B are not mutually exclusive is

$$p(A \cup B) = p(A) + p(B) - p(A \cap B)$$

As an example, if a single card is drawn from a well-shuffled deck, what is the probability that it will be a heart (H) or queen (Q)? Heart and queen are not mutually exclusive since the joint occurrence $(H \cap Q)$ is possible, namely, the queen of hearts. If the probability of heart $[p(H) = 13/52]$, is added to the probability of queen $[p(Q) = 4/52]$, the queen of hearts is counted twice, once with the hearts and once with the queens. The rule for determining the probability of A or B when these events are not mutually exclusive eliminates this error by subtracting out one occurrence of the joint event. Thus

$$p(H) = 13/52$$

$$p(Q) = 4/52$$

$$
\begin{aligned}
p(H \cup Q) &= p(H) + p(Q) - p(H \cap Q) \\
&= p(H) + p(Q) - [p(H) \times p(Q)] \\
&= 13/52 + 4/52 - [13/52 \times 4/52] \\
&= 13/52 + 4/52 - 1/52 \\
&= 16/52 \\
&= 0.3077
\end{aligned}
$$

Whenever you seek to determine the probability of this *or* that you must first determine whether or not the events are mutually exclusive and then use the appropriate rule. There is no convenient trick or clue to determining whether two events are mutually exclusive; simply ask yourself whether it is possible that both could occur at the same time.

When A and B are independent, we can determine the probability of the joint occurrence $(A \cap B)$ by multiplying $p(A) \times p(B)$. Many times, however, events are related (not independent), which means that the probability of a particular outcome is affected by the occurrence of a previous event. Under such circumstances we must use a probability value for the second event, which takes into account the influence of the first. The general rule for determining the probability of A *and* B when these events are not independent is

$$p(A \cap B) = p(A) \times p(B \mid A)$$

Note: The notation $B \mid A$ reads "B given A." Thus $B \mid A$ is the probability of occurrence of B under the condition that A has occurred or is simultaneously occurring.

If two cards are dealt from a well-shuffled deck, what is the probability that both will be aces? The probability that the first card will be an ace is $p(A_1) = 4/52$, but the probability that the second card will be an ace is $p(A_2) = 3/51$ since, after the first ace is drawn, there are 3 aces left in a deck totaling 51 cards. These two events are not independent because the outcome of the first affects the probability of the second. When sampling is done without replacing the selected individual prior to the next draw, the probability of the subsequent outcome is changed by the preceding outcome, unless the population is infinitely large. The probability that two cards drawn from a well-shuffled deck will both be aces is

probability that the first card will be an ace: $p(A_1) = 4/52$

probability that the second card will be an ace given that the first card was an ace: $p(A_2 \mid A_1) = 3/51$

$$p(A_1 \cap A_2) = p(A_1) \times p(A_2|A_1)$$
$$= 4/52 \times 3/51$$
$$= 12/2652$$
$$= 0.0045$$

Suppose that two cards are dealt from a well-shuffled deck, what is the probability that they will consist of a king *and* a queen? (Note: order of occurrence not specified.)

$$p[(K \cap Q) \cup (Q \cap K)] = [p(K) \times p(Q|K)] + [p(Q) \times p(K|Q)]$$
$$= [4/52 \times 4/51] + [4/52 \times 4/51]$$
$$= 16/2652 + 16/2652$$
$$= 32/2652$$
$$= 0.0121$$

Sampling without replacement is an obvious clue that the successive events are not independent. There are situations not involving repeated sampling in which the variables of interest are related and therefore also require use of the rule for non-independent events. If 30 percent of people have green eyes [$p(G) = 0.30$], 10 percent of people are red-haired [$p(R) = 0.10$], and 90 percent of red-haired people have green eyes [$p(G|R) = 0.90$], what is the probability that any given person will be red-haired *and* green-eyed? Is being green-eyed independent of being red-haired? The answer is no. The way to spot that red hair and green eyes are related is to note that there are two probability values for green eyes, one for the population at large [$p(G) = 0.30$], and another for red-haired persons [$p(G|R) = 0.90$]. This tells you that being red-haired has an effect on the probability of being green-eyed, that is, the two are related. Thus

$$p(R) = 0.10$$
$$p(G) = 0.30$$
$$p(G|R) = 0.90$$
$$p(R \cap G) = p(R) \times p(G|R)$$
$$= 0.10 \times 0.90$$
$$= 0.09$$

The following relationship is always true

$$p(A) \times p(B|A) = p(B) \times p(A|B)$$

One can determine the probability that green-eyed people will be red-haired [$p(R|G)$] as follows

$$p(\text{R}) \times p(\text{G}|\text{R}) = p(\text{G}) \times p(\text{R}|\text{G})$$
$$0.10 \times 0.90 = 0.30 \times p(\text{R}|\text{G})$$
$$\frac{0.10 \times 0.90}{0.30} = p(\text{R}|\text{G})$$
$$p(\text{R}|\text{G}) = 0.30$$

Whenever you seek to determine the probability of this *and* that you must first determine whether or not the events are independent and then use the appropriate rule. Be alert to whether sampling is being performed without replacement and/or whether a given outcome has a different probability under different circumstances.

Review Exercises

1. If a single card is drawn from a well-shuffled deck, what is the probability that it will be
   (a) a seven or eight
   (b) a jack or spade
   (c) an ace or black suit
   (d) a spade or picture card

2. In a group of 1000 people, 200 are blonde-haired, 450 wear glasses, 500 are men, 700 are over 30 years old, 150 are short, 310 are friendly, and 900 drink beer. If these variables are independent, what is the probability that a given person will be
   (a) blonde-haired and friendly
   (b) blonde-haired or friendly
   (c) short or wearing glasses
   (d) over 30 or friendly
   (e) a woman who does not drink beer and who is also short or blonde-haired
   (f) short, friendly or blonde-haired, and over 30

3. During a 50-day period, it rains on 20 percent of days, is hot on 40 percent of days, and is hot and rainy on 10 percent of days. What is the probability that a given day will be hot or rainy?

4. In a sample of 100 rabbits, 55 are spotted, 45 are female, and 13 are spotted females. What is the probability that any particular rabbit will be
   (a) spotted or female
   (b) male or not spotted

5. In dealing cards without replacement from a well-shuffled deck, what is the probability that
    (a) the first will be a queen and the second an ace
    (b) the first will be a heart and the second a spade
    (c) the first two will both be picture cards
    (d) the first five will be the ace, king, queen, jack, and ten of hearts in that order
    (e) the first five will be an ace, king, queen, jack, and ten in that order
    (f) the first five will be the ace, king, queen, jack, and ten of the same suit in the above order

6. If the probability of being blind is 0.05, the probability of having kidney trouble is 0.21, and the probability of having kidney trouble if blind is 0.44, what is the probability that a person
    (a) will be blind and have kidney trouble
    (b) will have kidney trouble and be blind

7. If the probability that any individual will become schizophrenic is 0.02, and if the probability that one will become schizophrenic if one has a schizophrenic twin is 0.19, what is the probability that
    (a) you and your twin brother will both become schizophrenic
    (b) your twin brother and you will both become schizophrenic

8. Among brown-eyed people the proportion who have sex appeal is 0.20, whereas among people with sex appeal the proportion with brown eyes is 0.32. Brown-eyed persons make up 64 percent of the population. What is the probability that a given person will have sex appeal and be brown-eyed?

9. You wish to go from Chicago to Toronto and can either drive, fly, or hitchhike. If you drive you have 0.01 probability of being in an accident and, if so involved, a 0.30 probability of being killed. The probability of a plane crash is only 0.001, but if it crashes, there is a 0.99 probability of being killed. Hitchhikers have 0.05 probability of being hit by a car, 0.02 probability of being hit by a bus, and 0.01 probability of being hit by a bicycle, and in each case a 0.50 likelihood of being killed. Which is the safest way to go?

10. A zebra has the following problem: if he goes to the waterhole, he has a 0.40 chance of being attacked by a lion and a 0.10 chance of being attacked by a leopard. If he stays where he is, there is a 0.15 chance of attack by a lion, a 0.02 chance of attack by a leopard, and a 0.25 chance of dying of thirst. If attacked by a lion, there is a 0.10 chance of escaping alive and if attacked by a leopard there is a 0.01 chance of escaping alive. Should he go to the waterhole or stay put?

11. Nick entered two pigeons, named A and B, in a race in which a total of ten birds competed.

    (a) What is the probability that his birds will be the first two to finish the race?

    (b) If three of the ten are lost during the race and never seen again, what is the probability that A will win the race?

12. Five firemen, A, B, C, D, and E, are asleep in their bunks; their pants are hanging on wall pegs. The alarm rings and each reaches out blindly and grabs one pair: A grabs first, B second, and so on. What is the probability that

    (a) everyone will get his own pants

    (b) A or B will get his own pants

13. At a gambling casino one has the choice of playing cards, dice, or roulette. Over any time period the probability of winning money is 0.40 at cards, 0.25 at dice, and 0.10 at roulette. Mary and Barbara both play cards and roulette, and do so independently of each other. What is the probability that both will win money at cards or roulette?

14. At a chicken farm there are 50 red, 20 black, 20 white, and 10 barred chickens. Ten percent of the red chickens are roosters, half of the white and half of the black ones are roosters, and eighty percent of the barred ones are roosters; the rest are hens.

    (a) If a hawk kills a chicken, what is the probability it will be a red hen or barred hen?

    (b) Starting with the original population, a fox comes and kills one chicken; later in the day a different fox comes and also kills one chicken. What is the probability that the two dead chickens will consist of a red rooster and a white hen?

15. Four people enter a Mexican restaurant. The menu is in Spanish but none of them can read or understand a word; further, the waiter does not speak or understand a word of English. The people order independently by pointing to items on the menu. The food is such that 80 percent of the dishes are hot, 25 percent are awful-looking, and 40 percent cause indigestion. What is the probability that

    (a) all four will choose a dish that is hot or awful-looking

    (b) the four dishes selected will consist of one awful-looking and three that cause indigestion

16. A field of horses starts off on a cross-country race. The field consists of 4 whites, 7 chestnuts, 1 spotted, 3 sorrels, 8 blacks, and 2 buckskins. Twelve of the horses are female. The first obstacle is a hedge and one horse tries to run through it and gets scratched to death by the thorns and

is out of the race. The second obstacle is a pond jump and one horse drowns and is out of the race. The third obstacle is a steep hill climb and one horse has a heart attack and dies and is out of the race. The fourth obstacle is a jump over some bales of hay and one horse has hay fever and sneezes to death and is out of the race. What is the probability that

(a) the first horse to drop out will be a male or buckskin
(b) all four horses that drop out will be chestnuts
(c) all eight blacks will finish the race
(d) the first two that drop out will be a white female and a buckskin female in that order
(e) the first two that drop out will be a male black and a male chestnut

17. Irene leaves the bar with a tray containing 4 scotches, 6 ryes, 3 gins, 1 bourbon, 4 colas, 5 ginger ales, and 10 beers. As she leaves the bar she is jostled and one drink is spilled. She then starts toward your table but trips and another drink is spilled; then, as she gets up she is pinched and a third drink is spilled. What is the probability that

(a) all the spilled drinks will be gins
(b) the first two spilled drinks will consist of a beer and a pop (soft drink)
(c) the bourbon will reach your table
(d) the three spilled drinks will consist of a bourbon, cola, and beer

References

Aldiss, B. *The Eighty Minute Hour: A Space Opera.* New York: Leisure Books, 1975.

Andrews, F. M., Klem, L., Davidson, T. N., O'Malley, P. M., and Rodgers, W. L. *A Guide for Selecting Statistical Techniques for Analyzing Social Science Data.* 2nd ed. University of Michigan, Institute for Social Research, 1981.

Bakan, D. "The test of significance in psychological research." *Psychological Bulletin 66* (1966): 423–437.

Bates, F. C. and Horvath, T. "Discrimination learning with rhythmic and non-rhythmic background music." *Perceptual and Motor Skills 33* (1971): 1123–1126.

Cicchetti, D. V. "Extension of Multiple-Range Tests to Interaction Tables in the Analysis of Variance: A Rapid Approximate Solution." *Psychological Bulletin 77* (1972): 405–408.

Clauser, C. E., Tucker, P. E., McConville, J. T., Churchill, E., Laubach, L. L., and Reardon, J. A. *Anthropometry of Air Force Women.* Report no. AMRL-TR-70-5, Aerospace Medical Research Laboratory, Wright-Patterson Air Force Base, 1972.

Cohen, J. *Statistical Power Analysis for the Behavioral Sciences.* 2nd ed. New York: Academic Press, 1977.

Comstock, G. W. and Partridge, K. B. "Church attendance and health." *Journal of Chronic Disease 25* (1972): 665–672.

D'Amato, M. R. *Experimental Psychology: Methodology, Psychophysics, and Learning.* New York: McGraw-Hill, 1970.

Edwards, A. L. *Experimental Design in Psychological Research.* New York: Holt, Rinehart, & Winston, 1960.

Ferguson, G. A. *Statistical Analysis in Psychology and Education.* 5th ed. New York: McGraw-Hill, 1981.

Glass, G. V. and Stanley, J. C. *Statistical Methods in Education and Psychology.* Englewood Cliffs: Prentice-Hall, 1970.

Glass, G. V. and Hopkins, K. D. *Statistical Methods in Education and Psychology.* 2nd ed. Englewood Cliffs: Prentice-Hall, 1984.

Guttman, L. "What is not what in statistics." *The Statistician 26* (1977): 81–107.

Hays, W. L. *Statistics.* 3rd ed. New York: Holt, Rinehart, & Winston, 1981.

———. *Statistics for the Social Sciences.* New York: Holt, Rinehart, & Winston, 1973.

Horvath, T. "Correlates of physical beauty in men and women." *Social Behavior and Personality 7* (1979): 145–151.

———. "Physical attractiveness: The influence of selected torso parameters." *Archives of Sexual Behavior 10* (1981): 21–24.

Horvath, T., Kirby, H. W., and Smith, A. A. "Rats' heart rate and grooming activity in the open field." *Journal of Comparative and Physiological Psychology 76* (1971): 449–453.

Howell, D. C. *Statistical Methods for Psychology.* Boston: Duxbury, 1982.

Kendall, M. G. *Rank Correlation Methods*. 4th ed. London: Griffen, 1970.

Keppel, G. *Design and Analysis: A Researcher's Handbook*. 2nd ed. Englewood Cliffs: Prentice-Hall, 1982.

Kerlinger, F. N. and Pedhazur, E. J. *Multiple Regression in Behavioral Research*. New York: Holt, Rinehart, & Winston, 1973.

Kirby, H. W. and Horvath, T. "Self-licking deprivation and maternal behaviour in the primiparous rat." *Canadian Journal of Psychology 22* (1968): 369–375.

McConnell, J. V. *Understanding Human Behavior*. 2nd ed. New York: Holt, Rinehart, & Winston, 1977.

Meyers, L. S. and Grossen, N. E. *Behavioral Research: Theory, Procedure, and Design*. 2nd ed. San Francisco: Freeman, 1978.

Morris, D. *Manwatching: A Field Guide to Human Behavior*. New York: Abrams, 1977.

Neft, D. S., Johnson, R. T., Cohen, R. M., and Deutsch, J. A. *The Sports Encyclopedia: Football*. New York: Grosset & Dunlap, 1974.

Reynolds, V. *The Biology of Human Action*. San Francisco: Freeman, 1976.

Roscoe, J. T. *Fundamental Research Statistics for the Behavioral Sciences*. New York: Holt, Rinehart, & Winston, 1975.

Tanur, J. M., Mosteller, F., Kruskal, W. H., Link, R. F., Pieters, R. S., and Rising, G. R. *Statistics: A Guide to the Unknown*. San Francisco: Holden-Day, 1972.

Warren, J. M. and Warren, H. B. "Reversal learning by horse and raccoon." *Journal of Genetic Psychology 100* (1962): 215–220.

Winer, B. J. *Statistical Principles in Experimental Design*. New York: McGraw-Hill, 1962 (1st ed) and 1971 (2nd ed).

Index